TENOR

TENOR

HISTORY OF A VOICE

JOHN POTTER

YALE UNIVERSITY PRESS
NEW HAVEN AND LONDON

For information about this and other Yale University Press publications please contact:

U.S. Office: sales.press@yale.edu yalebooks.com
Europe Office: sales@yaleup.co.uk www.yalebooks.co.uk

Set in Minion by J&L Composition Ltd, Filey, North Yorkshire
Printed in Great Britain by TJ International Ltd, Padstow, Cornwall

Library of Congress Control Number 2009920776

ISBN 978–0–300–11873–5

A catalogue record for this book is available from the British Library

10 9 8 7 6 5 4 3 2 1

For Penny, Alice and Ned

CONTENTS

ILLUSTRATIONS

PREFACE

Our response to the human voice is intensely personal; we all possess one and this enables us to empathize with singers in a way that perhaps we can't with other musicians. Occasionally a great tenor will produce a similar reaction in many admirers, but voices often become the subject of fierce debate, with individual fans hearing contrasting or conflicting personal versions of the singer they are listening to. This is potentially hazardous for those who write about voices. There is probably no way to write purely objectively about tenors, and it is certainly impossible to write about all of those that have made a significant contribution to what one might call the tenorocracy. This book divides into two parts: the post-gramophone era where you can hear what I'm talking about, and the pre-twentieth century part where you can't. I have treated the earlier chapters as a piece of historical research and I have tried to chart the evolution of the voice by looking at points where important changes seem to have taken place, usually driven by extraordinary singers of the times. It's as objective as I can make it, but is inevitably informed by my own biases (to do with having spent a lifetime singing only one very small area of the tenor repertoire, mostly in Europe). The second part is just as much of a challenge because everything I write about can be heard and discussed by you, the reader. There is a risk of sounding like a record reviewer (which I'm not really qualified to be) and I have generally tried to avoid giving opinions of my own, preferring to quote those of others rather than sit in judgment on such illustrious performers. I have thought of the post-gramophone chapters as extrapolations on the French, Italian and German strands of tenorial history, but as the twentieth century leaves us and the twenty-first progresses, I am conscious of a complex relationship between countries, styles and history. As an acknowledgement of this (and of the futility of trying to establish historical absolutes) I have included chapters on French, British and Russian tenors who are part of the wider tradition but also distinct from it.

There is very little new to be said about most of the tenors in this book, and I have not attempted a comprehensive biography of any of them – that has been done succinctly and elegantly for the most significant singers by such writers as Alan Blyth, Elisabeth Forbes, Harold Rosenthal, Desmond Shawe-Taylor, and the many contributors to Grove, MGG and K&R, and at length in the case of some of the greatest tenors by Shirlee Emmons, Michael Henstock, Jürgen Kesting, Michael Scott, and others. Instead I have tried to understand what it is in the careers of certain tenors that makes them historically significant (their background and training perhaps, odd events in their lives, a particular technical approach or their contribution to the creation or interpretation of particular roles, for example). This inevitably means that some excellent singers, the favourites of many perhaps, do not get much of a mention. To make up for this I have put together a Biographical List of Tenors, which I think of as a 'tenorography', so that anyone can follow up particular singers that interest them (and which I may not have dealt with in sufficient detail myself), with the aid of the basic research tool that I used to write the book. The tenorography consists of essential information about several hundred tenors and combines the function of bibliography and discography, listed by individual singer. It contains many more tenors than I have been able to deal with in the main body of the book and should enable readers to redress the balance where they think I have gone astray. The discographies are intended to be points of departure for further listening, but where books or articles contain extensive discographies I have noted this. I hope that the Biographical List will become a starting point for those interested in further research.

The Biographical List of Tenors is available on the web via www.yalebooks.co.uk where it will be updated from time to time. Updates or corrections can be emailed to tenorvoice@john-potter.co.uk.

Chapter 2 is an extended and updated version of 'The tenor-castrato connection' *Early Music* XXXV/1 (February 2007).

Anyone writing about singers has the good fortune to be able to call on some very fine writers and researchers, and I'd like to pay tribute to some of those who have inspired me over the years. The historical writings of John Rosselli, Rodolfo Celetti and Henry Pleasants are essential background reading; the work of Michael Scott is similarly vital for those interested in early recording; the encyclopaedic knowledge and infectious enthusiasm of J. B. Steane is a model of how to convert sound into words – he is one of the few writers on singing who can actually move the reader. Very few successful singers have the time or inclination to write, a notable exception being the tenor Nigel Douglas, whose two books of *Legendary Singers* are full of unique insights. For those who would like a more comprehensive discographical judgment, a combination of the works of Douglas, Scott and Steane will provide plenty of material. Finally, I owe a debt to the collecting fraternity (and especially to those who have written for *Record Collector* over the years): without their devotion to singers of the past much of what we now know would have been lost.

I owe a great deal to family, friends and colleagues: to my son Ned who as my research assistant did much of the initial work on the Biographical List of Tenors; to successive heads of the Music Department at the University of York, Nicola Lefanu, Roger Marsh, and William Brooks, who have always given great encouragement and granted me the occasional research term; to all those who have shared their research, their thoughts and their tenorial enthusiasms, especially Doug Fox, Anna Maria Friman, Margit Limpert, Nicky Losseff, John Kennedy Melling, Alice Potter, Dan Shea, Werner Schüssler, Neil Sorrell, Eric Wimbles, Richard Wistreich and Stefan Zucker. I am also very grateful to the librarians at the British Library, the Cambridge University Library and the J. B. Morrell Library at York, and to Timothy Day, who as Curator of Western Art Music at the National Sound Archive was a constant source of information and inspiration during my Edison Fellowship (for which I have to thank the trustees of the British Library). Elizabeth Haddon made many helpful comments on an earlier draft, and Richard Wigmore as the reader for Yale University Press improved the structure. I should also like to thank Vanessa Mitchell and, at Yale University Press, Stephen Kent, and especially Malcolm Gerratt for persuading me that I would enjoy writing a book on tenors. None of it would have been possible without the support of my wife Penny, whose tolerance for tenorial excess appears to be infinite.

CHAPTER I

THE PREHISTORY OF THE VOICE

What is a tenor? We know today's tenors as heroes of the operatic stage, often flamboyant personalities with rich and powerful voices, who move us with their interpretations of Wagner, Verdi, Puccini, Rossini or Mozart. We associate the voice with the great Passion settings of J.S. Bach, the oratorios of Handel and Mendelssohn. Anyone reading these words is likely to know tenors who are members of choirs or vocal ensembles, which may sing anything from renaissance music to barber shop. The voice itself is not easy to describe but most music lovers will recognise one when they hear it. The word can mean both the voice and the line of music that it sings, with a range that may overlap with basses at the bottom and altos at the top.

The plethora of tenorial enterprise that we now take for granted has not always existed: in the beginning there were just singers. The modern tenor voice is the product of many centuries of evolution: a process that began slowly in the early medieval period with voices that might have sung in a tenor range, and accelerated rapidly from the eighteenth century onwards to become the complex voice of today's opera houses and concert halls. The categorisation of voice types came relatively late in this time frame, leaving us to speculate on what sort of voice preceded the tenor and formed the seed bed for the phenomenon of the twenty-first century.

One way of defining the tenor voice is by range or preferred *tessitura* (that part of the voice where the singer is most comfortable). The physiognomy of the voice has almost certainly not changed significantly for many thousands of years, so the proportion of men potentially able to sing in the modern tenor range is likely to have been the same for as long as people have been able to sing.[1] For most of that time the world seems to have been content not to identify the tenor as a voice worthy of note and distinct from other voice types. We know (from the frustratingly small amount of surviving evidence) that for the Greeks and Romans song was an integral part of cultural life, and that many of the so-called 'barbarians' who replaced them were singers of sagas of great length and sophistication. We know too, that elements of ancient vocal wisdom were passed on to the early Christians in the first few hundred years of our era, including Jewish ritual songs that may have formed the basis of what we now call Gregorian chant. None of this music was written down, so we have only passing references to actual singing, and the only thing we can be reasonably sure about is that the concept of singing as performance is deeply rooted in our culture, even though the contexts in which 'performances' occurred may be unrecognisable to us today.

This may or may not imply a cultured way of singing. Successful tenors of today make a highly cultured sound which is usually the product of a rigorous training regime undertaken over a number of years. When we put on a recording or go to a performance it is quite clear to us what a tenor is, but in our search for the antecedents of this voice we need to suspend completely our idea of what a modern tenor sounds like. As we shall see, the *sound* of the modern voice is something that came relatively late in historical terms; for many hundreds of years before this, performers singing in the tenor range probably used a voice that sounded much closer to their speech. This has important implications when we try to imagine what medieval or renaissance tenors sounded like. Our voices are like our faces, part of the essence that defines us as individuals. With modern training some of this individuality is sacrificed in order to produce a voice of the *genus* 'tenor', so that we recognise the voice rather than the person. Of course we can still distinguish between individual tenors, but what we hear first and foremost is the tenor sound. Once we start to delve into the voices of history we find that this preoccupation with sound only becomes crucially important from the nineteenth century onwards, at about the same time as institutionalised instruction became widely available. We are familiar today with the voices of 'early music' which tend to be lighter and more agile than those who sing more mainstream repertoire. But we must remember that the concept of 'early music' was developed in the latter part of the twentieth century within the existing traditions of the times. Although many early music tenors are clearly different from, say, Verdi tenors, they have generally been trained to explore elements of baroque or renaissance *style* by applying many of the benefits of a modern *technique*. It is technique that creates the sound world, and we should bear this in mind when listening to a modern tenor singing Monteverdi's *Orfeo*, for example. What we are accustomed to hearing is perhaps a reduced version of the modern voice rather than the evolving voice of the seventeenth century.[2]

If pre-Romantic tenors were not concerned with making a highly cultured beautiful sound, what was it that defined the voice while western polyphony was developing over a period of a thousand years or so? What was this tenor who did not sound like a tenor? In at least one important respect he was similar to his modern counterpart: he sang in what we think of as the tenor range and he wanted to make the words as clear as possible. The sources from which we deduce this focus overwhelmingly on clarity of text, and relatively rarely mention beauty of sound.[3] This latter point is hard for modern singers to grasp, as we have in our heads a very clear idea of what a tenor is supposed to sound like; but if we are to get inside the heads of tenors of the baroque and earlier we need to understand that the sound was less important than the delivery of the words. If we want a model to base our concept on, we can draw (with care . . .) some parallels with modern rock singers. We would not normally identify male rock singers as tenors even if they sing in the tenor range (which many do, frequently in a relatively high tessitura). This is because they are not trying to make a tenor sound, but are delivering the text in a way which is related to their speaking voices: what we hear is the person rather than the voice type. I would not want to take the comparison any further than this as rock singing is obviously conditioned by many additional factors, but it may give an idea of the scale of difference between pre- and post-Romantic singing.[4]

Twelfth-century tenors?

Until the development of notation we have very little idea of what was actually sung. Writing and notation are essential building blocks of modern musical culture, and it is only recently that we have begun to understand that their function in the pre- and proto-literate societies of the medieval period may have been rather different. The names of the first known composers have traditionally been huge landmarks in music history because it has been assumed that they wrote definitive works in much the same way as their modern counterparts. But in an oral/aural culture, the process of generating new work is driven by complex formulae and memorisation strategies, and what we see in the earliest manuscripts credited to a named 'composer' may only be the one version that happened to be written down.[5]

As it happens, among the first named composers we find the first real evidence of the solo tenor voice. Magister Léoninus, or Léonin to give him the current French version of his name, is one of the least-known figures in the history of western music, yet has come to be considered one of the most important, having apparently left behind a large body of music associated with his name. His name is virtually all we know about him, however: there are no works directly attributable to him, and there are no surviving references to him that date from his own lifetime. Part of the reason for his fame is that some of his works (if they were his in the first place, that is) were revised and 'improved' by Pérotin (or Magister Perotinus), a man who was perhaps his successor at Notre Dame de Paris, and whose musical instincts seem to have been much closer to our own. All of Léonin's works are for two voices; Pérotin re-worked some of these for three or four voices. Four-part writing would eventually become a kind of norm (budding composers still begin their studies by harmonising four-voice Bach chorales), and the larger Pérotin works are written in a style that has an affinity with the rhythmic constructions of twenty-first century minimalist composers such as Steve Reich. Pérotin's music is approachable, 'modern' sounding, often very rhythmic and exciting to perform, and has rather eclipsed the more elusive and wayward music of his illustrious predecessor. The vocal lines of these two musicians (especially those of Léonin) give the impression of having been so beautifully crafted for the voice that it is almost inconceivable that the creators were not singers themselves. The blurred edges between composer, singer and instrumentalist that characterised almost all musicians until the nineteenth century suggest that both men would have been very skilful in all aspects of music-making. Léonin in particular may well have been a virtuoso tenor with a technique (now lost to us) every bit as impressive as that required for Bach or Rossini.

The *tenorista*

The specialist singer of the lower lines later became known as the *tenorista*, a singer with a technique or natural aptitude for holding the long tenor lines on which the pieces were constructed. The lines themselves tend to be fairly narrow in range, but sustaining the same note often for a page or more requires precise tuning and an ability to produce a consistent vowel sound, providing a rock-like foundation for the upper part. These lines may have been sung by a solo singer, or on special occasions by two or three singers. This is the first time we encounter the word 'tenor' to refer to a particular vocal line. It comes from the Latin *tenere* meaning 'to hold', and in classical Latin this meant literally holding on to something. It first appears in music to mean holding pitch, and this is presumably why the term tenorista was applied to those singers who held the long chant lines. Tenoristae were considered to be an essential element of the Notre Dame choral establishment until well into the sixteenth century, maintaining the connection between the almost timeless chant repertoire and the developing styles of polyphony.[6]

The skills of the tenorista are a little mysterious, because contemporary references to the term assume that the reader will know what the writer is talking about. To our modern ears and eyes the upper part, known as the *duplum*, and sung by another specialist called a *machicotus*, makes a greater impression; we value virtuosity rather than stamina when it comes to singing. The fact that the tenoristae get special treatment and we rarely hear about those who sing the upper part, suggests that maintaining the integrity of the chant foundation was more important to medieval commentators than the vocal pyrotechnics employed by the machicoti over the top of it. We are also dependent on scores, and the art of the tenorista was primarily an oral one. His part is the foundation of the piece, and is usually a fragment of chant, sung extremely slowly. It is often untexted, with only a brief *incipit* to remind him what words to sing. He would have in his memory the entire corpus of chant for the church's year (learnt as a chorister over a period of some ten years), and would be able to identify the appropriate text and the notes associated with it. It was not just a case of having to breathe impossibly long lines (he presumably breathed when he needed to), but of understanding the structure of the piece and how to keep it together.

For the modern tenor the relics that these musicians have left us provide endless creative opportunities. The special skills of the medieval tenors have been lost completely: modern singers are unable to call on the countless formulae from which medieval machicoti could create the music anew every time and there is a reluctance to depart from what we now consider to be 'the score', but the lack of knowledge allows considerable room for performative speculation nonetheless. Today's tenors are not *tenoristae* or *machicoti* and have to make a considerable adjustment to their modern techniques to be able to cope with the different demands of each line. Evolving as it did from something improvised, the upper voice in two-part music has a freedom that is slightly jazz-like. There is a text, but the singer is perhaps not expected to reproduce it literally, and the lower voice has to wait until the machicotus voice has had his fun before he can move to his next note (which can produce tensions of its own). The 'writing', so free and apparently spontaneous, often seems only a small step away from simply making it up, and often the singers of the upper lines must have been doing exactly that. Notation was relatively new and as yet very imprecise; generations of singers had been used to memorising formulae – small cells of variable material – and the *Magnus Liber* probably represents a mixture of aide-mémoire, composition, the provision of formulae, and transcription from improvised performances.[7]

We have so far considered tenor singing in the context of the church because that has been where the earliest evidence survives, and the descriptions of singers tend to indicate function rather than voice type. From the twelfth century onwards there exists a substantial body of monophonic secular song throughout much of Europe, but especially in northern and southern France, Germany and Spain. There were many famous singers and composers of these love songs (as they mostly were) with ranges usually of not more than an octave and therefore comfortably within the reach of most voices. We can assume that many of them sung in the tenor range even though none can be definitely identified as being tenors. There is a slight refinement in the way these singers tend to be classified: rather than being described in terms of their musical functions, these men (and sometimes women) are associated with their role within the genre, so we talk about French *trouvères* and *troubadours*, and German *Minnesänger*. The love songs of these poet–composers are some of the earliest secular music to be written down, and the creators themselves are the first named creators of secular music. These repertoires, emerging during a period when musicians were beginning to see the wider potential of notation, often demonstrate a personal connection with their creators, especially towards the end of the thirteenth century when composers such as Adam de la Halle began to explore the possibilities of polyphonic secular music.

During the fourteenth century the *ars antiqua* gave way to the *ars nova*, a 'new art' characterised by greater rhythmic complexity and the development of secular polyphonic song. This would have had a number of consequences for the tenoristae. The technique of *isorhythm*, whereby the tenor line repeated itself in accelerating mathematical proportions, would have given the tenoristae additional responsibility for keeping the piece together; they were increasingly required to sing secular motets that may have had a chant tenor, which implies that they were more than simply clerical chant fodder; perhaps most significantly, freely composed tenor lines not based on chant would have given them a broader range of skills.

The term tenorista is common in the fourteenth century, but we also come across references to the more general term ' tenor'. In the motet 'Sub Arturo plebs vallata' we get a charming glimpse of a choir (perhaps St George's Chapel Windsor). The piece is one of a number of so-called 'musicians' motets' which celebrate music and its history and often refer to contemporary performers. In this case the composer Johann Alanus has set two texts, one containing a potted history of music and an analysis of the piece (plus the composer's name), the other being a list of musicians that have been a part of the choral establishment. This includes reference to those who do florid singing and a commendation of Edmundus de Buria (Edmund of Bury St Edmunds) as being *basis aurea tenorum* ('the golden basis of the tenors'). Edmundus would presumably have sung the third line upon which the motet is structured. This is a chant extract with the *incipit* 'In omnem terram' and Edmundus would presumably know that this was taken from 'In omnem terram exivit sonus eorum'.[8]

Music history is conventionally written in terms of composers and we often overlook the fact that in the medieval period musicians were expected to turn their hand to anything musical. Alanus was almost certainly a singer himself, and we have speculated that Léonin may have been one too. There is also a case for Guillaume de Machaut having been a tenor, though his significance is attributed more to his compositions and poetry. Machaut is one of the first composers of secular music who clearly had an eye on his reputation among future musicians. The latter part of his life was spent ensuring that all his significant works survived him in manuscripts that he personally supervised. For many years he was the court poet and secretary to Jean de Luxembourg before becoming a canon at Reims cathedral. At Reims he would certainly have sung with the choir, but nowhere is his singing actually described. His *lais* (solo songs, often with a range of more than an octave) are clearly intended for a tenor type of voice, and it is likely that Machaut would have sung them himself (especially as he is also assumed to have written his own texts). The works of Machaut are fastidious and elaborate, but not very virtuosic. They demand a flexible voice and a great deal of musicianship, but no special technique is required to cope with the notes.

The same cannot be said for the versions of these forms which were exported to Italy, and during the course of the fourteenth century we see a remarkable increase in the amount of virtuosic vocal music in the form of the madrigal and its related forms. The fourteenth-century madrigal is not the same as the more familiar sixteenth-century version, but is for two voices (exceptionally, three), the lower of which is reminiscent of the old tenorista parts and accompanies a more florid upper voice. The poems are colourful, often presenting us with the sights and sounds of the Tuscan countryside.[9] This is especially the case with the *caccia*, a song with a hunting theme which is mirrored in the canonic writing of the music which appears to chase itself. These pieces are usually written in the tenor range. Many of the composers are recorded as being singers and holding posts in churches for which they were expected to supply the music.

Similarly virtuosic two-voice settings of the mass and motets also survive, which confirms a flowering of vocal culture in sacred as well as secular music. In almost all of this music the upper voice looks like a tenor part. The compositional technique is quite different from the chant-based repertoires, which began life as a fragment of plainsong. In the *trecento* madrigal the upper voice is thought to have been written first. It is not hard to imagine the composers trying out the pieces before writing them down, and going on to perform them themselves.

One of the most prolific singer–composers was Paolo Tenorista (*d.* 1419). He is one of the few late *trecento* composers described as a tenorista, which suggests this was unusual, presumably because the rest sang in a range appropriate for the upper part (which would be much more useful to them as composers). In other words they were what we would think of as tenors.

The musicians whose portraits gaze out at us from the Squarcialupi Codex are known to us primarily as composers but many of them were famous during their own lifetimes as instrumentalists or singers. If they accompanied themselves on the lute (as many did from the fifteenth century onwards) they would have made a light, unforced sound closely related to their speaking voices. Both lines in these two-part pieces are often texted, suggesting a performance by two singers, but the second line is almost always much simpler than the upper part, allowing for a self-accompanying singer to be able to cope with both lines simultaneously. We should also remember that these musicians are likely to have been skilled improvisers and that an oral tradition continued to hold its place alongside notated music.

One of the most famous musicians of fifteenth-century Ferrara was the lutenist–singer Pietrobono de Burzellis (*c.* 1417–97), who was celebrated as a performer of both monophonic song and polyphony.[10] Nothing of his music survives as none of it was written down. His lute playing was said to be unsurpassed, and he is often referred to in connection with his tenorista. Tantalisingly, we do not know what the tenorista actually did. The modern assumption is that the tenorista played a sustaining instrument, in effect accompanying the lute. The evidence (such as it is) actually suggests the opposite; the tenorista tradition appears to be a purely vocal one, and it may be more appropriate to think of Pietrobono's tenorista as a singer whose unique knowledge and skills provided the basic material and structural framework over which the lute could improvise.

The earliest tenor soloists

Most of the surviving music from the medieval period is for male voices. Although there were nunneries which had female choirs, the vast majority of sacred polyphony was created by and for men. Men, therefore, were trained as musicians, and it is not surprising that the earliest surviving secular music is also for men. As musical part-writing evolved from the customary two or three parts into four or more, the highest parts would also have been sung by male singers, either boys, falsettists or high tenors. In secular music, for courtly or domestic consumption, the highest part would have been taken by female singers, and in the sixteenth-century Italian madrigal the focus is very much on the highest part, normally sung by a soprano. The earliest madrigal manuscripts and prints are a little misleading, however, and did not necessarily imply an all-vocal performance. When the madrigals of Arcadelt, Verdelot and Willaert, for example, were performed as they appear in modern editions, tenors would have been relegated to a supporting role on the inner parts. But quite early in the century there is evidence that polyphonic madrigals were also sung as tunes with accompaniment. A number of Verdelot's madrigals were produced by Willaert as a book of songs with lute accompaniment (1536). These are performable by either sopranos or tenors, and indicate a willingness to plunder any musical source for performance in whatever ways the musicians felt appropriate.

During the course of the century the madrigal eclipsed the simpler strophic forms such as the *strambotta* and *frottola*, as its flexibility of form and potential to be adapted to any type of poetry gave musicians considerable creative freedom. The boundary between composition and improvisation was always fluid, especially as the 'renaissance man' (like his often underestimated medieval counterpart) was usually both composer and performer. Manuscripts or prints from this period (or earlier) represented something between an aide-mémoire and plan of action: they were still far from representing a notional performance of the piece. Musicians would instinctively add ornaments and decoration to almost anything, and from the second quarter of the sixteenth century onwards instruction books begin to appear, codifying improvisatory practice and trying to impose some sort of order on this spontaneous creativity.[11]

For singers, the peak of creativity came with the metamorphosis of the polyphonic madrigal into a virtuosic solo song. The performer would take the tune of a madrigal and improvise upon it, a practice which must have been something between a jazz-like extrapolation and a cover version of the original madrigal. These re-workings could be played or sung (there are examples with and without texts) and suggest that a new class of dedicated soloist was emerging.[12] Frustratingly, we know very little about the performers of such music; what Howard Mayer Brown described as 'the first golden age of the virtuoso performer' is known to us only from a small handful of pieces, some didactic works and the occasional reference to the brilliance of the singers.[13]

The reasons for this are partly a matter of historiography – scores and writings survive, people and performances do not – and partly to do with the nature of performing and performances. It was still uncommon for singers to be described by voice type; they are singers or musicians first and foremost, able to compose, improvise and play instruments as well as sing to order. If male singers were valued for their speech-like clarity of diction and their ability to get round the notes very quickly, then there would not be much to distinguish a tenor from a bass except in terms of range. So the exceptional voices of Brancaccio and Palantrotti means they are described as basses, whereas if they had been tenors they are more likely to have been referred to as singers. Example 1, by Bovicelli, could not easily be sung by a bass, and the most likely singer would have been a soprano or a tenor.

Example 1 Bovicelli: *from* 'Angelus ad pastores' (1594)

Little is known about Bovicelli, beyond his *Regole, passaggi di musica, madrigali e motetti passeggiati*, published in Venice in 1594. He was clearly a competent composer, and the versions of other people's music contained in his treatise suggest that he was an impressive improviser. He is likely to have been a tenor, as the ornaments fit idiomatically to the voice (more so than other versions of this madrigal that are obviously intended for instruments). When this sort of virtuosity is combined with drama and spectacle the tenor soloist begins to emerge from anonymity, and we start to get many more clues about the nature of the voice.

Tenors and early works for the stage

This early period in the history of the tenor voice (from the last decades of the sixteenth century onwards) coincided with the beginnings of what was to become opera. This was both the opportunity for the tenor to flourish as a soloist, and the cause of his temporary demise. For the first time we can document and name actual singers, as tenors took leading roles in many early operas before composers succumbed to the lure of the castrati. Although this short-lived 'golden age' turned out to be something of a false start for the tenor, it marked an important period in the development of the voice. The tenor voice began to be perceived as something special. The theorist Giovanni Battista Doni, in discussing which voices are appropriate for generic roles such as god, angels, demons and the like, suggests the part of Jesus, whether pre- or post-resurrection, should be given to a fine tenor (he recommends the Roman Francesco Bianchi) because tenors equate more to 'a well-adjusted and perfectly organised body' than other voices.[14]

The position of musicians in society was a delicate one. To read notation and be able to improvise was the result of study, and having the wealth and leisure to learn implied a certain social status. The only employers were the church and the aristocracy, on whose patronage singers were entirely dependent for their livelihoods. Many musicians had aristocratic connections by birth, but in the hierarchical society of the typical renaissance court they were always beholden to a patron who was wealthier or more well-connected than they were themselves.

Aspiring to nobility (and indeed being an aristocrat) involved certain social and professional constraints. A gentleman would not undertake anything so vulgar as paid work, but was expected to be extremely skilled in a number of areas. In his early sixteenth-century etiquette *Il cortegiana* (Venice, 1528; Eng. trans. *The Book of the Courtier*) Baldesar Castiglione says:

> let the Courtier turn to music as a pastime, and as though forced . . . and dissimulate the care and effort that is required in doing anything well; and let him appear to esteem but little this accomplishment of his, yet by performing it excellently well, make others esteem it highly.[15]

He goes on to say that the best sort of music is that which involves singers accompanying themselves.

This is exactly what Jacopo Peri did in one of the earliest known performances by a named tenor soloist. Peri was born in Rome in 1561 to a family with aristocratic connections. He moved to Florence early in his childhood and by the age of twelve was singing in the church of Santissima Annunziata, becoming a composition pupil of Cristofano Malvezzi; six years later he was appointed organist at the Florentine Baptistry and was employed by the Medici court from 1588 onwards.

His easy grace and charm, and the confidence born of an aristocratic background, endeared him both to fellow musicians and the local nobility, though some of his rivals (notably Giulio Caccini) seem to have felt threatened by his success. As can be seen from his costume, designed for the role of Arion in the

1589 *intermedi*, Peri, known as 'il Zazzerino' (shock-headed) because of his long fair hair, was an imposing figure.

Intermedi were musical entertainments that took place between acts in renaissance plays, and were often on a grander scale than the plays themselves. The intermedio tradition is particularly associated with large-scale celebrations at the Medici court in Florence during the sixteenth century. They were elaborate and expensive, with as much attention given to sets and costumes as to the music, little of which has survived. The most spectacular was put together for the wedding of Ferdinando de' Medici and Christine of Lorraine in 1589, and it included performances by at least two composers who were known to be tenors: Jacopo Peri and Giulio Caccini.

Peri was praised throughout his life for his sensitive singing and ability to give life to the words, and this breakthrough in musical expressiveness was due as much to the fact that he was a tenor as it was to his skill as a composer. He was capable of extreme virtuosity, as demonstrated in Example 2, which he performed to his own accompaniment on the chitarrone in the 1589 *Intermedi.*

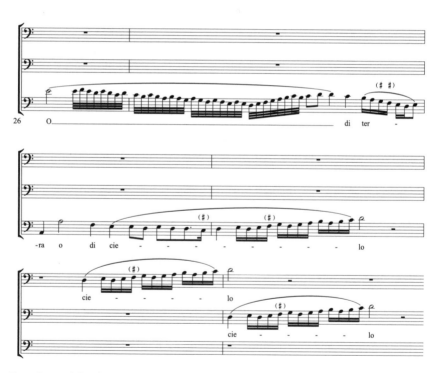

Example 2 Peri: *from* 'Dunque fra turbid' onde' (1589)

Here, perhaps for the first time, are all the ingredients for the creation of a star tenor: he sings complicated music which dazzles the fashionable audience, he accompanies himself brilliantly, he looks elegant and refined, writes his own music, and (curiously, in view of the most successful tenor manifestation of recent times) is supported by two echoing fellow tenors.[16]

This triumph undoubtedly confirmed Peri's reputation as a performer of substance, but it is as a composer that Peri is known to history, especially his contribution to the earliest operas. This was important on two counts: he was among the first to conceive of dramatic entertainment that is sung throughout, and (no less significantly) he is one of the musicians credited with the invention of recitative, in effect a dramatically heightened speech that carries the narrative in opera, obviating the need for spoken dialogue. It was Peri's practical experience as a performer that enabled him and his contemporaries to develop a concept of musical recitation in which the words were more important than the written notes. It only works in the hands of a charismatic singer: the recitatives in the earliest operas look very bleak indeed on the page. Peri's singing was unique; his younger contemporary Marco Gagliano said of him:

> Signor Jacopo Peri revived that artistic manner of singing that all Italy admires . . . there is no one who fails to give him infinite praise . . . I will say that no one can fully appreciate the sweetness and power of his airs who has not heard them sung by Peri himself, because he gave them such a grace and style that he so impressed in others the emotion of the words that one was forced to weep or rejoice as the singer wished.[17]

Peri wrote and sang in one of the earliest surviving operas, *Euridice*, in 1600, and also sang in Caccini's opera *Il rapimento di Cefalo* only a few days later. He was much in demand as a soloist both in his own works and in those of his contemporaries. It was his ability to personalise the narrative with an emotional weight that made his singing so appealing to his contemporaries. Severo Bonini said he 'would have moved to tears any heart of stone'.[18] The printed notes themselves are not sufficient, and in his preface to *Euridice* the composer draws attention to the singing of the soprano Vittoria Archilei, who adds 'long windings of the voice' and 'those elegances and graces that cannot be written or, if written, cannot be learned from writing'.[19] The expectation is that singers will improve on the composer's efforts in the new style, just as they did with the ornamentation of madrigals in the past, but anchoring their additions in the drama, not merely demonstrating virtuosity for its own sake. Peri's understanding that effective communication had to be grounded in emotional expression and textual rhetoric ensured that the tenor would become the principal narrative voice in the dramatic music of the future. This archetype would eventually manifest itself in the Evangelist roles in Bach's Passion settings, and would not be superseded until the operas of Wagner. The very essence of opera was thus symbiotically connected to the tenor voice from its inception.

Not all singers had Peri's sensitivity to text, and singers increasingly come under fire for excessive ornamentation (a trend that would also last until Wagner). One such tenor who comes in for early criticism is Giuseppe Cenci, known simply as Giuseppino. The writer Pietro della Valle, who mentions a number of the most successful tenors of the day, says of this singer:

> He sang with poor judgement because most of the time he put *passaggi* where they didn't belong; one never knew whether his singing was happy or sad, because it was always the same.[20]

The new style of singing was documented by Giulio Caccini – whose reputation, like Peri's, survived because of his more durable talent as a composer. Caccini was born in Rome around 1550, and like Peri had been a boy soprano. His father was a carpenter, a fact that perhaps made Caccini rather sensitive to the success of his more aristocratic fellow musicians. He came to Florence to study with Scipione della Palla, a singer of some reputation and to whom he gave credit for instruction in 'the noble manner of singing.'[21] Caccini was, by all accounts, vain and self-important, overly fond of women and gambling, never quite happy with his life however successful he became, and was often jealous of his rivals.[22] He took part in the first performance of Peri's *Euridice* but insisted that his family members and pupils who were also taking part should sing only music written by him. Of his two published volumes of monodies, the second may have been written in response to Peri's success as a monodist. The preface to Caccini's first volume, *Le nuove musiche*, is an important source of information about the new singing style. He went to some lengths to try to convince his readers that he was responsible for re-inventing singing. It is more likely, however, that Caccini articulated practices that had been around for some time. His assertion that singing is about 'speaking in tones' is central to the vocal aesthetic of the period, but it is probably no more than Peri and their contemporaries were already doing. Caccini's remarks were aimed at those singers who had not understood the restraint that he considered necessary for the new music.

One of the key concepts that he articulates is that of *sprezzatura*, a term which translates very approximately as 'negligence'. This concept, as Wiley Hitchcock points out in his commentary on Caccini's preface, had figured in

Castiglione's *The Book of the Courtier*, with reference to that effortlessness essential to the style of the gentleman.[23] Caccini describes it as 'noble', in keeping with his own courtly aspirations. The effect of this is to ensure that the rhythms of the poetry, and the expressive potential in individual phrases, are privileged over metrical rhythm. One reason for stressing this kind of rubato (and its associated courtliness) may be that part of the history of solo song is embedded in more popular (and rhythmic) genres such as the *frottola* and *villanella*. Caccini gives instructions for specific ornaments to enhance the printed notes, and cautions against display for its own sake. Unlike his fellow singer–composers, whose charismatic delivery was said to be an essential ingredient in their success, Caccini stresses that his scores have all the information for the successful performance by singers other than himself (an early example of the composer trying to assert control over 'his' music, and restrict the creative additions that future singers are likely to make). The history of performance from this time onwards is one of a subtly changing balance of creativity between composers and performers.

Caccini's other significance as a tenor is that he was one of the first to have an international career. He spent the winter of 1604–5 at the French court in Paris, together with his daughter Francesca and other family members and pupils, and his compositions were certainly known in England (two songs appear in Robert Dowland's *Musical Banquet* of 1610).

His most famous pupil was also a tenor of international repute, Francesco Rasi, born in Arezzo in 1574. Paradoxically, Rasi's compositions have been largely ignored by historians, possibly because his considerable reputation as a singer actually survived him.[24] He sang in almost every operatic production at the turn of the century: Amintas in Peri's *Euridice* in Florence (1600), Caccini's *Il rapimento di Cefalo* the same year, Monteverdi's *Orfeo* in Mantua (1607), and his *Arianna* (1608), as well as playing Apollo in Marco da Gaglinano's *Daphne*. Like Peri, he was of noble birth, so was in a position to spend his life fulfilling his chosen vocation without needing to try too hard. In common with his Florentine contemporaries he was a man of many parts, a master of the chitarrone and keyboard instruments, a composer of at least one opera and two books of monodies, and a writer of seven volumes of verse, as well as the most famous tenor of his day. These were simply the sum of his qualities as a gentleman (he did not like to be known as a jobbing musician).[25] One of Rasi's claims to fame is that he introduced the new style of singing to countries north of the Alps, appearing in Warsaw, Vienna, Salzburg, France and the Low Countries as well as all the important courts in northern Italy. Bonini (also an ex-Caccini pupil) says of him that he sang elegantly, and with the greatest passion and spirit. He was a handsome, jovial man, with a most pleasing smooth voice; his divine, angelic singing was enhanced by his joyous countenance and majestic presence.[26]

After studying briefly with Caccini in Florence Rasi quickly found himself in demand as a singer and chitarrone player. He may have been employed by Gesualdo, and his compositions were sought after by patrons in both Rome and Florence. Around 1595 he entered the service of the Gonzagas at Mantua, to whose court he remained attached for the rest of his life. The freedom to travel granted to him by his patron was an acknowledgment of the valuable cultural asset that Rasi represented. He performed in Warsaw for King Sigismund in 1597 (where he ran up enormous debts) and, together with Monteverdi, accompanied the Duke of Ferrara to Flanders in 1599.

Some indication of Rasi's skill as a performer can be seen in the music Monteverdi wrote for him in the role of Orfeo, which he first performed in 1607 and may have repeated in Salzburg in 1614. Orfeo's aria 'Possente spirto' was published in two versions, plain and ornamented. The reasons for this have never been fully established, but the ornamented version may represent something close to what Rasi actually sang (as opposed to the outline that the composer perhaps originally wrote) for the benefit of those who wished to remember it. If this is the case, it demonstrates the scale of the creative contribution that a singer was expected to make to the compositional process.[27]

Monteverdi and Rasi were colleagues at the Mantua court and would have seen a great deal of each other's music. Rasi sang in the lost *Arianna* the following year and was perhaps at the peak of his career by 1610, when he was sentenced to be hung, drawn and quartered for the murder of his stepmother's servant. Such was his importance to the Gonzaga court that he was pardoned but exiled from his home town of Arezzo.[28]

We can get an idea of what Rasi's performances may have been like by looking at his published songs, which combine virtuosity and a poetic sensitivity that characterised the best music of the time (Ex. 3).

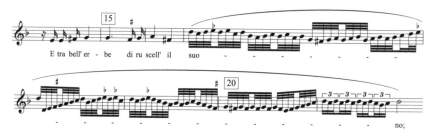

Example 3 Rasi: *from* 'Indarno Febo' (1589)

Monteverdi, though not known to be a great vocal performer himself, was a noted teacher of singers. Among his most famous pupils was the tenor Francesco Campagnolo, who lived with the composer in Mantua for a number of years at the end of the century. Campagnolo subsequently became internationally known, performing as far afield as the English court of Queen Anne, as well as in Rome, Salzburg, and in Hungary. By 1619 he was, together with Monteverdi, one of the highest-paid members of the Mantuan court.[29]

We can only guess at the sound these tenors made, but the fact that Monteverdi could teach singing while not being a singer himself is an indication that the kinds of skills and techniques required of a renaissance singer were rather different from those of today. The focus must surely have been on wider performance skills to do with rhetoric and virtuosity rather than sound quality in a more abstract sense. The picture is made the more complicated by the fact that some of the most famous tenors were also capable of singing in the bass register. This repertoire and its performers have been largely overlooked by historians, partly because the little surviving music is to be found in a small number of songbooks and not in any surviving large-scale works, and partly because it is very hard for today's tightly categorised singers to conceive of such a range. Vincenzo Giustiniani identifies four virtuoso tenors who were equally at home singing in both registers: Caccini, Giuseppino, Rasi, and the Roman tenor Giovanni Puliaschi. He claims that they all combined agility with an ability to make the words clear.[30] The wide range that these singers employed suggests that they made an open, speech-like sound which would have facilitated both mobility and clarity (a controlled but relatively uncultured sound compared with today's tenors and basses, perhaps).[31] Examples of music written for such a voice include two monodies in Caccini's 1614 collection and several by Puliaschi in his *Musiche varie* of 1618. [32]

The tenor voice had not yet settled into the distinctive range and sound-world that would eventually become the modern voice, but the potent combination of dramatic declamation and extreme virtuosity associated with early seventeenth-century tenors was a defining characteristic of the earliest operas. A successful tenor employed by an Italian patron in the first quarter of the century might well have imagined that his particular voice embodied the vocal persona of the future. In time this would indeed be so, and Italy would be the country that would see the most important developments in the tenor voice; but after the remarkable careers of the first star tenors, there was to be a long hiatus in tenorial evolution. The dramatic music in which the new voice flourished was invariably based on classical mythology, so far removed from the present as to seem almost magical. Gods and goddesses, semi-mythological shepherds and the like from the *intermedi* onwards, were not expected to behave like normal human beings; it was therefore perfectly acceptable for them to sing rather than speak their lines. Artificial beings need not be gender-specific either, and when courtly establishments began to employ castrati in their chapels it was only a short step for these extraordinary singers to add a new dimension of artifice to the evolving genre of musical drama. Over the course of the eighteenth century the tenor voice in opera would be eclipsed by the castrati, who took on the leading roles as lovers and heroes, while tenors were first shunted sideways into lesser character roles, and then type-cast as kings or generals as opera split into two sub-genres of *seria* and *buffa.*

This temporary thwarting of tenor evolution can be neatly charted in the music of Claudio Monteverdi. His earliest operas have substantial roles for tenor, and the *Vespers* of 1610 also includes movements that require specialist virtuoso tenors; there is a substantial repertoire of tenor duets, and in the 1624 *Combattimento di Tancredi e Clorinda* the tenor narrator is the leading role. His last opera, however, *L'incoronazione di Poppea,* has a castrato in the role of Nero. Monteverdi's successor at St Mark's Venice, Francesco Cavalli, occasionally wrote leading roles for tenors, but by then the majestic singing of the tenor-bass of earlier in the century was reduced to the tenor-falsetto bleatings required for the travesty role of Ceffea in his *Scipione* of 1667. None of Carissimi's one hundred and fifty cantatas is for tenor, and it is only with Alessandro Scarlatti that we begin to see renewed interest in the voice in Italy.[33]

High tenors in England and France

The development of the tenor voice as a distinct vocal entity took a different course outside Italy. Although Italian music was known in England at this time, Italian singing seems not to have made much headway. English aristocratic life centred on London and the monarchy, and there was not the artistic competition that drove Italian musical and cultural life. Italian musicians were traditionally welcomed at the English court, but they were regarded as exotic oddities, competent musicians and good teachers who were often little more than an ornament to the social and musical scene. There had been solo and polyphonic songs sung at the Tudor courts, and the decades either side of 1600 saw the rise and fall of the English lute song school. This domestic secular music was poetically expressive but undemanding vocally and required none of the virtuosity of contemporary Italian music. The songs can be sung comfortably by the tenor voice when accompanied by a lute, though when translated to the piano in early twentieth-century editions they were as likely to be sung by light baritones. Listening to a modern lute can give us valuable clues about renaissance singing technique. The most striking aspect of hearing a modern tenor accompanied by a sixteenth- or seventeenth-century instrument is the balance: the singer is likely to be too loud. His renaissance equivalent would almost certainly have sung with a similar dynamic range to that of the instrument: in modern terms from *pp* to *mf*.[34]

The civil war in England (1642–6) inevitably caused some disruption in the musical and cultural life of the country, but there were plenty of songs written for a tenor-like voice in the interregnum. There are parallels with late sixteenth-century Italy: musicians being generalists and expected to be competent as singers, players and composers, but history claiming them simply as composers. William and Henry Lawes, now known for their theatre music and songs respectively, were both 'musicians for lutes and voices' to Charles 1, and almost certainly sang tenor (the range that most of their songs are written for).

The main focus of English music was the masque, an aristocratic entertainment on a more modest scale than Italian *intermedi* but which featured songs in the context of dance and drama. The genre encompassed a wide variety of vocal styles from the folk-like to the rhetorical and mildly virtuosic, none of which generated singers of particular note. After the restoration of the monarchy in 1660 there are more obvious French and Italian influences at work. Purcell's 'opera' *Dido and Aeneas* was an inauspicious start for the voice that would eventually dominate the genre, but he did write significant music for male voices, especially for a higher voice that he called a counter-tenor. These lines have often challenged modern singers, who have been unsure whether they are high tenor parts or are meant for falsettists. They in fact divide into both varieties, the lower of the two being within range of conventional high tenor if modern performers use lower seventeenth-century pitch.[35]

Things were better for the tenor voice in France, however. While the English tenor was failing to get off the ground and the Italian tenor was being overtaken by castrati, the French *haute-contre* flourished. This was a voice similar to the high tenor of Purcell, a tenor with a mixed voice extension that could sing as high as D or E. By the middle of the sixteenth century the voice that in England and Italy would be assigned to the tenor line is called the *taille* in France and this continued to be the term for modest tenor roles until the nineteenth century when Italian terminology became the norm. The voice that would then be called *ténor* was the successor to the haute-contre, the high tenor for which Rameau wrote many leading roles. French composers never fully embraced the castrato (and the alto castrato was often compared unfavourably with the haute-contre). Although eighteenth-century Italian tenors were able to sing in the haute-contre range, the sound and the voice production were quite different. Italian singing involved moving seamlessly into falsetto (some were more successful at this than others) and in handbooks right up the end of the nineteenth century the joining of these two registers is a central requirement for good singing. As will be seen in Chapter 3, Italian singing eventually extended the chest voice upwards, and today's tenors rarely use falsetto at all, preferring to exploit the power that can be gained by chesting high notes. The haute-contre involves neither of these techniques, but produces high notes in a mixed register without actually making the transition into pure falsetto.[36]

The French had little time for virtuosity that was unrelated to the text, and a distinctively French sound developed based on the exigencies of the French language. The singers were able to add ornamentation, but this was elegant rather than extravagant, and preserved the stresses and quantities of spoken French. The custom of seeking pleasant and euphonious texts for *airs de cour* came to preclude the setting of harsh or markedly dramatic words or phrases, and only a limited amount of repetition was permitted.

There was much debate about the pronunciation that French singers were supposed to use. Bénigne de Bacilly's *Remarques curieuses sur l'art de bien chanter* of 1668 is part ornamentation treatise and part language tutor. He favours a forceful declamation similar to that used by actors rather than a delivery based on normal speech, and his strictures give the impression that sung French is almost a foreign language, bearing little relationship to everyday speech.

He does favour high voices over low ones (basses are only suitable for polyphony) and the *airs* that he writes about were designed for sopranos, falsettists or tenors. The songs are charming, and suit modern light, high tenors well, especially if they are accompanied by theorbo (Bacilly's accompanying instrument of choice).[37]

The genesis of national styles

This is a very different world from that of Italian singing, and is indicative of a fundamental divide that would characterise aspects of the singing of the two countries for generations to come. Bacilly is aware of the comparisons that were often made between French and Italian singing, and the importance of language to those distinctions: 'the Italian language permits more freedom than the French, whose strictness (which is perhaps excessive) tends to hold composers in check and often prevents them from doing everything that their genius would inspire'.[38]

Bacilly had studied with Pierre de Nyert, a courtier and singer who had visited Rome in 1633 and become profoundly interested in exploring the dramatic possibilities of Italian declamation without losing the textual subtleties of French singing.[39] The contradictions inherent in the two styles were not to be fully resolved until the nineteenth century, and despite the

Italian influence on French singing the two traditions developed in quite different directions, which might be considered to be the basis of separate national styles.

The argument for a French national style is clear: the singing was significantly shaped by the spoken language, to the extent that tenors brought up in this tradition would often find it difficult to transfer their skills into other languages. The resistance to Italian singing also ensured a strong French vocal identity, but compounded the isolation from the vocal traditions developing elsewhere in Europe.

Italian singing rapidly became internationalised; its expressive potential rooted in rhetoric rather than in the structure of the language meant that it easily translated itself into other languages and contexts. The function of singing was much simpler: it became an end in itself. The two traditions would intertwine at various points in the future, and as far as the tenor voice is concerned they had one essential thing in common: an instinct to explore the upper tessitura, and it was this that would ultimately bring the two strands into alignment in the singing of Duprez in the nineteenth century.

CHAPTER 2

HANDEL, MOZART AND THE TENOR–CASTRATO CONNECTION

The increasing tendency to think of the tenor as a high voice was partly the result of a number of individual singers who were judged to be particularly charismatic, with unique abilities to move their listeners. This phenomenon occurred both in the French realm of the haute-contre, where the high tenor flourished under both Lully and Rameau, and in Italy, despite being reduced to secondary roles in the age of the castrato *primo uomo*. Lully's haute-contre parts rarely go above A, and he used a succession of singers, from Louis Dumesny (who made his début in *Isis* in 1677) to Denis-François Tribou, who first appears in *Phaëton* in 1721. Tribou was a higher tenor still, and went on to create the roles of Hippolytus (1733) and Castor (1737) for Rameau. On Tribou's retirement in 1738 Pierre Jélyotte took over many of his roles, and took the voice itself to top D. In turn he was succeeded by Joseph Legros, for whom Gluck revised the castrato role of Orfeo in 1774, and who became an enthusiastic promoter of the works of Haydn and Mozart after his retirement in 1783. In Italy there were similar excursions into the upper reaches of the voice with tenors such as Gregorio Babbi and Angelo Amorevoli, although they achieved similar results by different means.

In 1768, Joseph de Lalande, reflecting on the career of the illustrious haute-contre, explained Jélyotte's relationship to his Italian contemporaries in terms of the differences between the two types of voice:

> I have said that the *tenor* of the Italians was the *haute-contre* of the French. ... The *tenor* goes from C to G in full voice and to D in *falsetto* or *fausset*: our *haute-contre*, ordinarily, after G goes up in full voice to B *flat*; while the tenor after G enters into falsetto; but that is not without exception: Babbi goes up to C in full voice, the same as Caribaldi until the age of 48. Amorevoli, who was a little older, went up to D. In Paris, Geliot had the compass of Amorevoli, and Legros had that of the first two; these qualities of voice, in all countries, are very rare.[1]

'Full voice' in this context should be taken to mean mixed head and chest voice, and not the full chest voice that Italian tenors would develop later. Both voices were described as powerful, but the haute-contre sound seems not to have travelled well. This is perhaps because the technique was likely to sound strained as singers approached their absolute top, making it unsuitable for extravagant virtuosic display. Lalande complains that the successors of Legros 'were obliged to shout to reach the pitch of the haute-contre'; the Italian tenors, on the other hand, were able to be expressive and artistic as well as agile close to their absolute ceiling.[2] Italian tenor technique was also very similar to that used by the castrati (as we shall see), and after Legros the haute-contre began to lose ground. The relationship between French and Italian singing would remain one of the most fascinating aspects of tenorial history, but the immediate future was to be Italian.

The history of singing from the sixteenth century to the first quarter of the nineteenth is (broadly speaking) one of increasing virtuosity, as both composers and singers tested each others' limits in terms of taste and agility, the former bearing in mind that singers would always seek to 'improve' on their efforts and the latter creatively exceeding the notes on the page whenever they got the opportunity. The continual pushing at the boundaries of virtuosic vocalism also tended to expand singers' upper ranges, the increasing size of venues, louder instruments and the colourful tonal palette of the baroque making an extended lower tessitura impractical (though not unknown). The process seems to have occurred to some extent in all voice types, though not always at the same time. By the middle of the eighteenth century the castrati were taking virtuoso singing into realms that we can now barely imagine, but as the century wore on there were remarkable developments in both soprano and tenor singing as these voices came to equal, and eventually supersede the *musici* (as they were euphemistically called) in terms of success if not of outlandish virtuosity. The tenor voice in particular saw a brief but extraordinary flourishing of extremely high singing, in which the best singers could unite the registers to combine 'the power of a man's voice with all the sweetness and charm of a woman's'.[3] The decline of this mixed-register singing overlaps with the final demise of the castrati and the evolution of the modern tenor, for whom the sweetness and charm came to be replaced with powerful top notes sung in what we call chest voice.[4] These three apparently separate developments were in fact closely connected with each other.

The high tenor voice is elusive, as composers rarely notated the highest available pitches, preferring to leave them to the ornamental discretion of individual singers. Composers were generally conservative in their estimate of singers' ranges and were careful to keep within a written tessitura that was comfortably manageable over an entire evening.[5] By the end of the eighteenth century there was a substantial gap between the highest composed notes and the known ranges of many singers, which could be exploited by those who were able to disguise the register change into falsetto and use this very special tone colour for additional improvised ornamentation. Descriptions of high tenor singing make it clear that this sound was powerful and thrilling (perhaps more like a modern operatic counter-tenor than a traditional cathedral alto); French treatises of the period frequently make the point that the high voice previously known as haute-contre was the equivalent of a normal high tenor.[6]

As tenors became more proficient at such heights the notated tessitura increased too, reaching a peak with the soprano F that Bellini required from Giovanni Battista Rubini in *I puritani* in 1834/5. This compares with the soprano G that Garaudé's treatise of 1841 gives as the highest usable note for tenors in their '2me régistre' or 'sons de tête'.[7] Many tenors became famous not only for the heights at which they could sing, but the ease with which they could pass imperceptibly from chest to head voice, a key tenet of eighteenth-century teaching (and earlier). Rubini, the most celebrated of these *tenore contraltini* and first real tenor superstar, could change registers (like his English contemporary John Braham) without anyone being able to hear the join.[8]

Handel and his tenors

The musical scene in London in the early years of the eighteenth century was dominated by Handel. One of the budding composer's earliest experiences of tenors was with his friend and fellow-composer Johann Mattheson. Mattheson later claimed to have influenced Handel's compositional style, especially his melodic writing, but perhaps a more subtle influence was

Mattheson's singing. He had learned a more refined and Italianate style than was the norm in many German opera houses and had written his first opera in 1699. The two first met in 1703 when both were employed at the Hamburg opera; both applied for Buxtehude's job as organist at Lübeck, composing complex fugues while they journeyed together for the auditions. Neither took the job, perhaps because the successful candidate was expected to marry the aging composer's daughter. They fell out briefly the following year over a performance of Mattheson's *Cleopatra* in which the composer himself took the role of Antoninus with Handel playing harpsichord continuo. After Antoninus' death in the third act Mattheson expected to take over the harpsichord part but Handel refused to leave the instrument. The two headstrong musicians then fought a duel, Handel (according to Mattheson) escaping certain death when the Mattheson's sword struck a large button on his coat. Honour having been satisfied they made up their quarrel and Mattheson subsequently took the leading tenor roles in Handel's first two operas, *Almira* and *Nero*, produced in Hamburg in 1705.[9]

Handel's Italian years 1706–9 exposed him to some of the finest singers in Europe. The best of these were, of course, castrati, and he would have immersed himself in the world of extravagant vocalism that was the norm for these extraordinary singers. He would also have encountered tenors that were in a different league from Mattheson and he certainly built up contacts that he would find crucially important in the future. By the time he became established as an opera composer at the King's Theatre in London he had access to, and budgets for, the best singers to be found. Tenors were not yet able to achieve the same status as castrati but their music and their star quality were on an upward trajectory. He was able to secure the services of the first stellar Italian tenors Francesco Borosini, Annibale Pio Fabri and Giovanni Battista Pinacci. Borosini's most famous role was that of Bajazet in *Tamerlano*, which Handel re-wrote in 1724 for his particular dramatic and vocal talents and which is generally considered to be the first substantial true tenor role to exploit the potential of the voice.[10] Borosini's strengths included considerable agility in the lower and middle parts of his register, going to down to a baritonal A or G. Pinacci must have had a similar range; hired by Handel for the 1731–2 season, he probably made his London début also in *Tamerlano*. Handel recomposed the bass parts of Hercules in *Admeto* and Lotario in *Flavio* for him, as well as giving him several other roles. He was a versatile singer, and took on roles originally sung by both Fabri and Borosini as well as the bilingual *Acis and Galatea*. He was often criticised for bellowing, but obviously had Borosini-like low notes.[11]

Perhaps the most famous of Handel's tenors was Annibale Pio Fabri, whose range was such that he could sing bass roles or mezzo-soprano parts transposed down an octave, as was the case when he came to London in 1729.[12] Fabri had the classic Italian tenor career path; born in 1697, he sang female roles as a child in Rome and then learned with the great castrato Panzocchi in Bologna. He was an accomplished composer and by the late 1720s he was successful all over northern Italy. Handel brought him to the King's Theatre, where he sang in *Lotario*, *Partenope*, and *Poro* as well as Sextus in *Giulo Caesare*, in the tenor version originally written for Borosini. The roles in these operas required him to be agile over his entire range of two octaves. Burney considered his singing so fine that it could make up for a male soprano lead – one of the earliest examples of a tenor registering with critics as the equal of castrati.[13]

Handel was very happy to use home-grown tenors where these were up to the job. Some of the more successful British singers had training and even careers in Italy. The Scotsman Alexander Gordon's earliest known performance was in Messina in 1716 and he appeared at the Teatro di San Bartolomeo in Naples in the 1717–18 season. By 1720 he was in London where he sang Tiridate in Handel's *Radamisto* in the first King's Theatre season in 1720. Despite Handel's intention to write him a part in *Giulio Cesare* (and he may also have been the original choice for Bazajet), Gordon gave up singing in 1723 to give himself over to his other great passion, the research into Roman antiquities in the north of England. Gordon did not always get on with Handel: once, dissatisfied with Handel's continuo playing, he threatened to jump into the harpsichord, whereupon the composer offered to advertise the event, saying that more people would come to see him jump than to hear him sing.[14]

It was his English works, however, that caused Handel to look to native singers, especially those who could bring a sense of drama to his oratorios. Thomas Lowe was an accomplished singing actor, for whom Arne wrote most of his Shakespeare settings as well as several operatic roles. Handel wrote several substantial tenor parts for him, including the title role in *Joshua*. Lowe also alternated with John Beard as Macheath in *The Beggar's Opera*.[15] Beard was the singer most associated with Handel's tenor roles; he had sung in *Esther* while still a treble and made his operatic début in the revival of *Il Pastor Fido* with Handel's own company in 1734 (significantly for the greater importance of the tenor voice, replacing the castrato Carlo Scalzi). He went on to take part in ten operas and almost all the oratorios, notably *Samson* (1743), *Belshazzar* (1745), *Judas Maccabaeus* (1747) and *Jephtha* (1752). Beard must have been a remarkably flexible singer, with the agility to cope with florid Italian operas as well as the gravitas required for the oratorios. He also sang ballad opera and pantomime, which must have involved the suspension of much of his technique and an ability to communicate in speech as well as song. As manager of Covent Garden from 1761 he was responsible for Thomas Arne's most successful stage works, *Artaxerxes* and *Love in a Village*. He sang in them both, accompanied in the latter by his own dog.

Haydn and Mozart: Friberth, d'Ettore, Raaff and Adamberger

Haydn and Mozart explored a higher tessitura generally, although apart from the title role in the early *Mitridate* which has a number of high Cs composed for Guglielmo d'Ettore, Mozart did not like to write above B flat for tenor. This is a little higher than Handel, and assuming singers' patterns of ornamentation remained much the same one can imagine that the ornamental range went perhaps to D.[16] The wealth of the Esterházy court ensured that Haydn had access to some of the best singers of the day. His writing for Karl Friberth, his friend, sometime librettist and principle tenor soloist for many years, displays extremes of pitch and an angularity of line, with wide leaps and extended arpeggios. Haydn extended Friberth in both directions (Ex. 4).

l'al - tra pro - va la___ lar - ghez - za, lar - ghez - za

Example 4 Haydn: *from* 'Questa è un'altra novità', *Lo Speziale* (1768)

In *L'infedeltà delusa* (1773) Nencio's aria in Act 1, scene VI ranges from bottom B flat to top C; in *L'incontro improvviso* (1775) Haydn takes Friberth down to bottom G, and in *Il ritorno di Tobia* (1784) he has several high Ds as well as a bottom A (Ex. 5).

Example 5 Haydn: *from* 'Quel felice nocchier', *Il ritorno di Tobia* (1784)

Mozart's first professional experience of tenors was exasperating, when as a precocious fourteen-year-old he had to endure the eccentricities and vanity of d'Ettore in the title role of *Mitridate*. The Sicilian tenor had little confidence in the young prodigy and tried to get the prima donna Antonia Bernasconi to substitute arias by Gasparini instead; he had no qualms about substituting a Gasparini aria himself, as well as obliging the composer to re-write one of his arias four times.[17] D'Ettore clearly had room at the top, however:

l'om - bra mi - a pre - ce - de - rà,   l'om - bra   mi - a pre - ce - de -

rà,____ l'om - bra mi - a pre - ce - de - rà,____ l'om - bra mi - a pre - ce - de - rà.

Example 6 Mozart: *from* 'Vado incontro', *Mitridate* (1770)

Later on there were tenors whom Mozart did respect, even love, such as
Anton Raaff, although the first time he heard him, in 1777, he was not
impressed by his performance. Raaff's acting had never been up to much and
at the age of sixty-three he was singing on borrowed time. He had intended to
become a priest, and had his first singing experience in Jesuit church dramas as
a boy before being sent by the Elector of Bavaria to study with the castrato
Bernacchi in Bologna. He subsequently spent ten years in Naples, where he
became the leading tenor in Farinelli's company. By the time he met the young
Mozart Raaff was one of the most distinguished singers of his day. In contrast
to d'Ettore, he was amazed at the talent shown by the youth. Although he must
have been aware that Mozart sometimes found him wanting, their relationship
blossomed into one of deep mutual respect. Raaff was a product of his age, and
like d'Ettore and every other tenor before him was accustomed to getting his
own way, even to the extent of refusing to sing anything he felt did not do him
justice. The twenty-one-year-old Mozart had to handle him carefully:

> One must treat a man like Raaff in a particular way. I chose those words on
> purpose ['Se al labbro mio non credi' K295], because I knew that he already
> had an aria on them: so of course he will sing mine with greater facility and
> more pleasure. I asked him to tell me candidly if he did not like it or if it did
> not suit his voice, adding that I would alter it if he wished or even compose
> another.[18]

Some negotiation ensued, with Raaff asking for the piece to be shortened as
his stamina is not what it was. Mozart agreed to 'arrange the aria in such a way
that it would give him pleasure to sing it. For I like an aria to fit a singer as
perfectly as a well-made suit of clothes.'[19] The following year Mozart heard
Raaff sing a concert aria by J. C. Bach in Paris and was obviously moved by the
singer's interpretation; although the excessive ornament of the Bernacchi
school was not to Mozart's taste, he appreciated that 'in bravura singing, long
passages and roulades, Raaff is absolute master'. The two had by now become
firm friends:

He likes me very much and we are very intimate. He comes almost every day to see us [. . .] But the time flies so quickly in his company that you simply don't notice it. He is very fond of me and I like being with him; he is such a friendly sensible person with such excellent judgment and he has a real insight into music.[20]

He compares Raaff favourably to Joseph Meissner (who had played Fracasso in *La finta semplice* in 1769 and whose vibrato Mozart found irritating). Mozart went on to compose the title role in *Idomeneo* for Raaff in 1781, by which time the singer was sixty-seven. Reading between the lines of his letter to his father of December 1780 it is clear that it was a frustrating experience for both of them:

Raaff is the best and most honest fellow in the world, but so tied to old-fashioned routine that flesh and blood cannot stand it. Consequently, it is very difficult to compose for him . . . Raaff is too fond of everything which is cut and dried, and he pays no attention to expression. I have just had a bad time with him over the quartet . . . Raaff alone thinks it will produce no effect whatever. He said to me when we were by ourselves: '*Non c'è da spianar la voce*. . . . *It gives me no scope.*' As if in a quartet the words should not be spoken much more than sung. That kind of thing he does not understand at all. All I said was: 'My very dear friend. If I knew of one single note which ought to be altered in this quartet, I would alter it at once. But so far there is nothing in my opera with which I am so pleased as this quartet; and when you have once heard it sung as a whole, you will talk very differently. I have taken great pains to serve you well in your two arias; I shall do the same with your third one – and shall hope to succeed. But as far as trios and quartets are concerned, the composer must have a free hand.'[21]

In this exchange we get a glimpse of just how advanced Mozart's thinking was: he wants control of the music and is striving for dramatic effect; he will not yield to the singer's demand for opportunities for vocal display, and the reference to the quartet being 'spoken' is a foretaste of the demands Verdi and Wagner were to make on their singers more than half a century later. On the other hand, if he thought the singer's suggestions might improve the drama Mozart was always ready to negotiate. The part of Arbace in *Idomeneo* was taken by Domenico de' Panzacchi, for whom Mozart wrote the brilliant 'Se il tuo duol'. Mozart seems to have got on well with Panzacchi, an older tenor of the traditional Italian school, which perhaps explains why he succumbed to a bravura aria when something less spectacular would perhaps have been more appropriate. When Panzacchi asked for an extended recitative Mozart was happy to agree:

> we must do what we can to oblige this worthy old fellow. He would like to have his recitative in Act 3 lengthened by a couple of lines, which owing to the *chiaro e oscuro* and his being a good actor will have a capital effect.[22]

Valentin Adamberger

The tenor most associated with Mozart's work is Valentin Adamberger. Born in Munich in 1743, Adamberger, like Raaff before him, had his first musical experiences courtesy of the local Jesuit school.[23] He was taught by Johann Walleshauer, another Munich tenor, who changed his name to Giovanni Valesi while working in Italy in the 1750s and who himself sang for Mozart in the first performances of *La finta giardiniera* (1775) and *Idomeneo* (1781).[24] Adamberger may not have had the caché of Raaff in his prime, but he was a successful tenor of international repute, appearing in London in 1777. A German tenor was something of a novelty outside the German-speaking world at this time (and the often curmudgeonly Earl of Mount Edgcumbe was unimpressed, noting that he 'had a disagreeable nasal voice, but sung with considerable science'[25]). As he did with all of his singers, Mozart crafted the music to fit the tenor's voice. We also get a sense from the correspondence that it gave the composer great satisfaction when he got the equation between voice and music absolutely right; his favourite arias invariably turn out to be those where the music fulfils his own artistic criteria while at the same time pleasing the singer. This was the case with Belmonte's aria 'O wie ängstlich' in *Die Entführung aus dem Serail* which the composer was working on towards the end of 1781. He wrote to his father:

> Would you like to know how I have expressed it – and even indicated his throbbing heart? By the two violins playing octaves. This is the favourite aria of all those who have heard it, and it is mine also. I wrote it expressly to suit Adamberger's voice. You see the trembling – the faltering – you see how his throbbing heart begins to swell; this I have expressed by a crescendo. You hear the whispering and the sighing . . .[26]

The first performance (at the Vienna Burgtheater in July 1782) was a success despite a hissing claque that hoped it would fail, but the second came close to disaster:

I was relying on the closing trio, but as ill-luck would have it, Fischer [the bass playing Osmin] went wrong which made Dauer [the tenor playing Pedrillo] go wrong too; and Adamberger alone could not sustain the trio, with the result that the whole effect was lost. . . . I was in such a rage (and so was Adamberger) . . .[27]

Adamberger seems to have been a supportive colleague and Mozart must have known him well; the letters contain references to their dining together and give the impression that they were often in each other's company. The tenor also performed several concert arias, including (transposed) those written for soprano, and he took part in Mozart's *Messiah* performance in 1789.[28] In 1784 he was supposed to sing the part of Tobias at a charity performance for Haydn in Vienna but withdrew at the last moment even though Haydn had cut the top D that he had originally written for Karl Friberth (see Example 2 above). Fortunately Friberth was also on hand on this occasion to save the day.[29] Adamberger retired from the stage in 1793 at the age of fifty, but continued to sing in the court chapel and to expand his successful teaching practice almost until his death in 1804.

Castrati as teachers

The lightness and agility required by late eighteenth-century writing for tenors is something that results from the ornamental technique of the castrati, who had some two centuries of experience of increasing virtuosity and joining registers artistically. Many (if not most) singers of the period were taught by castrati, but there is a particular connection between the *evirati* and tenors. Mozart himself took lessons from Giovanni Manzuoli while in London 1764–5, and, like Handel and Haydn before him, was steeped in the Italian tradition (although he would often weary of ornamental excess). Many of his tenors had castrati as teachers.

For much of the eighteenth century castrati defined the art of singing; it was the eventual loss of their irrecoverable skills that in time created the myth of *bel canto*, a way of singing and of conceptualising singing that was entirely different from anything that the world had heard before or would hear again. The male voices we hear today singing in the soprano or contralto range – countertenors – share only a certain overlap of range with castrati; the physiological and acoustic make-up of castrati and countertenors are completely different.[30] The optimum age for castration was before the age of seven, well before most treble voices have developed, though the operation was often carried out later than this. The large number of mutilated poor children contributed to the creation of musical charity schools at which the boys were prepared for a future as musicians if they showed sufficient talent or at least a life off the streets if they did not.[31] Training was rigorous and extensive and made the best possible use of the 'enhancements' in physique that castration produced, as the boys got older. Contemporary caricatures and descriptions often depict adult *musici* as large men with barrel chests, which would have given them much greater reserves of breath than unmutilated singers. Their larynxes in effect atrophied, remaining small and child-like. The extra breath supply meant a critical increase in subglottal pressure, which would have given them an unanswerable advantage over uncut singers: they would have the potential to command a very wide dynamic range with the means to control it, and they would be able to sing very long phrases (many of them could sing complex divisions for more than a minute without drawing breath). Castrati could – and did – sing in falsetto in their upper range, but their basic 'chest' voice was that of a potentially very powerful treble.

This 'natural' facility was soon exploited by composers and, more especially, by the singers themselves. Many became teachers, passing on the rapidly developing tradition; one of the earliest schools was that founded in Bologna in 1706 by Antonio Pistocchi (later to be the teacher of Annibale Pio Fabri). Among his most successful pupils was the *musico* Antonio Bernacchi, who himself became a teacher in Bologna, where he taught the legendary castrati Senesino and Carestini, as well as the tenors Panzacchi and Raaff. The teachers of the earliest castrato successes were invariably male, often not themselves castrati and likely to have been tenors if they were singers at all (basses being relatively rare and women teachers almost unknown in the eighteenth century); the institutions attracted some of the finest singing teachers and composers from all over Italy, including Alessandro Scarlatti and Nicola Porpora. Porpora (a tenor of sorts) came to be acknowledged as the finest singing teacher of the century, his students including the two stellar castrati Farinelli and Caffarelli, the influential teacher and tenor Domenico Corri, and the young Haydn (whose knowledge of singers and singing was comprehensive).

Since the greatest singers of day were often *musici* it is not surprising that voices of many tenors-to-be were nurtured by a *musico* from an early age. The career paths of Annibale Pio Fabri, Michael Kelly, Anton Raaff, Charles Incledon, John Braham and a host of other successful tenors show a very similar pattern, singing female stage roles as a boy while being taught by castrati (Pistocchi, Aprile, Bernacchi and Rauzzini respectively in these cases). This early link between castrati and potential tenors not only determined the nature of tenor technique but was a major factor in the transmission of ideas about singing from generation to generation. There was often considerable pressure even into the early nineteenth century for good trebles to be castrated in the hope that they would retain their voices into adulthood.[32] There were mutual advantages in the teacher–pupil relationship: the boys sang in roughly the same range as the castrati so a lot could be learned by imitation. Trebles who went on to become successful castrati would absorb teachings that dated back to the early seventeenth century or even earlier. The most talented youths would live with their teachers and study a relatively narrow repertoire of skills in great depth over several years. When boys' voices broke the castrati inevitably found themselves passing on their knowledge and experience to a relatively large number of young tenors (virtuoso basses were not unknown but the most spectacular vocal *fioriture* needed the greater range and higher tessitura of upper voices). This transition was also mutually beneficial: the fledgling tenor voice was not that dissimilar to that of the castrato an octave or so lower, so the principles of good singing could still be applied as the new voice developed. It was not uncommon for the voices of trebles who would become tenors not to break in the more drastic way that is sometimes the case for basses (in fact, the term 'break' is not really an appropriate one for many adolescent tenors, whose voices often seem just to sink into a lower tessitura[33]).

Michael Kelly

This was the experience of Michael Kelly, the Irish *buffo* tenor who was Mozart's first Don Basilio, and whose early career clearly shows the importance of castrato teaching for young tenors. While he was still a treble his talent was recognised by Venanzio Rauzzini on one of the great *musico*'s visits to Dublin. Rauzzini suggested he study in Italy, and Kelly duly took himself off to Naples, where he seems to have met another legendary castrato, Giuseppe Aprile, quite by chance (as he himself put it, 'It is really curious to observe upon what trifling circumstances the greatest and most important events of our lives depend'[34]). In Naples Kelly had become friends with the dancer Richard Blake and the two Irishmen bumped into Aprile one evening in a room above a billiard hall in the Strada di Toledo. Aprile asked the boy to sing to him the next day, and was sufficiently impressed to invite him to Palermo to study without payment (the only time Aprile ever made such an offer). In the meantime Aprile gave him daily lessons and sent him to a local singer for lessons in *solfeggi*.[35] After four months master and student set off on the three-day boat journey to Sicily and Aprile accommodated Kelly in an apartment in his own *palazzo*. During his five or six hours daily study with Aprile Kelly's voice 'fell gradually into a tenor' and he began to study songs written for the star tenors of the day, Giovanni Ansani and Giacomo David.[36]

Kelly's *Reminiscences* give a colourful and action-packed picture of Italian social and cultural life at the turn of the century. He was obviously a gregarious and charming fellow for whom doors opened effortlessly. The fact that he was a student of Aprile was sufficient for him to be invited to the best households in Palermo where he sang, played, flirted and gambled to his heart's content. When the time came for him to leave, his teacher provided him with letters of introduction to potential patrons in Florence and his career began with an engagement at the Teatro Nuovo in 1781. He was subsequently booked for operas in Graz, Treviso, Venice and Brescia, where he fled in fear for his life half way through a performance of Cimarosa's *Il pittore parigino*, having upset the owner of the theatre. Two years later he was fortunate to be recruited for the new Italian opera company in Vienna, where he met Salieri, Haydn and Mozart, and performed with some of the most famous singers of the day, though he never quite achieved the top rung of the international ladder.

In 1791 Kelly and David were both in London, where Italian singers were all the rage. Some of the home-grown stars could hold their own with the public but these tended to be sopranos of considerable personality, such as Nancy Storace. Kelly, despite his Italian adventures and international reputation, seems very much a jobbing musician compared with David. The Irishman, affable and gregarious to a fault, is to be found singing glees with other less celebrated singers; David is always given an aria and gets the lion's share of the critical acclaim. Both men sang in Oxford on the occasion of the award of an honorary doctorate to Haydn in July of that year but it was Storace that turned the hearts of the 'young gentlemen in black gowns'.[37] 'David . . . possessed a clear and flexible voice with an extensive falsetto,' William Parke tells us, and it was for him that Haydn wrote the role of Orfeo in *L'anima del filosofo* (1791), which shows him to have had a strong lower register going down to bottom A.[38]

John Braham

This pattern of boy soprano/adolescent tenor exposed to intensive castrato teaching at an early age was repeated in the case of many singers around the turn of the century. John Braham, perhaps the greatest British tenor of the early nineteenth century, was also successful as a child singer. Unusually (for a tenor who was to have so much success with music at the very heart of the Church of England) Braham was Jewish, and it was his singing in the Great Synagogue in Duke's Place that launched his career as a boy soprano. His parents having died when he was young, Braham was taken up by the financier and philanthropist Abraham Goldsmid, who paid for the boy to have lessons with Meyer Leon, the cantor at Duke's Place. Without the help of Leon, who had another life as the opera singer Michael Leoni, it is possible that Braham might never have considered working outside the Jewish tradition. Leon had sung at Covent Garden, and even angered his Jewish friends by singing *Messiah*.[39] With such a role model, and one who by all accounts was a sophisticated musician, Braham was encouraged to sing professionally himself, and it was Leoni who facilitated his appearances at Covent Garden at the age of thirteen before his voice had broken.

Braham then went to study with Rauzzini in Bath for three years. Rauzzini's teaching clearly focused on the joining of registers: Braham's treble range of two octaves evolved into an even larger compass from a Mozartian bottom A to a soprano E. So famous was he for passing imperceptibly from chest voice into falsetto that in 1818 the *Musical Quarterly* set up an experiment to see where he made the break:

> Mr Braham can take his falsetto upon any note from D to A [above middle C] at pleasure and the juncture is so nicely managed that in an experiment to which this gentleman had the kindness to submit, of ascending and descending by semitones, it was impossible to distinguish at what point he substituted the falsetto for the natural note.[40]

This is a significant insight into the sound of the early nineteenth-century tenor: we cannot know what the actual sound was like, but it is clear that even informed listeners could not tell the difference between registers in the best tenors.

Braham's début as a tenor at Drury Lane in 1796 was welcomed as a potential replacement for the 'degrading and disgusting form of the castrato', though he was criticised for an 'excessive weight of ornament', an excess often associated with *musici*.[41] The influence of Rauzzini's teaching was clearly responsible both for his remarkable range and his extravagant use of embellishment. In 1798 he and Nancy Storace (who later bore him a son) embarked on a series of concerts that took them to the great musical centres of northern Italy, where Braham was such a success that Giacomo David is said to have exclaimed, 'There are only two singers in the world, I and the Englishman.'[42] In Venice Cimarosa wrote *L'Atemisia* with Braham in mind, though the composer died before the work was finished. In Milan he had a spectacular triumph over the *prima donna* Elisabeth Billington, then at the height of her powers and considered to be one of the greatest English sopranos of the day. The Billingtons, acutely aware of the public's attention to the new star tenor, contrived to have one of Braham's most impressive arias cut. Public outrage at being deprived of Braham's virtuosity obliged the conductor to reinstate the aria on the following night. Braham, aware that Mrs Billington always meticulously rehearsed her embellishments, memorised her ornaments during the rehearsal and added all of them to his own first aria, which preceded hers.[43]

On his return to London, Braham sang at both the English opera at
Covent Garden and the Italian opera at the King's Theatre. For the English
operas he would often compose his own parts. His collaborators included
Bishop, Attwood and fellow singers Charles Dibdin and Michael Kelly. His
successful collaborations with Dibdin included *The Cabinet* and *The English
Fleet in 1342*, which featured a favourite duet between himself and fellow
tenor Incledon, and resulted in his being paid 1000 guineas for the copy-
right, the highest such sum paid to date. This was also the first occasion on
which Braham wrote for the oboe, and he asked William Parke if he could
borrow his oboe concertos to study his writing for the instrument. To
Parke's surprise, his own variations on 'Rule Britannia' turned up in the
overture.[44]

Braham went on to gain and lose a considerable fortune, but never lost his
power to move those who heard him. He was well aware of his status as the
foremost English tenor, and growing up, as he had done, in an age where the
performer was always right, he sometimes treated composers with a wilfulness
that Mozart had been all too familiar with. Weber was an admirer, but did not
find it easy to work with the ageing tenor for the first perfomances of *Oberon*,
being required to add new music at Braham's request and compromise many
of his original ideas. The florid style was not to everyone's taste by the second
quarter of the century (Weber also found his ornamentation excessive) but
Braham was probably the last tenor to sing Handel in a way that combined
dramatic presence with traditional virtuosity. Leigh Hunt found his singing
powerful and moving:

> When he stood in the concert-room or the oratorio, and opened his mouth
> with plain, heroic utterance in the mighty strains of 'Deeper and deeper
> still', or 'Sound the alarm', or 'Comfort ye my people', you felt indeed you
> had a great singer before you. His voice now became a veritable trumpet of
> grandeur and exaltation; the tabernacle of his creed seemed to open before
> him in its most victorious days; and you might have fancied yourself in the
> presence of one of the sons of Aaron, calling out to the lost of people from
> some platform occupied by their prophets.[45]

Lord Mount Edgcumbe was also impressed by his Handel, and despite his
earlier criticism of Braham's poor (for which read 'excessive') taste in embellishment, considered his mature work to be close to perfection:

> I have already expressed my unqualified admiration for the manner in
> which Braham executed this difficult and impassioned recitative ['Deeper
> and deeper still', from *Jephtha*] requiring so much pathos and varied

feeling: it is not too much to say, it was *perfect*, and this alone would establish his reputation as a first rate singer.[46]

Braham had a tendency to be wooden on stage, especially when he had no business to do, but he was not without a sense of drama. Joseph Heywood of the *Cornhill Magazine* wrote in 1865 of Braham's awkwardness in getting up to sing, but was utterly convinced by his declamation:

> Braham said 'But the children of Israel went on dry land' and then paused; and every sound was hushed throughout the space. And then, as if carved out upon the solid stillness, came these three little words: 'through the sea'. Our breath failed us, our pulses ceased to beat, and we bent our heads, as all the wonder of the miracle seemed to pass over us with those accents. Awful, radiant, resonant, triumphant, he sat down, while the whole house thundered its applause.[47]

Example 7 Handel: 'But the children of Israel', *Israel in Egypt* (1739)

No modern tenor would dare to make such a rhetorical pause – it would be considered absurdly over the top and tasteless. Braham knew his audience and he knew his art, and he pushed both of them to the limit. The traditional castrato technique not only gave him a great range and considerable virtuosity, but also enabled him to perform with power and conviction. He never forgot his teacher, and he and Nancy Storace paid for the monument to Venanzio Rauzzini that still stands in Bath Abbey.

Charles Incledon

Charles Incledon, one of Rauzzini's other great tenor successes, had sung as a boy in Exeter Cathedral.[48] He later impressed Haydn, who thought he used his falsetto excessively, trilling on high C and running up to G in Shield's *The Woodman*.[49] He was not quite so successful in disguising the break, as Leigh Hunt noted in 1817 when reviewing the singing of the tenor Pearman:

> Pearman's falsetto will remind the public of Incledon's, which it surpasses in reach and sweetness. He plays upon it like a flute. His transition to it

however from the natural voice is not happy. It is not indeed so violent as Incledon's who in his leap from one to the other slammed the larynx in his throat, like a Harlequin jumping through a window shutter; but it is poor and unskilful; neither does he seem to care upon what sort of words or expression he does it, so as the note is such as he can jump to it.[50]

Incledon was a charismatic, naïve and difficult man. He was able to sweep audiences along with his passion and enthusiasm (his laugh in Handel's 'Haste thee nymph' (*L'allegro*) was so infectious that the audience could not resist joining in) and William Parke, who experienced his singing from very close quarters as principle oboist in the Covent Garden band, never once heard him sing out of tune. He was unable to sight-read but his ear and memory were such that he only had to hear a piece once and it stayed with him for ever. He specialised in English opera, appearing many times at Covent Garden between 1790 and 1815, and sang in the first London performance of *The Creation* in 1800. He was something of a *bon viveur* but not a generous man. Parke remembered the occasion when Incledon invited a group of fellow musicians to dine with him on John Dory. When the guests arrived all except Incledon and his wife sat down to a large dish of herrings. With no John Dory apparently forthcoming several people helped themselves to second helpings of herring, eventually revealing the more exotic fish at the bottom of the bowl, by which time all except the Incledons were too full to eat any of it.

He was a founder member of the Glee Club, which met every other Sunday evening at the Garrick's Head coffee house in Bow Street. The order of the day was convivial singing followed by supper, and it was a chance for fellow professionals and talented amateurs to get together to make music for fun.[51] Incledon's idea of fun also extended to practical jokes. He and Irish actor Jack Johnstone were particularly fond of a brew known as 'flannel', made of beer, eggs, sugar and brandy, which was to be had from The Brown Bear in Covent Garden Market. On winter nights they would tell the admiring ladies who visited their dressing rooms that they were collecting contributions for the dying widow of a fellow thespian so that they could buy her some heart-warming flannel. They would then send their dresser out to the Bear with the donations extracted to get a quantity of flannel for their own consumption, sometimes presenting a glass to the subscribers as a token of their gratitude.[52]

Incledon's gullibility sometimes saw the boot on the other foot. In 1804, in the middle of a run of *The Beggar's Opera* he found himself unable to perform because of 'extreme hoarseness'. Desperate to resume his Macheath, he tried patent lozenges to no effect. Then some of the actors urged him to try an amulet, but to suck it rather than wear it. Incledon bought one and sucked all day, and after a few sucks first thing next day told his wife that the cure was working. He continued to sing the praises of the remedy till one day he was brought a message purporting to be from the amulet-seller refunding his money as he had sold him a pebble by mistake. Incledon was very angry but took comfort in the fact that one of the lozenge-sellers had agreed to take 40 pounds worth of tickets in return for a letter the tenor had written, saying it had been the lozenges that had cured his hoarseness.[53]

Castrato singing treatises: Tosi and Rauzzini

What, then, did the castrati actually teach? Porpora, the teacher of so many of the best castrati, is said to have made his students study the same page of exercises for five or six years, after which he pronounced them ready to sing anything.[54] This legendary page has not survived but we do have writings by several castrato teachers, the earliest of which is Pier Francesco Tosi's *Opinioni de' cantori antichi e moderni o sieno osservazioni sopra il canto figurato*, published in Bologna in 1723. Tosi was not an operatic superstar (certainly not a singer of the calibre of Pistocchi or Siface whom he recommends highly) and his treatise was written when he was in his late sixties, the fruits of a life-time of performance, teaching and observation dating back to the time of Purcell. So authoritative was it that annotated versions appeared in English (by John Galliard in 1743) and German (by Agricola in 1757), and it was much drawn upon by Mancini (1777) and Hiller (1780).[55]

Tosi makes a number of assumptions about technique. The student will understand that there are two registers: *di petto* (the chest) and *da testa* (the head), and that being able to move seamlessly from one to the other is a central aim of all good singers. He talks a lot of basic common sense that we would recognise today: about not singing too much in the nose or throat, breathing in the right place and pronouncing words properly. There are two areas in which Tosi's singers differ fundamentally from their modern counter-parts: he talks a great deal about ornamentation, ranging from *portamento* to high velocity divisions, and he refers to techniques that we no longer use such as *messa di voce*, literally the placing or setting up of the voice which took the form of a swelling and dying on the same note. This apparently simple exercise would be practised for more than an hour each day. Messa di voce is funda-mental to pre-twentieth century singing and (like portamento) is referred to in almost all singing manuals until the twentieth century. It enabled a consis-tency of tone colour and facilitated breath control, neither of which concepts receives much consideration in Tosi (or in any treatise until the nineteenth century).

Tosi's is the first, and perhaps (because of its wide dissemination) the most authoritative of the castrato treatises. The later (and more successful) castrati

Rauzzini and Crescentini also wrote sets of exercises with introductory material that Tosi would have recognised. Venanzio Rauzzini was born in 1746, fourteen years after the death of Tosi, and may have studied in Naples with Porpora.[56] Rauzzini had early success in Italy as composer, harpsichordist and singer (the young Mozart composed 'Exsultate, jubilate' for him in 1773 as well as the *primo uomo* part in *Lucio Silla*). In 1774 he was engaged at the King's Theatre in London, where he lived for three years before moving permanently to Bath. Until his death in 1810 he continued to compose and perform and he became increasingly successful as a teacher.

Rauzzini's *Solfeggi*, 'composed and dedicated to his scholars',[57] are not designed for amateurs, despite the author's reference to 'dilettanti' in his introduction. Even the most basic exercise would be beyond someone lacking a good basic technique and considerable musicianship. They are not, strictly speaking 'solfeggi', as he says they should be sung on 'a' as in 'arm', an exercise more usually called a vocalise at this time (as opposed to singing solfège syllables). His two-page preface advises singers not to attempt more than their natural 'facility' will allow, pointing out that everyone's voice has a unique configuration: what is easy for some may be very difficult for others. He says it is fine to listen to star singers (he includes the tenors Braham and Viganoni among his examples) but cautions against imitation; singers should find their own individual style, and their teachers should choose songs appropriate for individual students. One should keep the voice steady, 'gradually swelling the notes, ascending and descending LEGATO and APPOGGIATO [literally 'supported'], taking breaths in proper places.' The mouth should be open wide enough to display the teeth (but not too much) and words must be articulated distinctly; singers should aim for expression and precision.

Almost all of this makes a kind of sense to modern singers, but when we look at the exercises themselves it is immediately clear that Rauzzini is talking about a very different kind of singing from that of the twenty-first century. The exercises (complete with elegant Haydnesque keyboard accompaniments) have no explanation of any sort beyond a general tempo indication ('cantabile', 'allegro vivace' and so on). A modern singer is likely to be somewhat at sea trying to understand the pedagogic logic behind these very elaborate songs without words. An analysis of the complete set reveals three broad sorts of material, which become progressively more difficult. There are long held notes; these are presumably intended to be sung with messa di voce, as in the 'swelling' referred to in the introduction.[58] Similar passages recur at various points, beginning with leaps of up to an octave and a fifth and later stretching this to two octaves and a note.

The point of this material is twofold: the messa di voce is a very effective means of developing control over the necessary musculature for breath

Example 8 Leaps from Rauzzini's *Solfeggi* (1808)

control, and performing this exercise in every part of the range helps the student to achieve consistency of tone and control. The wide leaps presuppose a lightness of tone (as in the Haydn examples above): the muscles of the vocal tract have to respond quickly to get from the highest to the lowest part of the voice, and this is often problematic for richer, heavier voices.

The second sort of material consists of arpeggiated figures. These are initially over a single octave and progress to two octaves over the course of the book. This develops flexibility and also contributes to consistency over the whole range. Scale passages, the third basic teaching element, have a similar function. These begin with an octave or less, interspersed with long notes and arpeggios but become progressively extended to two octaves of chromatic and diatonic scales. As students work through the pieces all of these elements are progressively combined and fragmented, becoming in musical terms the *passaggi* and graces that Rauzzini and Tosi would have considered essential elements of eighteenth-century singing. The final exercises have long notes joined by intervals of up to a diminished 16th, two-octave arpeggios and runs and ornamental passages covering a range of two octaves and a third from bottom G to top B flat. These are very similar to the examples we have seen from Haydn and Mozart, and also very like the exercises composed and annotated by Crescentini in his *Vocalises* of the early 1820s.[59] It is this sort of exercise that Braham, Friberth and d'Ettore would have grown up with, and which would have enabled them to develop extraordinary agility over a very wide range, mirroring the technique of their teachers.

It is hard to imagine such tenor singing today, since the tenor falsetto was soon to be eclipsed by the upward extension of the chest voice.[60] The ease and power with which the traditionally taught tenors could sing in a very high tessitura is hinted at by Mount Edgcumbe, complaining about the 1834 performance of *Messiah* in Westminster Abbey:

There being no good counter-tenor, the song 'He was despised', which is generally given to that voice, was assigned to a female contralto, a Miss Masson, who sung it correctly, but without feeling. As it is within the compass of a tenor, Harrison, Knyvett, and others having sung it, Braham might have taken it, and would have given it all its deeply pathetic expression, which was totally lost.[61]

Since the late twentieth century this aria has often been sung by a counter-tenor. The modern operatic counter-tenor is a far cry from the cathedral alto that Mount Edgcumbe expected to hear, and perhaps rather closer to the falsetto tenor that he suggests as an alternative. Curiously, the counter-tenor is preferred today as a substitute for castrati, although all the evidence suggests that mezzo-sopranos were almost invariably chosen when castrati were no longer available. Today's counter-tenors do not sound anything like castrati, but they may well give us an insight into what an early nineteenth-century tenor may have sounded like at the top of his range. It may be this kind of sound that Mount Edgcumbe had in mind for 'He was despised'.

Giovanni Battista Rubini

The most famous (and one of the last) examples of high tenor singing was the soprano F that Bellini wrote for Giovanni Battista Rubini in *I puritani*. Arturo's aria in *I Puritani* has to be heard over chorus, orchestra and fellow soloists:

un so - lo j -stan - te l'i - re fre - na - te, po - scia sa - zia - te la cru - del - tà

Example 9 Rubini's top F in *I puritani* (Bellini, 1835)

Rubini, like so many of the tenors discussed above, began his career as a boy soprano, initially in the local monastery choir then playing female stage roles in Romano (near Bergamo). He made his début as a tenor in 1814 at the age of twenty. Later the same year the legendary Neapolitan impresario Domenico Barbaia heard him sing in Venice, and offered the young virtuoso a contract at the Teatro San Carlo in Naples, where he also took lessons from Nozzari. Over the next ten years he sang in all the major Italian opera houses, some-what in the shadow of the great Rossini tenors David, Garcia and Nozzari whose roles he would later assume. In 1825 he made his début in Paris singing three Rossini roles. His greatest success, however, was in the music of Bellini and Donizetti, who both wrote major roles for him. By all accounts he was an indifferent actor with a face scarred by smallpox and with the usual tendency to embellish extensively without regard to the drama that his roulades might be obscuring. It was Bellini who encouraged him to act, and to find an emotional connection between the singing and the character he was playing.

Henry Chorley heard Rubini every time he appeared in London and considered the tenor to be a genius, writing that

> no one . . . so entirely enchanted our public so long as a shred of voice was left to him; no one is more affectionately remembered.

His singing

> did not create a success for him so much as an ecstasy of delight in those who heard him. . . . He ruled the stage by the mere art of singing more completely than anyone, woman or man, has been able to do in my time. . . . The traditions of his method died with him.[62]

Chorley was right: although Rubini did publish *12 Lezione di canto* his method merely regurgitates in very concise form the conventional wisdom handed down for centuries. As a key to unlocking a traditional technique it is useless without a Rubini to explain it.[63] He retired in 1844 after successes in most of Europe and having been honoured by the Tsar of Russia. The last ten years of his life were spent at Romano in the villa he built for himself, which still stands as the Museo Rubini.[64]

CHAPTER 3

NOURRIT, DUPREZ AND THE
TENORINO D'HIER

At the beginning of the nineteenth century the international opera circuit flourished as never before, with well-funded series throughout Europe and in North and South America. The most successful singers travelled extensively, lured from contract to contract by increasingly skilled negotiation. Like the castrati who had taught many of them, the great tenors of the period were often widely cultured and likely to be composers, instrumentalists or conductors as well as singers.

The Garcia dynasty

Manuel Garcia, for example, who created the role of Almaviva in Rossini's *Il barbiere* and founded the Garcia musical dynasty that spanned the whole of the century, was all of the above as well as an energetic entrepreneur and successful teacher. Garcia was born in 1775, the son of a Sevillian cobbler. Details of his early childhood are sparse (and not helped by his own attempts to re-invent his origins); he almost certainly sang as a treble in Seville and by the early 1790s he was working in Cádiz as singer, composer and conductor.

After success in Málaga and Madrid as both composer and performer (he sang the Count in the Spanish première of Mozart's *Figaro* in 1802) he moved to Paris in 1807, where he made his début at the Odéon in Paër's *Griselda* (in a role previously made famous by Nozzari).[1] Remarkably (both because he was by this time in his mid-thirties and because he would in time become a great teacher himself), Garcia seems to have created his career without ever having formal singing lessons. He had a wide range (he sang the Count in *Figaro* and also the title role in *Don Giovanni*) and a natural facility that reviewers often criticised as excessively florid. It was not until he worked in Italy between 1812 and 1816 and met the highly respected tenor and teacher Giovanni Ansani that he acquired the skills that would enable him to cope with Rossini. Ansani taught him how to project, and perhaps how to achieve the heavier sound that Mozart had recognised in all Italian singers as long ago as 1770, and presumably gave him the pedagogical rigour that would enable him to teach so authoritatively.[2]

He arrived back in Paris to sing at the Théâtre-Italien in 1816, having created the roles of Norfolk in Rossini's *Elisabetta, regina d'Inghilterra* and Almaviva in *Il barbiere di Siviglia* during his stay in Naples.[3] In 1818 and 1819 he was in London, where he caught the eye and ear of Leigh Hunt in *The Examiner*. His florid extravagance was all too much for the dilettante poet and critic, who thought him

> running about in vain with his gratuitous high notes, like a dog that scampers ten miles to his master's one; and in this respect indeed, it must be allowed that we heard Cimarosa to disadvantage; for the progress of the melody was scarcely perceivable through the dust of Signor Garcia's gambols.[4]

Garcia was later to publish brief manuals for the use of his students, so we have an idea of what he learned from Ansani. Having begun a career without benefit of pedagogy it is not surprising to read that he believed anyone with intelligence, a good ear and the patience to work methodically at the right exercises could become a good singer. He understood that flexibility and agility should be deployed with a control that would enable finely nuanced performances that were more than mere virtuosity. He identified the three conventionally agreed registers (chest, medium and head) and advocated exercises combining messa di voce with portamento. Some of his published exercises are extremely virtuosic, as his reputation would predict.[5] He had started a short-lived singing school in London in 1824, but it was not until his voice failed him after a traumatic three years in Mexico 1826–9 that he finally established his own singing school in Paris. Among his students were his two daughters, Maria and Pauline, his son Manuel II and the tenor Adolphe Nourrit. The younger Garcia went on to become the most celebrated teacher of the nineteenth century, initially taking over his father's school before moving to London rather than risk staying in Paris after the 1848 revolution. His scientific approach to singing teaching was comprehensive and he was one of the first to observe the lower larynx technique known as the *voix sombre* or *sombrée*. This had the effect of darkening the tone and was a significant factor in the enrichment of vocal colour that occurred in the newer, more powerful 'post-bel canto' tenors.[6]

The tragedy of Adolphe Nourrit

The combination of working in Italian opera houses while consulting famous tenors of an earlier generation was a recipe that brought success to many tenors. Having the basis of a technique already in place, and enough of a career to be regularly engaged with real music, would have mediated the strict exercises that traditional lessons entailed. The formula did not guarantee success, and in the case of Adolphe Nourrit had terrible consequences. Nourrit's attempts to come to terms with the newest developments in Italian singing aggravated a fragile mental state and ended with his early death. Described as 'perhaps the greatest singing actor among all the dramatic tenors of opera history', Nourrit was also one of the most intelligent of tenors.[7] His experience sheds some light on the difference between French and Italian singing styles and technique, and brings into sharp relief the dilemma facing tenors at a time of radical changes as the old elegant lyricism began to give way to sheer power and dramatic declamation.

Louis Nourrit, Adolphe's father, was also a tenor and combined the business of a diamond merchant with a successful career at the Paris Opéra. He had a beautiful voice as a child and when his voice broke studied at the Conservatoire with Pierre Garat, an Italian-influenced Salon singer and teacher, before making his début at L'Académie in 1805. Although Nourrit *père* was not particularly ambitious he replaced Lainez as first tenor ('qu'on appelait alors *haute-contre*'[8]) at L'Opéra in 1812, becoming the star singer from 1817 until his son took over in 1821. Adolphe was born 1802. Louis hoped he would go into the family diamond business and be secure rather than indulging himself in the theatre, but young Adolphe was very musical at school and had a beautiful but small treble voice. On leaving school he did indeed go into the diamond brokerage business, but would spend his evenings going to the theatre, especially to see the great actors Talma and Mara, whose roles he would try to recreate in his own room when he got home.[9] He finally persuaded his father to let him have solfège and harmony lessons, and one day

Garcia overheard him practising something from Gluck's *Armide*; to Adolphe's great delight the famous teacher (as he was then becoming) eventually persuaded Louis that his son should study with him and leave business for the theatre.

Learning the traditional way could not be done quickly, but once achieved would equip the singer to cope with whatever music he came across. All of the pedagogical works of the period follow the same structure, beginning with exercises on single notes and eventually progressing to scales and improvised embellishments. The really creative ornamentation required for cadenzas, involving models and formulae that could generate newly improvised material, came towards the end of the process. Garcia gave Nourrit customised one-line exercises that he could fish out of his pocket even in the street, but after eighteen months of rigorous study Adolphe became desperate for some real music and began to pester Garcia to let him sing an aria. Both Quicherat and Legouvé tell the story of how Garcia appeared to agree, knowing that Nourrit had not yet got far enough with his studies. He complimented Nourrit on his cadenza and asked him to do two more, after which Nourrit ran out of ideas. Garcia then exclaimed 'After three cadenzas! A real singer must be able to improvise ten – or even twenty if he so desires. For the only true singer is the one who is a true musician'.[10] The virtuosic exercises that singers spent so much time practising were not simply to increase their agility but also to provide models for improvisation; singers' careers could be won or lost by the novelty and sheer creativity that they brought to their cadenzas.

Garcia taught Adolphe at the same time as his daughter Maria, later to become the great diva Maria Malibran. Both were to die before perhaps reaching the peak of their careers, Malibran after a riding accident in England, Nourrit in a moment of insanity in Italy. Nourrit continued to study Talma's style of declamation (Quicherat desribes him as 'le Talma de la scène lyrique'[11] while Garcia trained him and Maria in the Italian tradition, culminating in Nourrit's successful audition for the Théâtre-Italien in 1821. Nourrit was nineteen when he made his début in Gluck's *Iphigénie en Tauride*. He was a great success, noble and gracious but with a dramatic vigour, according to Quicherat. Talma heard him and was so impressed with his acting that he said if he ever gave up opera he would be welcome in Talma's own troupe.[12] He quickly established himself as something of a Gluck specialist, but it was with the arrival of Rossini, keen to hire real Italian singers and to work with those disposed towards the Italian style, that Nourrit's career really took off. In 1826 he created the role of Néocles *in Le Siège de Corinthe*, setting the seal on a relationship with Rossini that would endure for the remaining years of his life. Nourrit's status was acknowledged by the Conservatoire, which created the post of *professeur de déclamation pour la tragedie lyrique* for him in 1827. Two years later he created Arnold in *Guillaume Tell*, to great acclaim. In 1831 Meyerbeer wrote *Robert le diable* for him, a role requiring dramatic skill and vocal virtuosity (both these roles have pre-poitrine high Cs). Like both Garcia and Rubini, he also sang the title role in *Don Giovanni*, transposing as necessary, as he was considered perfect for the part dramatically.

Nourrit was a complex and cultured man with many intellectual and aesthetic interests beyond his performing career. Widely read and with a keen sense of the poetic, he contributed words and ballet scenarios to several Meyerbeer operas; the composer wrote after the first performances of *Les Huguenots* that Nourrit had contributed more than either of its authors. His youthful interest in the careers of the leading Parisian actors, especially the tragedians Mars and Talma, gave to his acting a physicality that was rare among opera singers. This, combined with his strongly felt political beliefs at a time when Paris was on the edge of social and political turmoil, imbued his performances with an integrity that perfectly caught the revolutionary *Zeitgeist*. In 1830 he was one of the first to man the barricades in the so-called Revolution of the Three Glorious Days, leading the cast of *Guillaume Tell* into the street with Arnold's cry of 'Ou l'indépendence, ou la mort!'[13] When the Opéra reopened after the troubles he was to be seen leading chorus and orchestra in flag-waving renditions of 'La Marseillaise and 'La Parisienne' night after night. The star of *La Muette* (the mute girl) was the legendary dancer Lise Noblet, and Nourrit was more than able to hold his own in such company. He went on to collaborate with choreographer Marie Taglioni on many projects including the Ballet of the Nuns in Meyerbeer's *Robert le diable*.

As well as his opera triumphs he had a successful career in the more rarified ambience of the *salons*, where he introduced the songs of Schubert to French audiences for the first time. Quicherat tells us that one day Nourrit was visiting the house of a Hungarian banker and entered the room as Liszt was playing his transcription of 'Erlkönig'. Nourrit was transfixed by the music and asked Liszt to repeat it, whereupon Liszt said it would be much better if Nourrit would sing it himself. This was the beginning of a life-long devotion to Schubert which on several occasions saw Nourrit and Liszt performing Lieder together.[14]

Nourrit's career was at its height when Gilbert-Louis Duprez returned from his triumphant years in Italy and was engaged as joint first tenor at L'Opéra in 1836. The prospect of having two of the most famous tenors in the world in the same troupe was thought to be an inspired commercial decision, and Nourrit at first generously accepted the situation, even handing over some of his own roles to Duprez. Nourrit's disturbed mental state was beginning to cloud his thinking, however, and his actions after this point are refracted through his psychological problems. He realised he could not accept the presence of Duprez (for whom he had considerable admiration rather than mere envy) and decided that since Duprez had perfected his craft in Italy, then he himself should go to Italy and try his luck there.

At first all went well, with Nourrit reacquainting himself with Rossini, Hiller, Liszt and a host of other leading musicians of the day. He was also introduced to Donizetti, and it seems to have been as a result of this meeting that he decided to reinvent himself as an Italian singer with Donizetti as his teacher and mentor. The two worked together in Naples often for several hours each day, perfecting the Frenchman's Italian accent. Nourrit became obsessed with all things Italian, intending to make his voice indistinguishable from the native product. His wife Adèle, who had remained in Paris with their six children, was shocked at the change when she visited him. Nourrit had convinced himself that the key to becoming a successful Italian tenor was to eradicate his French nasality and sacrifice (if necessary) his lifelong dedication to clarity of diction and the primacy of the text in favour of consistent tone production. Adèle afterwards wrote to him of her alarm at hearing how loud and devoid of nuance his voice had become; she had had to shut the door on his practice sessions.

The voluminous Nourrit correspondence includes complaints from Adèle about the 'disadvantages' of Donizetti's teaching. These are crucial insights into the differences between the French and Italian styles: 'his head voice is gone, his *mezza voce* is gone. . . . He is darkening it as Donizetti required . . . it is nothing new that the development of the chest voice extinguishes the head voice and the half-voice. Rubini almost never uses the chest voice.'[15] What a vivid and tragic picture this paints: Adèle by her own admission knew very little about music and singing, but she knew her husband, his singing and what it meant to him. Common sense eventually prevailed enough for him to begin to modify Donizetti's ideas and try to regain some of the 'Frenchness' that he had tried so hard to eliminate from his singing. But it was too late: five days after his thirty-seventh birthday one of the most compassionate, creative and intellectual performers of history climbed to the top of the Villa Barbaia, opened the window and jumped.

His death shocked the musical world. His body was transported back to Paris via Marseilles, where the mourners included Chopin, who played the organ at a memorial service, and George Sand. Chopin played Schubert's 'die Sterne', one of the songs that Nourrit had introduced to France.[16] At the funeral service in Paris a desperately unhappy Gilbert-Louis Duprez was one of the soloists in Cherubini's Requiem.

The ascent of the chest voice

By the second quarter of the nineteenth century there were very few remaining castrati, and more importantly for the future of the tenor voice, the number of castrati teachers also declined considerably. We begin to read of a more powerful variety of tenor whose singing owes less to the teaching of castrati than to the new sounds that tenors were beginning to find in their own voices. The most obvious change (because it was unmistakable and frequently commented upon) was raising the pitch at which they crossed the *passaggio* or 'break' from chest to head voice. Giovanni David, the creator of Rodrigo in Rossini's *Otello* in 1816 (with its many high Cs and Ds), had apparently begun to abandon the practice of singing high notes in his head voice from about 1814 onwards.[17] Domenico Donzelli famously wrote to Bellini in 1821 that he sang in chest voice to high G and had a further octave in head voice above that for 'decoration'.[18] Chorley's description of Donzelli's voice is revealing:

> He had one of the most mellifluous robust low tenor voices ever heard – a voice which had never by practice been made sufficiently flexible to execute Signor Rossini's operas as they are written, but who even in this respect was accomplished and finished, if compared with the violent persons who have succeeded him in Italy, each one louder and less available than his predecessor.[19]

His apparent inflexibility may have been due to a lower larynx position, which would also account for the richness of his sound. In the future these would be the characteristics of most tenors as the need for virtuosity gave way to dramatic declamation and depth of tone colour. Not all who attempted the new technique lived to tell the tale: in 1821 the tenor Americo Sbigoli, attempting to imitate Donzelli in a performance of Pacini's *Cesare in Egitto*, burst a blood vessel and died on stage.[20] Donzelli himself went from strength to strength, and in 1823 the *Allgemeine Musikalische Zeitung* reports that 'He has a beautiful, mellifluous tenor voice with which he attacks the high A in full chest voice without once resorting to falsetto.'[21] Significantly, Donzelli had been a pupil of Adamo Bianchi, Giuseppe Viganoni and Gaetano Crivelli, all of them tenors.

Duprez and the death of the capon

The most celebrated move in this direction was Gilbert-Louis Duprez's achievement of a chested to C in Rossini's *Guillaume Tell*, which he perhaps first attempted in 1831 at the Italian première in Lucca, and which stunned the Paris Opéra audience in 1837. The aria in question has several high Cs approached by leap, which were still presumably sung in the traditional way as it is the chromatic approach by step that caused all the fuss. The composer had intended this passage to be sung in head voice (as Nourrit had sung it), and he hated Duprez' stentorian version, remarking that it sounded like 'a capon squawking as its throat is cut'.[22] Rossini was known for his wit, and it is possible that he was fully aware of the irony in this remark, which was perhaps intended as a reference to the now inevitable extinction of the old castrati-influenced singing.

Example 10 Duprez' chested top C in *Guillaume Tell* (1829)

This was the point of no return for tenors, a change in the very nature of the voice and a defining characteristic of the best (and worst) tenor singing ever since. Duprez had been a precocious child, able to solfège anything at sight by the age of nine, and appearing at the Comédie française while still a treble.[23] He spent ten years of his childhood and teenage years studying singing and composition at the school of Alexandre Choron, who could be so moved by the young boy's voice that he was prone to spontaneous weeping. So beautiful was his singing that the composer Paër suggested that Gilbert-Louis should be considered for 'sopraniser à la chapelle Sixtine'. Duprez' father rejected the idea, and it was perhaps with some relief that the boy recorded the day his voice broke on 17 April 1823.[24] Choron, though himself a 'taille moyenne' (literally a medium tenor), would have given his young students a thorough grounding in traditional principles; Duprez left his tutelage a lyrical *tenore di grazia* and was engaged to sing at the Odéon. After the theatre closed in 1828 he went to Italy, where he met with considerable success. Duprez had a real gift for languages; French singers often found it difficult to suppress their accent when singing in foreign languages but his Italian diction was unusually good, and he was frequently hailed by the local press as 'vero Toscano', 'vero Napolitano', or 'vero Romano'.[25] In 1845 we find Chorley ecstatic about the elderly Duprez' rendering of 'Thy rebuke' from *Messiah*:

I have not heard since Braham's time – till Mr Sims Reeves came along – the great tenor solo . . . so perfectly sung and said as by M. Duprez. He had had to fight for every word of his English; whereas our English singers seem . . . to fight against their own language. . . . This great French tenor, in the strength of his feeling for dramatic truth, propriety and (most of all) his determination never to present himself without doing the best of his best, could master an unfamiliar style of music and a barbarous language . . . and could sing when his voice was half gone. . .[26]

In his youth Duprez was something of a tough negotiator, often ensuring a place in the cast for his wife, the soprano Alexandrine Duperron. His Italian odyssey tired him vocally; this may have been because he pushed himself hard and gave too many performances, or it may have been because of his experiments with the *voix sombre*.[27] The lowering of the larynx to create additional resonance is particularly effective in the chest register: the result is a more consistent sound and greater volume, sufficient to enable a modern singer to be heard over an orchestra with no extra effort. Crucially, it presupposes a concern for tone colour for its own sake: it will no longer be sufficient to deliver the text in the most communicative way. This is something still very new in the first half of the nineteenth century, and marks a fundamental change in the way singing is perceived. For tenors the new singing also involved an upwards extension of the chest register. Larger theatres, fuller orchestration and probably an increase in general noise levels everywhere all contributed to singers searching for increased power. The normal tenor range was from about the D below middle C to the G above it, and it was the upper end of this spectrum that excited both singers and, to a lesser extent, composers. Duprez was not the first singer to find this voice: Michael Kelly was known for his rich chest register and Domenico Donzelli, whom Duprez would have heard singing Rossini in Paris in 1825, became something of a mentor to the French tenor during his Italian period.

Duprez returned triumphantly to Paris a *tenore di forza*, and the prime exponent of the chested high C. He was contracted to the Opéra and went on to première works by Rossini, Halévy, Berlioz, Donizetti and Verdi among many others. His powerful high notes were something entirely new in singing and astonished listeners. Elwart, writing of the 1837 *Guillaume Tell* performance, says 'il excita au plus haut point le délire de l'Opéra, tout entire . . . tout fut anéanti dans le paroxisme de l'admiration'.[28] Duprez even referred to himself as *tenorino d'hier,* having discovered the 'ut de poitrine' (top C from the chest).[29] His voice eventually darkened to such an extent that he attempted baritone roles, often using both voices in the same performance.

He was not without a sense of humour: when Enrico Tamberlik first sang in French and was rumoured to be about to attempt a chested high C sharp, there were queues round the block and Duprez is said to have remarked, 'Here are receipts a semitone higher than mine.'[30] It was the beginning of tenors' competitive high chesting which continues to this day. Rossini liked Tamberlik's forceful top even less than he liked Duprez':

> Now comes Tamberlik. That jokester, wanting ardently to demolish Duprez' C, has invented the chest-tone C sharp and loaded it onto me. In the finale of my *Otello* there is, in fact, an A that I emphasised. I thought that it, by itself, launched with full lungs, would be ferocious enough to satisfy the *amour-propre* of tenors for all time. But look at Tamberlik, who has transformed it into a C sharp, and all the snobs are delirious! ... fearing a second, aggravated edition of the Duprez adventure, I cautioned Tamberlik ... to deposit his C sharp on the hall tree and pick it up again, guaranteed intact, when he left.[31]

But Tamberlik was a huge success in both England and France (and later, in Russia and Spain). He made his London début in 1850, singing roles by Rossini, Bellini, Donizetti, Verdi, Meyerbeer and others. He was a charismatic, forceful and robust performer, and Henry Chorley, who recognised his talent but did not place him quite in the top drawer with Rubini and Duprez, left an analysis of his singing 'by readers of the hour' for the benefit of those who would never hear him in life:

> One may tell those of the future that the voice, howsoever effective, and in its upper notes capable of great power, can hardly be called a charming one – though warm with the south – neither regulated by an unimpeachable method.[32]

Chorley was not keen on his 'habit of trembling' either, or his 'sense of measurement of time' but allowed that he was 'one of the handsomest men ever seen on the stage'.[33]

References to the new technique also appear in the didactic literature, confirming its increasing use alongside the traditional method. Duprez is cited in Heinrich Panofka's *L'Art de chanter* (1854) as a *tenor de force* or *robuste*, alongside Fraschini, Mario, Roger, Tamberlik and (curiously) Rubini, with a two-octave chest range from C to C (as opposed to *tenors légers* who sing the highest three notes in falsetto).[34]

Duprez himself published a singing manual in 1846; it is the modern work that his readers would expect from the singer whose performances were identified with the new full-voice tenor high notes. It could not have been written by a castrato.[35] He is curiously reticent about his own achievements, preferring to cite Nourrit, Levasseur and Damoreau when he needs a living example, and he has nothing to say about the science of singing. He appears to identify two styles: the *style large d'expression et de force* and the *style de grâce et d'agilité*. In the *style de force* high tenors can use chest voice for their entire range (though he claims that it is rare). He advocates pushing the chest voice as high as possible for maximum power but observes that uniting the registers combines the power of a man with the sweetness and charm of a woman. Vocalises should be sung full-voice with the dark A as in 'ame', 'pour sombre les sons'.[36] These exercises should enable interpretation based on phrasing, accentuation and style which can exist independently of the words, and it is through practising *vocalises* that the singer will keep abreast of new developments in vocal technique.

The *style de grâce et d'agilité* is difficult for heavier voices and should be practiced *mezza voce* to start with, though still trying to get greater force by taking the chest tones as high as possible. He supplies a more elaborate set of exercises for this second style, covering a range of two octaves C–C, and after a section on lyrical diction he provides a number of arias by named composers, with brief notes on the appropriate style.

By far the most substantial is his full page on Rossini, whom he credits with reforming the decadent singing which existed prior to 1814, when Rossini began his career as an opera composer. Rossini seems have had a natural affinity with all the tenors he worked with, the mutual creativity often leading to life-long friendships. He also sang himself in private: Hiller tells of an occasion when the Rossinis had invited David and Nozzari to lunch, after which the four of them sang canons by Salieri. The music was a little wearisome, but the singers constituted 'quite a passable vocal quartet.'[37]

Rossini's long periods of compositional silence (during which he enjoyed life to the full but was unable or unwilling to compose) have never been completely explained. One of the contributing factors may have been his inability to come to terms with the fact that the extreme virtuosity of his performers – and, by extension, their taste – was often at odds with his compositional instincts. Duprez tells us that Rossini thought that the rampant embellishments which all singers applied in the first decade of the century were fine in the hands of a Velluti, David, or Crivelli, but he felt that composers risked their reputations when third- or fourth-rate singers rendered their original constructs inaudible. Duprez suggests that it was this that probably gave Rossini the idea of making his own scores more elaborate; he was both composer and singer so he should have appropriate taste for his own music. The reform movement continued with Weber's *Freischütz* in Dresden (*c.* 1820), Bellini's *Il Pirata* (Milan 1826) and Rossini's own *Guillaume Tell* in 1826, in which words had a greater importance within melodies.

Rossini's experience of Duprez was mixed. The *tenor di grazia* that had emerged from Choron's tutelage was exactly what the composer appreciated. Duprez' encounter with Donizetti and Donzelli left him with a deeper and darker voice, and the relatively light and agile Rossini tenor became the *tenor di forza* that Donizetti so admired and Rossini was very wary of. Both composers got on well with the singer, but Donizetti perhaps appreciated rather more than Rossini the additional dramatic power that Duprez had learned in Italy.[38]

Duprez had a long career as singer and composer, and later as a writer of two works of autobiography as well as his didactic work. He taught at the Paris Conservatoire from 1842 to 1850 and three years later founded his own singing school. His career trajectory was satirised by Berlioz in 'How a tenor revolves round the public', the sixth chapter of *Evenings with the Orchestra*.[39] Although the composer gives a rather unflattering picture of the star performer of his day, the two did have a mutual respect and often found themselves in each other's company. Berlioz the critic frequently pointed to the coarsening of Duprez' voice as the singer got older, complaining that he could no long sustain long notes. He considered Duprez' compositions to be crassly melodramatic, and was baffled by a bit of re-composing that the tenor insisted on inflicting on one of the arias from *Guillaume Tell*, where Duprez would always sing an F instead of a G flat. When they were once travelling together on a train Berlioz took the opportunity to ask Duprez why he did it. Duprez did not really know, but promised to sing it correctly once just for Berlioz' sake. It was a promise he did not manage to keep.

The twenty-first chapter of Berlioz' *Evenings with the Orchestra* contains a moving account of a visit the two musicians made to the annual meeting of the Charity Children in St Paul's Cathedral in 1851. Berlioz was too late to get a ticket but John Goss, the organist of St Paul's, invited him to the organ loft where he donned cassock and surplice and pretended to be a choir member. Berlioz was profoundly moved by sight of six and a half thousand children singing 'in a gigantic unison' the hymn 'All people that on earth do dwell' and was hardly able to sing, much to the consternation of the singer next to him, who thought he kept losing his place. Leaving the cathedral, and overwhelmed by the occasion, Berlioz bumped into Duprez, who had also found the event highly emotional:

the great artist who in the course of his brilliant career has moved the hearts of so many, found many outstanding debts paid back to him that day – debts owed to him by France and paid him by these English children. I have never seen Duprez in such a state; he stammered, wept, and rambled, the while . . .[40]

The physical effort of the new singing took its toll on Duprez and although he continued to perform there were question marks over his stamina and reliability. In 1849 Meyerbeer had chosen Gustave-Hyppolyte Roger to play John of Leyden in *Le Prophète*. Roger had a lighter voice (Chorley described him as the 'cleverest and most mannered of French tenors'[41]) and had made his name in the operas of Halévy, Auber and Thomas. Duprez was not in fact even the composer's second choice of tenor for the part. The opera had had a long gestation period during which Meyerbeer's confidence in Duprez had waned, and he considered Fraschini and Mario before Roger. Mario was unavailable and Fraschini would have had to learn French, so the composer opted for Roger, for whom he re-wrote the part.[42] That same year Roger had heard Duprez sing *Otello*, when the 'terrifying old lion' (as he referred to him) electrified and moved the Parisian audience:

How he hurled his guts in the audience's face! For those are no longer notes that one hears. They are the explosions of a breast crushed by an elephant's foot! That's his own blood, his own life, that he is squandering to entice from the public those cries of 'Bravo!' . . . There is a certain nobility about it. . . . It's molten ore that he pours onto those broadened rhythms, and when he opens his mouth so wide it is to show us his heart![43]

Roger was a big-hearted man himself, surviving a shooting accident which led to the loss of his right arm. He continued to sing, making stage appearances with a mechanical arm.

Mario

Although he took on a number of Duprez' roles Roger could not really be said to have been his successor. If there was a tenor who combined something of the power of Duprez with the sweetness of Rubini it was the tenor known as Mario. Unusually for a tenor, Giovanni Matteo de Candia, born in the Sardinian city of Cagliari in 1819, was of aristocratic extraction; his father was Don Stefano de Candia, adjutant to Prince Charles Felix, later to become King of Sardinia. Father and son were political opposites; sent to the military academy in Turin, Giovanni befriended two of the architects of the Italian revolution, Mazzini and Cavour. On graduating he was appointed aide-de-camp to his father who was by then governor of Nice, and he found himself supporting fellow revolutionaries among the officers to the great anger of Don

Stefano, who attempted to have him arrested. In fear for his life, he deserted the army and fled to France, ending up with the expatriot Italian community in Paris and resigned to never working in Italy again. He seems to have had a beautiful, natural tenor voice, and had entertained family and friends since his youth. In 1837 he found himself singing at a soirée attended by Meyerbeer and the director of the Paris Opéra. The two were so impressed that Giovanni was persuaded there and then to become a professional singer (the newly-impoverished aristocrat swallowing his pride and realising that he had no choice but to work for his living). He agreed to go to Louis Ponchard and Giulio Bordogni (both tenors) for lessons and was coached by Meyerbeer himself in *Robert le diable*.[44] He agreed not to use the family name for political reasons, and after one convivial evening at Meyerbeer's he decided that Mario on its own was sufficient.[45] The following year Théophile Gautier described his voice as 'fresh, pure, velvety, with an admirable and youthful timbre', and despite his lack of stage experience he was sufficiently successful to take on further roles.[46] It was a late start, but Mario was soon successful in London, where he appeared regularly until his retirement in 1871, eventually conquering St Petersburg, New York and Madrid. No major roles were composed for him, but with an ability to take his falsetto up to soprano F he took over many of those written by Donizetti, Bellini and Rossini for Giambattista Rubini. Later he added heavier parts such as John of Leyden and sang the Duke of Mantua in the first London *Rigoletto* in 1848, one of several Verdi roles that he was quite at home in. His attempt at the Don in *Giovanni* was not a success but is an indication of his range as both singer and actor. Chorley was entranced by him, both as a personality – he was charmed by his genial aristocratic amateurishness and elegant appearance – and because of his effortless singing of an unparalleled variety of roles:

> There have been better singers, there have been better musicians, there may have been better voices than Signor Mario. There has been no more favourite artist on the stage, in the memory of man or of woman, than he.[47]

He also charmed his listeners in the salon, having a catholic knowledge of Lieder and Romances that included Schubert, Mendelssohn and Meyerbeer as well as his native Italian repertoire:

> By none have they been rendered more perfectly than by Signor Mario, the character of amateurship which pervaded his talent adding an elegance . . . to the speaking of the words and the delivery of the music. As a singer of Romances he has never been exceeded, rarely equalled.[48]

CHAPTER 4

THE TENOR AS ARTIST

It would be an over-simplification to suggest that the new breed of post-castrato tenor simply replaced those of the eighteenth-century tradition; above all, we should remember that recordings would not become widely available until the early years of the next century, so there were no universal models for young singers to aspire to. Tenors were still very much individualists in their basic vocal sound and technique, as they were in personality. The general tendency, however, was for singers not to have been taught by castrati (there were few of them left) and for serious study to start later, often at one of the new conservatories rather than with a private teacher. The traditional techniques and pedagogy were still acknowledged, but the teaching was generally in the hands of tenors or baritones who were by then at least once removed from the tradition itself. Perhaps because there was no question of preserving boys' voices into adulthood less attention was paid to children's singing, and boy sopranos no longer found themselves in an environment where it was automatically assumed that a good treble would make the transition to professional adult singer. The combination of public revulsion against the mutilation of children and a more general Europe-wide improvement in social conditions also lessened the need for music schools as a way out of urban poverty, although music would always provide an escape route for some. Many later nineteenth-century Italian tenors were from artisan stock, as George Bernard Shaw somewhat unflatteringly reminded his readers:

> if [my readers] had seen as much as I have of the results of picking up any Italian porter, or trooper, or gondolier, or ice-barrow costermonger who can shout a high C; thrusting him into heroic roles; and sending him roaring round the world to pass in every capital over the prostrate body of lyric drama like a steam roller with a powerful whistle, they would understand the immense value I attach to the competition of artists like Alvary. . .[1]

The gradual demise of the old way of doing things inevitably affected the relationship between performers and composers. Until the early nineteenth century singers were clearly in charge, able to ornament at will and order the re-composition of anything they did not like. As we have seen, Rossini was the first composer to challenge the right of singers to do whatever they liked with what they considered to be their music. By the simple strategy of writing in more ornaments he gave his singers fewer opportunities to stamp their own authority on an aria; this inoculation of composerly intent brought about a significant change in the power relations between composer and performer, and ultimately gave composers sufficient control to be able to exploit the dramatic (as opposed to the virtuosic) possibilities of the voice.

This shift in the perception of the singer's vocal persona was perfectly timed for the new generation of tenors. The lower larynx singing and powerful chested high notes made their voices less agile but gave them a wider range of tone colour – far more like the voice we know today. The mid-century composers such as Verdi were not interested in how florid their tenors could be, but how intensely dramatic, putting their vocal resources in the service of the music and not the other way round. The disappearance of castrati, and with it the element of gender ambiguity, also clarified the potential roles that tenors could play; Verdi was one of the first composers to become aware of this, refusing, for example, to cast Ernani as a contralto.[2] Bellini had already realised that basses would not make good romantic leads, and Verdi exploited the baritone for mature characters that a hundred years before might have been *opera seria* tenors. That left tenors free to be lovers, and Verdi recognised that there was something in the colour of the tenor voice that was particularly appealing. As John Rosselli put it, 'Sex goes a long way to explaining the rise of the tenor.'[3]

Verdi's essential requirement was a sound technique, and especially in his earlier works he called upon tenors who were schooled in the Italian tradition.

Carlo Guasco, who first sang Oronte in *I Lombardi* in 1843, is typical of the 'transitional' tenors. He started life as a surveyor but then after very little training became successful in the lyric roles of Rossini, Bellini and Donizetti (for whom he created Riccardo in *Maria di Rohan*). He was reluctant to take on Verdi's *Ernani* and barely survived the Venetian première, having been struck down with a pernicious hoarseness, but he eventually impressed the composer sufficiently to be offered Foresto in *Attila* in 1846. He retired in his mid-thirties having never quite felt at home in larger roles.[4] Gaetano Fraschini had greater stamina. He made his name in the operas of Donizetti, but Verdi thought his voice sufficiently durable to offer him Zamoro in *Alzira* (1845), Corrado in *Il Corsaro* 1848), Arrigo in *La battaglia di Legnano* (1849) and the title role in *Stiffelio* (1850). One of the first *tenori di forza*, he was in London in 1847, where his inelegant loudness worried Chorley (though not as much as his larger-voiced successors were to do):

> Fourteen years ago [he is writing in the early 1860s] we were little used to the coarse and stentorian bawling which the Italian tenors have of late affected. [Signor Fraschini] . . . seemed to become more and more violent in proportion as the 'sensation' failed to be excited. But he piled up the agony, forte on forte, in vain. . . . Alas! I already look back to Signor Fraschini as a moderate, if not intemperate Italian tenor, when compared with many who have since made the ears of right-minded persons suffer.[5]

Tamagno and Otello

FrancescoTamagno was one of the first tenors to record. His roles included Ernani and Adorno in *Simon Boccanegra* but it is as the creator of Otello that he is remembered today, his recorded legacy being a priceless connection with Verdi and the mid-century singing tradition.

The development of recording at the end of the century has been a mixed blessing for the historian of performance practice. Interpreting the first recordings is fraught with problems: many of the singers are old and possibly past their prime; the recording process, although a technological marvel for those experiencing it for the first time, was unable to capture a sufficiently wide frequency spectrum to do justice to the singing voice. The acoustic horn was a blunt instrument and left little room for subtlety, favouring louder voices and a lack of nuance at best. All of these factors have contributed to an underlying sense of disappointment that many historians seem to have felt when dealing with the certainties of actual aural history rather than inter-preting (sometimes very creatively) the silent sources before the recording watershed. The singing that we hear even well into the first decade of the twentieth century does not seem to be quite what we would predict from the earlier literature. Part of the reason for this is in our own heads – we *know* what we think good singing should sound like and our taste has been formed by listening to a potentially infinite number of models drawn from more than a hundred years of recording. All of our judgements on pre-gramophone singers have been filtered by this conditioning – and all of our writing has been speculation informed by silent literature.

We may argue about what Tamagno's recordings actually tell us but we do know what the singer himself thought about them (though he may have been in awe of the magical process itself as much as his own singing). Herman Klein recalled visiting the great tenor at his home in Varese on a hot summer's afternoon in 1904, shortly after Tamagno had taken delivery of a brand new gramophone from His Master's Voice complete with a set of his own records:

> It was most interesting; not merely hearing the records for the first time in the early days, but to watch Tamagno as he stood by his HMV machine, at times leaning lovingly over it, listening all the while with profound enjoyment to the tones of his own robust, colossal voice. From time to time he would ejaculate with a broad smile 'Che bellezza!' or 'Com' è bello, non è vero?'[6]

Otello, Verdi's first opera for fifteen years, was premièred at La Scala in 1887, and the sense of anticipation followed by clamorous triumph was vividly caught by commentators at the time. All were agreed that Victor Maurel as Iago was spectacular; Verdi and his librettist Boito had even considered calling the opera *Iago* – in the baritone voice the composer had found the perfect vehicle for his dramatic vision in much the same way as Wagner would re-discover the tenor.[7] The title role was one of the most taxing tenor parts ever written and was created specifically for the unique talents and vocal *persona* of Tamagno. The requirements of the role, an imposing physical presence capable of combining lyrical sweetness with a stentorian declamation that ranges from a rich baritonal middle to a ringing upper register, have made it problematic to cast ever since.[8]

Tamagno seemed to fare less well than Maurel at the time, the *Musical Times* attributing to him 'happy moments' – damning with faint praise – while Blanche Roosevelt accused him of bleating (as several critics had in the past). At the London performance a year later Shaw appreciated Tamagno's stage presence, observing that he was 'original and real, showing you Otello in vivid flashes'; he was less enthusiastic about the voice, calling it 'shrill and nasal' but was nevertheless impressed with what he called Tamagno's 'magnificent screaming'.[9] The 1903 recording of Desdemona's death scene, made after his retirement from the stage but when he was still a relatively young fifty-three, shows a consistent and fast vibrato that is presumably the bleating that his critics objected to. Tamagno makes a very open sound – I would not call it nasal – and manages to combine a strong legato line with absolute clarity of diction. In this sense he is firmly in the Italian tradition. The fragmented arioso sections enable him to show off the more modern declamation, using his huge dynamic range from a piercing forte to a whispered *mezza voce*. If his held 'ah!' before the word 'morta' can be described as shouting it is indeed magnificent. The final kiss, in which he interpolates an agonised gasp (and which cannot have been easy to do with his head in the acoustic horn), gives a spine-chilling hint at his histrionic depths.

The Tamagno recordings were the event of the year for the Gramophone Company. Tamagno was the first singer to be paid royalties; he earned 10 per cent and was given a £2000 cash advance. He also insisted that the records should be sold for £1 each, double anything charged previously, and that they should appear under a special Tamagno label.[10] Sadly, he had not long to enjoy the fruits of his negotiations: he died of heart failure two years later. Nellie Melba (whose 1904 recordings sold for a shilling more than Tamagno's) confirms the tenor's power at the top, claiming that his high C would actually rattle the chandeliers at Covent Garden. She also relates stories of his meanness, which he never overcame despite commanding extremely high fees. She was present when he surprised his illustrious American hosts one evening by collecting up the leftovers and taking them home. He had said that the lamb cutlets were destined for his dog, but in fact they ended up being given to his daughter the following day.[11] He was also famous for travelling steerage across the Atlantic and claiming the cost of a first-class ticket (something that his present-day successors have been known to do with airfares).

Tichatschek, Schnorr and Niemann: the evolution of the *Heldentenor*

The Rossini/Verdi trajectory of increasing control of what they saw as their material inevitably led to more direct influence by composers on the nature of the singing itself. Despite their attempts to revitalise singing, the Italian composers, steeped in the old tradition, did not try to re-invent it; that project fell to Wagner, and it is in the careers of Wagner's tenors that we see the old finally embracing possibilities that would carry the new vocalism into the twentieth century.

The Bohemian tenor Joseph Tichatschek seems in retrospect to have been a transitional figure, linking the tradition in which he studied with the new demands placed on him by contemporary composers. Born in 1807, he sang in choirs as a child but intended to become a doctor. While studying medicine in Vienna he had lessons with the tenor Giuseppe Ciccimarro, who recognised his talent and grafted a conventional Rossinian technique onto his natural sound. He joined the chorus of the Kärnthnor Theater and soon progressed to principle parts, eventually joining the Dresden Court Opera in 1838 and remaining associated with the city for the rest of his life.[12] He was an elegant singer, perhaps most at home in the lyrical roles of Mozart and Weber, but he also had ringing top notes and plenty of power. He is remembered today primarily as Wagner's first Rienzi (1842) and Tannhäuser (1845).

Wagner, even as he was writing Rienzi (his third attempt at music drama), was searching for something beyond the merely vocal, and although he thought Tichatschek in many ways a perfect singer he was frustrated by his complete lack of any sense of drama. He described Tichatschek's voice as 'a miracle of beauty' and 'a living wonder' but lamented that he could not express the 'ecstasy of humiliation' required by the role of Tannhäuser.[13] Wagner was a difficult man for singers to work with, demanding and fickle, yet he and Tichatschek remained friends until the composer's death. Tichatschek was intensely loyal, seeing something in Wagner's music that he knew was just beyond his understanding yet somehow appreciating it nevertheless; he continued to advocate the composer's work even when criticised by Wagner for his dramatic infelicities. Because of their firm friendship Wagner cast the tenor as Tannhäuser despite his reservations and the warnings of Schröder-Devrient that the part was beyond his comprehension.[14] He later sang Walther von Stolzing in *Meistersinger*, a role which probably suited him well, depending less on histrionics than on a sound technique. His Lohengrin at the age of sixty-three, standing in for Schnorr von Carolsfeld who had died unexpectedly, was not a success.

By all accounts Ludwig Schnorr von Carolsfeld was destined to become one of the great singers of the century. As was often the case, although he came from a musical and highly cultured background (his father was the Munich court painter Julius Schnorr von Carolsfeld and his mother a notable holder of musical soirées), he did not make the decision to become a singer until he was seventeen, after a spell at the Leipzig conservatory. He then began to study both singing and acting, moving to Karlsruhe to live and work with the actor Edward Devrient, making his début at the opera there in 1855. While still studying he had become profoundly moved by the music of Wagner, although his earliest roles were conventional repertoire works of Mozart, Donizetti and Bellini. He must have had an extraordinarily flexible voice, a lyric tenor that could deliver sufficient power when required to cope with the more strenuous roles of Tannhäuser and the Steuermann in *Der fliegende Hollander* which he played in 1857.[15] The following year he played Lohengrin to huge acclaim, having recovered from a heart problem. Some years earlier he had met the

Brazilian Danish soprano Malvina Garrigues and the couple discovered a mutual passion for Wagner. The two began to study *Tristan and Isolde* in 1858 just for the sake of it with no performance in view, and the opera came to assume an almost mystical significance in their lives. They married in 1860, after Schnorr had moved to the opera at Dresden, where Tichatschek was already installed as the senior dramatic tenor. The two tenors seem to have had a friendly respect for each other, the older singer having already drawn the attention of Wagner to the young phenomenon some six years earlier.

Schnorr had written to Wagner expressing passionate devotion to his music as well as his worries that Tristan was beyond him. Wagner was at first reluctant to meet Schnorr, fearing that his reported obesity – he was a very large man – might blind him to his artistry. Wagner arranged to see him as Lohengrin in 1862, and the effect on him was similar to his first encounter with Schröder-Devrient – he had found another perfect singer. Soon afterwards the two men spent two weeks together (with Hans von Bülow at the piano) experimenting with the Nibelungen works, during which time it emerged that it was only the curse on love in the third act of Tristan that troubled Schnorr. Wagner had finally met a singer whose ideas about music were as poetic and philosophical as his own, and who was perfectly tuned to the composer's aesthetic. He was deeply moved by Schnorr's integrity and very soon showed him how to cope with his Tristan problem.

It was agreed that they would work together towards a first performance of Tristan, but in the meantime Schnorr was engaged for *Tannhäuser* at Munich. There was only one stage rehearsal, which Wagner directed himself, shadowing Schnorr, standing beside him throughout and giving him a second by second account of the emotional states he required. The subsequent performance gave the composer 'a glimpse into my own creation such as seldom, perhaps never, had been vouchsafed to an artist.' [16]

It took almost three years for Wagner to get Schnorr and Malvina out of their Dresden contracts so that they could work exclusively with him on the music. In the rehearsals composer and tenor were of such a single mind that often hardly a word passed between them. The performances when they came were a magnificent success with the public, with Ludwig of Bavaria, and with the composer himself, who had finally discovered a tenor who was not only devoted to him but understood every dramatic nuance of his music. In the time they had spent together working on the opera all three had come to realise that they had an extraordinary spiritual and musical affinity that had the potential to take Wagner's new music drama into unimagined realms. It was the dramatic intelligence of Schnorr that appealed to the composer, who thought the tenor's talent almost magical, combining perfect vocalism with spiritual understanding.[17] Both understood that the old extravagant vocalism was no more, and that the unity of faultless technique and flawless acting was what the future would demand. Singer and composer were looking forward to securing the future of music drama, but the fourth performance of Tristan, a command performance before the king on 12 July 1865, was to be Schnorr's last; less than two weeks later the great tenor was dead, probably of typhoid, at the age of twenty-nine.

After such long and intense preparations of such new and difficult music it was perhaps understandable that word began to get around that Tristan had killed its creator. The stories of the tenor's death are extravagant and mostly unverifiable, but all are touched by his unbreakable attachment to Wagner and his music, which he is said to have sung repeatedly as he lay dying. The composer was devastated, and initially guilt-ridden at having perhaps worked the singer too hard:

> My Tristan! My Beloved! I drove you to the abyss. I am used to standing there. I have a head for heights. But I cannot see anyone standing at the edge. I am seized with frenzied sympathy. I grab hold to pull back and I push over just as we kill the sleepwalker when we shout out in alarm. It was thus – I pushed him over . . . My Tristan! My Beloved! [18]

Such was his grief that he began the diary known as *The Brown Book* to help him come to terms with the tenor's death. It was not just a personal blow, however, but the end of the composer's dream of forging a new vocalism around the unique talent of this extraordinary tenor. The two had discussed starting a singing school in Munich but in Wagner's despair the project did not materialise (and he initially even forbade further performances of Tristan, believing that he would never find another tenor who could step into Schnorr's shoes).[19]

Of course, there were to be other Tristans for him, the most notable of which was Albert Niemann, who first sang the role in 1876.[20] Niemann was perhaps the first true Heldentenor, with a real understanding of *Sprechgesang*, the declamatory delivery Wagner expected.[21] Born in 1831 he tried his luck first as an actor before going to Paris to study with Gilbert-Louis Duprez. His first exposure to Wagner was Tannhäuser in 1854, soon followed by Lohengrin a year later, and Rienzi in 1859, the year after he had first met the composer in person. Niemann was hugely successful, singing Siegmund in *Die Walküre* in Bayreuth, London and New York. He had a powerful stage presence and genuine acting ability, all of which appealed to Wagner even though the two bore each other only a grudging respect. They were, perhaps, too similar in character, both determined to be the centre of the musical universe and unwilling to admit their dependence on each other. Niemann eventually died in 1917, having given his last performance in 1892. Frustratingly, there are no known recordings of his voice.[22]

Wagner's attitude to singers was complicated by the conflicting demands of sound traditional technique and the artistic considerations of the *Gesamtkunstwerk*, in which the singing was only one element. He had been brought up to respect the Italian tradition, yet the visits to his mother's house of the Italian castrato Sassaroli, with his piercing laugh and high-pitched voice, frightened the young boy and left him with a certain antipathy towards things Italian.[23] On the other hand he grew to think that the German language was problematic for singers (it would have been one of the strands of study in his proposed singing school) and he understood the conflict between the seamless line that Italian singers could create and the need to make the text absolutely clear. He had little time for singing teachers, who were often suspicious of the new singing he was advocating; the answer to the vocal problems that many singers were to have with his music lay not in technical solutions, but spiritual ones. All of the tenor roles require considerable vocal and physical stamina.

Wagner does not write excessively high for tenor as that would compromise the relationship between musical declamation and the reality of speech; but for the same reason he expected tenors to be able to sustain long periods in the least comfortable parts of the voice, the so-called *passaggio* between the chest and head registers. The task is made doubly difficult by the dense orchestration the composer favoured. Tichatschek, Niemann and Schnorr all came close in their way to Wagner's ideal tenor, and by working intensively with them he was able to refine his ideas of a dramatic voice; in Bayreuth he had the perfect circumstances to experiment, and had the proposed Wagner and Schnorr singing school come to fruition the evolution of the Heldentenor might have been more lyrical (and Italianate) than subsequently was the case. For the first Bayreuth Festival in 1876 Wagner turned to the singing pedagogue Julius Hey, whom he had met in 1864 when considering the establishment of his Munich singing school. Hey was another kindred spirit who was able to articulate the connection between dramatic declamation and the old Italian legato style, and he coached Georg Unger, the first Bayreuth Siegfried, for a whole year before the first performance. His four-volume monumental *Deutsche Gesangunterricht* of 1885 is still in use in Germany today (condensed into a single volume).[24] Hey believed that there was nothing incompatible between the old and new techniques, and that the former was an essential prerequisite for the latter (although this did not prevent Wagner from insisting Unger repeat one particularly problematic phrase until he could sing no more).

The Heldentenor after Wagner

After Wagner's death in 1883 much of the radical forward thinking of the Wagner project came to an end as his legacy was left in the hands of his widow Cosima, who devoted her life to the preservation of the master's work and refused to allow any aspect to be developed beyond her own idiosyncratic (and extremely conservative) ideas of what the music drama should be. Hey's vocally benign oversight of the singers was replaced by the dogmatic Julius Kniese as vocal coach to the Festival. Kniese, aided and abetted by Cosima, seems to have wilfully misrepresented Wagner's ideas on declamation, believing that the legato line was a positive hindrance to the articulation of text. Cosima herself, in correspondence with the tenor Ernest van Dyck (coached by Kniese for the 1888 Bayreuth *Parsifal*), insisted on the primacy of language and diction, at the expense of the singing if necessary:

> Our stage differs from all other operatic stages in Germany in having drama at the centre of all the performances that are there given. We look upon music as the means, not the end. Drama is the end, and the organ of drama is language . . . and if there must be sacrifice at all . . . sacrifice rather the music (singing) to the poem than the poem (language) to the music. [25]

This is a far cry from the composer who loved Bellini and, as Cosima wrote in her diary in 1872, recalled with affection the singing of Rubini.[26] It cannot have been what the Meister had in mind but was something completely new, and indeed different not only from other German opera houses but also from most of the rest of the European and American operatic world.

The immediate effect of Kniese's teaching was to isolate Bayreuth from the main thread of Heldentenor evolution, which outside the Wagner enclave continued to acknowledge links with the more traditional teaching of Julius Hey. The difference between the two styles was brutally obvious to George Bernard Shaw, who complained of the 1894 Bayreuth *Parsifal* that the bass howled, the tenor bawled and the soprano screamed and none of them sang in tune. He contrasted this with the 'smooth' singing that he was used to hearing in England in similar repertoire, and likened Bayreuth declamation to the art of public speaking, 'a means of placing certain ideas intelligibly and emphatically before the public without any preoccupation as to beauty of voice or grace of manner'.[27]

The uncompromising Bayreuth style was carried forward by Alfred von Bary and Erik Schmedes, both of whom can be heard on disc showing at best clear and precise diction but lacking any sense of refinement.[28] The international style is represented by Hermann Winkelmann, Heinrich Knote, Karel

Burrian and Jacques Urlus, whose surviving recordings show remnants of a more legato tradition.[29] The Dutchman Urlus in particular was a sensitive musician, although his Met début as Tristan in 1913 was marred by vocal problems. Despite feeling unwell he had to go on as there was no understudy and lost his voice completely towards the end of the first act. His Isolde, Johanna Gadski, duetted with herself as Urlus turned his back on the audience and wept.

However stultifying Cosima's effect on the music, there were two permanent changes in the world of singing and singers for which Wagner was almost wholly responsible. The creation of an entirely new voice, the Heldentenor ('Held' means hero), changed the vocal landscape; but perhaps more important was the change in the nature of the relationship between singer and composer. Wagner's concept of *Gesamtkunstwerk* had no place for the old virtuosic vocalism, or singers adding improvised decoration to his meticulously wrought lines. Instead, they were offered an intellectual window into the composer's world as interpreters of the work at a far deeper level than the merely vocal. It is from this time onwards that singers can call themselves artists.

The extent to which Wagner was responsible for a new German national style is a more complex question. The new post-bel canto tenors with international careers were as likely to be French as Italian (and the centre of the operatic world for much of the century was Paris) but performances were almost invariably given in translation until well into the twentieth century.[30] The increasing status and mobility of star performers could sometimes lead to performances in a mixture of languages, and although Wagner's works offered more opportunities for native German singers (and led to singing in Germany being taken much more seriously), the extent to which the Heldentenor represented a distinct national style is debatable. Wagner certainly thought he was developing a new German style, and dramatic declamation was obviously very different from old Italian florid singing, but voices everywhere were getting bigger and less agile, and many of the best Wagnerian tenors were not actually German. Later in the twentieth century Heldentenors in particular would tend to specialise in Wagnerian and related roles, but the singers we hear on the earliest recordings tend to have much wider repertoires than many of today's star tenors.

Jean de Reszke

One of the most intriguing singers of the period was the Polish tenor Jean de Reszke. He was born in Warsaw in 1850 into a wealthy aristocratic family and first learned singing with his mother, Emilia Ufniarska, a soprano who had been a pupil of Garcia and his daughter Pauline Viardot. His brother Edouard and sister Josephine were also precociously talented, the three siblings making their first public appearance together at a soirée in 1869. Jean's voice broke early and by the age of fifteen he was having lessons at the Warsaw Conservatoire with the tenor Francesco Ciaffei, who considered him to be a baritone; Edouard also studied with Ciaffei and went on to become one of the great basses of the era. Ciaffei persuaded Jean, by then studying law, to take lessons with Antonio Cotogni (who would later number Battistini, Lauri-Volpi, Gigli and the 'last castrato' Moreschi among many other star pupils). Jean made his début at La Fenice in Venice 1874 and later that year sang opposite his sister at the Teatro Malibran. He italianised his name to Giovanni di Reschi and had considerable success in Italy and England in baritone roles, including Figaro and Giovanni.

He first appeared as Jean de Reszke at his Paris début at the Théâtre-Italien in 1876 as Fra Melitone in *La forza del destino*. It was a visit of his father from Warsaw that convinced him that his increasingly vibrant high notes meant that he might well be a tenor.[31] Edouard de Reszke had also made a successful Paris début (in *Aida*) and had taken lessons with Giovanni Sbriglia, and it was to the distinguished Italian teacher that Jean now turned for advice. Like all of the de Reszke brothers' teachers to date, Sbriglia was of the old Italian school, but enough of a pragmatist to apply the principles to the larger voices than would have been current in his youth (his pupils included Pol Plancon, Mary Garden and Lillian Nordica). He had an open mind about the tenor/baritone question and master and pupil set about exploring the possibilities with no fixed outcome in mind. The high notes continued to develop under Sbriglia's guidance and Jean eventually made his début as a *tenore robusto* in Madrid in 1878, again singing opposite his sister, this time in *Robert le diable*.

Although he felt comfortable with the change he did not have immediate success in Spain and briefly retired from performing to work on his technique and observe other singers in action. As luck would have it, the de Reszke brothers were trying out some music in a Paris shop when they were over-heard by Massenet, who was entranced by Jean's voice and booked him for the tenor role of Jean in *Hérodiade* which was presented at the Théâtre-Italien in 1884. So successful was he that the composer wrote for him the role of Rodrigue in *Le Cid* and his future as a tenor was assured with a five-year contract at the Opéra beginning the following year.[32] In 1891 de Reszke made his New York début as Romeo and began a period of unprecedented success at the Met which lasted until he stopped singing in the USA ten years later. His final season in New York included almost all the roles that he had by then made his own: Lohengrin, Faust, Le Cid, Vasco, Tristan, Roméo, Siegfried and Raoul. No tenor since has been able to match this achievement.[33]

Jean de Reszke's aristocratic charm, handsome bearing and engaging personality endeared him to audiences and critics alike. The more perceptive of them (such as George Bernard Shaw) sometimes wondered if he really stirred himself enough to fully realise his potential. Perhaps his background did deny him that hunger for success that drove so many of his less privileged fellow tenors, but if so it surely also informed a man whose generous behaviour to his fellows was rare in the competitive and highly charged world of the star singer. His performances were dogged by bronchial infections which caused him considerable pain and anxiety. Persistent bouts of 'flu and related illnesses, often resulting in hurtful critical notices, led him to retire from the stage while in his fifties and at the peak of his career; he gave his last performances in 1905 and devoted the rest of his life to teaching. This decision is one that has vexed historians of singing: here was perhaps the greatest tenor of his age at the top of his form and silent, at a time when lesser singers were competing to record their voices for posterity. De Reszke preferred history to judge him on his reputation: no recordings survive apart from a live Met performance of 1901 which is barely audible through the hiss.[34]

His fellow singers loved him. Nellie Melba, that connoisseuse of tenors, sang countless operas with the de Reszke brothers and was inspired by Jean since he almost single-handedly rescued her second Covent Garden season in 1889, guiding her through every nuance of *Roméo et Juliette*:

> he was a god – not only in his voice, which he used with an artistry which can only be called perfection – but in his appearance, his acting, his every movement. So utterly wonderful was he that when sometime later I found myself singing in *Lohengrin* with him without a rehearsal, I burst into tears in the last act . . . Jean de Reszke – so perfect, so gallant! Never has there been an artist like him.[35]

The two performed so often and so naturally together that it was only a small surprise to Melba when seven years later King Oscar of Norway and Sweden knocked on the door of her Paris apartment asking for a cup of tea and proceeded to sing duets with her – she playing herself and the king being Jean de Reszke.[36] David Bispham, who sang with de Reszke on many occasions including his last Met performance in New York in 1901, considered him irreplaceable, 'the finest artist of his generation, a tower of strength to our company and a vocal and physical adornment to the stage he elevated by his presence'.[37]

The critic Herman Klein was a friend, and wrote of his Radamès that he sang without a hint of vibrato and with vigorous declamation, that he was an ideal Lohengrin, an unsurpassable Faust and a superb Raoul.[38] Klein knew both de Reszke brothers well, and in his *Thirty Years of Musical Life in London* recalls many occasions when the three (often accompanied by Lillian Nordica and the baritone Jean Lassalle) spent time together discussing matters vocal. On one notable occasion the three men were joined in a restaurant by Tamagno, whom Lassalle challenged to sing higher in his chest voice than Lassalle could in his falsetto. The contest ended around a top D with both singers standing on chairs, and was declared a draw.[39]

De Reszke's breadth of repertoire was remarkable – he maintained the 'lighter' Mozart repertoire even as he was singing Lohengrin. Most of these roles he first learned in Italian; fluent in Italian and French as well as Russian and Polish, he also had good conversational English and German, and became famous for his exquisite diction in all of these languages once the 'Italian-only' taboo was finally broken at Covent Garden. De Reszke's linguistic ability was integral to his perception of style, and in his teaching he drew attention to the need for students to synthesise the best elements of the three great traditions. From the Italian one learned the legato line and the control that comes from agility, the French school gave charm and sobriety, while the German method taught 'energy of diction, the violence required in certain dramatic situations and a particular poetic vehemence, or exuberance . . .'[40]

He was perhaps the first to realise that the future of singing was truly international, and that the best singers of the future would have to absorb the essential elements of what had sometimes been thought of as discrete national styles by some of his contemporaries and predecessors. Ironically, the reverse may have appeared to be the case when he and Augustus Harris, encouraged by Shaw and Klein, persuaded the Royal Italian Opera at Covent Garden (as it had been since Handel's time) that operas should be given in their original languages rather than the ubiquitous Italian or in a vernacular translation. It was as a successful singer of the Italian and French repertoire that he first came to Wagner (and initially in Italian, of course). He was determined to sing Wagner in German, and was the first to do so at Covent Garden in the 1895–6 season. De Reszke's Heldentenor performances were sensational successes, uniting his unfailing musicianship with a charismatic stage presence and dramatic intensity not seen since Schnorr. Like Wagner's protégé, the Polish tenor saw the master's work as something almost sacred.

As well as being the first of a new breed of international tenors, de Reszke was one of the last routinely to have his own way with the music, as opposed to having an interpretation foisted on him by the conductor. Amherst Webber, the tenor's accompanist for much of his career, tells of the disappointment of Johannes Sembach, who had studied Lohengrin with de Reszke, on discovering that conductors simply would not allow him to incorporate many of the nuances suggested to him by de Reszke.[41] Jean de Reszke was a superstar of whom conductors and impresarios were in awe. He charmed promoters into agreeing to huge fees with the minimum of negotiation, and to his adoring audience he was a romantic hero figure such as had never before trod the operatic stage. He showed that it was possible to sing Wagner in addition to the lyric dramatic repertory rather than instead of it, and that Heldentenors need not shout their way to success if they kept the link with basic Italian principles.

De Reske's (almost) silent contemporaries

De Reszke had also been the foremost singer of the French repertoire, a significant fact which perhaps indicates that the nineteenth-century convergence of French and Italian styles – the Nourrit–Duprez–Rubini–Mario trajectory – had resulted in a singing style that was less distinctly French. It was perhaps the case that the more muscular roles of Gounod, Massenet and Auber tended to even out the distinction between line and language that had been so problematic when French singers attempted the Italian repertoire. De Reszke's most successful French predecessor was probably Jean-Alexandre Talazac, who created Offenbach's Hoffman, Massenet's Des Grieux, Gérald in Delibes' *Lakmé*, and Mylio in Lalo's *Le Roi d'Ys*. George Bernard Shaw wrote of his 1889 *Pêcheurs de perles* that he had 'a pretty and fairly steady mezza voce, besides some sweet headnotes; but the tremolo with which he uses his chest register will prevent him from attaining popularity here.'[42] This is a tenor we would love to be able to hear, but he died in 1896 at the age of forty-five. Perhaps there are clues in the singing of Edmond Clément, who was twenty-nine at the time of Talazac's death; he demonstrates elegance, control and an exquisite mezza voce which looks forward to those of his successors who would be influenced by Fernando de Lucia, such as Georges Thill.

Another voice that many historians believe to be an essential link to the tradition of Rubini and Mario is that of Angelo Masini. Ten years younger than de Reszke, he retired at about the same time as the Polish tenor and left no recordings. Masini had a big career but has been less visible to history perhaps because he did not appear in New York, nor at Covent Garden, and in the latter stages of his career not often in Italy either. He had great success in Russia, South America, France, Spain and Portugal, and sang roles as diverse as Don Ottavio and Lohengrin. This in itself is not remarkable, but the descriptions of his voice would certainly sound strange if applied to a modern Lohengrin. He was hailed as the heir of Rubini and was likened on more than one occasion to a soprano, such was his agility, flexibility, breath control and lightness of timbre. His lack of respect for the composer's score was often criticised: he was as creative with the notes as he was with the tempo, which audiences loved but critics and conductors thought tasteless and infuriating. Tamagno, who greatly respected Masini, said of him:

> A Nightingale . . . a violin! . . . you can have no idea of the sweetness, of the angelic softness of that voice. Never in my life have I heard anyone who so deeply enters the heart and wrenches the tears as he does, with that voice of paradise, that seems to come not from the mouth but from the air. [43]

The rumours of a de Reske cylinder also apply to several other singers whom we would dearly love to be able to hear, notably the trio of relatively young tenors who did not survive the 1890s: Julián Gayarre, Italo Campanini and Roberto Stagno. All had been pupils of Francesco Lamperti and went on to successful and significant careers without ever quite reaching the heights of de Reszke in public acclaim; all sang a remarkably wide variety of repertoire and were among the last to have such catholic tastes. They all died relatively young after periods of ill health or vocal problems: Stagno, the first Turiddu, died in 1897 aged fifty-seven; Campanini, the first Italian Lohengrin, had retired dogged by vocal problems two years before his death in 1896 at the age of fifty-one; Gayarre, who created the Duke in Donizetti's *Il Duca d'Alba*, Enzo in Ponchielli's *La gioconda* and was the first Italian Tannhäuser, died of respiratory problems in 1890 at the age of forty-one.[44]

The tenor voice in Spain is less visible historically since we tend to see the history of the voice in terms of the creation of new roles and the new demands that these may make on the singers. There has been a flourishing operatic tradition in the Iberian peninsular almost as long as in Italy itself, and there has been a succession of superb Spanish tenors since the elder Garcia. But Spanish houses have seen relatively few new creations as their repertories tend to be dominated by imported composers. Spanish tenors have almost always been measured in terms of how well they manage the great Italian or French roles. Spanish and Portuguese opera houses, however, have welcomed Italian tenors with open arms and wallets, and many tenors developed their careers in the Iberian Peninsular.[45]

Gayarre was born in Navara but studied in Milan with Lamperti at the Conservatorio di Milano. Over a twenty-year period after his début in Varese in 1869 he travelled the operatic world from St Petersburg to South America and sang a huge variety of roles. He began with Donizetti but within three years had a clutch of Verdi roles and Tannhäuser under his belt. By the 1880s his repertoire included Gounod and Meyerbeer, and he was being acclaimed as one of the great tenors of the century, helped by the ferocious rivalry between his fans and those of Angelo Masini, born in the same year, whose career and repertoire closely paralleled Gayarre's own.[46] The Gayarre legend took lasting form on the occasion of his final performance, of Bizet's *Les Pêcheurs de perles* at the Teatro Real in Madrid, in which he seemed to anticipate his own death, which did indeed follow a few weeks later.[47] Critical reactions to Gayarre's voice illustrate the difficulties of trying to imagine a sound from conflicting descriptions: are we to believe George Bernard Shaw, who heard his Raoul and called him a goat bleater, describing the tenor's voice as 'harsh, acute, piercing, disquieting; its finish and polish ... like those of a circular saw'? Shaw thought his acting 'aggravated rather than redeemed his vocal disadvantages'.[48] Or is Michele Uda's recollection of his Gennaro nearer the mark with 'The voice of Gayarre says everything; and the face ... radiates, contorts, suffers agonies with that of the character. ... The god-given throat, the prodigious lungs, the marvellous art of the sweetest *smorzature* in the ringing fullness of the chest, all played their part, but the heart predominated.'[49] Perhaps these are simply Italian and Irish-English impressions of the same thing, which one appreciated and the other did not. Gayarre was clearly a histrionic performer of great commitment but perhaps not a very large voice, who sang with vibrato and was able to modulate the power of his chest voice with dramatic fades (*smorzature*). Other commentators note his messa di voce, his agility and phenomenal breath control.[50]

Campanini's experience was even more eclectic. The son of a blacksmith, he fought for Garibaldi as a teenager before turning to singing. His military exploits presumably helped him endure a three-year stint in Russian provincial opera houses, before in 1870 he, too, became a pupil of Lamperti. Performances in northern Italian houses quickly followed, including *Faust*, *Don Giovanni*, and *Lucrezia Borgia* at La Scala in 1871, which was also the year of his Lohengrin at Bologna, the first performance of any Wagner opera in Italy.[51] Colonel Mapleson hired him for Drury Lane, but it was not long before Max Strakosch paid him much greater sums to appear in New York, where he took part in the American première of *Aida* as well as in performances of works by Wagner, Verdi and Mozart. He was a huge success, and over the next ten years acquired a repertoire ranging from Bach to Berlioz (whose *Requiem* and *Te Deum* he was the first to perform in the USA).

During this time he had begun to experience vocal problems and, worried about his increasing reputation for unreliability and inconsistency, in 1882 he retired to Parma to rest. The following year he was tempted back to New York for the opening of the Metropolitan Opera, and it was Campanini's 'No!' in the opening scene of Gounod's *Faust* that was the first voice to be heard by an audience from the Met stage.[52] Vocal problems still troubled him but he went on to sing eleven roles in the first Met season before retiring once more, this time for three years. He then turned his attention to the concert repertoire, more demanding in terms of travelling but easier on the voice than his operatic roles. His repertoire included *Messiah*, a rare choice for one who had sung Lohengrin, and indicative of his flexibility and musicianship.

Stagno was born into minor aristocracy in Palermo and cultivated a gentility that sometimes bordered on the pompous.[53] He made his début in Lisbon in 1862 as Rodrigo in Rossini's *Otello* and graduated to Meyerbeer, Verdi and the early Wagner roles. He became the companion of the soprano Gemma Bellincioni and the two of them premièred *Cavalleria rusticana* in Rome in 1890. They were scheduled to repeat the partnership in Giordano's *Fedora* in 1897 but Stagno died (to be replaced by the young Caruso). The role of Turridu is, unusually for a tenor, that of an anti-hero; it is forthright and lies high although never going beyond B flat, and demands stamina as well as an old-fashioned sense of line within a *verismo* context. Stagno was successful in the role, but perhaps it was as a powerful lyric tenor in the traditional Italian mould rather than as a revelatory *verismo* singing actor. The part was taken by Fernando de Lucia at Covent Garden two years later and eventually fell to Caruso, who brought more power to it. There may be a progression here, illustrating the application of power by succeeding generations of singers in the same role. In the mid-1890s, however, critics commended Stagno's almost limitless repertoire, his extreme virtuosity and his ability to sing comfortably in the very high tessitura required for Bellini and Meyerbeer. One critic commented on his messa di voce and wide dynamic range, and likened his ornamentation to that of a light soprano.[54]

Fernando De Lucia

Unlike the tenors discussed above, Fernando De Lucia left hundreds of recordings. As an approximate contemporary of them all he is a key figure in our understanding of what lyric tenors may have been like at the turn of the century. He was born in 1860, twenty years after Stagno, within sixteen years of Gayarre, Masini and Campanini and only ten years after Jean de Reszke. Both de Reszke and de Lucia died in 1925, having outlived the older trio by more than a quarter of a century.

Unusually, De Lucia went straight from singing in concerts and drawing rooms to a début at the Teatro San Carlo, Naples in 1885, having started his musical life as a double-bass player. After a number of performances in Bologna and Florence (where he first sang Don José, a role he was later very much associated with) he was signed up for a South American tour with the Ciacchi–Rainieri company. While there, he would have had ample opportunity to observe Stagno, who was appearing with Angelo Ferrari's rival company. As a student in Naples he would certainly have heard Stagno, Gayarre and Masini, who all sang at San Carlo at some point during the 1880s and he followed all three of them in seasons in the Iberian peninsular and South America. At various stages in his career he was likened to them all, and by all accounts they seem to have shared many characteristics.[55] They were all capable of moving their listeners by both singing and acting, they all had powerful high notes which might be delivered in head or chest voice, they all believed that the singing was at least as important as the music (or indeed that it *was* the music), and they were all creative virtuosi, able to amaze audiences with their *fioriture*. These are characteristics that we read of their legendary predecessors Rubini and Mario; they are not generally applied to de Reszke or Caruso. In hearing De Lucia, therefore, we can perhaps capture something of a vanished sound world.

He began as a lyric tenor and re-invented himself as a dramatic tenor – he was a fine and histrionic actor – but at the long-term expense of his voice. Canio and Don José – his two most famous roles and in which he showed his dramatic talents to the full – took their toll. He had mixed success in the USA, his passion being perhaps over the top for an 'Anglo-Saxon' audience, and he was in competition with Jean de Reske whose more baritonal qualities enabled him to cope with dramatic rôles with more restraint and subtlety. De Lucia performed Lohengrin five times at San Carlo and never repeated it, writing in his score 'an opera that I sang with adoration but abandoned because it ruins the voice'.[56] He received good notices – it was obviously an Italianate and lyrical performance such as Neapolitans might have expected (but which would have baffled any German tourists in the house) – but he was criticised for using excessive falsetto. This is a criticism that recurs throughout the singer's life, often combined with comments on his mannered delivery, particularly his frequent recourse to mezza voce diminuendos.[57] At the top of his voice – around B (he was not a stratospherically high tenor – he seems to have been able to shade his register changes between chest and falsetto with a mixed register mediating between them) he could be powerful in chest or equally dramatic with an instant retreat into mezza voce. He was also inclined to add fioriture even when they weren't called for, and his concept of tempo was extremely fluid – characteristics that did not endear him to conductors of the Toscanini caste.

De Lucia was one of the last tenors of the period to work with living composers, and his instinct for the traditional (but almost vanished) singerly freedoms often created tension between him and the modern score-orientated composers whose work he performed. He was Puccini's first choice for Rodolfo in *Bohème* (despite his tendency to 'improve' on the score), and sang the role at La Scala and San Carlo, having been too expensive for the première in Turin in 1896.[58] The correspondence between composer Mascagni, conductor Toscanini, publisher Ricordi and singer De Lucia (quoted at length in Michael Henstock's biography of the tenor) vividly reveals the unresolvable conflicts between composer and performer over the ownership of the music. For the moment, the composer was at the mercy of the singer. Tito Ricordi wrote to Mascagni:

> And everything possible was done regarding Sig. De Lucia, who at rehearsals accepted all the observations, [and] performed as required: only at the last rehearsal had I the – fleeting – suspicion that he was placating us! ... I sent Toscanini to repeat to him all the recommendations made a hundred times at rehearsals – and the first night De Lucia played a dirty trick and did it his own way! ... What should we have done? Dragged him out through the wings? ... or fired a revolver at him? ... Unfortunately these are miseries which one must endure in the theatre ... .[59]

It was not to last, of course. Toscanini, the composers' secret weapon, would eventually ensure that singers sang only what was written in the score, and the relationship between composer and performer soon assumed its modern form, with the score as authoritative artefact and the performer its interpreter. De Lucia sang at Caruso's funeral in Naples in 1921, at which thousands lined the streets. His own funeral four years later also drew thousands to pay their last respects. Naples lost a son, and singing too lost something irrecoverable: the tenor as creative artist linked to a tradition dating back hundreds of years into the musical past.

CHAPTER 5

CARUSO AND THE ITALIAN SUCCESSION

The Italian singing tradition evolved over a period of some three hundred years until the first decades of the nineteenth century. We cannot know what the style sounded like in its pre-nineteenth-century form but the evidence suggests that it was characterised by smoothness of line, flexibility of phrasing and an ability to sing with lightness and agility. We know that singers would improvise additional ornamentation, especially at cadences, which became opportunities for virtuosic display. Chest and head registers were expected to be joined seamlessly, with tenors by the end of the eighteenth century having wide ranges, typically from a baritonal A (about a third lower than a modern tenor) up to a falsetto D (about a third higher than most modern tenors). The music essentially belonged to the singer at the moment of delivery, the task of the composer being to exploit the talents of individual singers who would by their creative performance reveal the talent of the composer. Learning the trade was a relatively simple if time-consuming process; individual talent was nurtured but tenors were born and not created – there was one 'natural' way to sing and it could be applied to any individual fortunate enough to possess a good voice.

Gradually this picture began to be complicated by a dawning awareness that the key tenets of traditional technique could be enhanced by an awareness of what happens in the vocal tract. From the first quarter of the nineteenth century the pedagogical literature contains an increasing number of references to the lowering of the larynx, which gives increased resonance – greater power and projection – and a more complex frequency spectrum, which in turn means potentially richer tone. We cannot be certain of when tenors first started experimenting with their larynxes, but we are on surer ground with the upwards extension of the chest register and the eventual loss of falsetto. Although this seems to have started in Italy (Donzelli was perhaps the first major tenor to experiment with this heavier sound and Donizetti the first composer to encourage it), it soon became associated with French tenors, after Gilbert-Louis Duprez and his successors who took the voice into realms that it had never before inhabited. In particular they extended the chest voice upwards to produce the ringing high notes that we are familiar with today. The establishment of the Paris Conservatoire and Napoleon's deep appreciation of Italian culture ensured that traditional Italian teaching became enshrined in the new, now state-supported, pedagogy. A hybrid French–Italian tradition developed, with a distinct dramatic and lyric flavour that was in contrast to the heavier German singing which evolved from the mid-century onwards.

From then on the picture becomes yet more complicated. By mid-century Wagner's German tenors were making similar exploratory forays into virgin vocal territory, although the new elements of style and technique generally acknowledged the primacy of basic 'Italian' teaching (the Bayreuth school eventually becoming an obvious exception to this). Virtuosity still had a major role in pedagogy (which tended to lag behind compositional practice), even though singers of the new dramatic repertoire were not expected to be particularly agile in actual performance. The older repertoire, Mozart especially, continued to be performed alongside the modern works. Although many singers had a far wider variety of roles than their present-day equivalents, we see increasing specialisation towards the end of the century, with some Heldentenors, for example, being reluctant to take on more lyric roles if they considered themselves to be true Wagnerians. The lyric tradition continued to flourish, often benefiting from the increased power that all tenors were expected to display during the second half of the century, but there was an increasing awareness that the vast expansion of the repertoire meant that singers had to think carefully about which roles to avoid. Composers still tailored roles to specific singers and popular singers would be expected to repeat the repertoires that had made their reputations, but with a thriving operatic culture in cities from Moscow to Montevideo it was inevitable that the most popular works would have a life far beyond their first performances.

Successful tenors could choose what suited them, and their decisions were invariably governed by vocal pragmatism; those without huge reserves of power would steer clear of the later Wagner oeuvre but might sing Lohengrin or Tannhäuser, for example.

The industrial revolution, with its accompanying expansion of cities every-where and the complex social patterns that emerged, inevitably had an effect on music and musicians. It was relatively rare by this time for singers to attach themselves to an acknowledged master as a kind of apprentice; the tradition of boy sopranos taking women's roles in theatre productions (a traditional route for would-be tenors) virtually died out with the emancipation of women in music. In countries with a strong Catholic tradition (such as France and, more especially, Italy) boy sopranos were often given encouragement by their local church choir, where the ban on women lingered. The teacher was still some-thing of a guru-like figure, but was more likely to be teaching in one of the thousands of music schools that were founded in the nineteenth century. These varied in size and quality from the Paris Conservatoire, still driven by a Napoleonic agenda of national excellence, to the provincial Italian schools which fed local opera houses with anonymous but ever-hopeful young singers. The aspiring tenor was less likely to be from a comfortable bourgeois back-ground: singing was a way out of poverty, and towards the end of the century we see tenors thrust into the limelight from very diverse backgrounds, often of considerable deprivation.

During the early years of the twentieth century there is still evidence of discrete national styles to be discerned in the tenorocracy, although this is not the straightforward exercise in categorisation that one might expect. The Franco-Italian style continues to underlie what one might think of as the mainstream operatic technique, but it is coloured by the language of the singer, who is as likely to come from the Americas, Russia, Spain, Scandinavia or anywhere else in Europe. The Germanic influence is manifested in heavier voices, and these tend to come from northern Europe. Although modern tenors perhaps sound less distinctive than their counterparts a generation or two ago, there is still an individualism linked to their native language. It is this, rather than a more specific sense of national style, allied to the individual tenor's charisma, that gives a wider sense of identity to individual singers. At the end of the nineteenth century there is still a living tradition of contempo-rary music, with audiences in Italy, for example, enthusiastically welcoming new works by Puccini, Cilea, Giordano, Mascagni or Leoncavallo. It would not be so for much longer, but this parting of the creative ways was graced by one of the last and greatest exponents of the music of his own present: Enrico Caruso.

Enrico Caruso: first superstar of the gramophone era

Caruso arrived on the scene when opera houses were hungry for successful new performers as the great figures of the previous era (de Reszke and Tamagno among the tenors) came to the end of their working lives. It was his supreme good luck to mature as recording technology first became widely available, and to take his career to its height as the new technology evolved and improved but before electrical recording and the microphone reduced the need for singers to be completely self-sufficient vocally. The recording industry and its tenor superstar owed their phenomenal success to each other.

Nothing in history has changed music and singing more than the invention of the gramophone. The machine that could store and reproduce sounds brought music into the home of everyone who could afford one. This not only changed the way people listened to music: it permanently altered how they thought about it. By removing the human contact with the individual performer it created a kind of performance *in absentia,* in which for the first time it was possible to hear a performance without seeing it, without direct experience of the person. Even more bizarrely, it was possible to hear the same performance repeated identically for as long as the needle or shellac would last. Many of the unpredictable and often larger-than-life characters of musical legend would not prosper under the ruthless regime of the machine that could hear them but not see them. Success as a recording artist did, though, almost always ensure success as a live performer, and in Caruso's spectacular rise to fame these two vital elements went hand in hand.

Within a few decades the extraordinary variety of voices and styles revealed by the earliest recordings would give way to a much more rigorous and less tolerant idea of what singing was. Capturing sound means you can measure it, and measuring means you can make comparisons, conceive standards, emulate perceived greatness. The reproduction is taken for the reality and may even be preferred to it. As Friedrich Kittler put it, 'As a photograph of the soul, the talking machine put an end to the innocent doctrine of innocence.'[1]

We are able to hear Caruso's immediate predecessors and contemporaries on record, including not only Tamagno's famous Verdi recordings, but also fine performances by Giovanni Zenatello and Fernando De Lucia (like Caruso, both Neapolitans). De Lucia, as we have seen, was a significant figure on both sides of the Atlantic, though he attracted mixed reviews (Shaw was lukewarm on his Covent Garden creation of Turiddu, Klein more positive about his first Canio); he was not happy in the stratospherically high 'old' Rossini roles, and had a pronounced vibrato. There was more of a critical consensus in the case of Giovanni Zenatello. He began his professional career as a baritone but graduated to the dramatic Italian roles and was an especially fine Verdi interpreter (Scott considers him the finest Otello since Tamagno).[2] He was associated with La Scala for many years, creating Pinkerton for Puccini, as well as a number of roles by Cilea and Franchetti.

Toscanini's reign in Milan, and later at the Met in New York, was to change the expectations of audiences, performers and composers for ever. Taking Wagner as his paradigm, he saw all opera as drama rather than as just an expensive and sophisticated form of entertainment. There were to be no breaks in the action, no repetition of arias, no additions to the composer's score, and no singing just for its own sake. When Zenatello encored an aria in the middle of *Un ballo in maschera* Toscanini resigned from the company. The future had arrived. Zenatello's reputation future-proofed him to an extent – he went on to huge success across the opera world from Leningrad to central and south America, and in his retirement he devoted himself to teaching and to the opera at Verona, where he sang in the opening concert of the amphitheatre, later engaging Maria Callas for her Italian début in 1947.

The Toscanini view of opera as dramatic art is one we now take for granted, but his vision (perceived at the time by most audiences as being rather bleak) was given much greater substance after he moved to the Metropolitan Opera in New York and engaged Enrico Caruso, who would turn out to be a singer unlike any heard before. Caruso was born into a poor Neapolitan family in 1873. He went to work as a mechanic at the age of ten, singing in local choirs in the evenings and eventually ending up, as a teenager, in a factory weaving jute. After the death of his sickly but supportive mother Caruso told his father that he would have no more manual labour but would devote himself to music. Conscripted into the army, he was fortunate to have a commanding officer who recognised his talent, and gave him time off for singing lessons, finally allowing him leave altogether on the condition that his brother took his place.[3]

He made an inauspicious start to his new career. He was a starving Napolitano who could barely speak Italian and who could not tell whether he was a tenor or a baritone, and he often found himself with singers who were a good deal more sophisticated than he was. His teacher, Guglielmo Vergine, did not want to take Caruso on at first, famously likening his voice to the wind in a chimney. Yet eventually he was persuaded, and in time arranged for his pupil's début as Wilhelm Meister in Thomas' *Mignon*. It was a disaster for the young tenor, who was completely outclassed by the rest of the cast and had his contract swiftly cancelled. Caruso never sang the role again.[4] That might have been the end of the sensitive soul's attempt to make it as a tenor, but, as happens to many singers, a series of lucky breaks enabled him to pick himself up. He was offered work in a number of provincial theatres in Italy and Egypt, where he was able to attempt Gounod's *Faust*, Turiddu in *Cavalleria rusticana*, as well as *Rigoletto*,

Traviata and Puccini's *Manon Lescaut*: the perfect set of roles to launch the career of any dramatic lyric tenor. Things moved quickly after that: by 1897 – still only twenty-four – he was singing to Puccini, who asked rhetorically if he had been sent by god.[5] He was soon in demand by the last generation of Italian composers to have a symbiotic connection to singers: Cilea asked him to première Federico in *L'Arlesiana*, Giordano secured him for *Fedora*; his was the perfect voice for the mature *verismo* composers: manly and powerful, yet sweet and lyrical – everyone's ideal of Italian manhood in tenor form.

It was the first performance of Franchetti's *Germania* in March 1902 which led to the next and most historic break for the young tenor. His performance at La Scala was attended by William Barry Owen and Fred Gaisberg of the Gramophone Company. It was a triumph, and the two talent scouts booked Caruso to record ten songs a few days later. His fee was rejected straight away by the company but Gaisberg was too embarrassed to tell the tenor, who walked off with £100 for the afternoon's work. It was the first instalment of the vast sums he would earn in the future; those two hours' worth of songs, recorded in a hotel room with the piano perched on a pile of packing cases and a horn suspended five feet from the floor, secured the future of the company, legitimised the genre, and marked out Caruso as the most marketable commodity in music. Within three months the company's investment had earned them £15,000.[6]

The following year he appeared at the Met and quickly established himself as the voice that everyone wanted to hear. He was to return for sixteen more seasons, singing thirty-seven different roles.[7] Secure in his technique, he began a long period of consolidation in which he took on no more newly composed music but explored the great French and Italian lyric dramatic roles of the past. He was the perfect singer for a new age in which opera would become something monumental, akin to a museum exhibit in the reverence accorded a core repertoire involving a small number of roles – to which very few would be added in succeeding generations.

Caruso's was the first twentieth-century voice: he sings with a lyricism which the romantic repertoire requires but adds a power and a richness that is not so much elegant as forthright. He has the 'sob' reminiscent of Tamagno's, but the younger tenor's sound world is of a different order altogether. There is no refined note-spinning; everything is projected and energised in the service of the character, a true *verismo* tenor. Thanks to his recordings, which tended to be vibrant rather than subtle, his appeal went far beyond the opera cognoscenti; his humble origins, perceived sincerity and lack of upper-class condescension meant that anyone could identify with him. As Michael Scott put it, Caruso's was the voice that the ordinary man fancied he heard as he sang in his bath.[8]

The history of singing changes with Caruso, not just the audience response but the singing itself; all tenors from the 1920s onwards who attempt the dramatic lyric French and Italian roles – the core operatic tenor repertoire – would routinely need to apply more power, and it was the fate of most of them to be measured against the almost mythical master. His death in 1921 at the age of 48 was a shock not only to the musical world but to millions beyond it who had followed his career in the press or bought his records. Early signs of failing health were not taken as seriously as they might have been; Caruso was a workaholic and something of a hypochondriac but always bounced backed from what he at first considered temporary setbacks.[9] From the end of 1920 onwards he was increasingly debilitated by pleurisy, finally realising that despite several operations he was unlikely to survive. He chose to return home to die, and the city of Naples and the whole of Italy mourned the passing of a man whom they loved as a singer and as a person.

The splintering of the *spinto*

Caruso's retention of a certain stylistic elegance which he combined with a powerful timbral richness meant that he had inherited both dramatic and lyric roles from his predecessors; he was a unique and particularly robust variety of *spinto*, however, and there was no obvious successor who could take on everything that the great man had made his own. A spinto is a lyric tenor with a reserve of power to give an extra dramatic push ('spinto' being the past participle of the Italian 'spingere', to push). J. B. Steane nicely illustrates the difference between a lyric tenor and a spinto in a discussion of tenorial taxonomy, pointing out that in the case of Giovanni Martinelli 'push came to shove' when he strayed into the *robusto* roles of Otello and Tristan, and thereby hinting at the awkwardness of over-categorisation.[10]

The terms 'lyric', 'spinto', and 'robusto' are sometimes helpful in describing individual tenors but less so in characterising specific roles, as the greatest singers bring a deeply personal quality to their interpretations and can often reveal new dimensions to a role through their own vocal peculiarities and constraints. Puccini's Rodolfo, for example, has been successfully undertaken (although those of a particularly taxonomic disposition may disagree . . .) by tenors of such varying power and timbre as Tito Schipa, Gigli (lyric tenors) and Martinelli (a spinto) as well as more modern tenors such as Pavarotti and Domingo who often seem to defy classification altogether. There is also a progression that many tenors make as they get older, sacrificing grace and agility perhaps but gaining a depth and fullness that might bring heavier roles into consideration as well as a more complex approach to those they already know. As we have seen, some lyric/dramatic/spinto tenors have been able to make the transition to the heavier Verdi roles and early Wagner, the territory more easily negotiated by Heldentenors.[11]

Steane calls for a new term to describe the voice that Caruso's might have become had he lived (and which he considers was subsequently realised in the voice of Jon Vickers).[12] The problem with more precise categorisation is that there are always exceptions, and we are dealing with singers who at their best are in any case very different from each other. If the tenor voice is to develop in the future it is surely going to be in the way that individual singers approach what has become a very limited repertoire. It is beyond dispute that there has been a gradual increase in power (the volume at which they could comfortably sing) among *all* significant tenors during the nineteenth and twentieth centuries. This has meant that *all* roles tend to be reinterpreted by larger voices with each succeeding generation, until we arrive at the twenty-first century, when there are so many tenors who overlap into more than one area of repertoire that the traditional subdivisions no longer mean very much.[13]

The first 'modern' tenor in this sense was Caruso: he was the first tenor who could (potentially, at least) sing everything. If we are to draw lines of influence from him to the present, then we should perhaps think in terms of a looser relationship between voices and roles, and be wary of over-categorising and comparing individual tenors.

The Met and the Italian succession: Martinelli and Pertile

The confidence of New York in the last decades of the nineteenth century ensured a permanent and wealthy audience for opera, and a series of hard-headed but creative managers saw the Met's reputation continue to grow, largely fuelled by the best singers from Europe until the outbreak of war made the transatlantic trip problematic. Before 1900 there had only been sixteen American singers in leading roles, and the artistic thrust of the company was divided into German and Italian wings, the house at times featuring solely European repertoire and singers. The Met could afford vast fees, confident that sponsors would pick up the bill. Singers were an investment: it was an expensive and time-consuming operation to get them to cross the Atlantic and the journey was not one you would undertake for just a concert or two. Star singers, certain of attracting the necessary box office, were generally engaged for whole seasons at a time. This meant a variety of roles and the chance to build up a real relationship between performer and audience, which for the most successful singers meant serious socialising as well.

Caruso had established his reputation so firmly in New York that it was to the Met that the public, promoters and aspiring tenors looked for the next generation of Italian tenors. The vacuum left by his death had a polarising effect on the subsequent generation of tenors, both in terms of the roles they took on and the houses in which they played. The Met was a powerful magnet for Italian tenorial talent, with first Giovanni Martinelli, then Beniamino Gigli and Giacomo Lauri-Volpi having great success there. One potential successor, Luca Botta, hailed as a young Caruso by Gatti-Casazza and Frances Alda, had died of cancer in 1917 at the age of twenty-five after a tragically short career that included Puccini and Borodin at the Met.[14] There was an extraordinary affinity between Italian tenors and the American public. Such was also the case with Irish tenors, but the greatest singers, such as McCormack and Caruso, could draw on audiences well beyond their respective expatriate communities.

With Italian tenors deserting the homeland for transatlantic riches, those who stayed behind were inevitably drawn to La Scala, to which Toscanini had returned in 1920. From 1921 onwards it was Aureliano Pertile, only ever a lukewarm success in New York, who became Toscanini's preferred tenor in Milan.

Legend has it that Aureliano Pertile and Giovanni Martinelli were born within a few weeks and a few streets of each other in Montagnana in 1885. Pertile's birthdate is relatively certain, but Martinelli may well have been two or three years older. Martinelli was the son of a cabinet-maker and learned the clarinet as a child. His vocal talents were not properly revealed until he joined that bizarrely musical institution, the Italian army. He made his début in 1908 and played several small parts in provincial theatres before his first serious role in Verdi's *Ernani* in 1910. Invited to audition for the Opera in Rome, he impressed Toscanini and Puccini, who offered him the first performances of *La fanciulla del West*. He made a successful Covent Garden début in 1912 as Cavaradossi and the following year sang in *Bohème* at the Met. He was an instant success and was befriended by Caruso, who presented him with the costume he had worn for the part of Canio in *Pagliacci*. Martinelli became one of the company's longest-serving tenors over the next thirty-three seasons, eventually becoming an American citizen. He stepped into many of Caruso's dramatic roles (Samson, Don Alvara, Eléazar), though initially with some trepidation, later remarking that 'You can take Gigli, Pertile, Lauri-Volpi and me, roll us all into one and we would still be unfit to tie Caruso's shoelaces.'[15] He was clearly conscious of the tenorial competition – all four were rivals in the post-Caruso market. Perhaps more than any of them Martinelli seemed to posses something of Caruso's dramatic charisma, especially in Verdi; many think him to be one of the finest Otellos of the century. His voice had a steely strength, less rich and baritonal than his predecessor's but with a similar lyric warmth.

Aureliano Pertile sang his first adult role in 1911 in Vincenza in Flotow's *Marta*. This was followed by success in Milan and Turin and the following year he was engaged for *Manon Lescaut, Ballo, Mefistofele* and *Cavalleria rusticana* by the Teatro Municipal in Santiago, and *Tosca* and *Rigoletto* in Valparaiso. Opera flourished in post-independence Chile and the country's opera houses had a tradition of taking Italian singers. Pertile's first south American trip turned out to be the first of several highly successful tours. He returned in 1918, this time to Montevideo, Rio and Sao Paolo, as well as Buenos Aires' famous Teatro Colón; in between he had become an international success in his own country. He had a disappointing season at the Met (and never returned to New York) but his *Mefistofele* at La Scala under Toscanini in 1922 established him as the conductor's (and the country's) favourite tenor. His voice is not often described as beautiful, but he had a highly developed dramatic sense which translated itself to an urgent delivery, heavily nuanced (and with noticeable vibrato), unlike Martinelli's dramatic but more traditional sense of line. Pertile was particularly suited to verismo roles which needed instant emotional engagement, and in many ways hinted at tenors to come. Toscanini clearly appreciated his musicianship and no-nonsense attitude to the composer's notes (although perhaps not always his portamento) and his chosen repertoire almost guaranteed him success on his home ground. Martinelli was something of a playboy and fitted the American image of what a tenor should be like. Covent Garden audiences, having little time for extra-curricular detail, welcomed both tenors.

Giacomo Lauri-Volpi

The third candidate for Caruso's crown was Giacomo Lauri-Volpi, a controversial and temperamental tenor whose bearing had something of the aristocratic demeanour of de Reszke but whose singing harked back to that of the legendary Rubini. Born near Rome in 1892, Giacomo Volpi (the Lauri came later) eventually outlived most of his rivals and was still performing shortly before his death in 1979. In 1915 he was still undecided whether to become a lawyer or to take the riskier path as a singer, and signing up to fight was an altogether more glamorous option than either. He distinguished himself in the trenches, becoming a much decorated infantry captain, at one point stunning the Austrian enemy into silence by singing while the Italian army replenished its ammunition.[16]

Before the war he had studied at the Accademia di Santa Cecilia with baritone Antonio Cotogni (sometime teacher of de Reszke), who was by then in his eighties and a crucial link with earlier nineteenth-century tradition. Cotogni, born in 1831, made his stage début in 1852 and sang for both Rossini and Verdi; in his highly successful career he had encountered singers who had known and worked with such iconic singers as Rubini and Mario, and when he retired from the stage he became one of the country's most authoritative singing teachers.[17] Cotogni died in 1918, so Lauri-Volpi briefly resumed his studies with Enrico Rosati before making a spectacular début in *I puritani* at Viterbo under the name of Giacomo Rubini. The adoption of this particular pseudonym is an indication of where Lauri-Volpi saw himself in terms of both singing and success, and it is tempting to think that his earlier encounter with Cotogni was a fortunate coincidence that encouraged him to exploit his extraordinary facility at the top end of his range.

Lauri-Volpi quickly went on to successes (under his own name) in Italy and South America, making his Met début in 1923. He became one of the Met's star Italian tenors, giving the first US performances of *Turandot* and *Luisa Miller*. He was very sure of his place in the post-Caruso tenorocracy, and once installed at the Met he refused to sing for less than Gigli's fee, eventually agreeing to ten cents more on one occasion.[18] When the depression hit the Met in the 1930s Lauri-Volpi returned to Italy, and when war broke out he again took up soldiering, becoming one of the few tenors to have fought in both wars. He was by then a favourite tenor of the Mussolini family, and *Il Duce* promoted him to full colonel. His association with Fascism eventually made it impossible for him to stay in Italy and he moved to Spain towards the end of the war (he had married Spanish soprano Maria Ros in 1921).

His most significant role in the war years was Otello, which would not normally be attempted by a lyrico-spinto. His 1942 La Scala performance was criticised by those who would have preferred a conventional robusto interpretation, but his supremely confident and characterful vocal intelligence brought a unique dramatic sensitivity to the part.[19] By the late 1940s he had resumed his international career and he sang with Maria Callas in *I puritani* in Rome in 1952, when both singers impressed with their top Cs. Three years later he took part in the revival of Donizetti's *Poliuto* at the Baths of Caracalla (where the cast included hundreds of soldiers, several horses and five lions).

Lauri-Volpi was one of the truly original singers of the first half of the century. Apart from his year of study with Cotogni he was to all intents and purposes self-taught. Unlike almost all of his contemporaries (and most tenors since) he did not study other singers' recordings to improve his own technique, believing that his artistic integrity would be compromised; correspondingly, he had little time for anyone who claimed to have been influenced by Lauri-Volpi.[20] In this sense he was old-fashioned, and he took a similarly unfashionable attitude to composers' scores, having no qualms about interpolating ornaments and cadenzas, especially if it gave him opportunities to demonstrate his effortless soprano E. This was not something that endeared him to Toscanini, whose adherence to the written notes would always be an unacceptable constraint to singers brought up in the old tradition. Lauri-

Volpi was a genuinely cultured man (writer of five books) and did not suffer fools gladly; in the age of Shaw's singing bricklayers and crooning gondoliers his arrogance and intelligence marked him out as a cut above the conventional tenor innocent. His technique may have declined over his long life, but it was sufficient for him to release a final recording of operatic arias at the age of eighty-one.[21]

Tito Schipa

Lauri-Volpi's near-contemporary Tito Schipa was another tenor whose distinctive singing is very hard to categorise. In some respects he was the supreme *tenore di grazia* of the first half of the century, but his repertoire, though narrower than some, was (like Lauri-Volpi's) broader than one might expect from such a seemingly light voice. He was born Rafaele Attilio Amedeo Schipa in 1889, and, small of stature, was known to his childhood friends as 'titu'('little one' in the dialect of Lecce, close to the southernmost tip of Italy). Lecce was a long way from the centre of things and Schipa's earliest years were spent in dignified poverty, relieved by the rewards that came to him as people became aware of his extraordinarily beautiful treble voice. He was taken under the wing of local maestro Alceste Gerunda, who had been a friend of Paolo Tosti (Queen Victoria's singing teacher) since they both studied under Mercadante. Gerunda trained him for six years, from treble to tenor with a sideline in harmony and counterpoint, and provided him with a sure foundation before he travelled north to Milan for further study with Emilio Piccoli.[22] He made his début in *La traviata* in Vercelli in 1910, after an apprenticeship that is reminiscent of the old master–student relationship of the eighteenth century, a slow maturation which surely contributed to his vocal longevity. [23]

Thereafter he appeared in theatres all over Italy, making his La Scala début in 1915 in *Prince Igor*, after a successful South American tour the previous year. At this stage he was still singing dramatic parts – the lighter Verdi, Massenet and some Puccini, and in 1917 he created the role of Ruggiero in Puccini's *La rondine*. Two years later his American career took off with the first of many seasons at Chicago; his Met début followed in 1932, after Gigli had resigned rather than take a pay cut, and by then he had sung in most of the USA's opera houses. In 1937 he made the first of several films. Although he still kept the later dramatic works in repertoire, he found his true métier during this period to be the lyric Mozart and the lighter French and Italian roles (his first Met opera was *L'elisir d'amore*).

The American public loved him and he loved them, entertaining his fans with his love of animals and incautious financial investments.[24] The naivety that these otherwise charming incidents demonstrated took a darker form with his involvement with Fascism, heeding the call from Mussolini's son-in-law to return to Italy to sing for the cause in 1941. His European and South American reputation recovered after the war, but he never quite regained his star status in the USA (and is one of the few internationally successful tenors of the period not to have appeared at Covent Garden).

Schipa's voice is well-represented on record. It undoubtedly shows signs of wear and tear from the 1950s onwards (he died in 1965) but he never lost the stylish sense of line that was obviously instilled into him at a very early age. His was not a dramatic voice, but he could seduce and charm the ear with his elegant shaping of a phrase. He had exquisite diction and a distinctive tone that was sometimes peculiarly less than pure but nevertheless beguiling. For many he is *the* tenore di grazia.

Beniamino Gigli

All of the above-mentioned singers have one thing in common: they have been compared at various points in their careers to Beniamino Gigli.[25] Gigli was born in Recanati, Le Marche, two years before Lauri-Volpi and the year after Schipa, and like the latter sang as a treble in the choir of the small *duomo*. His father was the sacristan and a cobbler, which at least meant that he did not have to go shoeless. He left school at twelve and had a number of temporary jobs, playing saxophone in the town band and singing at every opportunity. Determined to sing professionally, he moved to Rome where he entered the service of the Countess Spannochi, who recognised his talent and arranged for him to have free lessons with Agnese Bonucci. In 1912 he was called up for military service, but the Italian army once more recognised the vocal talents of its conscripts and assigned him to a telephone switchboard. His tour of duty was safely completed before war broke out, and the same enlightened colonel who had originally 'auditioned' him for the army suggested he audition for the Accademia di Santa Cecilia, who gave him a scholarship to study with Cotogni and Rosati.[26]

Cotogni's great talent as a teacher was to insist on a disciplined practice regime while allowing the natural voice to develop with minimal intervention, which is why both Gigli and Lauri-Volpi used their short periods of study with him to find their own individual vocal personae (which were, of course, completely different from each other within the framework of an ancient tradition).[27] Soon after graduating he won the 1914 international competition at Parma, later discovering that one of the judges had written on his report that at last they had found *the tenor*.[28]

Then began one of the most remarkable success stories in the history of the voice. He made his début in *La gioconda* at Rovigo, and soon had Italian houses queuing up to employ him. Notable early successes included Faust in Boito's *Mefistofele*, which led to his playing the role in the La Scala Boito memorial concert after the composer's death in 1918. The following year he made a triumphant Met début (again as Faust), beginning an association with the New York company which would last into the '30s. He inherited the lyrical works from Caruso's corpus (leaving the dramatic side to Martinelli). Audience response was electric wherever he appeared, and he seemed to have the stamina of a team of oxen, singing at any and every opportunity just as he had in childhood. It was not just his finely controlled and lyrical delivery, but his huge and very obvious commitment that impressed people, and the sense that he was bestowing upon them something of his infinitely profound vocal heart. Gigli would have a go at *anything* that did not require a huge voice, and he treated all music in the same way. This is what all his contemporaries did, of course, but because he sang with such emotional engagement, the smoothing out of stylistic compositional differences is particularly obvious.[29] He took to recording with a similar relish to Caruso, and became a household name on three continents.

Gigli is a controversial figure in the tenor pantheon. His significance as one of the most popular voices of the century is unquestioned, but the appreciation of his singing is tempered by a widespread dislike of his interpolated sobs, and a feeling in some quarters that he was at heart an instinctive musician who lacked the sophistication, intelligence and taste that his vocation demanded. Furthermore, he associated himself unashamedly and pro-actively with Fascism, which leaves a certain distaste among many commentators. Such was Gigli's commitment to the cause that the usual excuses of naivety or musicianly misjudgement are very hard to apply in his case. The sob is more easily excused: paralinguistic rhetoric had probably been part of the singer's stock-in-trade for generations. A look at Garcia's suggested interpretations of Mozart or Rossini will confirm that sobbing and the like had been a legitimate part of expressive singing since at least the heyday of Garcia *père* a hundred years before; he was simply in touch with a tradition that in age of easy consumption by iPod we now find self-indulgent and all too obvious.

There is a value to Gigli's work that we would be foolish to ignore. His innocent enthusiasm for singing and making people happy was the same naivety that saw Italy as his fatherland whatever the political regime. Just as he was unable to see the musical differences between Schubert and Sullivan, he was unable to register the wider implications of Fascism. All of the Italian tenors between the wars were compromised by their response to a situation which most of them were not remotely competent to understand. The one who probably did realise the implications (because he was a cultivated, educated man) was Giacomo Lauri-Volpi, but he was of the class that stood to benefit most from a despotic government that was committed to order, the arts and the suppression of democratic expression. None of that should blind us to the simple commitment of Gigli to share with his audience his understanding of what he knew better than anyone on earth at the time: the emotional and communicative power of the voice.

CHAPTER 6

THE ROMANTIC TENOR HERO

At the beginning of the twentieth century it helped to be Italian if you were a tenor, but it was not essential. Among the competitors and successors of Caruso and his compatriots were singers from the rest of Europe and from the USA (and as the century progressed, from Hispanic America). The European line could also include a darker German influence that often eluded Italian tenors: while there were many robust Italian tenors, most were too anchored in the lyric tradition to make the final push into Heldentenordom. This was the period when our current idea of the tenor as romantic hero evolved. Tenors had been stars long before the twentieth century, of course, but the new technologies of sound, vision and radio were to revolutionise the popular idea of the persona behind the voice. A select few transcended singing altogether, living out their lives in public and becoming celebrities to rank with pop stars.

Alessandro Bonci

Alessandro Bonci was at one time considered a serious alternative to Caruso. History has not been so kind to Bonci, largely because of the uneven quality

of his recorded output. Many of his recordings of the French and Italian repertoire show a stylistic elegance which is too often tempered with a fast vibrato
and wayward tuning. Vibrato in tenors – as in all voices – varied enormously;
critics complained of regular or excessive vibrato in the singing of Rubini and
Mario, and in early recordings there is a characteristic tremulousness in the
singing of tenors such as Fernando de Lucia, Fernando Valero and Alessandro
Bonci.

Born in 1870, the son of a comb-maker, Bonci was a sickly child who grew
only to five feet two inches (which would later put him at a disadvantage with
sopranos such as Melba who thought him too short even in high heels). He
had a fine treble voice and sang in local church choirs until his voice broke,
after which the young tenor went to the Conservatorio Rossini at Pesaro (nine
miles away on foot) where he studied with Felice Coen for five years. He then
felt confident enough to go to Delle Sedie at the Paris Conservatoire (an indication of how international its reputation had become), who presumably
added a modern depth to his traditional Italian sound. His long period of
training gave him a rock-solid technique, and once he had made his début (as
Fenton in *Falstaff* in Parma in 1896) he was soon taken up by La Scala (*I puritani*) and by the end of the century had appeared to great acclaim in Spain,
Portugal, Austria, Germany and Russia. In 1900 he appeared at Covent Garden
in *La Bohème* and *Rigoletto*, returning to London in alternate years 1903–7,
adding *Don Pasquale*, *La sonnambula*, and *Il barbiere* to his increasing list of
lyric roles.

In 1906 he made the first of his many visits to the USA. Oscar Hammerstein
engaged him for *I puritani* at his new Manhattan Opera hoping he would
draw audiences away from Caruso at the Met. Bonci was indeed a success, and
in a move reminiscent of the Nourrit/Duprez rivalry in Paris three-quarters of
a century before, the Met management persuaded him to join Caruso, singing
Bohème on alternate nights.[1] Both were hugely successful, and although they
were quite different in style (Bonci was lighter than the fast-maturing Caruso),
the public and press were quick to dream up a rivalry that perhaps did not
exist. Bonci was certainly a sufficiently big star not to feel seriously threatened
by Caruso; his contract specified that he be paid in gold coin, deposited in a
specific bank in Florence.[2]

He subsequently had a successful career in north and south America, and
after retiring from the stage taught singing in Italy and the USA. His teaching
was very much in the old Italian tradition. Pietro Buzzi dedicated his translation of Mancini's *Osservazioni practiche sul canto figurato* to him, which
together with Bonci's response to it, is an indication of the esteem in which
traditional singing teachers held the great tenor.[3] He was an elegant singer and
a man of refinement who was greatly appreciated by many of the singers who

worked with him.[4] Modern listeners may feel that his voice lacks the sheer dynamism of Caruso; he sounds as though from another age, whereas in the singing of his great contemporary we can hear something of the sound of his successors.

The Celtic Connection: McCormack, O'Sullivan and Tom Burke

The tenor who might have rivalled Caruso was John McCormack. McCormack's background was not a musical one, and it was as a largely self-taught amateur that in 1903 he entered the Feis Ceoil, an open singing competition held in Dublin. He won the gold medal and resolved to devote his life to singing rather than to the post office job that his father had in mind for him. In the audience to hear his performance was the young James Joyce, who also had pretensions as a singer. Inspired by McCormack, Joyce entered the Feis the following year but could only rise to the bronze medal.[5] The two young tenors appeared on the same bill at least once in 1904 and were both coached by Vincent O'Brien, McCormack's only real singing teacher until he went to Milan to study with Vincenzo Sabatini.[6] Sabatini thought his voice almost perfect and probably taught him very little, but the young Irishman's Italian travels enabled him to learn the language and gave him some much needed experience in small Italian theatres. He auditioned unsuccessfully for La Scala and decided to try his luck in London, where he was offered the part of Turiddu at Covent Garden in 1907. Supported by a substantial Irish contingent, McCormack's singing was judged a success; of his acting, one commentator reported that 'It is kinder to say nothing except that he was just himself, a simple and sincere Irish singer, incapable of interpreting the Sicilian way of life.'[7]

From then on his future was assured, playing *Rigoletto* and *Don Giovanni* that same season and *Rigoletto* and *Traviata* in Naples in 1909. The same year he made his début at the Met, through the persuasive advocacy of Luisa Tetrazzini. He was a huge hit with the American public, but it was as a concert singer that he had his greatest successes. In a six-month period 1912–13 he gave twelve concerts in New York, playing to a total of 58,000 people, including 7,000 at the Hippodrome, from which a further 5,000 were turned away.[8] His popularity was almost unprecedented for a singer and he seems to have touched people's hearts in a way that only the greatest singers can, with a mixture of simplicity and elegance underpinned by great conviction. Vocally, he was entirely different from Caruso, whose singing had originally inspired him and whose friend he later became. He was not a powerful singer (at his initial Covent Garden audition worries were expressed that his voice might not be large enough), and if there was a model at the back of his head it may well have been Fernando de Lucia. Gerald Moore, who accompanied his farewell tour in 1938, tells of his speech-like phrasing and rhythmic flexibility, and a reluctance to rehearse. This was not just laziness on the tenor's part – his performances always had a freshness and spontaneity which gave the listeners the impression that they were hearing him for the first time. [9]

In contrast to the mellifluous McCormack was his fellow countryman, the 'loud and dreadful' John O'Sullivan.[10] Born in 1877, O'Sullivan came from a middle-class Cork family but moved to France in early childhood after the death of his father. He entered the Paris Conservatoire as a baritone, leaving it without graduating in 1902. Over the next few years he discovered his upper register and made his London début at the Lyric Theatre as Tannhäuser in 1908. Returning to France he expanded his repertoire to include many of the robusto roles and made his American début in 1918 with the Chicago Opera under Cleofonte Campanini (younger brother of Italo). Back in France his Tannhäuser elicited a letter from Jean de Reszke, congratulating him on his performance and commending his future as a Heldentenor.[11] He did not fulfil the future imagined for him by de Reszke but stuck mostly to the larger Verdi, Berlioz, Gounod and Meyerbeer roles, in which he had considerable success in Europe and on the South American circuit.

In 1829, back in Paris for a season which included *Tannhäuser, Samson, Les Huguenots,* Berlioz's *Faust* and the centenary performance of *Guillaume Tell,* he met James Joyce, tenor manqué and now an author of international repute. In a manner which recalls Hugh Walpole's obsession with Lauritz Melchior,[12] Joyce became infatuated with O'Sullivan and his voice, and to the tenor's embarrassment insisted on writing letters to promoters and conductors (including Beecham) to promote his career or complain at what he saw as plots to end it. Joyce was especially fond of O'Sullivan's upper register, and counted the high notes in his *Guillaume Tell* performance: 'I have discovered that Sullivan sings 456 Gs, 93 A flats, 54 B flats, 15 Bs, 19 Cs and 2 C sharps. Nobody else can do it.'[13] Joyce's campaign was perhaps fuelled by a certain paranoia on the part of O'Sullivan who thought his career disadvantaged by what he called the 'Italian ring' of Martinelli, Lauri-Volpi and the other post-Caruso Italians, but even O'Sullivan was surprised by the crude vigour with which Joyce promoted his interests. This included an Irish claque at the Opéra, which the author himself would lead, shouting out approbation for his fellow Irishman and raining insults on his Italian competitors.[14]

O'Sullivan's voice was certainly loud, but far from dreadful (although perhaps not 'one of the most dramatic tenor voices on record'[15]). Even without the Joyce connection his work would stand as a testament to a solid and successful career despite not being compared to Caruso; O'Sullivan was his own man, a cultured Irish Frenchman who mastered some fifty dramatic tenor roles.

A third (and perhaps now one of the least known) tenors of Irish extraction from the first half of the twentieth century was Tom Burke. Burke was born in 1890 to an Irish working-class family in Lancashire in the north of England, and by the age of fourteen he was mining coal down the pit. The British coalmining communities were close-knit and mutually supportive, and music often flourished as a respite from the hard labour underground. There was a strong tradition of choirs and brass bands, and the young Tom won medals for his cornet playing. After his voice broke he began singing in pubs and discovered that he had potential as a tenor. At the age of nineteen he walked the thirty miles to Blackpool to see Caruso, and later sang to the great tenor, who suggested he study in Italy. After a stint in local opera houses Burke's first big break arrived when Gigli withdrew from the première of Mascagni's *Lodoletta* and Burke created the role of Flammen opposite Toti dal Monte. In 1918 Nellie Melba heard him sing the Duke in *Rigoletto,* and insisted on his partnering her at Covent Garden the following year. The reopening of Covent Garden after the war was a triumph for Tom Burke and he very quickly endeared himself to some of the greatest names in opera. He sang in the first English performance of *Gianni Schicchi* and Puccini was apparently heard to say 'I have never heard my music more beautifully sung.'[16]

Burke looked set to conquer the world. He set off for a tour of the USA and was able to charge the highest fee ever paid to a singer from England. It was the first of many misjudgements; he was promoted as the new John McCormack and the tour was not a success (the old McCormack still had plenty of life left in him, as did his legions of fans). Burke became extremely discouraged and did not sing for eighteen months before being persuaded to join Chicago Opera. Here again he had tremendous success, singing opposite Mary Garden, Tito Ruffo and Igor Kipnis among many other famous names. In 1927 he returned to the United Kingdom, a hugely successful star with an extravagant lifestyle to match. His Albert Hall concert was a sell-out, and he appeared again at Covent Garden before going on to sing in Paris, Berlin and Vienna. If Tom Burke had been able to sustain his career at this level, 'posterity would have ranked him – along with Tauber, Martinelli, Gigli, Schipa and Lauri-Volpi – as one of the really great tenors of the twentieth century.'[17] The singing came easily to him; although he had lessons during his Italian period with Ernesto Colli and De Lucia he was essentially a natural singer, and although working in the pit had given him a certain aptitude for hard work it had not prepared him for a life where anything could be his for the asking. He became increasingly arrogant, fell out with conductors and even once made the king wait to congratulate him after a Covent Garden performance. He took to drink and soon alienated conductors, promoters and, worst of all, audiences. His career evaporated as quickly as it had begun, and with the Wall

Street crash so did whatever wealth he had left. He entertained the troops in the World War II, with few of his audience aware that that they were listening to what had been one of the great voices of the century.

After the war he returned to Lancashire and was reduced to singing in clubs (one of his own was raided by police and shut down). For the ten years before his death in 1969 he lived alone, forgotten by all except friends and family. There are few parallels for such a dramatic decline, and hearing his surviving recordings one cannot help but wonder what the world has missed. He was known as the Lancashire Caruso, and was often compared with his great contemporaries McCormack and Tauber. A romantic figure with a powerful voice, in flair and exuberance he was undoubtedly their equal, and had he gone on to sing Otello, Radamès, or even early Wagner, there is no knowing what he might have achieved as his voice got older and darker.

An adopted Viennese: Alfred Piccaver

Alfred Piccaver also lived his latter years in obscurity in England, though his fans in Vienna never forgot what many considered to be the greatest tenor of his time. Piccaver was born in Lincolnshire but his family emigrated to the USA when he was two. A precocious singer after his voice broke, like Burke, he too was entranced when he first heard Caruso at the Metropolitan Opera in 1905, having won a scholarship to the Met's Opera School. Two years later he attended a summer school in Hallstadt, Austria with fellow Met students, where he had the great good fortune to be spotted by the director of the German Theatre in Prague. He was immediately offered a contract despite his lack of experience, and over the next three years developed into a formidable artist. In 1910 Mattia Battistini asked him to stand in as Alfredo in *Traviata* and was sufficiently impressed to offer him *Rigoletto* at the Hofoper in Vienna. His success was immediate and lasting: two years later he returned to Vienna and international success in the major Italian and French roles. The Viennese public took him to their heart, as had the Prague opera-goers before them. Nigel Douglas, in his touching tribute to his former teacher, quotes a Prague newspaper on the imminent departure of the twenty-six-year-old tenor:

> Round the hearts of the girls in Prague a wistful sorrow is stealing. Soon, too soon, will come the time of parting. As yet, they are still happy. Out there, in the beautiful gardens of the city, the lilac is in bloom; in the streets at midday a gentle sun shines down. The air is light and gay as the new dresses that they are wearing – and Alfred Piccaver is still within the city walls.[18]

Piccaver's handsome features, smooth line and warm sound completely seduced the Viennese public. Lotte Lehmann, who sang with him on many occasions from 1916 onwards, when asked who her favourite singer was, replied 'Oh Piccaver! It was like being surrounded by velvet.'[19] The two often appeared opposite each other in Puccini, Richard Strauss and Massenet, their forty-six performances of *Manon* creating a Viennese legend that they always sang together. In 1917 the Emperor appointed Piccaver *Kaiserlicher und Königlicher Kammersänger*, a rare honour for a young foreigner, and when war broke out he was allowed to remain in the country provided he continued to sing at the Opera.

Piccaver's relationship with the Opera's management was not an easy one (although it never affected his popularity with opera-goers). Despite success in Chicago and London (where the *Daily Sketch* called him Caruso's successor and announced that 'the greatest tenor in the world is an Englishman') he always returned to his beloved Vienna.[20] In the 1930s he was as popular as ever, the informality and friendliness of his recitals delighting his adoring fans. Nigel Douglas recounts the story of one occasion where the audience refused to leave, even after the management had turned the lights out. In the absence of an electrician to turn them back on again Piccaver borrowed a torch and returned to the stage to sing seven encores. [21] Like Burke, Piccaver was prone to cancelling at the last minute, but unlike his fellow 'Englishman', Piccaver was all charm and was easily forgiven.

The second world war was less kind to Piccaver. In London at the time of the Anschluss, he decided not to return to Austria. He lived anonymously in Putney, giving occasional lessons and even rarer concerts. Lord Harewood recounts an expedition to hear Piccaver in Wimbledon in 1942, noting that 'the velvet and the long sensuous phrasing were still there, even though he was in his late fifties'.[22] Intriguingly, he recorded a tape of warm-up vocalises in 1955 when he was seventy-one years old; these are a remarkable window on the basic exercises that enabled him to maintain a flawless technique for so long. That same year he was invited as a guest of honour to the reopening of the Vienna State Opera. He never returned to England and died in Vienna three years later. Vienna had never forgotten him, even though he had not sung there for more than two decades. He was given a state funeral, in the course of which the cortège halted in front of the opera house, while the Vienna Philharmonic played the funeral march from Beethoven's *Eroica*.[23]

Heavier northern lights: Jussi Björling and Nicolai Gedda

The relationship of singers to their audiences changed fundamentally with the availability of cheap recordings. Instead of having to travel to see a tenor who would be known only by his reputation, fans could in effect buy into a singer's reputation, and own a piece of their favourite singers. While this process can and does happen during the lifetime of certain tenors, the permanence of recording means that it can survive beyond their life and career in the case of singers who generated a substantial or particularly interesting body of recordings.

The Swedish tenor Jussi Björling is a case in point. His voice is notoriously difficult to describe, and even the most eloquent critics appear to flounder when trying to articulate what this extraordinary tenor means to them.[24] Nigel Douglas evokes something of the Björling magic when he says

> His voice possessed all the sweep, the ease and the power of the finest Latin singers, and the beauty too – but it was another beauty than theirs, not the uncomplicated beauty of the golden Mediterranean sunshine, but the haunting beauty of the more melancholy and introspective North. The most telling description of ... Björling's sound was ... written to me by a lady listener ... 'To me ... it is a voice heavy with unshed tears', and when an instrument like that is harnessed to a style and technique ideal for the extravagant outpourings of the Italian composers it can produce a magic all of its own.[25]

It was a truly magical voice, and listeners are still being seduced by it almost fifty years after his death in 1960. In many ways he was the ideal tenor: not conventionally handsome and somewhat rotund, but able to transport listeners by the exquisite sound that he wielded in such a consistent and sensitive way. His technique seems to have been almost flawless, giving him complete control of his singing and an absolutely secure basis for his interpretation of the great lyric and dramatic roles. Films of him in action show how effortless his singing was, and how efficiently he used the acoustic space in the vocal tract: he creates the maximum physical volume between the larynx and the lips, which enables him to access the greatest possible frequency range, giving him control of tone and text. He was a complete singer (as John Steane put it, his voice 'glowed with health'[26]), and it is perhaps not surprising that Dorothy Caruso told him that he was the only successor of her legendary husband.[27]

Björling was born into a musical family and was trained as a treble, like his two brothers, by his father David, an opera singer of some distinction. The three Björling sons and their father toured Sweden and the USA as the Björling Male Voice Quartet when Jussi was still a child. As a teenager he failed his first audition for the Stockholm opera chorus but was fortunate enough to sing to the Swedish tenor Carl Martin Oehmann, who took up his case with the opera's general manager John Forsell, telling him that he had heard 'the best Swedish tenor voice of the century'. Björling ended up with a bursary and never looked back, beginning an association with Forsell as teacher and mentor, and with the Stockholm Opera that lasted the rest of his life. [28] He also had some lessons from the Scottish tenor Joseph Hislop, who taught in Stockholm from 1936 to1948. Hislop thought him a delight to teach, recalling that 'teaching Jussi was like pouring water on blotting-paper – everything stuck and was absorbed immediately'.[29]

The Swedish tenor's smooth quality was remarkably consistent over his entire range, and he was well suited to those operas which required both lyricism and power. He was also capable of something close to crooning, as can be heard on the recordings he made under the pseudonym Erik Odde.[30] Frequently compared (especially by his countrymen) to Gigli and Caruso, he was particularly at home in Puccini and Verdi (excluding Otello) as well as the Massenet and Gounod roles. Most of his success was in northern Europe and the USA, the Italians perhaps reluctant to acknowledge his vocal genius because of his lapses in pronunciation (a curious failing, given his exquisite musicianship and legendary memory); his only Italian appearances were two performances at La Scala, a bizarre statistic for a tenor considered to be one of the greatest interpreters of the Italian operatic repertoire.

Björling began his career with Mozart and Rossini in Stockholm under the guidance of John Forsell, and in 1936 sang Radamès in Vienna, after which he was invited to Paris, London and Chicago, returning to Sweden during the war years and conquering America with performances at the Met once the war had ended. Towards the end of his short life he was considering Lohengrin and Otello, but died of a heart attack before he had done more than occasional excerpts in concert programmes. He was not the most elegant figure to take the stage (Desmond Shawe-Taylor describes his stage presence as 'rather a matter of deportment than of acting'[31]) yet his singing captivated both fellow performers and audiences alike. His death shocked a Swedish nation that had taken him to their hearts and made him almost into a folk hero; the very personal sense of grief felt by so many colleagues, collaborators and friends can be sensed in the *Minnesbok* or Memorial Book compiled by many of them after his death.[32]

As a man and as an artist he was an inspiration to opera-lovers the world over, despite (or perhaps because of) never entirely forsaking his provincial Swedish roots. The latter part of his career was clouded by alcoholism, which allied to his reluctance to rehearse often made things difficult for his fellow musicians and, perhaps more seriously, for record producers. Björling's career coincided with the widespread adoption of the LP format (the first great technological advance which succeeded in persuading listeners to re-invest in music they may already own) and there is a rich recorded legacy, which might have been richer still had he not towards the end of his life been too often incapacitated by drink. His problem was attributed to the pressures of a perfectionist needing constantly to produce the goods, and so close was his singing to a kind of perfection that the many fans who even today keep his memory alive are not troubled by the human weakness in such a great artist.

The career of fellow Swede Nicolai Gedda paralleled that of Björling in certain key aspects. Gedda was also a protégé of Carl Martin Oehmann, with whom he studied for three years while beginning his career with the Opera in Stockholm. Oehmann taught him the fundamentals of efficient supported breathing from the diaphragm and how to place the voice. This is a difficult concept for non-singers to understand. Almost all of the resonance a singer generates happens within the vocal tract, which is the acoustic space between the vocal cords (or folds) and the lips; and yet singers will often talk of head and chest resonance, and, as Oehmann did, of 'placing the voice in the mask' or front of the head or sinuses. This apparent dichotomy occurs because singers are aware of sensations in their chest and parts of the head, which feel like crucial areas of resonance. In fact, the so-called head and chest resonances are not acoustically significant, but they are convenient terms to refer to what singers feel when they are singing. So when Oehmann talks of the mask he means the sensation that singers feel of the sound being directed behind the eyes or above the nose. In practice this means that the singer is adjusting the shape of their vocal tract, based on signals they are getting from parts of the head outside the vocal tract which are not themselves acoustically important but which trigger specific vocal tract adjustments.[33]

Like Björling, Gedda possessed (or was given) a fine technique, and had the great good fortune to be in Stockholm in 1952 when Walter Legge was visiting in connection with the EMI *Boris Godunov* project. Legge unexpectedly found himself hearing huge numbers of hopeful singers, the first of whom was Gedda. It was an extraordinary encounter, as Legge recalled many years later:

> He sang the *Carmen* Flower Song so tenderly yet passionately that I was moved almost to tears. He delivered the difficult rising scale ending with a clear and brilliant B flat. Almost apologetically I asked him to try to sing it as written – *pianissimo, rallentando* and *diminuendo*. Without turning a hair he achieved the near-miracle, incredibly beautifully and without effort.[34]

Legge not only gave him the part of Dmitry in Boris, but persuaded Karajan to give him the Bach B Minor Mass and La Scala to take his Don Ottavio. Walter Legge also encouraged him to sing operetta, and Gedda became one of the century's most sophisticated exponents of the genre.

Gedda was born in 1925, the son of a Swedish mother and Russian father. He grew up bilingual and became trilingual after the family moved to Leipzig in 1929, when his father became cantor at the Russian Orthodox church. He was a gifted linguist, later adding a working knowledge of English, French and Italian, bringing his basic fluency to a total of six languages; this undoubtedly contributed to his ability to sing a vast repertoire in its appropriate language. He never became the hero Swede, but his career had a wider international dimension than that of Björling (whose success was primarily in Sweden and the USA during his lifetime) and he is said to be the most-recorded tenor of the twentieth century. His instinct for language meant that he mastered the Russian lyric roles – so difficult for non-Russian speakers – with ease, and he was also able to sing a huge French repertoire ranging from Gounod to Bizet and Berlioz, being frequently compared with the great French tenor Georges Thill; and unlike Björling he did sing Lohengrin.

After successes in Paris, London and Salzburg he made his Met début in 1957 in Barber's *Vanessa*, beginning a twenty-year relationship with the New York audience, for whom he became the most versatile and intelligent of all tenors. He also continued to study while in New York, finding that Paola Novikova (who had been a pupil of Mattia Battistini) gave him a connection to the older Italian tradition. His sound is rich without being overpowering, and he is one of the few tenors to be consistently acclaimed for his effortless high register; his mezza voce (rather than head voice) at the top is something he credits to Novikova.[35] As well as his opera and operetta engagements Gedda was a much admired recitalist, with a multi-lingual repertoire that matched his stage roles. His sound technique ensured a long career, during which he has been recognised as one of the most versatile tenors of his era. He was a prolific visitor to the studio, with more than 200 recordings to his name covering opera, oratorio and song. His relative lack of recognition in the twenty-first century may have something to do with his sheer competence in so many genres, combined with a retiring modesty which may have inhibited his operatic acting. His voice is nicely characterised by John Steane, who referred to his sweetness and instantly recognisable smiling quality.[36]

Spain: Iberian Italy?

One of the tenors with whom Gedda was sometimes compared is the Spaniard Alfredo Kraus.[37] Both had multi-cultural backgrounds which gave them a linguistic and textual sensibility that enabled them to become fine interpreters of the French repertoire, a rare achievement for tenors who were not French. Language is only part of the equation, however: if singers are to empathise with repertoires beyond their own language, then some sort of cultural affinity is essential. The four main linguistic areas that tenors may have to grapple with are Italian, French, German and Russian. French singers in particular have historically found it problematic to modify their native nasality when singing Italian, and some German singers have similarly found it difficult to find the appropriate accent and inflections for other European languages. Idiomatic Russian has proved near to impossible for all but a very few Western tenors. The two nationalities that seem to have the closest linguistic affinity (in singing terms) are Italy and Spain. There are cultural similarities too: both countries have historically had a thriving operatic infrastructure, with theatres in most major cities (though there are fewer of them in Spain). There is one major difference, which is that Spain has added very little to the core operatic repertoire, whereas it has produced some of the world's greatest opera singers.[38]

Gayarre's successors

The most famous Spanish tenor of the late nineteenth century was Julián Gayarre, and such was the power of the Gayarre myth that tenors for generations to come would be compared with him. Gayarre symbolically bestowed the succession on Francisco Viñas, presenting him with his Parsifal costume after Viñas' stunning début as Lohengrin at the Teatro del Liceu Barcelona in 1888. He had been, like Gayarre and Fernando Valero, a student of Melchiorre Vidal and he became one of the most significant singers of Wagner in Italian (with considerable success in Italy). The Viñas Wagner recordings summon up a vocal world that is now lost to us. As we saw in Chapter 4 above, all the evidence suggests that Wagner appreciated the fundamental principles of Italian singing but wished to apply them in the service of music-drama as he conceived it rather than to facilitate vocal display. In Viñas we hear a master of the traditional Italian legato line, with all the stylistic subtlety that carefully judged rubato and portamento can produce. Wagner would have been less keen on his willingness to indulge in the occasional octave transposition or interpolated high note, but he probably would have forgiven him the odd appoggiatura. This is Wagner-singing before the Helden *Fach* was fully formed (in its post-Wagner sense) and the world only knew varieties of lyric tenors (from *grazia* to *spinto*).[39] Spain produced many fine 'Italian' heroic tenors in the early part of the twentieth century, several of whom so identified with the tradition and the repertoire that they Italianised their names. Among the last to resist the fashion for singing Wagner in his own language were Isidoro de Fagoaga and Giovanni Voyer (born Juan Boyer), both of whom died in 1976. There was also a significant Otello tradition, represented by the first Spanish Moor, Angelo Angioletti (born Jaime Bachs), Antonio Paoli, and Icilio Calleja.[40]

Hipólito Lázaro

In the dramatic-lyric mainstream there was direct competition between Italian and Spanish tenors. International stars such as Anselmi and Schipa were hugely popular in Spain (Anselmi's heart is preserved in the Museo del Teatro Real in Madrid by his own request), but the Spanish tenorial talent was often the equal of the Italian paradigms. Hipólito Lázaro was a potential rival for Caruso, and Lázaro himself was certainly not troubled by doubts on that question, on one occasion telling his audience to pay attention as they were listening to the greatest tenor in the world.[41]

Born in Barcelona in 1887, he had very little formal teaching and his vocal talents were not revealed until his military service. A short period of intensive study with Ernesto Colli in Milan was followed by his Italian début with *Rigoletto* in 1911. He was particularly successful as Folco in Mascagni's *Isabeau*, the composer appreciating his higher register, and both Mascagni and Giordano subsequently created roles for him. He made successful débuts at Covent Garden (under the name of Antonio Manuele), La Scala, the Teatro Colón, and finally the Met in 1918. Here he again sang *Rigoletto*, inviting comparison with Caruso who had made his own Met début in the same opera. The New York Times was impressed:

> Mr Lázaro has a voice of fine quality, warm and rich and powerfully resonant, with a complete avoidance of the 'white' tone too frequently [found] in tenors of his youth and slenderness. There was at times a nasal effect from overmuch use of vibrancy in the 'mask' of the face, as singers say, and an occasional forcing of a high note a shade above pitch. The Duke's airs . . . gave him every opportunity, and . . . in the last act he took with ease a ringing E-flat in the 'Donna e mobile' and the entire air had to be repeated.[42]

The critic has captured the essence of Lázaro – powerful top notes and no shame about adding more when he could, but a hint of forcing and perhaps excessive vibrato. His tone would darken over the years and the vibrato become less all-pervasive, but all of these characteristics can be heard in his surviving recordings.[43] Within a year the Caruso camp was seriously rattled, and embarrassed by comparisons between Lázaro and the legendary Rubini, but the death of the great Italian in 1921 put an end to any competition between the two.

Miguel Fleta

Lázaro's chief rival turned out to be another Spaniard, Miguel Fleta, whose richer tones and wilder lifestyle captured the Hispanic imagination on both sides of the Atlantic. Fleta's birthdate is variously given as 1893, 1897 and 1899, and little is known about his early life. He studied at Barcelona Conservatory where he met the soprano Luisa Pierrich, who took him off to Italy for further training; he made his début in 1919 at the Teatro Comunale Trieste, in Riccardo Zandonai's *Francesca da Rimini*. Fleta was a great admirer of Zandonai's Mascagni-esque style and created the role of Romeo in his *Giulietta e Romeo* three yeas later in Rome. In the meantime he had had considerable international success, including a first visit to Buenos Aires in 1922. He was to go on to become a star in South America, where he and Lázaro attracted rival groups of fans which recalled the battles between the Masinists and Gayarrists of the previous generation. He appeared in *Tosca* at the Met in 1923 and went on to do several classics of the French and Italian repertoire, but he had the misfortune to be competing against Gigli, Martinelli and Lauri-Volpi, and when an opportunity arose in his second season to sing at the Teatro Apollo in Madrid he broke his contract and returned to Spain (where he was pursued by the Met's lawyers). In 1926 he premièred Puccini's posthumous *Turandot* at La Scala under Toscanini (a curious partnership, given Fleta's old-fashioned rhythmic waywardness and tendency to improve on the composer's score). Fleta was a huge hit with the public, and he delighted in giving of himself until he could sing no more. This generosity extended to bringing on a piano after the curtain calls and singing encore after encore, which he even did in the middle of a performance of *Carmen*, having sung a particularly successful Flower Song.[44]

A lack of care took its toll, however, and within a few years his vocal powers were exhausted; he died in 1938, almost forgotten except to his newfound Falangist friends. Fleta's was a remarkable voice – one of the most characterful of the era. Although he is not often compared with Schipa, he does have something of the originality of the Italian. His warm tone, exaggerated rubato, extravagant portamento, exquisite mezza voce and ability to spin out unfeasibly long diminuendos were almost more Italian than the models he aspired to; as Michael Scott put it, he 'makes de Lucia seem virtuous by comparison'.[45]

Antonio Cortis

The third pre-Kraus Spanish success story was Antonio Cortis (or Corts, as he was christened). Born (on board ship) in 1891, Cortis sang in choirs as a child and had some musical training at the Royal Conservatory in Madrid, though considered Caruso to have been his only teacher. Exactly what he meant by this is not clear; he first met the Italian star at the Teatro Colón in 1917, when he sang the *comprimario* role of Beppe opposite Caruso's Canio in *Pagliacci*.[46] The story goes that Caruso was taken with the young Spaniard and suggested the two should go to New York together. Cortis declined the invitation and returned to Spain for the birth of his daughter. He never did appear at the Met, and despite eight successful Chicago seasons remained in the shadow of his many competitors. His sound is not unlike that of Caruso, thicker and more rounded than that of Lázaro or Fleta, and at home he became known as the Spanish Caruso. He is perhaps the most complete singer of the three, but his non-appearance at the Met has tended to marginalise his historical reputation.

Americans in Europe

The Metropolitan Opera's position as a barometer of international operatic success inevitably made it a magnet for European tenors, and from the mid-twentieth century onwards it has also represented the apogee of ambition for American singers too. New York's first exposure to serious European opera was in 1825 when Manuel Garcia's company put on *Il barbiere* at the Park Theatre. Thereafter the city saw many international stars in very similar French and Italian repertoire to that of the European houses, in a highly competitive theatre environment. The Met opened its doors in 1883 (with Italo Campanini in Gounod's *Faust*) as a response to a number of wealthy opera enthusiasts who were unable to get boxes at the Academy of Music. It was a showcase for the best European singers (only sixteen Americans had sung leading roles there before 1900, none of them tenors). It was not until the Canadian-born tenor Edward Johnson took over the company in the mid-1930s that American artists began to be taken seriously by the management.[47]

There had been American tenor successes earlier in the century, and some even exported their art to Europe.[48] Riccardo Martin (born 1874) studied with Sbriglia and Jean de Reszke in Paris and was one of the first American-born tenors to be contracted by the Met, making his début in *Mefistofele* in 1907 and later premiering three American operas there. He made his Covent Garden début in 1910 as a robust Pinkerton much appreciated by the *Musical Times* correspondent.[49] The Italian connection was a natural one for aspiring American tenors; the émigré Italian community included a large number of musicians and European (i.e. Italian) pedagogical principles were well-known to American singers. Carlo Bassini, singing teacher and sometime professional violinist, published several books on singing including a dedicated tenor tome in 1866. This is a comprehensive resource that would not have been out of place at the Paris Conservatoire, and is full of traditional Garcian wisdom.[50] Archer Cholmondeley went so far as to change his name to Mario Chamlee, and did most of his training with Italian teachers before he crossed the Atlantic. Heavily influenced by Caruso, he made his Met début as Cavaradossi and returned many times to sing verismo roles and had some success in Europe.[51]

Charles Hackett

Charles Hackett was the first American tenor to have a truly international reputation. Born in 1887, he seems to have developed a natural tenor voice and had lessons with Arthur Hubbard in Boston before moving to New York in 1911, where he soon got plenty of work at churches and small-scale concerts. Hackett was ambitious, though, and the next year set off for Florence to study with Vincenzo Lombardi. The two years he spent with the teacher of Fernando de Lucia familiarised him with a number of key roles, and turned him from a jobbing singer into one who understood the finer points of the Italian tradition. He sang in *Rigoletto* and *Il barbiere* in provincial theatres before making his La Scala début in Thomas' *Mignon*. After repeating *Mignon* in Rome, Hackett was contracted for the 1917 season to the Teatro Colón, where he sang an astonishing number of roles including Lohengrin, and gave the local première of Puccini's *La rondine*.

He was not the only tenor in town: also working at the Buenos Aires theatre were Antonio Cortis and Enrico Caruso. Caruso befriended both young hopefuls and insisted on being Hackett's best man at his wedding. Hackett made his Met début two years later (again with *Il barbiere*) but after three successful seasons concluded (as many fellow tenors were to do) that with so many star European tenors on the books he would be better off going in the opposite direction. His subsequent European engagements included Melba's farewell performance at Covent Garden. He became an accomplished recitalist and during the 1930s sang for Chicago Opera as well as returning for several seasons at the Met. He died suddenly in 1941 after minor surgery, one of the most successful American tenors and still in his prime.[52]

Roland Hayes and George Shirley

Born the same year as Hackett, Roland Hayes also made his reputation primarily as a recitalist, but in his case it was because the professional options open to an African-American singer were extremely limited. In 1917, against huge odds, Hayes became the first black American to record classical music. The son of former slaves, he was born on a farm in Georgia, and showed musical promise at an early age. A youth of great tenacity, after many setbacks he attended Fisk College, making his first records as a member of a quartet from the famous Jubilee Singers in 1911. He became an efficient and successful promoter, first of his own concerts and then of his recordings, since it was impossible for a black tenor to record for the heavily stratified major labels. After touring in the USA he sailed for England in 1920, intending to study and work in Europe before going on to Africa to investigate the origins of black

American folk music.[53] After a difficult year in London he received a summons to sing for the king and queen after a much acclaimed Wigmore Hall recital. A month later he sang for Nellie Melba, whose enthusiastic support led to recitals all over Europe. He returned to the USA in 1923 and sang with the Boston Symphony Orchestra under Pierre Monteux, the first time a black soloist had appeared with a major American orchestra. From then on success came more easily, though he was always at risk from racism in the USA. In his youth he had sung for silent movies behind a screen so that the audience were not aware of his colour, and in 1942 he left Georgia after an incident in a whites-only shoe store.[54]

Hayes' recorded legacy is surprisingly diverse, considering the constraints on his repertoire. He was famous for spirituals, but would sing opera arias and more esoteric composers such as Machaut and Monteverdi, both of whom suited his light and elegant voice very well. In a 1918 advertisement for his self-produced recordings he describes himself as 'the Greatest Negro Tenor' and lists 'Vesti la giubba' and 'Una furtive lagrima' alongside 'Swing low, sweet chariot' and 'Steal away'.[55] He went on to become an outstanding interpreter of Lieder and French song, and continued singing till his eighties, dying in 1976 at the age of eighty-nine, one of the most distinguished singers of the century.

The series of black socio-musical 'firsts' continued with George Shirley, who grew up in Detroit, where he became the first African-American to be appointed to a high school teaching position; after he was drafted he found himself the first black member of the United States Army Chorus; finally, he became the first black tenor to sing leading roles at the Met. Shirley has always been conscious of the immeasurable contribution that African American singers such as Marian Anderson and Roland Hayes have added to the American cultural heritage. It was no problem for him to sing spirituals even as late as the 1990s, and in performing Hayes' 'Little boy, how old are you?' he was simply acknowledging, as did Hayes himself, an honesty and directness in the composition that mirrored that of a Schubert Lied.[56] Shirley's career, perhaps even more than that of Roland Hayes, has shown that the operatic world can be colour-blind: he not only conquered the Met, but triumphed in most of the world's major opera houses.[57]

Charles Kullman and Richard Crooks

Charles Kullman's career featured fewer firsts but as much distinction. Born in 1903 to émigré German parents, Kullmann (as he was then spelled) won a singing competition while studying medicine at Yale. His potential revealed, it was not long before he won a scholarship to the Juilliard School, followed three years later by another scholarship to study with the tenor Thomas Salignac at the American Conservatory at Fontainebleau. He returned to the USA in 1928 (where his concerts included the American première of Monteverdi's *Orfeo*) but was back in Europe two years later and soon singing for Klemperer, Blech, Kleiber, and Furtwängler in Berlin, Vienna, Salzburg and London. He made his inevitable Met début in 1935 (in Gounod's *Faust*) and remained associated with the company for twenty-five years. While in Germany he had a small role in *Bomben auf Monte Carlo*, the first of five films that he made in either English or German between 1934 and 1947. Kullman's voice is Italianate and lyrical, with sufficient power to tackle *Lohengrin* and *Parsifal,* though he could not be called a Heldentenor. His German ancestry clearly steered him towards the German repertory where this was within vocal range, but he was equally at home in the Italian and French dramatic repertoire. Kullman responded well to both the microphone and the film camera – both showed him to his best advantage and brought his artistry within reach of large numbers of people.

The tenor who best illustrates the communicative power of the evolving technologies, and who as a result probably touched most American hearts, was Richard Crooks. He was born in 1900 and as a boy was something of a star treble, good enough to appear beside Ernestine Schumann-Heink in a performance of Mendelssohn's *Elijah* at the age of ten. After his voice broke he began to get work as a tenor and was signed up to Victor in 1923 after a series of concerts at Carnegie Hall with the New York Symphony Orchestra. His New York appearances included the American première of Mahler's *Das Lied von der Erde*. Crooks also decided on a European route to operatic success and made his début as Cavaradossi in Hamburg in 1927.[58] After several appearances at important European houses his triumphant Met début as Des Grieux in 1933 earned him thirty-seven curtain calls. From then on he was able to choose his work carefully and, like McCormack before him, realised the power of the concert platform in an era characterised by an apparently inexhaustible supply of European stage stars. More especially, he discovered that his voice was ideally suited to the microphone, and he became the 'Voice of Firestone' on Monday evenings from 1932 until his retirement in 1946. His relaxed manner, warm and uncomplicated singing endeared him to millions, who also went out to buy his records.

Crooks has been compared by many to Mario Lanza in his ability to move easily from operatic arias to popular song, but a more apposite comparison is surely John McCormack (or more recently the Scottish tenor Kenneth McKellar). His diction and commitment to textual narrative perfectly match his warm sound, which never becomes an end in itself.[59] Richard Crooks was one of the last great classical tenors to be able to do this, before pop singing was overtaken first by the crooning of his friend Bing Crosby, and then by the far more direct post-Presley speech-orientated delivery that we now expect. In Crooks' singing we hear many of the traits of traditional lyric tenor singing: floated high notes with controlled diminuendos to mezza voce, profligate use of portamento and rubato and perfect diction, all of which illustrate exactly how communicative such singing could be.

The cantorial tradition: Jan Peerce and Richard Tucker

Religious institutions have historically been fertile seedbeds for adult male singers, especially in Europe. In the case of many Italian and French opera stars the Catholic Church has been a major provider of educational and musical opportunities. In the United Kingdom the 'English' choral tradition owes its very nature to the high standards of cathedral and college choirs, and a similar tradition exists with German boys' choirs which are often attached to churches. In the context of two thousand years of history, with religion for most of that time embedded in the socio-political and educational establishment, it is perhaps not surprising that very few European tenors admit to being inspired by a personal faith. In the USA many singers come from families whose reason for immigrating to the USA was historical religious or political persecution in Europe. Against this background, and the more recent phenomenon of born-again America, it is also no surprise that many American singers claim to be guided by a strong religious faith. Opera, of course, knows no religion except itself, so there are no doctrinal problems with opera singers attributing their success to something beyond their own innate wondrousness (and in a fundamentally egocentric world this can sometimes be refreshing).

The influx of European musicians into the USA as a result of the second world war had a number of significant effects on music-making and, more especially, on music teaching. American universities and conservatories benefited from émigré German and Italian teachers in particular, and this brought a new disciplinary rigour to singing pedagogy. The tendency of tenors to identify strongly with what they feel is their *Fach* dates from this period, perhaps carrying with it something of the ideological and pedagogical certainties that prevailed in Europe before the war. This has meant that post-war American tenors have tended to be more specialised than their European counterparts (who, by and large, have a broader approach to repertoire and technique). The war also saw a strengthening of the cantorial tradition in the USA, where many cantors sought refuge and continued to flourish. The singing of the Ashkenazy cantors in the Hapsburg and Russian traditions dates from the early nineteenth century, and the meticulous study required has often been likened to the training of an opera singer. In Europe, Joseph Schmidt and Hermann

Jadlowker are perhaps the two most famous tenors who benefited from cantorial training before they began their secular stage careers. The two most
prominent American tenors with cantorial backgrounds are Jan Peerce (born
Jacob Pincus Perelmuth) and Richard Tucker (born Reuben Ticker), and who
became brothers-in-law in 1936 when Ruby Ticker (as he was then known)
married Pinkie Perelmuth's sister Sara. Both had grown up singing lighter
music and finding success on radio; both became cantors, subsequently
attributing their stamina and technique to cantorial discipline and their
success to God.[60] Both were also held in high esteem by Toscanini, and to work
with such willing acolytes must have been a relief to the maestro after a
lifetime of trying to keep subversive Italians in check.

Peerce, the older of the two (born in 1904), began singing in dance bands and
after taking part in the first live (as opposed to virtual) Radio City Music Hall in
1932 he rapidly became a radio star (his 'Blue Bird of Happiness' was a big hit
in 1936). In 1938 Toscanini, a keen listener to music on radio, heard him broadcasting part of *Die Walküre* and recognised a fine future spinto; he booked him
to sing Beethoven's 9th with the NBC Symphony Orchestra, and subsequently
booked him for more Beethoven as well as Verdi and Puccini. He was having
lessons with Giuseppe Boghetti (who had taught Marian Anderson among
others) and made his stage début as the Duke in Philadelphia, and went on to
début at the Met as Alfredo in 1941. He stayed with the Met until 1968 and went
on to sing on Broadway in the 1971 *Fiddler on the Roof*, finally retiring in 1982.

Richard Tucker sang alto in his local synagogue before his voice broke, and
became a cantor at the Brooklyn Jewish Centre. His rich, full sound developed
during this period and his teacher Paul Althouse (an American tenor who had
sung at the Met) saw no incompatibility between his cantorial studies and his
opera training.[61] Tucker at first refused Edward Johnson's offer of supporting
roles at the Met, and the gamble paid off when he finally made his début in *La
gioconda* in 1945. He stayed for nearly thirty years, and became an American
tenor who could hold his own with the best of his European contemporaries
such as Franco Corelli. He sang most of the French and Italian dramatic repertoire, and waited till his voice matured before singing the heavier Verdi roles. It
was Toscanini who first offered him *Aida* in 1949, a performance that was
broadcast simultaneously on radio and television. He went on to become one of
the country's great Verdi interpreters (often partnering Robert Merrill). Tucker's
voice was a magnificent instrument, in the European post-Caruso mould, and
he flung himself into every role he attempted (around thirty at the Met). His
death at the age of 61 in 1975 was a shock to musicians and audiences alike. He
is the only singer to have been accorded a funeral at the Met, his coffin left on
the stage as the curtain descended for the last time on one of the greatest
American tenors of the century.[62]

Tenors still come up through the cantorial tradition. Neil Shicoff (born 1949) also sang in the synagogue as a child. When he matured into a tenor he was taught for two years by his father, the baritone cantor Sidney Shicoff, a notable singer who might have considered an operatic career for himself. After Neil Shicoff was unsuccessful at his first Julliard audition he studied cantorial singing at Hebrew Union College for three years before deciding on an operatic career. He went on to become one of the most successful American dramatic tenors.

The popular voice

All of the tenors discussed in this chapter have had huge popular appeal to a wide public. Some tenors were able to achieve a level of fame that took them much more deeply into the public consciousness, thanks to their particular affinity with the mass media of radio, film and, later, television. The development of sound recording technology was quickly followed by film, which was, ironically, initially silent. Despite the lack of words and music the new medium had many parallels with opera: it was expensive, dramatic, larger than life and happened in dedicated public theatres. The showing of silent films was, of course, far from silent: they normally had live music playing throughout, a concept derived from opera and which eventually became the sound track, reflecting the action and manipulating the emotions in very similar ways to an operatic score.

It was surely only a matter of time (and technology) before the old art form realised the possibilities of the new. From the start, the collaboration involved compromise, and as things turned out, opera on film has never managed to replicate the theatrical experience. The reasons for this include the inability of film to capture the atmosphere created by the vocal and theatrical experience of live productions, and the ossification of opera as a genre, which makes it very difficult for film-makers to have an impact on the repertoire without alienating its core audience. There was also a more mysterious and less quantifiable social dynamic at work: opera, despite its mass appeal in some parts of the world, remained essentially an élite event, whereas the commercial development of the film industry was geared from the start to the mass market. It was perfectly suited, in fact, to the musical, which was unencumbered by nineteenth-century tradition and repertoire, and would become a sub-genre of film in its own right. The voices required for film musicals (or musical films) tended to require something closer to a light baritone, but there were also roles for lyric tenors who could take on lighter repertoire without sacrificing too much of their vocal identity.[63] The new medium also permitted a different kind of celebrity, which became a phenomenon in its own right, transcending whatever talent may have created public interest in the first place. For singers, it meant a return to a kind of physical presence that sound recording had removed from performance: if the charismatic tenor hero could be seen as well as heard, then the public might be prepared to buy into the whole person, not just the voice.

The earliest attempts to match sound and vision before the advent of electrical recording were clumsy, as realistic synchronisation was impossible. There were ingenious solutions that had a certain appeal to marketing executives, such as the 1908 recording of the sextet from *Lucia di Lammermoor* with a celebrity line-up which included Caruso, which could accompany a film of actors miming the action (miming was thus part of the genre right from the start). Giovanni Martinelli was an early success in real sound recording in 1926, making a series of twelve short films for Vitaphone.[64] Film was not a comfortable medium for the star operatic tenors of the earlier part of the century, however – an operatic or concert career still had to be made in the theatre itself. The screen, like the microphone, likes some performers and not others, and the genre attracted several tenors who were also charismatic screen actors.

Among the earliest singers to have a successful film career was the Heldentenor Leo Slezak, who turned out to have a gift for comic timing that saw him through more than a dozen major roles in the 1930s and 1940s, as well as parts in more than thirty more. Lauritz Melchior similarly made an effortless transition into movies (eventually becoming an American citizen). Their fame was a marketing advantage of course, but both tenors used their carefully nurtured talent to great effect. A natural bonhomie combined with a certain gift for narrative and an ear for timing stood them in good stead on the big screen. Both tenors had children who also went into show business, Walter Slezak becoming a film star in his own right, and Ib Melchior going into production.

Jan Kiepura

Some singers became show business personalities whose fame extended far beyond their singing, and if they could marry another star they became twice as marketable. Jan Kiepura, born in Poland in 1902, made his début at the Vienna Staatsoper as Cavaradossi in 1926, the same year as making his first (silent) film *O czem sie nie mysli*. After operatic success at La Scala as well as in north and south America, he found himself increasingly in demand for film roles and in 1934 played opposite the soprano and film star Martha Eggert in *Mein Herz ruf nach dir*; two years later the couple were married, becoming one of the most famous show business couples on the circuit.

Kiepura is one of the few tenors to have had success both at the Met and on Broadway (where they both starred in *The Merry Widow*). The couple moved to New York during the war, and afterwards returned permanently to the USA in 1953, shortly after which Kiepura became an American citizen. Kiepura's voice was seductively rich, and he sang all of the important Puccini and Massenet roles, as well as the lighter Verdi such as *Rigoletto*. He was an instinctive communicator, and had a charismatic stage and screen presence which perhaps owed more to his natural gifts than anything he would have learned from a teacher. Kiepura was one of the first great tenors of the century to suffer from the law of diminishing critical returns that afflicts those who create mass appeal: however fine the surviving recordings, the singer is considered to have trivialised his art and is unlikely to be taken seriously by posterity.

Radio stars: Joseph Schmidt and Ernst Groh

From the beginnings of film it was clear that the tenor hero should ideally have a compelling physical presence (such as the charismatic Wagnerian rock singer Peter Hofmann, for instance); some tenors were not physically prepossessing but used their bulk to great effect (Lauritz Melchior comes to mind) or had such vocally redeeming features that audiences could forgive them for being short and fat (many contenders here, starting with Gigli). Parallel with the evolution of recording and film was the development of radio. Like electrical recording it depended on the microphone, but unlike the stage or the movies it did not require physical presence. It did demand a particular expression of the vocal personality, however, and there were certain singers who, for one reason or another, were less successful in the physical world but had significant careers in the mass market that radio was able to capture. One of the most fascinating (and tragic) of these was the Romanian Jewish tenor Joseph Schmidt, whose career in radio eventually led to a highly successful film career until World War II intervened and he died of a heart attack in a Swiss refugee camp at the age of thirty-eight.

His family moved to Czernowitz at the outbreak of World War I, and he grew up fluent in German and Hebrew as well as Romanian. He sang in the local synagogue and became a cantor, and like so many singers, when called up for military service in 1926 his talents were recognised and enjoyed by his fellow soldiers.[65] He entered the Berlin conservatory and was well placed when Radio Berlin began opera broadcasts in 1929. Schmidt had a particular reason to appreciate opera on radio: he was less than five feet tall; the stage tenor hero roles, with his leading ladies towering over him, were just too difficult to contemplate. His voice was not a large one, and he probably could not have sustained a major stage career even if he had had a more substantial frame. As it was, he was able to sing some three dozen roles for Radio Berlin from 1928 to 1933, when Hitler prohibited Jews from making radio broadcasts. By then, however, he had already made four films, the latest of which, *Ein Lied geht um die Welt* (known in English as *My Song Goes Around the World*), was so popular that Goebbels is said to have considered making him an honorary Aryan. It was partly autobiographical – about a singer who was so short of stature that he could only sing on the radio – and it confirmed his status as a star. He toured widely, including the United States (where he was marketed as 'the pocket Caruso'), and made many recordings. These, together with his films, reveal him to have been a sensuous singer more in the Gigli mould than a Caruso, with exquisitely legato phrasing that was well suited to the microphone. As a Jew he was eventually banned from singing in Germany and Austria, and in 1942 he was interned in Switzerland while trying to make his way to America and safety. He had a heart attack, after which he was sent straight back to work, accused of shirking. Another heart attack followed almost immediately, and he was silenced for ever.[66]

Herbert Ernst Groh was similarly small of voice and as a result went into operetta, but was increasingly able to find success on the radio (with Norddeutscher Rundfunk) and in recordings from 1930 onwards. As with Schmidt, he was eventually able to translate this into a film career, resulting in eight films of his own and several more where he overdubbed the singing of other actors. Groh studied in his youth with Karl Beines, who had taught Richard Tauber. Tauber remained an influence on the younger singer, and both tenors demonstrate a personable charm and an evenness of tone that came from not having to project to the back of an opera theatre.

Richard Tauber

It is Tauber whose quixotic presence overshadows all other popular tenors of the first half of the century. He was born to theatre folk in a hotel in Linz in 1891; his father was an actor and his mother was a singer, working at the Landestheater. The boy was an unplanned and illegitimate arrival; his mother needed to keep working and his father was touring extensively in the USA, so the infant Richard was sent to foster parents in the country. From his father's return a year later the child lived the life of a theatrical nomad, experiencing stage life from the inside as he accompanied his parents wherever they happened to be working.[67]

The young Tauber was a musically precocious child, and from an early age wanted to be a singer. Having been raised in the theatre he became a confident youth and would sing Wagner for anyone who would listen (and some who wouldn't). His rendering of Lohengrin's Narration must have been bizarre in the extreme and it failed to help him find a singing teacher until the Freiburg teacher Carl Beines persuaded him to try something 'less noisy'.[68] In the meantime his father had encouraged him to consider becoming a conductor, and enrolled him in the Hochschule at Frankfurt, where he studied piano, composition and conducting (all skills that he would use in the future).

Beines' two years of work completely re-focused Tauber, and he left his Wagner obsession behind to become a lyric tenor. He made his début in 1913 as Tamino in Chemnitz, thanks to the good offices of his father who was the Intendant at both the town's theatres. This led to a five-year contract with Dresden Opera, where he sang all the major Mozart roles and gained a repu-tation for mastering scores with incredible speed, enabling him to fill in at very short notice if opportunities came his way. He is said to have learned Gounod's *Faust* in forty-eight hours, and he made his Berlin début in 1915 as Bacchus in Strauss' *Ariadne auf Naxos* with only two days' notice and only a cursory piano rehearsal with the composer.[69] His most famous rescue opera-tion was in 1926, when he gave the German première of *Turandot* at only four days' notice. One Wednesday he was about to leave the Dresden theatre (where he had returned for *Die Fledermaus*) when news came that Curt Taucher was ill and would not be able to play Calaf at the opening night on the Saturday. Tauber was the only tenor who could have performed such a feat, and with such élan that the press could hardly believe what they were seeing and hearing.[70] Only the most extraordinarily gifted singers can learn such complex roles in such a short time.

Tauber had the nerve and the ability to pull off the most challenging roles but during his time at Dresden discovered a penchant for operetta. In 1921 he sang Franz Lehár's *Zigeunerliebe* at the Salzburg Landestheater, and in 1922 he rescued *Frasquita* from possible failure in Vienna. From then on, all of Lehár's tenor leads were composed for Tauber. The relationship between the young singer and the aging composer was one of mutual admiration, even love. Lehár wrote to Tauber: 'You are singing like a god. I believe you have the most beautiful voice in the world! The sound of it stimulates me to compose and write my music for you. You are always in my thoughts.'[71] The Tauber sound stimulated listeners too, and the 'virile initial upward thrust' of a Tauber Lehár tune brought a new focus to the composer's later works.[72] For Tauber, the lure of operetta and the stardom that went with it were irre-sistible; it was, after all, what he had grown up with. He made his first film in 1929, and went on to become a hugely successful musical film star with *Land of Smiles, Blossom Time* and *Heart's Desire* among many others, securing millions of fans throughout the world. He was not conventionally handsome, but his charm seemed to overwhelm people, especially women. He lived the life, breaking the hearts of many of those who fell in love with him on the way.[73]

Despite his success he never forsook the lyric roles that he also enjoyed, and he was delighted when Covent Garden asked him to sing *Magic Flute* under Beecham in 1938; he returned in 1947, not long before his death from lung cancer, to sing Don Ottavio in Mozart's *Don Giovanni* with Elisabeth Schwarzkopf and the Vienna Staatsoper. 'Yes, I sing for both worlds,' he said, 'One world keeps me in comfort and the other gives me a good cold glass of beer ... I sing opera every year in Vienna for pennies: this fills me up like petrol in a car to carry on for another year until I return.'[74]

An Englishman, an Irishman, and a Scotsman

Britain had its own media-star tenors, most of whom did not have the international profile of a Tauber or a Lanza, but successfully negotiated careers that depended on their singing with a classically-based technique. They were not crooners, even though their repertoire may have overlapped with that of some 'popular' singers. Webster Booth and his wife Anne Ziegler actually starred with Tauber in the 1945 film *Walz Time* as a pair of gypsy troubadours.[75] Booth began playing minor roles with the Doyly Carte Opera Company (as Leslie W. Booth) in 1923 but then auditioned successfully for Covent Garden and became a proficient oratorio soloist. After he met Anne Ziegler while filming *Faust* (based on Gounod's opera) the two paired up to become a British version of 'America's singing sweethearts' Jeanette MacDonald and Nelson Eddy, their glamorous image underpinned and legitimised by their backgrounds in 'serious' music.

Irishman Josef McLaughlin enlisted in the Irish Guards as a teenager and then spent time in the Palestinian Police and Royal Ulster Constabulary before touring the United Kingdom as the Singing Bobby. Although self-taught he wanted to be an opera singer until John McCormack steered him in the direction of lighter music. He became Josef Locke when his full name would not fit onto a poster for promoter Jack Hylton, and thus foreshortened he was taken on by the Grade brothers. He signed a contract with EMI in 1947 and became a successful recording artist and regular fixture on Royal Variety Performances. In 1992 a re-release of his 1947 hit 'Hear my Song' reached the Top Ten album chart. He was frequently hailed as 'Ireland's greatest tenor'.[76]

Gravitating towards lighter music was not always a career choice based on personal ambition. The Scots tenor Kenneth McKellar grew up listening to Caruso, Gigli and Tauber, but did not discover his own voice until he joined the choir at the University of Aberdeen. He then won a scholarship to the

Royal College of Music, where he developed his elegant combination of a smooth legato line and crisp diction. His voice was perfect for Handel, Mozart, and lyric stage roles, but a spell with the Carl Rosa company convinced him that opera was not his true vocation. He left to concentrate on Scottish traditional songs, especially those featuring the poems of Robbie Burns. In 1966 he became one of the few genuine tenors to be entered for the Eurovision Song Contest. Unsurprisingly, he was not considered commercial enough to win, but had he done so he might have become a significant international star along the lines of some of today's tenors. His many recordings of the Scottish traditional repertoire have elevated him to a unique position in Scottish consciousness.

All of the tenors discussed above who were successful in light music played to some extent on the romantic associations of their ethnic backgrounds – it was important that Tauber was Viennese, Booth was seen to be English, Locke became an Irish institution, McKellar famously appeared on television Hogmanay celebrations in his kilt. Wales, too, had its emblematic singer in the comedian Harry Secombe, whose tenor voice and Welsh accent was very much a part of his performing persona. The USA had a romantic star of its own in the Italian-American Mario Lanza, whose image reflected the glamour of the American dream.

Mario Lanza: screen star

Mario Lanza was born Alfredo Cocozza in 1921, the year of Caruso's death. He grew up in South Philadelphia, a strong-willed child obsessed with music and sport. Recognising his talent, his mother arranged for him to have singing and language coaching as a teenager. With a career as a singer in prospect he changed his name to Mario Lanza (a version of his mother's maiden name). He sang to Koussevitzky, who invited him to the Berkshire (now Tanglewood) Festival in 1942, but before his career could take off he was drafted into the army airforce. This turned out to be fortunate, as his talent was spotted by a sergeant who was recruiting singers for a morale-boosting show called *On the Beam*. This led to his joining the cast of the Moss Hart production *Winged Victory*, which was then filmed, introducing Lanza to Hollywood. Lanza would sing on any occasion and it was only a matter of time before he was heard by the right people. He was given a contract with RCA without even a formal audition, while he was still in the military; he would stay with RCA for the rest of his career. After his discharge he moved to New York and started lessons with Enrico Rosati, who had been one of Gigli's teachers in Rome. Rosati immediately realised that he might be hearing a successor to his famous pupil, pronouncing: 'I've been waiting for you for thirty-four years. But I must tell you something. No one can actually teach you to sing. You had the greatest teacher of them all. God was your teacher.'[77]

After a year's study Lanza signed to the Columbia Concerts agency, who arranged a spectacularly successful tour for him. His big break came in 1947 when he replaced Ferruccio Tagliavini for a recital at the Hollywood Bowl, after which he was signed up to MGM. In 1949 his first film, *That Midnight Kiss*, made him a star almost overnight. The year before, he made two professional operatic appearances in New Orleans as Pinkerton in Puccini's *Madame Butterfly*; in the future his stage was to be the movie theatre, and he never again returned to the operatic stage. His ten-year film career included *The Great Caruso* (1949), and the sound-track for *The Student Prince* (1954), which became the first million-selling soundtrack album. Lanza did not spare himself in his relentless pursuit of the screen-star lifestyle, and he died at the age of thirty-eight.

Lanza's voice hypnotised a generation of singers, and together with Caruso he is the singer most often cited as a formative influence by such stars as Domingo, Pavarotti and Carreras. His voice was a superb natural instrument, and for those who can see and hear beyond the self-destructiveness of his lifestyle he was an inspiration. Quite simply, he moved people, vast numbers of people, and he did it not by devaluing the music, but by the sensual power of his voice.

Critics are often dismissive of the success of singers who become popular through what appears to be commercial exploitation. The laws of supply and demand are subtle and complex when applied to music. It is certainly the case that the recordings of some singers – Mario Lanza and Joseph Schmidt are prime examples – have remained commercially viable, but because Schmidt and Lanza are not associated with great operatic roles they are somehow perceived as being of lesser artistic worth, even though their earliest vocal achievements pre-date their recording successes. The same is true of many of those whose recordings are now harder to find, such as Jan Kiepura and Webster Booth. Enlightened listeners may like to listen 'blind' to recordings of these 'commercial' singers and compare them with their more critically successful counterparts, and may be surprised at the similarities. The artistic use of a microphone is a sophisticated skill – it is in no sense 'cheating' in the hands of an accomplished performer. The post-Three Tenors rush to market personable young tenors is entirely different: these are in the main singers who have little experience of live unamplified performance and cannot be compared to the 'popular' tenors of earlier eras.

CHAPTER 7

SPLENDID ISOLATIONISTS?

THE BRITISH ISLES IN THE TWENTIETH CENTURY

With a small number of notable exceptions, the twentieth century appears to have been dominated by Italian tenors, with public imagination captured again and again by the voices of a succession of extraordinary stars from Caruso to Pavarotti. Actual history is more complicated than that, of course, and individual countries had their own characteristics which sometimes bypassed the mainstream altogether. Britain had a thriving domestic musical scene, but was seemingly incapable of producing singers either vocally or temperamentally suited to international tenor stardom, and (together with France and Russia, discussed in the following chapters) reflects a colourful individuality that applies to many countries within the wider story of tenor history.[1]

The lyric tradition in England

In the eighteenth and nineteenth centuries the musical links between England and the rest of Europe were often tenuous even though singers and composers from the mainland frequently visited London to teach or perform. The obsession with continental stars probably made it more difficult for British singers, but those who were talented and persistent enough to seek out training in Italy (or with Italian teachers in France) benefited their singing considerably, though not always their careers. The English scene was complicated by the development of ballad opera from the 1728 première of *The Beggar's Opera* onwards. John Gay's play with tunes was in part a satire on the foreignness of Italian opera, then in full swing in London. It was a huge success and created a useful market for singers who could act as well as sing, and who did not need to be especially virtuosic (in vocal terms it is a forerunner of the modern musical). English composers who did not feel at home in Italian opera also began to develop a homegrown variety influenced by Gay's model. For singers, this added layer of opportunity also had the effect of adding to the distance that separated them from the operatic culture of the rest of Europe, a trend that would last into the twentieth century and would see relatively few British tenors making a mark on the international stage.

The London opera houses were a mixed blessing for English singers: there were occasional opportunities, but an institutional commitment to visiting international stars meant the competition was fierce. Covent Garden became one of the handful of top opera houses in the world and singers tended to use it as their only benchmark; this rather narrow view meant that many British singers, even when they did get opportunities to sing in Europe, were focused on success at home rather than on an international career for its own sake.

For an ambitious singer in Italy or Germany the opportunity to experience great singing (in opera or concerts) as a listener or as a performer was never very far away, and with it the chance of rigorous training. Britain was isolated from this informal cultural infrastructure and in these circumstances it took extraordinary ambition and persistence for singers to think beyond the English Channel.

Opera had been slow to develop in England from the time of Handel and even when it was in the height of upper-class fashion was still perceived as something not quite British. Handel's lasting influence was in fact not the Italian operas that had been so successful in his own lifetime, but his oratorios in English. These appealed to the Victorian obsession with self-improvement, requiring discipline and decorum rather than the outpourings of emotionally incontinent continentals. Aspiring nineteenth-century tenors were more likely to have grown up with amateur performances of *Messiah* than the operas of Rossini or Verdi. The positive effect of this was the development of a peculiarly English lyricism – even those who discovered that they might be Heldentenors would have cut their teeth on Handel. The sensuality of Italian and French dramatic singers, and later the sheer physicality of German and

Scandinavian Heldentenors, were almost entirely absent from the tradition that evolved in the British Isles. The exceptions were either from the Celtic countries or lived outside the United Kingdom altogether.

Sims Reeves

There were international successes, of course, as we have seen with the example of John Braham. Braham's successor was Sims Reeves, who was born in 1818 into a musical family and showed sufficient promise to train as a singer rather than enter the medical profession as his parents intended him to do. He began his career in 1838 as a baritone, but after studying in Paris with Mario's sometime teacher Giulio Bordogni and then with Alberto Mazzucato in Milan, he made his début at La Scala as Egardo in *Lucia di Lammermoor*. Like Braham before him, Reeves was able to sustain a long career thanks to the soundness of his traditional technique during a period when tenors were increasingly under pressure to produce richer, more powerful sounds. Chorley thought him 'probably the best English tenor who has ever existed' and was puzzled by the fact that his return to England from Italy did not ensure Reeves' success on the Italian stage in London.[2] Perhaps because his formative musical experiences were very domestic (his teenage years were focused on his local church choir), Reeves seems not to have had a great flair for the stage and became more successful on the English oratorio scene. He did have notable stage successes, however, including the role of Faust in the first performance of *La Damnation de Faust* under Berlioz himself in 1848. Herman Klein reflected fondly on Reeves' reputation in his 1931 *Gramophone* article 'Sims Reeves: Prince of Tenors', drawing particular attention to his fastidious diction, having first heard the tenor in 1866.[3] David Bispham was a little less flattering in his assessment; the American baritone did a concert tour with Reeves when the illustrious tenor was almost sixty-eight years old and together with the other younger soloists in the troupe was charged with the task of 'keeping our chief amused and pleased, never crossing him in any way, taking walks or drives with him, playing billiards and otherwise causing him to forget that he was a tenor'.[4]

Reeves was famous for two idiosyncrasies as well as his compelling singing; he was extremely reluctant to give encores and he would often fail to turn up for engagements. These habits cannot have made him easy to deal with, and the fact that he had such a long and distinguished career despite wilfully creating the circumstances that could alienate both audiences and promoters suggests that his singing was something absolutely out of the ordinary. Encores were a measure of success, and Sims Reeves must have been extra-ordinarily confident of his own status if he felt he could do without them. His not turning up could have had unfavourable contractual implications, but according to Bispham his contract guaranteed him forty guineas even if he did not appear.[5]

Reeves' repertoire as he got older fell back on the English material that had served him well: songs by Braham, Dibdin and Balfe rather than anything too foreign. He published a short compendium of his thoughts on singing towards the end of his life. It shows a grounding in traditional principles but one gets the impression that he did not think very hard about how he did it – his musings are those of a star singer rather than a pedagogue. Perhaps the most interesting section is his paragraph on vibrato, which he calls 'the tremolo'. The evidence from early recordings shows a very wide variety of vibrato in tenors – some singers have almost none at all, others have the persistent trembling that may be what commentators from Mozart to Shaw complained about. Sims Reeves excoriates the 'five out of every six modern singers [who] are afflicted with it', calling for rigorous correction for those who use it.[6] The implication is that singers of his generation would have sung with a much straighter tone than those who succeeded them.

Edward Lloyd and Ben Davies

Sims Reeves died in 1900 at the age of eighty-two, having formally retired in 1891. That same year his younger contemporary (and in some respects, successor) Edward Lloyd retired at the age of fifty-five.[7] Reeves left no recordings behind him but between 1904 and 1911 a surprisingly youthful-sounding Lloyd recorded a number of sides including the 'Prize Song' from *Meistersinger* and selections from his song and oratorio repertoire.[8] Lloyd did not have the caché of Reeves, never having trod the operatic stage and always insisting on singing in English, but his reputation was considerable as a recitalist and oratorio soloist. Bispham recognised him as the successor of Sims Reeves, and wrote that 'No other tenor upon the concert stage was his equal; all acknowledged his superiority.' The recordings bear out Shaw's description of his voice as 'homogeneous … from top to bottom, and charming in its colour', though he goes on to say that it is not quite as beautiful or pure as that of Reeves.[9] Klein, who knew both singers' performances well, remarks that Hans Richter thought Lloyd was the first tenor to do justice to the 'Preislied', which Lloyd sang at his farewell concert at the Albert Hall, and which for Klein recalled the accomplishment of Jean de Reske.[10] As well as espousing the music of Wagner in concert, Lloyd was one of the great Handel singers of his time, appearing at every Triennial Festival between 1874 and 1900. He also gave more first performances than any tenor of the last decade of the century, including Sullivan's *Martyr of Antioch* and *Golden*

Legend, Gounod's *Redemption* and *Mors et vita,* Elgar's *Caractacus* and *Dream of Gerontius,* and works by Parry and Stephen Adams (including 'The Holy City'). Lloyd's place in the history of British tenors is a significant one – his recordings are one of the earliest aural windows onto the lost world of pre-1900 English singing. It was his misfortune to have had to follow in the footsteps of the more charismatic Reeves, whose historic reputation is perhaps higher because of frustration at the lack of a recorded legacy. Lloyd's recordings show exquisite control but a blandness that one imagines would be foreign to the likes of Mario and de Reske.

Lloyd must have been of Welsh extraction despite his wholly English upbringing. The principality may have produced more tenors per head of population than any territory of similar size on earth. The origins of the Welsh bardic tradition are lost in the distant mists of the oral culture in which it flourished, but its legacy is the Eisteddfod, especially since its re-founding as the National Eisteddfod in 1880. These meetings of poets and musicians (the word means 'session') gave a central place to a performance culture at a time when the country was supplying most of the British Isles with coal. The choral tradition thus extended down into the pits, and many early twentieth-century tenors began their careers in coal mines. A remarkable number of these were 'natural' tenors who only needed singing lessons for style, rather than technique. One reason for this may be the pitch inflections of the Welsh accent (even more obvious in Welsh English speakers than in Welsh itself) which has a distinctively musical character.

Ben Davies was fortunate not to have to work in the pits as his father (who died when Davies was seven) had been an engineer and a Nonconformist preacher. Unusually he sang alto in his local choir (where he read from tonic-solfa notation) but by the age of nineteen was a promising tenor. An unexpected first prize at the Swansea Eisteddfod in 1877 encouraged him to think of a career and with the help of family and friends he was then able to go to the Royal Academy. He impressed Charles Santley and Carl Rosa, and he began a career in musical theatre and English opera. He preferred concerts to the stage, however, and although he did appear at Covent Garden he rebutted Augustus Harris' attempts to get him to sing Siegmund in 1895. He made frequent visits to the Cincinatti Festival, where he was compared with Lloyd, and was a favourite singer of Queen Victoria.

Walter Hyde: English Wagnerian

The English appetite for Wagner (whether in German or English) met with a significant response from British tenordom in the first decades of the twentieth century. Walter Hyde was a notable Wagnerian, singing Siegmund in Richter's first English *Ring* cycle at Covent Garden in 1908 and repeating the role at the Met the following season. He had studied with Gustave Garcia (son of Manuel) at the Royal College of Music and was an indefatigable worker, at one point managing Loge, both Siegfrieds and Walter in the same week. He was aware of the importance of languages and could sing Wagner roles in both English and German, his willingness to perform in either language standing him in good stead when he was asked to sing Lohengrin in any language except German for the opera in Budapest.[11] He also supported new music, giving the first performance of Delius' *A Village Romeo and Juliet* in 1910 and Debussy's *Pelléas et Mélisande* the following season. After the war he appeared at Covent Garden in a wide variety of roles from Mozart to Mussorgsky, and became a director of the British National Opera Company, finally retiring from the stage and becoming a professor at the Guildhall School of Music in 1926.[12]

John Coates and Gervase Elwes: Elgar's early interpreters

One of the tenors to follow in Lloyd's footsteps as *Gerontius* was John Coates. Coates came from a musical family and was an enthusiastic treble as a boy. The death of his father at the age of thirty-seven set back his musical ambitions, but the young Coates continued to take music seriously, even studying French, German and Italian in his spare time. He seems to have had very few formal singing lessons apart from a few sessions with William Shakespeare in 1893, and (perhaps because of this) his adult voice evolved into something between a tenor and a baritone. He had some success in musical comedy before an operation on his throat in 1896 seemed to re-focus his voice as a firm tenor, making a more serious career a real possibility.

In 1901 Covent Garden engaged him for Stanford's *Much Ado about Nothing*, which was not a critical success for the composer but allowed Coates to impress his patrons. It was suggested that if he should go abroad to study and work, he might return to England with 'the *cachet* of a continental reputation' sufficient to take on roles previously sung by Jean de Reszke.[13] Coates then took himself off to Paris for some lessons with Julius Bouhy and some months later auditioned for the opera in Cologne, where he amazed Julius Hofmann by singing Lohengrin's Narration in German and the cavatina from *Faust* in French.[14] Hofmann engaged him for *Lohengrin* and *Roméo et Juliette* immediately, both of which were hugely successful and led to engagements in Leipzig, Berlin and Hannover. Had Coates taken up the offers of permanent contracts that then came his way from Cologne and Frankfurt he might have then developed a substantial European career as a dramatic tenor. As it was, he returned to England only to be offered small parts at Covent Garden, and was destined to sing Tristan, Lohengrin and Radamès with touring companies. His concert career took off, however, and he became one of Elgar's favourite interpreters of Gerontius, first singing the part in 1902 at the age of thirty-seven. After the war (in which he served as a captain, even though above military age) he returned mainly to concert performances, especially the recital repertoire. For a period of some five years he worked with pianist Gerald Moore, including a taxing tour of the USA, championing contemporary composers such as Cyril Scott as well as Lieder and French song. Moore considered their partnership to be among the most valuable experiences of his life, and for Michael Scott he is 'one of the finest English singers on record'.[15] As is almost always the case with singers who broaden their scope to take in the ballad repertoire and lighter music, Coates' posthumous reputation has belied his true value as an artist.[16]

Elgar's other favourite Gerontius was Gervase Elwes, who was just a year younger than Coates, and the two tenors enjoyed a friendly rivalry until Elwes' untimely death in 1921. Elwes was a man of great charm whose inherited wealth relieved him of the need to be over-ambitious. He sang as an amateur to start with and only gradually realised that singing was his true vocation, like Coates making a late entry into the profession (having had a brief career in the diplomatic service). Also like Coates he was unsure whether he was a baritone or a tenor, a question that was answered for him by Julius Brouhy, to whom he went for lessons in 1901. Brouhy offered him a choice between theatre or concert singing in England:

> I said the latter, and he told me he had asked me because if I wanted to work for the stage he would cultivate my voice as a baritone, but if the latter, then as a tenor, and for the reason that the tenor parts in opera were very hard and required a very big voice, whereas the tenor parts in oratorios in England were not so high. I said that I did not think that my voice was big enough for the theatre, but he said it certainly was, and that it was not so much the size of the voice but the production that really told. So now I am regularly taken in hand as a tenor . . .[17]

Elwes did not enjoy Brouhy's opera class but studied with him until 1903. His wife then persuaded him to study with Victor Beigel (who would later teach Lauritz Melchior) and Beigel moved into Elwes' country house for the summer, giving two lessons a day in between croquet and fishing. It was Beigel who encouraged him to sing Brahms, and eventually became his accompanist. Reassured by both Beigel's sound instruction and his musicianship, Elwes went on to become an accomplished recitalist, giving the first performance of Vaughan Williams' *On Wenlock Edge* and Quilter's *To Julia* cycle, among many other new British works. He could also tackle larger works, notably Mahler's *Das Lied von der Erde*, which he sang in English under Henry Wood. He declined to sing opera or ballads, but was acclaimed as an oratorio soloist.

Elwes was a practising Roman Catholic and brought a religious commitment to the part of Gerontius, which he sang more than one hundred times, becoming together with his friend John Coates, one of the work's foremost interpreters. On one occasion Coates deputised when Elwes refused to modify the Marian references in the text, and it was Coates who stepped in once again for what became Elwes' memorial concert at the Albert Hall, after Elwes was fatally injured falling from a railway platform in Boston a few weeks before. Elwes' career was a very English one, not just in its geographical reach but in terms of its artistic and musical restraint. Never having had to earn his living, and already being at home in the upper reaches of English society, he had a life that was not complicated by social and financial ambitions. This left him free to explore the limited musical options that were to his taste, and this he did supremely well.

A Serenade of Tenors

Similarly constrained but in many ways more perfectly formed was the career of Heddle Nash. For many critics Nash was the ultimate English lyric tenor; John Steane considers him the best English lyric tenor on record and his Gerontius 'one of the most worthy achievements of British singing'.[18] After serving in the war he studied briefly at the Blackheath Conservatoire before going to Milan to work with Giuseppe Borgatti. He made his début there as Almaviva in *Il barbiere*, but in the typical English fashion he returned to England in 1925 and hardly ever stirred himself outside the British Isles thereafter. He was a refined, elegant singer, as can be heard in his many surviving recordings and particularly suited to Mozart (his Don Ottavio at Covent Garden in 1929 was reckoned to be the finest since John McCormack). He settled down into a routine of opera runs (he was a favourite at Glyndebourne), oratorios and recitals. His voice has something of the quality of Schipa or De Lucia, but his English reserve prevented him from realising the full expressive potential of the French and Italian repertoire. Occasionally he would bring a note of Italian extravagance to his English repertoire: one critic commented after hearing Nash sing Gerontius after a run of *Bohèmes* that 'certain phrases made him fear that at any moment Gerontius would tell the angel that "her tiny hand was frozen."'[19]

Heddle Nash was one of the four tenors chosen by Vaughan Williams to perform his sixteen voice *Serenade* in 1938, the others being Walter Widdop, Parry Jones and Frank Titterton.[20] Jones was the son of a Monmouthshire butcher, who began his working life in a Welsh coalmine. Funded by well-wishers he was able to attend the Royal College in London and then study with Colli in Italy, Karl Scheidemantel in Germany and John Coates back in England, all of which experience gave him an enterprising musical outlook. He was one of the survivors of the torpedoing of the *Lusitania* in 1915 and after the war he sang with the D'Oyly Carte and Beecham companies before becoming a founder member of the British National Opera Company. Although he rarely sang outside Britain, his ability to cope with complex scores brought him an international repertoire. He sang in the first performances in England of Berg's *Wozzeck*, Schoenberg's *Gurrelieder*, Busoni's *Doktor Faust*, Kodály's *Psalmus hungaricus*, Hindemith's *Mathis der Mahler* and Shostakovich's *Lady Macbeth of Mtsensk*, among many others. His recording career included the first complete *Elijah* in 1930 and the first recording of Stravinsky's *Les Noces* (in English, as 'The Wedding') under the composer in 1934.

Frank Titterton was less adventurous but no less successful in his own way. He was a strong singer who stuck to concert performances and salon music, but also included, like Lloyd and Tudor Davies, the 'Prize Song' (in English) as well as Puccini (sung in Italian) in his recorded repertoire. In 1931 he took part in a curious attempt at historical reconstruction, recording eight sides of music associated with Sims Reeves. Herman Klein in *The Gramophone* is rather baffled by this but does give Titterton credit for a brave attempt to imitate a singer he had never heard.[21]

The tried and tested path of Royal College of Music (Gustave Garcia), war service and then British National Opera Company (where he created the role of Hugh in Vaughan Williams' *Hugh the Drover* in 1924) also served Tudor Davies. This fine Welsh tenor was one of the earliest to record Gerontius under the composer, and he joins the list as one of the role's great interpreters.[22] He worked with various English opera companies (though his Rodolfo opposite Melba in 1922 did not lead to further roles at Covent Garden) and gave up the stage for concert work from 1950 onwards.[23]

Operatic tenors between the wars:
Joseph Hislop, Walter Widdop, Frank Mullings and David Lloyd

Joseph Hislop, sometime coach and friend of Jussi Björling, was born the son of an Edinburgh house painter in 1884. He sang in Edinburgh cathedral as a treble, but later chose to train as an engineer. Engineering took him to Gothenberg, where he started to have lessons with Gillis Bratt, who had himself studied with Manuel Garcia. Hislop subsequently successfully auditioned for the Royal Opera House in Stockholm, and made his début there in *Faust* in 1914. The world then lost an engineer and gained a musician who became one of few British tenors of the 1920s and 1930s to have an international career at the highest level. He was the first modern British tenor to sing at La Scala (Edgardo in *Lucia di Lammermoor*), and he sang Verdi and Puccini at Covent Garden, Chicago Opera and many other leading houses. After he retired from performing in 1937, he taught in Stockholm until 1948, when he returned to England to teach at the Guildhall School of Music. His students included not only Björling, but also Birgit Nilsson.

Hislop was a fine lyric tenor who, unusually for a British singer, was at home in several languages. Klein lamented his lack of recognition in his home country, castigating Covent Garden for not making more use of him, and comparing him with Jean de Reske.[24] Hislop is one of many English (and French) singers between the wars that John Steane categorised as 'Splendid Isolationists', fine singers all (in the case of the tenors he cites) but limited in their scope and influence.[25] Ironically, one of the reasons for Hislop's lack of work in England is because his international opera commitments meant he had no need to do the English oratorio circuit. Bach and Handel, especially the latter, were the mainstays of English music festivals, and many tenors flourished in the concert environment, opportunities for English opera singers being somewhat limited by Covent Garden's need to focus on the best foreign singers.[26] The reluctance of British singers to sing in any language other than their own had obvious repertoire limitations, precluding much of the mainstream repertoire and privileging lighter English music, which time has not been kind to. There was a technical and interpretative isolation too – English singers had fewer opportunities to work with the best international stars and were rarely in the forefront of interpretative developments, which often makes their recordings sound a little old-fashioned compared with their European contemporaries.

After Tom Burke and Joseph Hislop the most successful English tenors between the wars were Walter Widdop and Frank Mullings. Widdop, born in 1892, was a working-class lad from the Yorkshire town of Halifax, the son of a stonemason, who had no thought of singing beyond his local church; it was not until the age of twenty-one that he learned to read music and started to have singing lessons. His studies were interrupted by the war, which he survived by being placed in the Entertainment Corps by an enlightened commanding officer. Spectacular progress after the war enabled him to make his Covent Garden début as Siegfried in 1924 at the age of thirty-two; he was immediately hailed as a great British Heldentenor and went on to sing Siegmund, Tristan and Tannhäuser, as well as premièring Stravinsky's *Oedipus Rex* under Ansermet in 1936.[27] It was a very late start, and it was perhaps unrealistic to expect an international career; his Wagner, while powerful and impressive, lacked the depth of tenors who spend years studying the music, and he was no actor (Beecham famously accusing him of making love like a hedgehog).[28] It was nevertheless a source of frustration to many critics that such a singer seemed doomed to a life on the English oratorio scene rather than taking German opera houses by storm.

Mullings was a similarly heroic beast, much favoured by Beecham for whom he sang Tristan, Tannhäuser, Siegfried and Canio in the years after World War 1. He also was a favourite oratorio soloist, and stuck resolutely to English. Klein described him as 'the most rumbustious of all our tenors'.[29]

Listening to recordings of these singers is a fascinating experience: they all have large and wonderful natural tenor voices; what they seem to lack is the polish that comes with experience and study, and the depth of character informed by a lifetime of dedication and self-belief.

The arrival of two major new opera houses (Sadlers Wells in 1931 and Glyndebourne in 1934) was a major boost to British tenors, who now had the possibility of serious roles besides whatever they might be offered at Covent Garden. Among those to benefit from the increased opportunities was the Welshman David Lloyd. Born in 1913, Lloyd was of coalmining stock and came to professional singing thanks to his success in local Eisteddfods after his voice broke. He won a scholarship to the Guildhall School of Music to study with Walter Hyde and went on to sing at Glyndebourne in 1938, making his début under Fritz Busch as Macduff in Verdi's *Macbeth*. From then on he specialised in Verdi and Mozart roles, with success at Sadlers Wells and in Europe before and after the war.

British tenors from the mid-nineteenth century to shortly after World War II seem to suffer from a lack of ambition and a sense of unfulfilled potential, in the case of even the most successful singers. The reasons for this are not hard to discover, but underlying the matters of history and convention that determined the nature of singing there were even more fundamental factors that inhibited the growth of a robust vocal culture. The British Isles are simply too small and were too culturally focused on London to develop the infrastructure to sustain a serious singing profession. There were no provincial opera houses that were sufficiently well-endowed to be able to offer career opportunities to young singers. Since opera had historically been the engine of creative vocal endeavour it is not surprising that both the singing and what was sung in Britain was somewhat adrift of the mainstream. The preferred repertoire almost always included lighter British music, with more serious singers often displaying a predilection for both Wagner and Handel, a combination that was much less common elsewhere. There was a real repertoire problem: Britain produced no Gounod, Massenet, Puccini or Mascagni to provide the roles that might have generated the singing. A tendency to start late, often unsure if they were tenors at all, a lack of genuine stage experience and a reluctance to take other languages seriously were all impediments to a wider career for those who did embrace the continental repertoires. Many, however, retired to teaching posts at the London music colleges and were to become a significant influence on future generations. English tenors such as Hislop and Piccaver who did have international careers tended to live in mainland Europe, and thus managed to escape the inward-looking English scene. Those that stayed comfortably within the English musical environment inevitably marginalised themselves in terms of the development of the tenor *Fach*. English taste was of a top-down variety that was very conservative and sometimes absurdly refined. Henry Wood, perhaps the most significant choral conductor of the period, would rather hear the seventy-seven-year-old Sims Reeves with his voice 'nearly vanished' but its diction and phrasing intact than Caruso 'overblowing and squirting out top notes'.[30]

The Italian tenor who had the most success in England between the wars was probably Dino Borgioli, who was one of Toscanini's favourite tenors at La Scala before he settled in London in 1933, after marrying Australian singer Patricia Moore. He had some success in the USA in 1934, singing at the opening of the San Francisco opera house and later in Chicago and at the Met, but preferred to work in England, where he became a director of the New London Opera Company. His elegant, Schipa-like sound was appreciated at both Glyndebourne and Covent Garden, especially in Verdi and Puccini, and he was considered to be a more subtle singer than the other tenor to whom he was sometimes compared, Beniamino Gigli.[31]

The British public and press were generally wary of the histrionic, as a review of Frank Titterton's performance (in English) of the 'Flower Song' from *Carmen* confirms; his 'singing with a manly tone, to my mind, is streets ahead of the snivelling, sobbing and suffering sounds produced by most of the foreign operatic tenor "stars."'[32] English singers are often described as manly, with the implication that 'foreign operatic stars' might be somewhat less so. From a British perspective opera was a foreign art form that was extravagant and exotic, an élite entertainment that did not sit easily with British upper-class containment and understatement, however fashionable opera became.

Post-war revival

After the war British tenors began to have more international success in the traditional repertoire, though the system could still throw up curious one-off successes that did not travel well or very far. James Johnston was one of the most remarkable of the new British tenors to emerge as artistic life began to re-establish its infrastructure. Like Parry Jones (and Max Lorenz) he was the son of butcher, and after a meteoric career of hardly more than ten years he returned to his Belfast butcher's shop, satisfied that he had quit while he was ahead. He was ten years older than his near-contemporary David Lloyd but outlived him by more than twenty years, becoming the leading British operatic tenor in the late '40s and '50s. Like so many of his predecessors he began singing as a baritone and with very little formal training. Between 1945 and 1958 (when he returned to butchery) he gave more than 850 performances in twenty-four roles at both Sadlers Wells and Covent Garden. Of all the late starters Johnston was by far the tardiest, being in his mid forties when he made his Sadlers Wells début in 1945. So impressive was he that Malcolm Sargent preferred him over Heddle Nash when he came to record *Messiah* the following year.[33] His progress from then on was spectacular, taking part in the belated first English performance of Verdi's *Simon Boccanegra* at the Wells in 1948 and singing *Traviata* opposite Schwarzkopf and *Trovatore* with Callas at the Garden. Then, after a performance of *Carmen* in 1958 he decided to return from whence he came, and from then on entertained his customers while providing their Sunday beef. Johnston has inevitably been compared with McCormack, but perhaps it is to Michael Kelly that we should look for a precedent: a tenor who loved music but who loved life even more. Both were very much the exception in the world of their fellow tenors.

Charles Craig made a slower start but had a more enduring career. He was rescued from the Covent Garden chorus in 1951 by Thomas Beecham, who took him under his wing and paid for lessons with Dino Borgioli. Success still eluded him, but finally he made a sensational Covent Garden début in 1959 as Pinkerton, following it up with a highly-acclaimed Cavarodossi. During the '60s he graduated to Radamès and Otello, both roles taking him to international success and making him the finest British Verdi interpreter of his day. Richard Lewis was another British tenor to have real international stage success, appearing in the USA and South America; he created Troilus in Walton's *Troilus and Cressida*, Mark in Tippett's *Midsummer Marriage*, and took part in the first UK performance of Schoenberg's *Moses und Aaron* at Covent Garden in 1965. That same year Alberto Remedios made his Covent Garden début as Dmitri in *Boris Godunov*. The son of a Liverpool docker who had studied at the Royal College of Music, Remedios had begun his career with lyric parts but found himself gravitating towards heavier roles. He sang Mark in the revival of *Midsummer Marriage*, but he is perhaps most famous for his recordings of Wagner with English National Opera in the 1970s, which made him the country's premier (and most italianate) Heldentenor. Lighter voices also managed to find serious international careers: Gerald English (born 1925) was active in contemporary music and also pioneered much earlier music. The lyric tenor Stuart Burrows (born 1933) was especially well suited to Mozart's Tamino and Don Ottavio, both of which roles he has sung with distinction in the USA and Britain.

Peter Pears and the post-war succession

The lack of a serious operatic repertoire in English had always meant that British singers would struggle to match continental singers in mainstream roles, but after World War II homegrown tenors found themselves with an extraordinary opportunity to transform the repertoire: one of the most important opera composers would turn out to be British. In the works of Britten, Tippett and a host of younger composers in the second half of the century, British tenors would at last come into their own. The second half of the century was dominated by the towering figure of Peter Pears, who brought a remarkable intelligence to everything he performed whether on the stage or in the concert hall. Not everyone considered Pears' voice beautiful; his voice had a 'clear, reedy, almost instrumental quality [which is] capable of wide variety of expression and . . . is displayed with great flexibility, if no wide range of colour'.[34] Like Dietrich Fischer-Dieskau, Pears used his voice in the service of the music, not the other way round. His lifelong collaboration with Benjamin Britten not only inspired a new generation of British tenors but produced singable new stage roles which have revitalised and extended the canon, and a number of cycles which have found a ready place in the tenor songbook. His operatic roles, Peter Grimes especially, were models that were unsurpassed for many years. He modestly credited his reliability and stamina to his occasional lessons with Lucy Manén, but the textual insights that the new singing required come from the intelligence of the individual singer and are not something that a singing teacher can provide.[35] He was also a fine Evangelist in Bach's Passions and a keen enthusiast for English renaissance and baroque music. He was not, by any stretch of the imagination, an 'early music' singer, but his questioning intelligence and his advocacy of a singing that could encompass anything from madrigals to grand opera, inspired many young singers to experiment. Although he was at Oxford for only a short time, his intellectual approach to singing fitted well with that of choral scholars leaving the universities of Oxford and Cambridge.

Pears' approximate contemporaries – the generation of English singers born around the first two decades of the twentieth century – included a number of elegant and intelligent tenors. Wilfred Brown (born 1921) had relatively little training as a singer but was an accomplished linguist and brought a delicacy to the singing of Lieder and French song. Alexander Young (born 1920) was a noted oratorio singer who also gave many fine stage performances of new works, including the first UK performance of Stravinsky's *The Rake's Progress*. Many of Pears' contemporaries and successors (he can hardly be said to have had rivals in a conventional sense) have taken on the Britten roles and creatively extended the interpretative possibilities that were so rooted in the partnership between Britten and his tenor.

The mantle of Pears fell in the first instance on Robert Tear, who was one of many singers to come out of King's College Cambridge, but one of the first to transcend the English choral tradition (he was born in Wales) and create an international career in opera. Tear worked with the English Opera Group and shared many of the Britten roles with Pears. He created Dov in Tippett's *Knot Garden* but also explored the earlier dramatic repertoire, making his Covent Garden début with Lensky in 1970. One of the most intelligent of singers, he has since performed all over the world. More recent British tenor successes have included Philip Langridge, Ian Partridge, Anthony Rolfe-Johnson, John Mark Ainsley, Ian Bostridge and Mark Padmore, all of whom have brought new insights into operatic roles and the interpretation of songs.

These are sophisticated singers with broad musical and intellectual interests. Unlike their purely operatic counterparts they tend not to be primarily concerned with making beautiful sounds (though they do that too); they are engaged with a search for musical meaning that is not constrained by the dedicated opera tenors' need to confine themselves to a small number of commercially viable roles. While international opera stars strive towards a kind of perfect vocalism in which they can only be distinguished from each other by personality, it is in the more commercially modest achievements of some of their less famous counterparts that new developments in tenorality can be heard. The performances of Monteverdi by Rolfe-Johnson and Ainsley matched instinctive musicianship with a creative intelligence derived from their acknowledgement of earlier singing styles, and Langridge has excelled both in Britten and in post-Britten roles. Although the subject of his PhD thesis is somewhat remote from singing, Ian Bostridge underpins his performances with meticulous research that has led to remarkable performances across a range of media and genres, and many hail him as the finest British tenor of his generation. Mark Padmore, another alumnus of King's Cambridge who made his mark in baroque music, has revitalised the song recital with particular attention to Lieder.[36] All of the current crop of British tenors (which I will leave history to judge) share an ability to go beyond what they have been taught; this may mean a harder and longer road to success, but it bodes well for the future.

CHAPTER 8

FRANCE AND THE DECLINE OF LINGUISTIC LYRICISM

France had been as important as Italy during the nineteenth century, but the Duprez experience had served to re-energise the Italian tradition and in retrospect must have seemed something of an anomaly. The less forceful French style that had its roots in pre-Duprez elegance continued to flourish within France, but became increasingly un-exportable as the Italians carried all before them.

The Conservatoire tradition

Paris, like London, continued to be a magnet for opera singers of all nationalities from the nineteenth into the twenty-first centuries. The Paris Conservatoire was a very different institution from the English music colleges, however. Students received a rigorous, all-round musical education, grounded in a tradition that went back to its Napoleonic roots. Above all, it epitomised French musical artistry, and the seriousness of intent that succeeding generations were expected to show towards the national cultural heritage: all French tenors would study there if they could, even if they started at one of the provincial outposts. The singing teaching had absorbed the Italian bel canto tradition and morphed it into something uniquely French, adding a linguistic fastidiousness to the legato line. The result was generations of tenors whose singing was imbued with clarity, elegance and restraint – a sophisticated collection of attributes that perfectly suited the lyric and lyric-dramatic French repertoire, but which would too often prove insufficient for the more macho Italian (and German) roles as the twentieth century wore on.

Success at home was relatively easy to achieve for Francophone singers: there were two major opera companies in Paris and La Monnaie in Brussels as well as provincial companies in both France and Belgium. Like some wine, however, French singing did not travel well, and was particularly unsuccessful at the Metropolitan Opera in New York, with very few tenors contracted for more than one season. This process repeated itself over many years, as the Met's talent scouts never quite grasped the management's reluctance to make room for anything that was not Italian or German. They would make regular trips to Europe, be seduced by leading French stars in their home environment, and then be surprised to find that New Yorkers preferred the less complicated, less delicate, more romantic Italians.

Height and depth

The legendary Gilbert-Louis Duprez taught at the Paris Conservatoire from 1842 to 1850 and then founded his own school in 1853. Up until his death in 1896 he was still consulted by many tenors anxious for the master's approval. Among those to work with him was Léon Escalaïs, son of a farmer from Narbonne, who had first studied at the Toulouse Conservatoire before moving to the Paris school, where he graduated in 1883. Escalaïs, like his mentor, had phenomenal high notes. Building on his *Tell* (on which he was coached by Duprez) he was soon in demand for the more robust roles of Meyerbeer and Halévy. Successful in Paris, he hoped for a triumph in Milan, but his Eléazar was a disaster and he never returned to La Scala. He became a success in France, but like many of his countrymen was unable to make much of an impression abroad. His one trip across the Atlantic did produce the remarkable achievement of four repeats of 'Di quella pira' from *Tell*, unleashing an unprecedented torrent of top Cs, but no subsequent visits.[1] His 1905/6 recordings hint at what Duprez may have sounded like: the high notes are brilliant without sounding forced, and join seamlessly with his middle register. Despite the power there is still a sense of a text being enunciated, rather than brute force for its own sake.[2]

Charles Dalmorès was a rare transatlantic French success. He began his career as a horn player (as Fritz Wunderlich was later to do) and was thought to be too valuable an instrumentalist to study at the Conservatoire as a singer.

He persisted with his bizarre ambition and after his vocal début in Rouen in 1899 (having been appointed horn professor at the Lyon Conservatoire five years before) he was contracted first to La Monnaie in Brussels and then to Covent Garden, where he gave the British premières of works by Saint-Saëns, Massenet and Charpentier. In 1908 he sang Lohengrin at Bayreuth and by the second decade of the century was singing Tristan in Chicago, becoming at one stage the highest-paid tenor in the USA after Caruso. Unlike many Wagnerians, he was also said to be a fine actor.[3]

The Belgian Fernand Ansseau, less powerful and more lyrical than Franz, stepped into many of his roles at La Monnaie and in Chicago. He was never a Wagnerian, but his rich lyric-dramatic tenor suited the French repertoire and Verdi very well. He started life as a baritone but studied with Flemish tenor Ernst Van Dyke for three years and made his début as Jean in Massenet's *Hérodiade* in 1913. Ansseau was a man of simple tastes and in 1920 joined a very select bunch of tenors of any nationality to turn down an offer of a Met contract from Gatti-Casazza. Three years later, however, he joined the Chicago company, where he had a fruitful collaboration with Mary Garden. The Chicagoans were not particularly concerned with what language their stars sang in, which gave the singers a certain linguistic leeway. During a perform-ance of *Tosca* opposite Mary Garden he sang 'Recondita armonia' in Italian, followed by the love duet in French (which was what Garden preferred). He reverted to Italian for the second act as Vanni Marcoux would only sing in Italian, and then followed Garden back into French for Act 3.[4]

French dramatic singing developed further with René Verdière, René Maison and Paul Franz. All French dramatic tenors managed *Samson* and most undertook *Lohengrin*. Verdière was also a successful Otello, and Maison was one of the few French successes at the Met (helped, as a Belgian, by being bilingual in French and German). The greatest of them all was Franz who became a truly great Wagnerian, giving the first *Parsifal* at the Opéra in 1913. Franz was born François Gautier and sang as an amateur baritone while working as a clerk on the railways. He failed to get into the Conservatoire but in 1908 won an amateur singing competition as a tenor, having changed his name to Franz. He was by then over thirty, and mature enough to cope with the heaviest of roles. He went on to make his début at the Opéra in 1909 in *Lohengrin*, in which his physical presence, effortless delivery and flawless pronunciation attracted impressive notices from the press. He became a favourite at Covent Garden, retiring from the stage in 1938, having become a teacher at the Conservatoire that had rejected him more than twenty years before.

The lyric tradition

A high tensile power is present in many of the Conservatoire-educated tenors who recorded in the first decade of the century, such as Agustarello Affre and Georges Imbart de la Tour, but the pre-Duprez lyricism is also much in evidence. Léon David and Edmond Clément were both Conservatoire students of Belgian tenor Victor Warot, whose pedigree went back to the mid-nineteenth century (he was born in 1831). David was at home in both French and Italian lyric repertoires, frequently singing *Rigoletto* and *Traviata* as well as *Werther, Manon* and even *Carmen.* His greatest successes were in France and Belgium (he gave the La Monnaie première of *La Bohème* in 1900 with Puccini present), and had an invitation to sing with the Boston Opera not coincided with the birth of his son, he might have been a rare French success in the USA.[5]

Edmond Clément's experience at the Met shows just how difficult it was for French tenors to make an impact. As the leading tenor of the Opéra-Comique, he was engaged to sing French roles in the 1909 season. Gatti-Casazza then insisted that in future seasons he would have to learn Italian roles as there was little demand for French opera. Clément refused and never again sang with the company, although he was appreciated by the American public and subsequently sang in Boston Opera for two years. He resented the imbalance between the two strands: 'Italian tenors do not sing French operas. Why should French tenors sing Italian operas. . . . Still, I realise now that to make a career at the Metropolitan under its present direction it is necessary to learn Italian and to sing Italian.'[6] Both these tenors had light, bright voices with exquisite phrasing and control, coupled with a lightness at the top facilitated by artistic use of the head voice; the controlled *diminuendi* in which they changed smoothly from full voice to *mezza voce* were musical rather than the dramatic effects that their Italian counterparts would have wanted.[7]

Between the wars

The interwar years were notable for the number of successful 'French' tenors who were not actually of French origin. Cézar Vezzani, José Luccioni (a pupil of David and Escalaïs) and Gaston Micheletti were Corsican; Miguel Villabella was born in Bilbao, and Giuseppe Lugo was Italian. This cosmopolitan infusion may well have contributed a subtle layer of sophistication to French tenor singing. Villabella and Lugo could presumably have worked in their home countries but were happy in the French cultural environment; the Corsicans came from a country heavily influenced by Mediterranean culture (and which together with Wales has probably produced more singers per hectare than any other in Europe).[8] The result of this musical melting pot is perhaps less easily defined and therefore less marketable outside France. Of this group only Luccioni had real international success, with a small number of transatlantic appearances; after the second world war he had more success as a film actor. They all make a recognisably French sound, Villabella in particular having soaring top notes, for which he uses a *voix mixte* that takes him easily to top D.

Vezzani's career was a significant one, and it illustrates how successfully the Francophone cultural infrastructure could sustain careers within itself. Little is known about his early life, but his family moved from Bastia in Corsica to Toulon in mainland France after the death of his father; mother and son subsequently moved to Paris and Vezzani ended up studying with Agnès Borgo, a Conservatoire-educated dramatic soprano whom he later married. The two were invited to Boston Opera but the war intervened; Vezzani was called up and was wounded (a rare event in the tenor soldiery), though not seriously enough to prevent a return to the stage at the end of hostilities. His instinctive Corsican fire may have made him difficult to deal with, and in the early '20s he seems to have had terminal problems at the Opéra-Comique with whom he started his career, and rarely appeared in Paris thereafter. He was able to maintain a successful career in Belgium and France, working in some two dozen provincial houses as well as French-speaking north Africa. His recorded legacy shows him to have been a powerful singer with a consistent vibrato (though not as much as his fellow Corsican Micheletti), capable of making the text absolutely clear throughout his compass; being taught by a Wagnerian soprano clearly did him no harm vocally but perhaps left him not the subtlest of singers. He excelled in the French dramatic repertoire, and recorded extracts from *Lohengrin* (though he may not have sung the role onstage).[9]

Georges Thill

One tenor who did not flourish at the Paris Conservatoire was Georges Thill, who found the teaching of André Gresse uninspiring. In theory a singer can learn from a singer of any voice (or even none, in some cases), but as we have frequently seen in these pages, there has often been a historical correlation between tenors and high-voiced teachers, whether they were castrati, sopranos or other tenors. Gresse was a bass of impressive pedigree (his father Léon, also a bass, had been a stalwart of the Opéra until his death in 1900) and no doubt passed on to Thill the Conservatoire ethos of disciplined application of traditional principles. Very few tenors seem to have been successfully taught by basses, and it was only when Thill started to study with Fernando De Lucia that his technique came into focus.

Thill was born into a middle-class, musical family in 1897, and sang as an amateur as a youth until his stockbroker uncle suggested he audition for the Conservatoire. Until then his knowledge of singing had been gleaned from listening to recordings of Caruso (whose voice his own did not remotely resemble). Impressed with the progress made by his friend Mario Podesta at the feet of De Lucia, Thill moved to Naples in 1921 and began two years of study with the ageing maestro.[10] De Lucia's voice was also nothing like Thill's and his teaching was every bit as traditional as that handed down by the Conservatoire, but in Thill De Lucia found a protégé to whom he could pass on his own vocal secrets. As Thill already had a working technique, the two were able to work slowly and thoroughly on both French and Italian repertoires, exploring the necessary links between technique, articulation and emotional expression. De Lucia had no method, but responded to his students in a pragmatic way, correcting faults as necessary.[11] Eight months after Thill arrived in Naples he found himself attending the funeral of his one-time idol Caruso, and hearing his new mentor singing a valedictory 'Pietà Signore' by Stradella.[12]

Thill returned to Paris but at first success came slowly, as he tried out a variety of roles that he felt he should be able to do as a former student of De Lucia. He began to be offered dramatic roles that would in the past have gone to Paul Franz, who was then moving into Heldentenor territory, and by 1927 he was firmly established at L'Opéra with a number of heavier roles that included Lohengrin. The following year he became the first French singer to be invited to the amphitheatre at Verona, where he achieved a triumph with *Turandot*, which he went on to repeat at La Scala the next year. His international reputation was then virtually guaranteed, and he made successful débuts at Buenos Aires' Teatro Colón in 1929 in six French and Italian operas, and the Met two years later (*Roméo et Juliette*, *Faust* and *Aida*). Until his retirement in the late 1940s he was the star French tenor, helped by a series of successful recordings and a willingness to sing almost anything that was thrown at him. He later regretted being unable to say no to works that were very taxing, citing his performances of *Tell* and *Carmen* on consecutive nights as examples of poor judgement on his part, but he became an institution in France as a handsome, charismatic figure who represented all that was best in French singing. Ironically, in 1949 he applied for a teaching post at the Conservatoire, and after giving a specimen lesson was rejected on the grounds that the methods of De Lucia were not appropriate. French singing, even at its best, was apparently not good enough for itself.[13]

The last decades of the twentieth century saw a continuing decline in the style of singing associated with the French language. In the first decade of the twenty-first century even the classic French dramatic repertoire (which remains popular with the record-buying public) has become almost the exclusive property of young Italian or Italian-influenced South American stars. The Swiss tenor Hughes Cuénod has the distinction of being one of the oldest living tenors of international reputation. Born in 1902, he studied in Geneva and Vienna and went on to specialise in character roles, accumulating an extraordinarily eclectic repertoire from medieval and baroque music through to contemporary works over most of the twentieth century. At the time of writing, he is still living in Switzerland at the age of 106. His remarkable career has succeeded in part because of his keen musical intelligence, extremely catholic musical tastes, and an ability and willingness to take on new challenges. He thus managed to achieve a colourful profile despite the gradual disappearance of the traditional French tenor, which in many respects he resembled. His was a light voice (at its best in Mozart), not weighty enough for the French dramatic repertory but perfect for the mélodies of Poulenc, Roussel and Honegger, with whom he frequently collaborated. His reputation as a recitalist saw him undertake many tours of the USA, and he made his Met début as the Emperor in *Turandot* in 1987 at the age of 85 (he is still the oldest Met débutant). Of the younger generation of Francophone tenors only Michel Sénéchal has established himself in the Cuénod mould.

Cuénod has lived long enough to see the French style almost completely succumb to Italian internationalism.[14] Of those who continued to assert the old lyric style, the most high-profile has probably been the French-Canadian Léopold Simoneau, who died in 2006 at the age of ninety. Considered by Steane to be the finest Mozart tenor since John McCormack, he had successes in France and Italy, and managed the obligatory lyric tenors' single season at the Met.[15] Among the last practitioners of the older French style, with its exquisite attention to textual nuance, was the Monégasque tenor Alain Vanzo, who died in 2002 at the age of seventy-three. Vanzo had all the qualities of elegance and restraint that connoisseurs of French singing admire and which are no longer sufficient in the age of the stadium tenor. Like so many of his peers he made just one appearance at the Met (in 1977 with the Paris Opéra company). Even though his repertoire expanded to include a number of Italian roles, the public preferred the larger voices and personalities of tenors such as Alfredo Kraus and Nicolai Gedda (neither of them Italian, but masters of Italian style and technique). Vanzo's voice was a direct descendant of Edmond Clément's, effortlessly ascending to high C with a mixed head voice/falsetto technique that predates the chested the high notes that have come to dominate modern tenor singing (and which, ironically, can be traced back to the Frenchman Gilbert-Louis Duprez).[16] The true inheritor of the Duprez mantle is perhaps Roberto Alagna. The son of Sicilian parents but born and raised in France, his vocal experience (even in the French dramatic repertoire) has been entirely Italian, as it became for Duprez a century and a half before him.

ЛАУРЕАТ СТАЛИНСКОЙ ПРЕМИИ
ЗАСЛ. АРТ. РСФСР, ОРДЕНОНОСЕЦ
С.Я.ЛЕМЕШЕВ

CHAPTER 9

RUSSIA AND THE PRESERVATION
OF LOST TRADITIONS

Russia has also evolved very differently from the rest of Europe; having been one of the key stops on any successful tenor's itinerary during the late nineteenth and early twentieth centuries, the country became virtually cut off from the mainstream of Western singing until the Cold War began to thaw. This resulted in an isolation that preserved its own traditions, based on vocal fashions that prevailed before the Revolution.

Italian singing may have been problematic for the French, but it was embraced wholeheartedly by the Russians towards the end of the nineteenth century. While the most of the rest of Europe and the Americas succumbed to Italian singing in the twentieth century, elements of something older survived in Russia after cultural and political links with the West were severely restricted once the effects of the Revolution began to bite. For those interested in the archaeology of the tenor there is a special fascination with the tenors of the Russia empire. The survival of the feudal system until more than one hundred years after the last vestiges of it had vanished from western Europe meant that cultural life was in the hands of aristocratic amateurs until late in the nineteenth century, when the social polarity finally began to dissolve sufficiently among musicians for singers of all classes to be offered lessons at the St Petersburg Conservatory. The models on which these young musicians based themselves were the successful touring stars from the west, especially those from Italy, where the best young Russian tenors would aspire to study. There had always been plenty of money available for the aristocratic enjoyment of opera, and tenors from Rubini onwards would make the trip to the Bolshoi in Moscow (founded in 1825 and rebuilt in its present form in 1856) or the Mariinsky in St Petersburg (founded in 1860 and now the Kirov).[1]

The Revolution of 1917 and the subsequent establishment of the Soviet Union, after a brief period of enlightenment in the post-war years, reinforced an inherent tendency towards conservatism by virtually isolating Russian singers from the rest of the world. Deprived of contact with such centres of tenorial culture as the Met, Covent Garden and La Scala, the Russian tradition developed with a rigour of its own, based on traditional principles that were applied by the conservatoires established in all the states of the union as part of a political agenda to foster education in the arts. When contact of sorts was resumed in the Kruschev era the west was treated to the sound of tenors that recalled a much earlier period in the history of the voice. This process of revelation took another leap forward with the fragmentation of the Soviet Union into its constituent republics at the end of the twentieth century, as opera companies that were formerly state-supported found themselves with little or no funding. The more entrepreneurial of these then looked to the west, and companies such as the Chesinau from Georgia found themselves touring provincial European theatres. In doing so they opened a window for their audiences onto a singing tradition that has its roots in the singing of almost a hundred years ago. The increasing availability of CD transfers has added considerably to our knowledge of the era.[2]

Pre-revolutionary Russians

The early history of Russian tenors is incomplete and under-researched.[3] At the moment, modern history of the Russian tenor begins with Mikhail Medvedyev, the creator of Lensky in Tchaikovsky's *Eugene Onegin*, and Nikolai Figner, who first sang Hermann in *Pique Dame*. Medvedyev was a dramatic lyric tenor with a wide repertoire that spanned Otello (which was compared with Tamberlik's), Tannhäuser, Raoul and Faust, as well as Hermann (many thought his better than Figner's). As a teenager in Kiev, he was discovered by the composer and teacher Nikolai Rubinstein who took him to the Moscow Conservatory, where he was taught stagecraft by the actor

Samarin (from the Moscow Maly Theatre) and singing by the ex-patriot Italian Giacomo Galvani. He gave the Lensky première at the Conservatory in 1879, while a third-year student. He quickly became successful in Russia and then in the USA, where he toured a programme of Tchaikovsky songs and set himself up as a promoter. Returning to Russia after mixed fortunes in the west, he tried again as an impresario but from 1911 onwards became a full-time teacher. Recordings of him exist, including one of 'Der Leiermann' from Schubert's *Winterreise* (sung in Russian).

The somewhat chaotic memoirs of baritone Sergei Levik, whose teacher he was, contain many descriptions of his teaching methods, which seem to have been inspirational rather than dogmatic. 'Italomania', as Levik put it, infected both private and conservatory teaching. Students would be taught in classes, using a mixture of the idiosyncratic methods favoured by individual teachers, and the exercises of Bordogni, Conconne and Panofka (which were in use at the Paris Conservatoire). Levik seems not to have quite understood exactly what the 'advanced Italian method' was, perhaps because it was the only 'method' taught, so seemed the natural thing to do. He points out that with no radio and with performances difficult to get to for most people, it was only those with a naturally good voice who considered training for a singing career. As a result, they were two-thirds of the way to being competent before they started with their teacher.[4]

The Conservatories of Moscow and St Petersburg had famous women teachers, and many taught privately, especially sopranos, retired from the stage and often very old. This is unlike the Italian tradition, where the teachers of tenors were almost always other tenors once the castrati were no longer on the scene. However, the teaching of tenors by high voices that they would not be able to imitate may go some way to explain the lyrical qualities of many Russian-trained tenors.

Nikolai Figner entered the St Petersburg Conservatory in 1878 and went on to Naples for further study, making his début there in 1882 at the Teatro Sannazaro in Gounod's *Philémon et Baucis*. After successes in northern Italy he toured South America where he became a friend of the young Toscanini, with whom he sang Catalani's *Edmea* at La Scala Milan. There he met his future wife, the soprano Medea Mei. The two joined the Imperial Opera in 1887, Figner making his Russian début in *Aïda* at the Mariinsky and going on to give the first performances in Russia of the latest Italian operas. He also sang Lensky in Tchaikovsky's *Eugen Onegin* and in 1890 premièred *The Queen of Spades* with Medea (who was pregnant at the time). Tchaikovsky was very fond of the couple, believing Figner to be the ideal Hermann, and wrote parts of the opera at their house. *The Queen of Spades* made stars of them both, and in 1892 Tchaikovsky repeated the success, writing *Iolanta* for the husband and wife team. The following year, a few months before his death, he dedicated his *Six Romances* opus 73 to Figner, who went on to become one of the most distinguished tenors and teachers. He was one of the last tenors to have a successful career in both east and west before the revolutionary fog descended. He died in 1918, having lost most of his possessions to revolutionary fervour.

Ivan Yerschov was some ten years younger than Figner, which meant that his voice is better preserved on record and that he was better equipped to survive the Revolution, finally retiring from the Mariinsky in 1929 after thirty-four years. There he had sung all of the great Wagner roles as well as Otello and many Russian works. Like Figner, Yerschov began his studies at the St Petersburg Conservatory and then went to Italy, returning to Russia in 1894 and the following year joining the Mariinsky where he spent the rest of his life. He had the *mezza voce* that seems to come easily to Russian singers, but he could also turn on the power for Otello and a curiously lyrical Forging Song. Not quite a Heldentenor, he was something of a superspinto (a reminder of the limits of categorisation, as Sergei Levik cautions), and was often compared to Tamagno. He was, according to Levik, an impressive stage presence, with a remarkable ability to synthesise his vocal and histrionic talents.[5]

His successor in lyric roles was the Moscow-trained Leonid Sobinov, who also began his professional life under the Tsar and ended it under Lenin. He came from a middle-class background and had begun a career as a lawyer before his teacher Alexandra Gorchakova (an early example of a female teacher of tenors) suggested he audition for the Bolshoi. He was awarded a two-year contract and made his début as Sinodal in Rubinstein's *Demon*. He then took on the Russian repertoire including Lensky, where he was favourably compared with Figner. In 1904 he first performed outside Russia at La Scala, where he impressed the Italian audience as Ernesto in *Don Pasquale*. He returned several times, between performances at the Bolshoi and Mariinsky, adding Gounod, Massenet, Puccini, Verdi and Wagner to his repertoire (his Lohengrin was compared with that of Yerschov). Conscripted in 1914, he was unable to continue at the Imperial Opera and was given the task of organising concerts for the wounded. He supported the Revolution and had various cultural posts under the new regime (he was the first elected director of the Bolshoi), but his life was touched by tragedy, losing one son in the civil war and the other to emigration. Although he was a much-decorated figure the true circumstances of his life under Soviet rule are only just emerging.[6] Sobinov's 1910 recording of Lohengrin's Farewell is an example of how Italianate the singing of the Russian houses was at this time – almost suspended on the breath, exquisitely shaped yet having the strength to delineate the character.[7]

Although the Tsar controlled the fate of the Mariinsky and the Bolshoi there was occasional competition from private opera companies set up by wealthy bourgeois individuals. One such was Savva Mamontov's Moskovskaya Chastnaya Russkaya Opera where Dmitri Smirnov made his début in 1903. He then studied intensively with Pavlovskaya who obtained an audition at the Bolshoi for him. He made a successful début the following year in *Demon*, an occasion which marked Rachmaninov's first appearance as an orchestral conductor. He found himself frequently sharing roles with Sobinov, who was by then the Bolshoi's leading tenor. Success in Paris 1907–9 under Diaghilev led to his being offered a contract at the Met. Here he had mixed success, his elegant exaggerations seeming rather old-fashioned compared with the larger and more straightforward sound of Caruso. His visit coincided with John McCormack's début season, and the Irish tenor fared rather better as a foil to Caruso than did the Russian.[8] Smirnov returned to Russia, but when the Revolution struck he chose to emigrate. He had a successful career in the west (although, ironically, dying in Soviet-occupied Riga in 1944). Sobinov and Smirnov were pre-revolutionary rivals before their career paths diverged; that rivalry continues to this day as record collectors debate their relative merits. Vocally they are dissimilar, Smirnov having a fast vibrato which is largely absent from the singing of Sobinov.

Post-revolutionary tenors

We live in a very different world from that of the Soviet Union, and from our perspective in a fragmented late capitalist society it is very easy to interpret the Soviet years as monolithic and alien. In an age when opera stars are made and unmade overnight, and whose main concerns are often their image and their bank balance, it is worth pausing for a moment to consider what merits the 'lost years' of the old Russian system might have had. It is a minefield for the historian, and Russian historians will be renegotiating that minefield for generations to come, after which non-Russian speakers may get to understand something of the era. In the meantime it may not be over-simplistic to suggest that the system did exemplify an alternative way of looking at things. Without getting into a sterile ideological debate we can look at video and aural footage of Soviet tenors and make an attempt to understand what they were trying to achieve. In the time of Verdi there was a direct connection between opera as an art form and the people – the theatres may have been stratified along class lines, but social divisions dissolved when it came to fêting the great tenor of the day, whoever he might be. Such a link between the genre and the ordinary person may still happen in opera houses in provincial Italian or German houses (possibly), but in the traditional centres of operatic excellence in

London, Milan, Vienna, Berlin, Paris and New York (for example) the audience is likely to have paid a great deal of money for a seat (despite support from sponsorship or government agency) and is unlikely to follow the stars back to their hotel.

Soviet ideology had a complicated take on art: the essentially 'bourgeois' nature of classical music was problematic, and the solution to the problem was to make it available for everyone. So, broadly speaking, instead of the exclusive private aristocratic performances of pre-revolutionary Russia, operatic singing would be brought within the educational and cultural reach of everybody. The system never did solve the problem of how composers were supposed to reconcile individual genius with compulsory art for all, but as far as the singing was concerned there was no question: the Communist party knew what good singing was when it heard it and believed that it should be available for all (and in Russian), whatever the nature of the composition. So every Soviet citizen would appreciate the Simpleton in *Boris Godunov* or Lensky in *Onegin* and would also enjoy Kozlovsky singing officially-sanctioned folksongs to the miners.[9] Underlying this is an assumption that the appreciation of high art is fundamental to the running of civil society. It is surely not a coincidence that Moscow and Leningrad had a number of opera houses and many strictly disciplined (if under-resourced) conservatories but nothing resembling a modern police force or the rule of law. The result was (at least in theory, if not always in practice) opera for all to a very high standard throughout the Soviet empire, isolated from the rest of the world but able in the fullness of time to produce artists of the stature of Angela Gheorghiu.[10]

There is a characteristic lyricism that informs much Russian tenor singing. There were more dramatic tenors, of course, but Wagner (with the possible exception of Lohengrin) had not had great exposure in Russia in the decade or so before the Revolution, and native Russian composers wrote serious roles for heroic basses. Tenors made their mark in the Romantic lyric operas of Puccini, Massenet and Mascagni and the voice was associated with sweetness rather than power. It may also be significant that they were as likely to have been taught by women as men (Sobinov and Alexandra Gorchakova, Smirnov and Pavlovskya, Kozlovsky and Elena Muravyova); this is not something that generally happened in the west until much later in the twentieth century and obviously exposed them to a different kind of model, one which recalls the castrato–tenor relationship of the eighteenth century. This was at a time when singers in the west were opting for a Caruso-like model of muscular vocalism, a model that was unavailable to most Russians from the 1920s onwards.

One of the prime examples of a true post-revolutionary tenor is Ivan Kozlovsky, who sings with the all lyrical ease and exquisite phrasing that is the hallmark of the Russian style. Kozlovsky joined the Bolshoi in 1927 and was a regular soloist there until 1954. He was the archetypal Soviet artist, apparently completely at home in the system which was all he knew (since Stalin, knowing his worth, refused to let him leave the country). He was a perfectionist and was able to develop his art without worrying about 'the market', knowing that if he got it right he would be appreciated by both his political masters and the public (which he undoubtedly was). For Kozlovsky, so integrated were life, politics and music that on his wall he hung a certificate from Stalin thanking him for his financial contribution to the purchase of an army tank.[11] His singing of the Simpleton in *Boris Godunov* was taken to represent the plight of the Soviet people, and in its *faux naïf* way is one of the most moving interpretations of the role. There are signs of an attempt to rehabilitate some of the early Soviet singers, about whom information was scarce and possibly open to misinterpretation; this is not so far the case with Kozlovsky.[12]

Kozlovky's singing may preserve something much older than the Soviet pre-war tradition. In 1954 he recorded (in Russian) Almaviva's cavatina 'Ecco ridente' from *Il Barbiere di Siviglia*.[13] It does not represent the tenor at his limpid best, but when he arrives somewhat breathlessly at the final cadence point he sings a cadenza that covers three octaves (Ex. 11).

Example 11 Kozlovsky's cadenza from 'Ecco ridente'

This is sung in the original key, although the pitch is a little wayward. Kozlovsky may just have been messing about, of course, but such a demonstration of bravura height and depth is relatively rare anywhere, and raises the question of where he got the idea from. He was also capable of being very free with his tempi, in a manner which the old Italian tradition required but which has become foreign to modern western singing.[14] Kozlovsky was born in the Ukraine and attended the Kiev Institute of Music and Drama from 1918 to 1920 under Elena Muravyova.[15] The opera house in Kiev was built in 1867 and rebuilt after a fire in 1901; many of the great tenors of the west would have sung there, and it is quite possible that Muravyova or her predecessor witnessed Masini or one of his contemporaries and passed on to her pupils an older Rossinian tradition than was customary for the Romantic repertoire. There was not much call for *The Barber* and its decadent virtuosity during the

Soviet period, but perhaps something stirred in Kozlovsky's memory when he came to record Almaviva in the 1950s.

Film footage of him in action confirms that his mouth opens little further than in speech. This is a characteristic of much older singing, and seems to draw the listener in rather than project outwards. 'The more you scream, the less you sing', he said, which is in direct contrast to his contemporaries, the post-Caruso Björling and Tauber (and even De Lucia, according to his pupil Thill) who opened their mouths a lot wider and were clearly focused on projecting their voices as far as possible.[16] It may be, as Jürgen Kesting suggests, that what we hear in Kozlovsky and his fellow Russians is something closer to eighteenth century 'bel canto' than the Caruso model that was applied in the west during the first half of the century.[17]

Kozlovky's Soviet contemporaries included Sergei Lemeshev and Georgy Nelepp. Lemeshev was a handsome and charismatic figure who has been compared to Tauber and Kiepura, having made a number of films. Vocally, however, as with many of the lyric Russians, it is the sound of McCormack (or perhaps Gigli) that he most resembles. His joining of the registers is surely something that harks back to a much older technique. Although he is perfectly capable of chesting high notes (the top C in 'Plus blanche' from *Les Huguenots*, for example) there are many examples of his going seamlessly into falsetto. In Auber's 'J'ai revu nos amis' from Act 3 of *Fra Diavolo* there is a remarkable example of immaculate register changing (Ex. 12).

falsetto -------------------------------- | chest voice -------------- | falsetto --------------------

Example 12 Lemeshev's alternating chest voice and falsetto in *Fra Diavolo* (Auber)

The first three bars are sung entirely in a virile falsetto; he then reverts to chest voice for five notes, changing back to falsetto for the remainder of the phrase. The difference between the two timbres is only obvious to a careful listener, and must have given Lemeshev enormous flexibility over a considerable range. He only goes up to B here but one feels he could soar much higher if required (or inspired). When this same elegant lyricism is applied to Lohengrin we may be hearing a kind of singing that Wagner might have appreciated: firmly grounded in the Italian tradition, yet with a warmth and declamation that matches beauty of tone to the requirements of the drama, and with an abundance of portamenti that would be alien to current German Heldentenors.[18]

Nelepp is different – firmer and more in the Yershov mould. Taken up by Glazunov, he made his début at the Mariinsky in 1929, singing there until moving to the Bolshoi in 1944. He brought more power to dramatic lyric roles and might have gone on to heavier roles had he not died at the age of fifty-three. Nelepp is another Soviet singer whose history is currently being revised, and as more recordings become available and more archives are opened up we can expect to see more pieces of the Russian jigsaw laboriously fitted together.

One obvious weakness of the Soviet system is that even singers who embraced the ideology without question would not flourish if they found themselves on the wrong side of cultural or political officialdom. Georgi Vinogradov may have been one such, having had a successful if limited career in radio before the war (a Russian Joseph Schmidt, perhaps), then in the Red Army from 1943 to 1951, after which he disappears from the radar, dying in 1979 a few days before his seventy-second birthday. A younger contemporary of Kozlovsky, Nelepp and Lemeshev, he never quite made it to the peak of Soviet stardom. The recent release of a four-CD set of his recordings reveals him to be a sweetly lyrical tenor, who on record certainly stands comparison with his more well-known rivals. It may be that, also like Schmidt, he failed to make the transition from radio to the stage, with the result that his career did not acquire the specific gravity needed for take-off. Little is known in the West about his life, and the fog of rumour includes various conspiracy theories that may have involved him in embarrassing the Soviet authorities.[19]

Kozlovsky and his contemporaries perhaps represent the most perfect integration of language and music, the two meeting in a vocal synthesis that Italian promises but Russian actually achieves. The same effect happens writ large with Russian Heldenenors. Nikander Khanayev's performance of Siegfried's forging song is one of the most energetic and electrifying on record; there are few singers who do not sound strained when trying to put across the metaphorical violence of this piece, but Khanayev's rendering, though loud and powerful as one would expect, has an air of menace that comes from the suggestion that if necessary he could sing at twice the volume and still have power to spare.[20] The combination of lyricism and power is one that appeals to modern audiences; it is one of the factors underlying the Italian domination of the current tenorocracy. In its Russian language version, this synthesis has an attraction that could yet make an impact on tenor singing in the twenty-first century.

CHAPTER 10

THE TWENTIETH-CENTURY HELDENTENOR

The Heldentenors of the late nineteenth century and the early part of the twentieth had all been possessed of large voices but were generally able to contain themselves sufficiently to sing certain lighter roles, in particular those of Mozart. Their first experiences, even if they had begun as baritones (which many of them did), were often in lyrical dramatic roles, from which they made their way to Verdi and Wagner as they got older. The German-speaking countries inevitably led the way (and even today the *Fach* acknowledges a German authenticity), but there are no barriers in principle to any country producing a Heldentenor. Scandinavia has been a particularly rich source for Heldentenors, as has North America, especially since World War II. All of the main twentieth-century Heldentenors are represented on record, although not all of them recorded the roles for which they were most famous at the time.[1]

Leo Slezak

Europe was a fluid geographical entity at the end of the nineteenth century and many of the eastern states were subsumed into the old Austro-Hungarian empire, which blurred the boundaries between German-speaking countries. Leo Slezak was born in 1873 in the Moravian town of Märisch-Schönberg, now in the Czech Republic. Although he was a contemporary of Caruso there were many who saw him as an heir of Jean de Reszke, able to sing a wide range of roles from the lyric to the heroic. The backgrounds of these two giants could not have been more different: Slezak was the son of a miller; he grew up in poverty, leaving school at fourteen and failing to settle in a multitude of jobs, ranging from gardening to selling insurance. The one proper trade that he attempted (also without distinction) was that of a blacksmith, which (as he would later joke) at least came in handy when he came to play the young Siegfried. Slezak was built like a blacksmith and had a correspondingly large natural tenor voice, though was of a gentle disposition. At the age of nineteen he auditioned successfully for the opera chorus in Brno. He could not read music (if he was a typical chorus member the director of the opera must have had a lot of patience); his early experience of being part of an opera company convinced him that he might have a future as a singer. He was taken up by the baritone Adolphe Robinson and his wife, who sponsored him for two years before he had to join the army. In time-honoured military fashion, an enlightened commanding officer recognised both the gentleness of his character and the richness of his voice, and ensured that he was free to sing for three nights a week. It was while learning to be a soldier that he also mastered Lohengrin (helped by Mrs Robinson's supportive repetiteuring), singing the swan knight to great acclaim in Brno, as a result of which he was offered a contract at the Berlin Hofoper in 1898.[2]

Slezak did not enjoy Berlin but he did get to sing in a variety of operas, including *Rienzi*, *Euryanthe* and *Meistersinger* (the lesser role of Kunz Vogelsang under Strauss, who thought him unmusical). The following year he accepted a two-year contract in Breslau, where he encountered *Tannhäuser* and Elsa Wertheim, the actress who was to give up her career to marry him. Slezak and Elsa were devoted to each other and remained so for forty years, the serious aristocratic Austrian ensuring that the rather more straightforward but often humorous Bohemian was able to carve out an international career for himself. In 1900 he sang Siegfried at Covent Garden and the following year joined Gustav Mahler at the Vienna Opera. Under the fanatically disciplined Mahler, Slezak refined both his singing and his acting, performing the Wagnerian heroic roles of Lohengrin, Erik, Stolzing and Tannhäuser, as well as Verdi's Otello, Ernani, Manrico and Radamès. Significantly, he also sang Tamino, and continued to broaden both the roles that he undertook and the dynamic range with which he sang them; he was by no means simply a larger-than-life Heldentenor.

In 1907 Slezak went to study with Jean de Reszke in Paris. It was de Reszke who taught him to spin out the high mezza voce which became his trademark. This is nowhere more evident than in his 1905 recording of 'Viens gentille Dame' from Boieldieu's *La Dame blanche* or the 1909 'Magische Töne' from Goldmark's *Die Königen von Saba*. It is impossible to imagine a modern Heldentenor relinquishing the source of his power in favour of a tone that might be considered almost effeminate by comparison.[3] In 1909 he made his New York début at the Met as Otello, where he was hailed as a more lyrical Tamagno (who had originally created the role). He stayed in New York for four years, taking part in the American première of Tchaikovsky's *Pique Dame* as well as the Wagner and Mozart roles that he had made his own. In 1913 he returned to Vienna, where he later sang in the Austrian première of *Turandot.* Throughout the '20s he remained Vienna's favourite tenor, broadening his performing to take in operetta and film. He turned out to be an accomplished screen actor (as did his son Walter). Slezak died in 1946, disillusioned by the war. He had grown up within the evolving nineteenth-century tradition, and the voice we hear on his recordings is that of a previous era; his sound and style are far too individual to be mistaken for a modern tenor.

Significant Scandinavians: Melchior and Svanholm

At the time of Slezak's death, in the American war-time comfort zone another Heldentenor was just beginning his second career as a movie star. Lauritz Melchior, first and possibly greatest of Scandinavian Heldentenors, was born in Copenhagen in 1890 and began his career at the Royal Opera School as a baritone singing smaller roles in *Traviata, Pagliacci* and *Carmen,* before being retrained by Vilhelm Herold as a Heldentenor.[4] He was a big, jovial bear of a man with an infectious sense of humour. His début in Copenhagen as Tannhäuser did not impress, and he returned to studying smaller roles with Herold. These included Heinrich in *Tannhäuser,* which he sang in Danish at the Royal Opera, opposite Slezak's eponymous hero singing in German.

In 1919, on a visit to London, his career changed rapidly as a result of a series of life-changing events that began in the men's room of the Savoy, when he found himself humming a tune while standing next to a fellow Dane who was staying at the hotel. His countryman, son of a wealthy Aarhus coal merchant, was about to leave, and placed at Melchior's disposal his suite in the hotel and Rolls Royce complete with chauffeur.[5] He then obtained an introduction to Henry Wood, who booked him for a Promenade Concert at the Queen's Hall the following year. That concert was attended by the writer Hugh Walpole, by then a successful novelist of independent means (he was of aristocratic descent), who was very much taken with the young Dane. Walpole believed (with extraordinary foresight) that Melchior could be the Heldentenor of his generation, and offered to help bring this about by funding singing lessons in London and putting the top floor of his own house at the disposal of the young tenor. Not one to look a gift horse in the mouth, Melchior was soon having three lessons a week with Victor Beigel, a friend of Walpole's who had once accompanied Jean de Reszke and was thoroughly familiar with the great man's technique. [6] Beigel was to become both friend and guru to Melchior, who was still having lessons from him at the time of his Met début in 1926. After two months, Beigel arranged an audition with Franz Schalk of the Vienna Staatsoper. Schalk pronounced that he needed further training in both singing and German, and advised him to seek help from the legendary Wagnerian soprano Anna Bahr-Mildenburg. She was impressed but thought he would take at least a year to realise his potential. Melchior then returned to England for German lessons before going back to Munich to study the essential Wagner roles with the soprano who had once been Mahler's mistress and was a close friend of Cosima Wagner.[7] His good luck followed him to Munich: he met the diminutive film starlet Anny Hacker, whom he called 'Kleinchen', and who would eventually become his second wife and business manager. His first recital elicited an invitation from Siegfried Wagner, who then engaged him to do Siegmund in *Die Walküre* when Bayreuth reopened in 1924.

The Bayreuth experience had a lasting effect on Melchior. He had been well prepared by Bahr-Mildenburg and impressed both Siegfried and Cosima Wagner, and his friendship with Walpole gave him easy entry into the Bayreuth élite (which included Adolf Hitler, who was moved to tears when he first heard the young Heldentenor sing Parsifal[8]). Melchior got on particularly well with Siegfried (he would be a pall-bearer at his funeral in 1930) and absorbed whatever he could of the musical and dramatic tradition handed down from Wagner's heirs. The Dane was not a great actor, but the criticisms he would later receive for his wooden stage demeanour can be in part attributed to his understanding of the authentic Wagner dramaturgy learned at Bayreuth. In the six years before his distaste for the politicisation of the Festspiel caused him to leave and never return, he studied and performed Parsifal, Siegfried, Siegmund, Tannhäuser and Tristan (this last under Toscanini), and these crucial years instilled into him a uniquely authentic understanding of the roles.[9] He appeared at Covent Garden every year from 1926 to 1939, and after a shaky start at the Met went on to become one of the most successful tenors in the history of the company, singing all of the heavier Wagner roles and becoming as iconic in New York as the Met itself. He was even considered a possible successor to Edward Johnson as general manager when the latter retired in 1949.[10] The job went to Rudolf Bing, who thought

Melchior's extra-Met activities unbecoming to an opera singer and did not renew his contract in 1950. There was another Scandinavian tenor on hand to fill his shoes, the Swede Set Svanholm. By then a hugely marketable star (shrewdly managed by his wife), Melchior was able to capitalise on his popularity by involving himself in radio, television and theatre work.[11] He was not the only well-known opera singer to find a second career in less serious music; at a time when light music had serious pretensions it was relatively easy for classically trained singers to take on stage and film musicals. Leo Slezak had set a precedent for Heldentenors, and Ezio Pinza, perhaps the most accomplished bass of the '20s and '30s, had a big success on Broadway with *South Pacific* in 1949; Helen Traubel, Melchior's wartime Isolde, had a post-Met career as a cabaret singer. Melchior eventually became one of the wealthiest tenors of the century, and a celebrity more famous even than his own singing.

Connoisseurs of great singing have sometimes been disappointed when the object of their devotion is thought to have diluted their art by moving sideways into something considered less challenging vocally. Melchior's metamorphosis into a show business personality may have something to do with his subsequent neglect, despite acclaim from some of the most perceptive of critics. Desmond Shawe-Taylor considered him to be the outstanding Heldentenor of the century, and John Steane draws attention to the 'incomplete recognition' of his vocal excellence (and goes on to describe the high points of his recording career, describing his *Götterdämmerung* recording as 'among the classics of the gramophone').[12] He was not without his faults, which included a reluctance to rehearse and a certain waywardness with both notes and rhythm, but he had in abundance the key attributes of a great Heldentenor: a thrilling, slightly baritonal sound that was even over at least two octaves, a beguiling mezza voce, immaculate diction, and above all stamina: his immense physical frame ensured an ability to sound as fresh at the end of the most demanding roles as he did at the start. In the mid-1960s he set up the Melchior Heldentenor Foundation to encourage new Helden talent to come forward, especially baritones who might be latent Heldentenors; he was very aware of the short supply and took a keen interest in possible future Melchiors.[13]

Set Svanholm was yet another Swedish tenor to come out of John Forsell's tutelage at the Stockholm Opera, where he made his début in 1930 in the baritone role of Silvio in *I Pagliacci*.[14] Svanholm had originally trained as a church organist, and his broad musical education and interests surely influenced the sensitivity and musicianship that he would later bring to his vocal roles. Over a six-year period he gradually became convinced that his attraction to the heroic baritone roles was restricting his upward development as a possible tenor. Eventually he announced to Forsell that he had discovered a new tenor.

'Who?' asked his teacher. 'It's me,' replied Svanholm and launched into 'Celeste Aïda'. Forsell needed no further convincing and arranged for him to début as a tenor in 1936, singing Radamès. Within a year he was singing Wagner, and in 1938 was invited by Bruno Walter to sing Lohengrin and Siegmund in Vienna; in 1942 he sang Erik and Siegfried at Bayreuth, and made his La Scala début as Tannhäuser (in Italian).[15] In 1946 he became the first Swedish Peter Grimes (and when he later became director of the Swedish Royal Opera he would introduce several contemporary operas including Britten's *Rape of Lucretia* and *The Turn of the Screw*).

Svanholm's Met début in 1946 was inevitably seen by the press as being potential competition for Melchior. The young Swede was not the dominating presence, physically and vocally, that Melchior had become, but he was an intelligent singer, heroic, handsome, and – especially important relative to the portly Dane – slim. The management found him much easier to deal with and he was also prepared to undertake a wider variety of heavy and heroic roles. His accession to the Melchior throne enabled him to return for the next ten years. He was also a huge success at Covent Garden, and sang Loge in the Solti *Ring* recording for Decca. His death from cancer at the age of sixty was a shock to the operatic world; his approach to singing was as much intellectual as instinctive, which gave a depth to the art of the Heldentenor that revealed itself in both his singing and his acting.[16]

German tenors: World War II and after

Melchior's remarkable talents were enhanced by considerable good fortune: as a young man he had a knack of being in the right place at the right time, and his years at the Met were unrivalled in no small degree because his German competitors were isolated by the war in Europe. All of the German tenors born in the last decade or so of the nineteenth century, especially those with larger voices who were to grow into the Heldentenor *Fach*, were destined to be in their prime in the compromised years of the mid-1930s and the '40s, when being successful in Germany was quite another thing from being appreciated abroad. With hindsight we can evaluate the recordings left behind by these singers, but can have no idea of the physical presence that they brought to the work, and one can only speculate on what the Heldentenor scene might have been like had the European and American opera houses been able to offer equal opportunities to all the Wagner singers of the era. The one who came closest in reputation to Melchior, Max Lorenz, had neither the Dane's gift for public relations nor his opportunities in the USA, and his career, like those of his German contemporaries, such as Gotthelf Pistor, Fritz Wolff, Carl

Hartmann, Paul Kötter and August Seider, was inevitably affected by the war and its aftermath.[17]

Ludwig Suthaus sang almost exclusively in Germany during the war years and in the '50s was discovered by Furtwängler, who considered him to be the greatest Heldentenor of his day (despite his apparent inability to act). Between 1952 and 1954 Suthaus and Furtwängler recorded *Tristan*, *Siegfried*, *Götterdämmerung* and *Die Walküre* and he finally achieved an international reputation before a car accident in 1960 led to his re-thinking the heavier roles, and eventually to his retirement in 1967.

Lorenz was more successful in the inter-war period. A butcher's son from Düsseldorf, he studied with Ernst Grenzebach in Berlin and became Melchior's most illustrious successor at Bayreuth. Grenzebach[18] had taught Melchior briefly and many other successful Wagnerians of all voices, but this pupil did not impress Siegfried and Cosima at his first attempt. Lorenz's audition at Bayreuth yielded only small roles and he considered giving up singing altogether until he won first prize in a singing competition run by the Berlin Philharmonic, which resulted in a contract with the Dresden Staatsoper, where he stayed from 1926 to 1931. It was not until 1932 that he returned to Bayreuth, by now under the control of Siegfried's widow, Winifred Wagner. His great success there in succeeding seasons proved an embarrassment after the war, and the eventual collapse of German artistic infrastructure undoubtedly caused a hiatus in his development as a Heldentenor, but he still managed to re-establish himself as one of the foremost Heldentenors of the time. Lorenz was not only a Wagnerian; his repertoire included Richard Strauss (Herod and Bacchus), Verdi (Otello) and Gottfried von Einem, whose Josef K he created in *Der Prozess* in 1953. It is arguable that the younger post-war Heldentenors looked to the singing actor Lorenz as a model rather than the inimitable Melchior.

Wolfgang Windgassen and Neu Bayreuth

In 1949 Winifred Wagner formally renounced her connection with the Bayreuth Festival, handing effective control to her sons Wieland and Wolfgang. The two Wagner brothers were determined to make a complete break with the past, and the evolving aesthetic of 'Neu Bayreuth' affected everything from singing to set design after the re-founding of the Festival in 1951.[19] After the constraints of the war years it was a time of plenty for Heldentenors; Bayreuth saw the likes of Hans Hopf, Helge Rosvaenge, Ramon Vinay and Gunther Treptow, but the tenor most associated with the new singing was Wolfgang Windgassen, who sang for nineteen seasons at the

Festival from 1951 to 1970 (a record only broken in 1996 when Siegfried Jerusalem completed twenty).[20]

Windgassen was the son of Fritz Windgassen, Heldentenor with the Kassel company, and grew up with Wagner in his blood. When the family moved to Stuttgart Opera, Wolfgang worked as an apprentice in the theatre for five years, learning opera production from the bottom up. Exposed to first-class singing on a daily basis, and increasingly aware that he had inherited his father's talents, the younger Windgassen became a pupil of the elder. He was conscripted into the army in 1937, but a cultured commanding officer ensured that he could continue to sing. The military enlightenment continued until the very end of the war when no able-bodied soldier was able to escape the fighting, but until then Wolfgang was left alone to develop his operatic career. He joined the Stuttgart company in 1945 and three years later sang with his father in a number of concerts celebrating Fritz's retirement from the stage. From this point on he stepped into his father's shoes and in 1950 he sang Stolzing for Knappertsbusch in Munich. A year later he was singing *Parsifal* at Bayreuth, and over the next nineteen years he sang all the major Wagner roles at the Festival.

Windgassen shared Wieland Wagner's aesthetic, and the two collaborated on the re-interpretation of Wagner's heroes as modern figures with a recognisable humanity. It was Windgassen who addressed the mourners at the graveside when Wieland died suddenly of cancer in 1966. In 1957 he made his Met début, but his lyrical Siegmund was not the macho hero that American audiences were used to, and Windgassen in any case preferred the total immersion of the German experience to the sometimes lonely and superficial life of a foreign opera star in New York. He returned to Europe and apart from a *Tristan* in San Francisco in 1970 never returned to the USA. He is perhaps best known for his recording of the Decca *Ring* cycle; he took over from the inexperienced Ernst Kozub at short notice, and deeply impressed both Solti and the producer John Culshaw with his freshness, stamina and commitment. Like Svanholm before him, he died unexpectedly, barely sixty years old, when at the peak of his intellectual and musical powers. If his attempts to continue Wieland's production aesthetics were not entirely successful, nothing could detract from his position as a unique link between old and new Wagnerian traditions.[21]

Windgassen was not a sensuous singer, but his lyricism in many ways returned Wagner singing to something that was perhaps more like the vocalism the *Meister* might have appreciated. His intelligence and deep understanding of the theatre enabled him to bring to bear a more contemporary and psychological approach to music drama. Having been brought up in the opera house as the son of a Heldentenor he also knew the importance of the understanding between producer and singer, and the legitimacy of the composer's intention. This made him a natural collaborator with Wieland Wagner, and the perfect singing actor to renew the tradition.

Sándor Kónya

Wieland also played a major role in the success of Sándor Kónya. Kónya was born in Hungary and after a musical childhood went to the Franz Liszt Academy in Budapest. His studies were interrupted when he was drafted into the army at the outbreak of war. He was captured and imprisoned by the British in Germany but managed to escape (the only tenor known to have escaped from a British prisoner of war camp). He managed to stay in Germany after the end of hostilities and studied at the Musik Hochschule in Detmold and also for a short time in Milan, but struggled to make ends meet in post-war Germany. In 1951 he finally auditioned successfully for the opera in Bielefeld (to which he had to hitchhike, unable to afford the train fare). He made his début as Turiddù and stayed with the company for three years before moving to Darmstadt, where his big break came in the form of a contract with the Stadtische Oper (now the Deutsche Oper) in Berlin. There he created the role of Leandro in Hans Werner Henze's *König Hirsch* and gave the German première of Menotti's *Saint of Bleecker Street*.

He was an italianate dramatic tenor at this time, but his potential in heavier roles was recognised by Wieland Wagner who invited him to audition for Bayreuth. Kónya had no Wagner under his belt and sang 'Vesti la giubba' (as Leo Slezak had done, finding himself similarly embarrassed many years before).[22] Wagner asked him to re-audition having looked at Lohengrin. The result was a triumph for Kónya in the 1958 production. He went on to sing Erik, Stolzing and Parsifal, becoming one of the most exciting young Heldentenors, conquering the Met in 1961 and Covent Garden two years later. He returned to the Met for fourteen further seasons, repeating his Bayreuth successes and adding the major Verdi operas. He avoided Tristan and the heaviest roles, preferring to spin his somewhat non-German lyricism around only the parts that would not compromise his fundamentally 'bel canto' sound (his Lohengrin was described by one authority as 'Pucciniesque'[23]).

Kollo, Jerusalem and Hoffmann

Windgassen was destined to be a Heldentenor from very early in his career, Kónya grew into the *Fach*. Three of the greatest German Heldens of the latter part of the century began their careers outside singing altogether: René Kollo was a pop singer, Siegfried Jerusalem a bassoonist, and Peter Hofmann a paratrooper before they felt called to the *Fach*. Born in 1937, 1940 and 1944 respectively, their formative years coincided with a more confident post-war Europe in which there was a sense that anything was possible, and that rules were made if not to be broken then to be creatively ignored.

Kollo came from a professional musical family of eclectic taste, and in his youth played drums and acted in stage and television shows. From 1958 he had singing lessons with Elsa Varena, who realised that he had potential as a class-ical singer. He made his tenorial début in Braunschweig in 1965 and was engaged as a lyric tenor by Düsseldorf Opera in 1967. His performance of the Steuermann at Bayreuth in 1969 opened up a Europe-wide career and he grad-ually began to take on the heavier Wagnerian roles. This led to acclaim for him as both Siegfrieds, a rare achievement in a tenor with no hint of baritone in his voice. Kollo was also a thinking singing actor, and gained a reputation for disliking dictatorial direction (his career managed to survive fallings out with Karajan and Wolfgang Wagner, among others). Kollo was a charismatic performer and his singing always retained its lyricism; he never lost the need to communicate with his audience, a legacy of his days as a popular entertainer.

His contemporary Siegfried Jerusalem also had a musical childhood, learning several instruments and becoming a professional bassoonist with the Stuttgart Radio Orchestra. He sang as a semi-professional baritone and his transition to tenor occurred when he found Wotan's music beyond him and his teacher Herta Kalcher suggested he try Siegmund's instead.[24] Jerusalem had been reluctant to take the step into possible insecurity that a singing career might bring, and his entry into the profession is one of the few cases of a tenor being created by *force majeur*. In 1975 the radio orchestra was recording Johann Strauss' *Zigeunerbaron* for television and the tenor Franco Bonisolli failed to appear. Bonisolli's behaviour was unpredictable, especially as he became more successful. Three years later he would throw his sword into the pit during a rehearsal of Karajan's *Trovatore* in Vienna, to be replaced by Placido Domingo; on another occasion he missed the high C customarily interpolated at the end of Manrico's aria 'Di quella pira' but came on before the curtain came down at the end of the scene and sang it anyway, on its own.[25] On this occasion Jerusalem saved the day by overdubbing the vocal part, having previously recorded the bassoon part with the orchestra. He was only just up to the part and took twenty-seven takes to get the high C at the end of 'Als flotter Geist'. As he would afterwards joke, he muttered 'shit!' after so many failures, to which the producer responded, 'We've got plenty of that. Now just sing the note. . .'[26]

The success of the recording gave him the confidence to give up his orches-tral job in 1977 and a year later he was singing Lohengrin in Munich. In 1980 he made his Met début, alternating with Peter Hofmann as the Swan Knight and then went on to sing all the major Wagner roles. A highpoint in his career came in 1990, when his Met performances of the *Ring* operas (singing Loge and both Siegfrieds) were recorded for television; he won a Grammy for his Loge a year later. He opened the 1993 Bayreuth Festival with his first Tristan to huge acclaim, and repeated the role for his Bayreuth farewell performance in 1999. According to Carla Maria Verdino-Süllwold Jerusalem 'creates one of the most thrilling Siegfrieds in history – a hero in the Windgassen–Thomas lyric tradition, a figure dramatically compelling in the Svanholm legacy.'[27]

Peter Hofmann, the third great German Held of the century, was described by Harold Rosenthal in 1976 as 'quite frankly the finest Heldentenor I have heard since the war. Forget about Svanholm and Windgassen and even Max Lorenz. This was the nearest thing to the authentic Heldentenors since Melchior and possibly Suthaus.'[28] Hofmann's story is fascinating and, ultimately, tragic. Born into a middle-class liberal family, he was a child of the '50s – that generation for many of whom rock 'n' roll was as important as classical music; he grew up with Wagner and Elvis Presley happily coexisting in his musical consciousness. He left school without finishing his education and when drafted into the army continued his military service as a paratrooper for seven years. In 1969 he went to the Karlsruhe Musikhochschule to study with Emmy Seiberlich. At this time he was a baritone, but things changed when his teacher introduced him to the American Heldentenor Jess Thomas at Bayreuth in 1967. Thomas recognised the ex-soldier's talent and suggested he might be a tenor, and by 1972 he was enough of a lyric tenor to make his stage début in Lübeck as Tamino.[29]

Over the next few years he refined his acting and developed his voice sufficiently to attempt many of the Wagner roles, moving to Stuttgart and also making his Bayreuth début. His big break came in 1976, when he sang Siegmund in Patrice Chéreau's landmark *Ring* production, conducted by Pierre Boulez. Chéreau's production was one of the most extraordinary *Rings* ever staged, the almost unknown French director requiring great risk-taking from the singers as well as acting skills of a very high order. The strikingly fit and handsome Hofmann caused ecstasy and outrage in equal measure with a passionate performance that climaxed with the removal of his shirt before being prepared for death by Brunnhilde. There had never been a more controversial production, and nothing could have done more for Hofmann's career.

In 1981 he attempted *Tristan* in concert under Bernstein, Lohengrin at Bayreuth and the Bolshoi, as well a highly successful Bayreuth centennial *Parsifal*. The following year he played Schnorr von Carolsfeld in the Richard Burton film *Wagner*.

Having conquered virtually all the mountains there were to climb, it is perhaps not surprising that Hoffman should turn to his previous life as a rock singer for further inspiration. He released his first album of rock classics in 1983, and went on to tour extensively, singing both in German and English. From then on he maintained parallel careers as a Heldentenor and rock singer, with huge popular success in both fields. Critical response to his pop singing has been mixed. Timing was perhaps a factor in the mixed reception his pop music ventures received in the classical press. Had he been born a few years later he would have missed the Elvis generation and his teenage years would have coincided with the Beatles, who were singer–songwriters rather than celebrities who sang other people's material. In his *homages* to Elvis, Hofmann's performances cannot help sounding like pastiche, whereas for the post-Elvis generation it was originality that counted: the Beatles transcended their influences. Pop singing for Heldentenors will always be a risky, self-indulgent enterprise; whether 'crossover' or covers, the question of originality versus imitation will not go away, and will inevitably lead to questions about how far a singer of one genre can sing in another and maintain his credibility. Hofmann came closer than many others to making the two work (and his rock singing was far less embarrassing than that of some of his illustrious successors). Sadly, both careers came to a premature end when he retired in 2004 to fight Parkinson's disease.

Heroic North Americans and the *Drang nach Deutschland*

The tenorial connection between North America and Europe has generally been mutually advantageous, although it has changed character over the years. The Europeans gained career advantage from appearing in the USA, and American productions felt legitimised by European singing. The American opera-going public has historically preferred the dramatic to the lyric (as the long line of European lyric failures at the Met attests) and a relatively small number have managed the lyrical 'bel canto' pre-Wagner roles; those who are successful, such as Chris Merritt and Rockwell Blake, are often more appreci-ated in Europe. As one would expect, there have been many American dramatic tenor successes such as James McCracken, Richard Leech, Neil Shicoff and the Canadian Paul Frey. The significant number of Heldentenors is a response on the one hand to the demand from students for specialised training, and on the other, to audiences who like their singers big, heroic and straightforward. In the post-war period those aspiring to the Helden *Fach* almost always studied and worked in Germany before becoming recognised at home. In the twenty-first century such is the confidence of American opera producers and performers that many productions now feature all-American (and American-trained) casts.

Jess Thomas

Among those who made the pilgrimage to Germany were James King and Jess Thomas. Both came from similar provincial backgrounds and rose to the heights of the profession through disciplined work and a dedication to the craft. Thomas was the first American Heldentenor to be accepted in Europe as being on a par with native German Heldens, and his success probably made it easier for North American tenors to achieve recognition in Europe. He grew up in rural South Dakota, and had a conventional and conservative American upbringing, excelling at school and completing a Psychology degree in 1949. He began a PhD in Psychology in 1952 but completed an MPhil a year later and became a school psychologist. He was an amateur singer at this time with an interest in opera but little opportunity to pursue it, until he auditioned for San Francisco Opera in 1957. The following year, on the advice of Stanford professor Otto Schulmann, he set out for Germany and within six months had a contract at Karlsruhe, where he became a student of Emmy Seiberlich. He sang a number of small roles before a lucky break came his way when Ken Neate failed to appear for final rehearsals of *Lohengrin* and at Seiberlich's suggestion Thomas stood in for him. Although the Australian tenor did appear in time for the first performance, the grateful Intendant allowed Thomas to take over the role from the third performance onwards. So enthusiastic were the reviews that Thomas soon had a viable future in Germany, with notable successes as Bacchus in *Ariadne auf Naxos* in Stuttgart and Munich, and as Parsifal in Bayreuth in 1961. A year later he returned to the USA to sing Stolzing at the Met, an astonishing triumph only five years after he left the country as an unknown part-time psychologist.[30] Thomas' extra-musical studies in psychology surely equipped him well to take on the great Wagnerian roles, to which he brought an emotional intelligence that meant he did not have to make his point by sheer volume alone.

James King

James King's career similarly blossomed once he left the USA, having come to the *Fach* relatively late in life. He grew up on a musical diet of Nelson Eddy and Grace Moore and served as a pilot in the war before going to Louisiana State University. There he was taught by choral conductor Dallas Draper, and sang in university productions as a baritone. He graduated in 1949 and became a singing teacher at the University of Kansas City where he stayed for nine years, during which time he began to suspect he was actually a tenor. He was finally convinced during a year of disciplined study with Martial Singher, a French baritone whose career had included twelve seasons with the Met. He auditioned successfully for several regional opera companies and was a prize winner in the American Opera Auditions in Cincinnati in 1961, which enabled him to go to Italy (where he made his début in Florence as Cavaradossi). There he heard that Sándor Kónya was leaving the Deutsche Oper in Berlin to work in the USA; King auditioned successfully and moved to Berlin where he threw himself into as many roles as he could. He very quickly established himself as a potential Heldentenor, and gradually acquired the key roles, singing Siegmund in the Bayreuth *Ring* of 1965. The next year he made his Met début on the occasion of the inauguration of its new Lincoln Center home, in Strauss' *Die Frau ohne Schatten*, an achievement to rank with that of Jess Thomas a few years before. King moved to the Bayerische Staatsoper in Munich for the rest of his career, and from there maintained an international profile that included La Scala, Covent Garden and many return visits to the Met.

Jon Vickers: a reborn Grimes

Germany became a cultural home for Thomas and King, and both were able to fuse their American work ethic with German ensemble practices. Canadian Jon Vickers was also grounded in a strong work ethic, but his fundamentalist Christian upbringing led him to a more critical engagement with the singing profession and its music. He auditioned for the Toronto Conservatory in 1950 and went to study with George Lambert.[31] Things moved slowly after he graduated, but in 1955 he was offered a Covent Garden audition which led to a three-year contract to sing *Un Ballo, Carmen, Don Carlo, Aida,* and *The Trojans*. He made his highly-acclaimed Bayreuth début as Siegfried in 1958 and two years later first appeared at the Met as Canio. He would return on countless occasions to the New York and London houses throughout his career, becoming a huge favourite on both sides of the Atlantic.

Vickers' success came despite the idiosyncratic approach that resulted from his fundamentalist upbringing, which caused him to wrestle with basic concepts such as Grimes' homosexuality and Wagner's apparently anti-Christian philosophy as expressed in *Tannhäuser*. He refused to play Grimes as a homosexual in Tyrone Guthrie's Met production of *Peter Grimes*, insisting on changes in the text to make it clear that he was portraying a universal human condition. In 1977 Vickers was booked to do *Tannhäuser* at Covent Garden, followed by a series of Met performances in the next season. A month before the first performance he withdrew on the grounds that the opera was offensive to his Christian faith. In the ensuing uproar many questions were asked about the singer's true reason for cancelling, especially since he had managed a much-acclaimed interpretation of *Tristan*, despite believing it to be 'an evil and wicked work'.[32]

Vickers was a complex character who had no truck with those aspects of the singing profession that transgressed his moral sensitivities. In another life he might have been a farmer or a fiery preacher, and his performances were always informed by the conviction that comes from moral certainty. He was rarely troubled by doubt. His Grimes may have upset the composer, but it showed that it was possible to interpret the character anew and without sounding like its creator, Peter Pears. Jon Vickers has no successors, either in terms of his massive voice or his views on how that instrument should be used.

Ben Heppner

In Ben Heppner (like Vickers, reluctant to call himself a Held) there exists a heroic tenor whose stylistic forbears are Fritz Wunderlich and Jussi Björling rather than Melchior or Vickers. His Tristan has an intense lyricism about it, and there is no hint of barking or shouting. Heppner was the recipient of the first Birgit Nilsson Prize at the Metropolitan Opera Auditions in 1988, and Nilsson was instrumental in getting him to play Lohengrin in Stockholm for his European début the following year. He subsequently went on to sing Britten (*Grimes* and the *War Requiem*) and made his official Met début in Mozart's *Idomeneo*. Adding Berlioz, Schoenberg and Mahler to his repertoire has also undoubtedly kept his singing fresh and nuanced, but it is for the heroic roles of Otello and Tristan that he has become known. His tastes are eclectic, and he is equally at home on the concert platform. Despite a vocal crisis in the 2002–3 season, he has come to be a Helden force to be reckoned with, in what is becoming a very small field.[33]

A future for the Heldentenor?

The great Heldens of the latter part of the twentieth century are now either dead or living in honourable retirement, and the heroic repertoire is not susceptible to the three-minute aria treatment that has served the post-Three Tenor market so well. Whether one is pessimistic or sanguine about the state of tenor singing in the first decade of the twenty-first century there will be a lingering question concerning the future of the Heldentenor in the minds of many who appreciate the voice. Not only are fewer tenors making the transition to more dramatic roles as they mature, but often those who possess the potential to assume heldenhood do not want to risk losing the more comfortable dramatic repertoire. As Jon Vickers once put it, 'I want to keep my Italian roles, because Italian caresses the voice while German exploits it.'[34] Of course, Vickers went on to become one of the finest heroic tenors of his day, singing

Tristan despite his misgivings and keeping Verdi and Britten in his repertoire. The first requirement of a Heldentenor is a powerful physique: Heldentenors tend to be big men, unlike the quasi male-model preferred by record companies. They need both physical and mental stamina: to quote Vickers again, 'Tristan is just inhuman in its demands.'[35]

In the past, a large physique has often seemed to mean a wooden demeanour and an unsubtle vocal delivery. There is no necessary connection between these attributes, however, and the likelihood is that demands for a more lyrical hero will eventually be met. Historically, voices have appeared and disappeared in response to demand, and the future Heldentenor will be no different in this respect. It is also possible that new Tristans will be discovered or created in exceptional circumstances. The British tenor Ian Storey is one such, studying the role full-time with Daniel Barenboim over six months before making his La Scala début in the role in 2007 at the age of forty-nine. Storey, like many British tenors of a previous generation, comes from coalmining stock and only became a professional singer in his thirties. The first tenor to make an impact on him as a child was Mario Lanza. The combination of early exposure to lyrical singing with mature entry into the profession has produced a genuine modern Heldentenor, capable of applying a sustained lyricism to a heroic role.

CHAPTER 11

POST-WAR LOSSES AND GAINS

In wartime, institutions fail and the arts inevitably become drawn into government propaganda machinery. Musicians often find themselves hapless victims of appalling circumstances which are beyond their control; high-profile tenors on the losing side are bound to be at risk from political misjudgements of their own and cynical manipulation by politicians. Historically, there has been a curiously positive relationship between tenors and the military, the origins of which may go back to the formality of *opera seria* when tenors were cast as soldiers, mature father figures or aristocrats and the like. As we have seen, in countries where conscription was the norm, many singers from the late nineteenth century onwards found themselves unexpectedly appreciated by music-loving superior officers, and their soldiering years did them no harm at all. Some tenors (Lauri-Volpi is the most notable example) positively enjoyed fighting and were distinguished soldiers. Most simply wanted to sing and keep themselves out of trouble, and some, such as Richard Crooks, enhanced their reputations by singing to the troops. Others were sufficiently aware of the political situation, and confident enough of their own position within it, to take pre-emptive action. This was especially the case with many of the singers who worked in Bayreuth in the interwar years, for whom the commitment to Wagner's musical ideals had to be set against the implications of his political thought for German nationalism. Lauritz Melchior is the supreme example of this, refusing to sing at Bayreuth once it became a tool of the Nazi propaganda machine. Very few tenors were prepared to suffer for their principles. An exception was Carlo Bergonzi, who was active in the Italian resistance and as a consequence spent the latter part of the war in a prisoner of war camp. The Spanish Wagnerian Isidoro de Fagoaga retired from the stage in protest against the bombing of Guernica and the Italian aid for Franco, but Gigli, Lauri-Volpi and Schipa, on the other hand, appeared to embrace Fascism and sang for both Hitler and Mussolini.[1] It is perhaps fortunate that it was not until the 1950s that Bergonzi (who began his career as a baritone) began to appreciate the artistry of Gigli. In time, it seems, the artistry of the greatest singers transcends their political naivety, both for fellow artists and the public at large; Gigli was back in action in Rome as early as 1945 despite the public demonstrations against him after the Allies took the capital in 1943, and the Anglo-Saxon world had forgiven all of them by the early '50s.

National styles versus internationalism

There was a certain sense of déjà vu in Europe after the war, recalling the aftermath of World War I, as opera houses and conservatories reopened and new singers began to emerge. Opera singing continued to produce exciting new interpreters of the canonic roles, spiced with the occasional new work, and for many it soon became business as usual. The post-war generation of tenors coincided with the replacement of the old shellac 78rpm by the new vinyl LP. In retrospect the singers seem to sound more modern, partly because of the medium itself: the sound quality, especially in stereo, had a greater depth, a wider dynamic range and far less surface noise, giving listeners a more realistic sense of the physical presence of the voice. It also perhaps encouraged more trenchant criticism – it was less easy to blame the technology for the short-comings of performance; there was less room for singers to be given the benefit of critical doubt. The hugely increased availability of recordings inevitably saw a tendency towards standardisation, which led to losses in key aspects of tenor singing, a trajectory which has continued into the CD era. In the early years of the twenty-first century the universal availability of almost any product in the western world has meant that even the most obscure tenors are available some-where on record if buyers look hard enough, but the mainstream of tenor singing has undoubtedly lost much of the individuality that it had a hundred years before. Standardisation is driven by commercial criteria: markets are identified and exploited by record companies; for singers, significant models become fewer and more similar. This pattern has persisted into the twenty-first century.

Post-war Italian superstars

This pessimistic view of what has been lost has to be set beside the quality of the singing that flourished, and in many ways the 1950s were a golden age for Italian singing, especially tenors. The quartet of Italian tenors who came to prominence after the war all attracted criticism despite their popular acclaim, but this can be seen as a healthy indicator that style and technique are still evolving. Mario Del Monaco's singing could be magnificent, according to John Steane, but was often unpleasant (the Flower Song from *Carmen*), insensitive ('Un bel dì di maggio' from *Andrea Chénier*) and unimaginative ('Celeste Aida'), mostly because he sang too loudly, and yet his 1955 Chénier was described by many as one of the most perfect interpretations of the role.[2] Giuseppe di Stefano was condemned on all sides for wilfully wrecking his voice by continually taking on roles that were too big for him, and yet his début at La Scala as Des Grieux still resonates with those who were there. Franco Corelli was also taken to task for singing too loud and then retiring too early, but consistently tops polls as one of the greatest tenors of the century; Bergonzi's refined elegance has been considered conservative, but this did not prevent him from becoming one of the century's favourite Verdi interpreters. These singers fulfilled a post-war public demand for charismatic Italian tenor heroes; they were the real thing, and their cumulative experience is still felt in the singing of many of their successors, even where there may be no obvious direct influence.

Del Monaco and di Stefano

The traditional scenario for the young middle-class proto-tenor is one of parental doubt, in which the young aspirant is destined for the law, commerce or other safe, self-improving career rather than the dangerous and potentially ruinous career as a singer. Mario Del Monaco is one of the few great tenors to have had precisely the opposite experience. He was born in Florence in 1915; his mother was a cousin of Caruso's mistress, the soprano Ada Giachetti, and Del Monaco grew up in an environment where the great tenor's achievements were readily acknowledged, and in which the thought of becoming a singer was by no means discouraged; the spirit of Caruso was alive and well in the Del Monaco household even before Mario discovered his tenor voice at the age of thirteen. He had mixed experiences with singing teachers, but the one that worked for him, and to whom he constantly returned, was Arturo Melocchi. Melocchi taught an extreme version of the low-larynx technique that most twentieth-century tenors have used in some form or another, which created the maximum acoustic space in the vocal tract. It requires the mouth to be opened very wide, almost as though yawning, and results in a rich muscular sound, usually at the expense of delicacy and agility. Too much downward pressure on the larynx is potentially harmful, and some pupils found the technique problematic; it revolutionised Del Monaco's approach to singing, however, from the time he first tried it publicly as Chénier at La Scala in 1949. This performance revealed a depth of power that extended the vocal possibilities of the role beyond the romantic histrionics of Gigli (who had last sung the role at La Scala two years earlier).

Del Monaco was not a subtle singer, in effect applying a Heldentenor technique to Italian dramatic and French roles. He was one of the century's finest Otellos, performing it hundreds of times in Europe and America (and so identified with the role that he was buried in his Otello costume). He also had considerable success with Puccini, investing the roles with greater power than perhaps the composer would have appreciated (though Verdi might well have enjoyed his Otello). Del Monaco, as a Heldentenor in all but name, would perhaps have gone on to become that rare beast, an Italian Wagnerian (he had sung Lohengrin – in Italian – at La Scala in 1957), but a motoring accident in 1963 seriously damaged his left leg. He did manage a remarkable recovery and successfully returned to the stage, but although he sang Siegmund in *Die Walküre* in 1966 and was invited by Karajan to sing Tristan, his true Helden potential was never realised; he retired in 1975.[3]

Risky though his technique might have been, it did not significantly shorten Del Monaco's career and he sang on even into retirement. Such was not the case with Giuseppe di Stefano, for whom technique was a largely a matter of experiment and instinct. He began singing seriously while interned in a Swiss refugee camp during the war, and made his formal début in *Manon* in Reggio Emilia in 1946. Des Grieux was the perfect vehicle for him, and he repeated the role for his La Scala début with a vocal and physical grace that seduced critics and audience alike. Two years later he made the first of many visits to the Met, and in 1951 had his first encounter with Maria Callas. The two of them formed one of the most enduring partnerships of the operatic stage, much of which survives on recordings from the 1950s. At this point in his career di Stefano was the perfect lyric tenor hero, his rich full sound and impressive stage presence offering an alternative vision to that of the ageing Gigli (who retired in 1956). But from the mid-'50s onwards the critical consensus is that his career began to falter as he took on dramatic roles that required him to expand his sound (especially at the top) beyond the reach of what turned out to be a limited technique. The result was, in the opinion of many, that his 'reckless and self-indulgent attitude towards his gift and his art not only prevented his voice from lasting but also kept him from exerting the lasting influence on the art of tenor singing that his early performance had promised.'[4] His career spanned little more than fifteen years. Another way of looking at this is that di Stefano simply did what he wanted to do with his singing, and when he felt that it was not working for him any more, he stopped. There are many tenors who continue to sing long after they have lost the wherewithal. At his best Giuseppe di Stefano was one of the most mellifluous and elegant singers of the century.

Franco Corelli

His one-time rival Franco Corelli also brought his career to what many considered a premature end, though rather more on his own terms. If any evidence were needed of the power of the tenor voice to move audiences we need look no further than Corelli's live recordings. One of a small number of tenors whose names are regularly put forward as the greatest of his century, Corelli was thought by his many fans to be perfect. In manner and appearance he was (like di Stefano) utterly unlike the cliché'd idea of the short, fat unprepossessing tenor of popular myth. Undeniably handsome, and possessing 'the most exquisite pair of legs ever seen on a tenor',[5] he cut a romantic figure even on the concert platform, appearing to be so confident of what he did, and so in the music, that he had little need of any extraneous gestures or rhetoric – what he did with his voice was enough. His singing seemed effortless – his torso hardly seemed to move however high the note or long the phrase. It was a big voice and not always lyrical, Corelli preferring to harness his considerable power with a consistency that his contemporaries such as Di Stefano might envy.

Unusually for one who would become such a sensational adult singer, Corelli did not sing as a child. He was born in 1921 in Ancona into a musical family (his brother and two of his uncles were all singers); his father worked in the shipyard, and he would perhaps have followed in his father's footsteps had he not been persuaded to attend the music high school in Pesaro. His tenor voice evolved into a substantial instrument which he found hard to control. Although he claims to have studied with 'half the voice teachers in Italy', the one certain thing we can say about his early career in the '40s is that he did not settle with a regular teacher.[6]

Without the benefit of consistent singing teaching in his formative years, Corelli's vocal development was determined to an extent by what he could learn from listening to records of Caruso, Gigli, Lauri-Volpi and other successful tenors. His habit of learning by analysing the performances of other tenors never left him (as Stefan Zucker put it, 'Corelli was a copycat'[7]). It was obvious to his friends (and to the judges who heard his competition arias) that he needed to study seriously, and his first steps towards this were with fellow student Carlo Scaravelli who was having lessons with Arturo Melocchi. Scaravelli was passionately interested in vocal technique, and would pass on to Corelli what he had learned after each lesson. Corelli did eventually have some lessons with Melocchi himself, having heard a live broadcast from La Scala of the famous Del Monaco *Andrea Chénier* in 1949, but the initial explorations of his own voice were made at one remove from the famous teacher and this seems to have made a great impact on the young tenor, enabling him to construct a technique for himself using elements of Melocchi's method.[8]

Taking almost complete responsibility for his own technique so early on meant that at a crucially important time for an aspiring singer he did not have a conventional teacher to guide him, to confirm (or not) that what he was doing was healthy and sensible. The advantage of this is that if a singer gets to know his voice in depth he may be able to explore his own uniqueness in ways that may not occur to a teacher. A disadvantage in Corelli's case is that he became almost obsessively interested in his own voice and technique; he suffered from stage nerves throughout his career and this fed his need for constant reappraisal of his own voice, which in the end caused him to retire from the operatic stage before he reached the age of fifty. In this respect he is very like de Reszke: each of them was considered by many to be the greatest tenor of his time, and at the point where they had conquered the highest musical peaks, both opted for a life without the demons caused by constant performance anxiety, leaving their fans bereft and bewildered.

Corelli's career effectively began when he won a competition in the Florence Maggio Musicale, the first prize of which was intended to include a part in Aida at Spoleto in 1951. Having worked for three months with Giuseppe Bertelli it became obvious that Corelli's technique was not yet robust enough to sustain the powerful legato lines needed for Radamès, and he switched to Don José in Carmen which was easier on the voice and temperamentally more suited to the young tenor. Corelli then went to Rome, before making his La Scala début in 1954 opposite Maria Callas in Spontini's *La vestale*. His Covent Garden début came three years later (in *Tosca*) and in the early '60s he triumphed in Berlin, Vienna and New York (*Il trovatore*) in rapid succession. At the beginning of his career he struggled to find high notes and chose his roles accordingly, gradually moving from the heavier dramatic roles to the more lyrical repertoire. By the late '50s he had found a way of crossing the *passaggio* in such a way that the higher roles such as Manrico and Calaf came more easily to him.[9]

He worked with some of the most successful divas of the age, including Leontyne Price (*Il trovatore*), Joan Sutherland (*Les Huguenots* and *Poliuto*), Leyla Gencer (*Poliuto* – in which Corelli interpolated a top D) and Birgit Nilsson (*Turandot* – a particular favourite at the Met and Covent Garden). He was not above upstaging his co-stars, most famously in the final duet in *Turandot*, opposite Nilsson as the eponymous heroine, who sings 'my glory is over' to which the tenor is supposed to reply 'no, it's just beginning'; Corelli sang instead, 'yes, it's over'. Nilsson attempted to turn the tables in the next performance by singing '*your* glory is over', to which Corelli replied 'no, it's just beginning'.[10]

Apart from being a truly international star (and his film version of *Tosca* has ensured him a certain immortality), Corelli's significance lies in how he relates vocally to his predecessors and contemporaries. He saw himself as being in the tradition of Caruso, Gigli and, more recently Lauri-Volpi, who became a friend and mentor. The fundamental influence, however, was surely the Arturo Melocchi/Mario Del Monaco connection. Corelli was well aware of the lack of subtlety in Del Monaco's singing, but he also appreciated the value of the Melocchi method if used with care. Corelli understood the significance of larynx position, but allowed his larynx to 'float', giving him more flexibility and control over a wider dynamic range and over the transition to head voice. All of his comments on singing suggest that he believed that once the basics were in place, especially as far as larynx position was concerned, then the peripheral details that are of such concern to so many singers and teachers, were much less important. His larynx theory certainly suited him, and helped him to incorporate other singers' stylistic traits.

Carlo Bergonzi

Carlo Bergonzi is another tenor who believed, like di Stefano and Corelli, that ultimately singers are the best judge of their own voices. Born very near Busseto (birthplace of Verdi), he was the son of a cheese-maker and sang in local choirs as a child. His singing ambitions were initially thwarted by the war, the last two years of which he spent in a German prisoner-of-war camp. On his return he studied in Parma with Ettore Campogalliani (who also taught Pavarotti) for three years as a baritone, making his début as Rossini's Figaro in Lecce in 1948. It was in his dressing-room during a performance of *Madam Butterfly* two years later that he realised that he was a tenor: Galliano Masini had mis-hit a top C and Bergonzi discovered that he could do a better one himself. Three months later he made his tenor début as Andrea Chénier in Bari.[11] Bergonzi taught himself thereafter, and like Corelli made a point of absorbing what he could from other tenors that he admired. Like Corelli he began by listening to recordings of great Italian tenors of the past: the obligatory Caruso and Gigli, but also Schipa and Pertile, as he himself put it:

> Caruso for the inimitable purity of sound; Gigli for a vocal technique that sang on the *piano* and carried the note, linking it to the *forte*; Schipa for his inimitable technique, achieved by no one else, that allowed him without having a beautiful voice quality, to become a great tenor; Pertile for vocal technique and technique of interpretation.[12]

Bergonzi clearly had a tenor brain to go with the voice, and using the power that he retained from his baritone beginnings, went on to become, like Mario Del Monaco, one of the most highly regarded Verdi interpreters of the century, although *Otello* was finally his undoing. He gave his American farewell performance in 1996 and went into semi-retirement without ever having performed the role on stage. In 2000, however, he agreed to a concert performance at Carnegie Hall but found himself unable to continue beyond the interval. It should have been a fine example of what a seventy-five-year-old singer could achieve (and Bergonzi would certainly have wished to impress the younger Pavarotti, Domingo and Carreras, who were all in the audience), but he was overtaken by *force majeur*.[13] Disasters of this sort can happen to any singer and Bergonzi was unlucky that his Otello gamble failed (it may have been due to something as banal as problems with the air-conditioning); for most of the half century of his career, his disciplined approach to his own instrument guaranteed him a sound technique. In retirement, he has become an inspired and inspiring teacher to many tenors, most notably the young Salvatore Licitra.

Alfredo Kraus and the lyric tradition

The post-war Italian star tenors dominated the market, and it is from this point that the public and critical sense of what a tenor was begins to narrow considerably. In the new world of mass communication *all* tenors were expected to be rich, full-sounding and dramatic – to be light and lyrical, however tasteful, was not enough. It was not just the French tradition that suffered in consequence: lyric tenors post-De Lucia and Schipa in Italy are also few and far between. The most successful exception was the Spaniard Alfredo Kraus. Kraus was brought up in the Canary Islands, the son of an Austrian émigré father who recognised his musical talent but initially encouraged him to study engineering. The musical gene eventually dominated and he followed his older brother (baritone Francisco Kraus) to Milan, where he became a pupil of Mercedes Llopart, who had had some success as a soprano in Italy and Spain between the wars (her achievements included the première of Wolf-Ferrari's *Sly* at La Scala in 1927, the year Kraus was born[14]). Llopart subsequently had a distinguished career as a teacher, mostly of women singers, and by the time of her death in 1970 she had numbered Renata Tebaldi, Montserrat Caballe, Anna Moffo and Renata Scotto among many successes. It is significant that Kraus studied with a woman, and his extended and easy high register (top D was no problem for him) may have been influenced by being taught by a high voice. Kraus also acknowledged the influence of Lauri-Volpi on his breathing technique (both could sustain impressively long lines) though he was critical of the Italian's 'reinforced falsetto'.[15] He also shared with Lauri-Volpi a romantic and aristocratic bearing that, combined with his instinctive lyricism, harked back to tenors of a previous age: the roles that he focused on were small in number and well within his capabilities: Mozart (whom he did not particularly like), Donizetti, Bellini, the lighter Verdi and the lyric French operas of Massenet and Bizet. The French repertoire suited him especially well, requiring restraint and grace rather than histrionic exaggeration. He was reluctant to take on the larger verismo roles, fearing that Puccini's heavier orchestration would put his technique at risk; there was also, perhaps, an element of musical snobbery in his choice of roles: he left the popularising to his 'Three Tenor' contemporaries, believing that 'Singers are artistic masters' and that 'If we try to popularise this art form, we go down to the lowest level.'[16] His caution served him well, and his technique enabled him to sing and teach for all of his adult life.

The stadium tenor: Pavarotti, Domingo and Carreras

The last decade of the twentieth century saw the coming together of three of the most successful tenors of their generation in the phenomenon known as the Three Tenors. The collaboration came about initially as a result of some creative thinking on the part of the Italian musical entrepreneur Mario Dradi. The germ of the idea was a celebration to mark the recovery from leukaemia of José Carreras and to raise money for his charitable foundation. The result was in the first instance a huge amplified open-air event, staged at the Baths of Caracalla in Rome in July 1990 immediately before the football World Cup; it launched Carreras, Domingo and Pavarotti to success that was extravagant even by the standards of international opera stardom, the ensuing commercial whole being even greater than the sum of the parts. The connection with sport was fortuitous but not inappropriate; the tenors, friends and colleagues, but each a star in his own right, were pleasantly competitive and the thirty-five or so concerts that they did together had something of the atmosphere of an international soccer friendly.[17] The events brought operatic arias to sports stadiums and generated vast amounts of money for the singers, their promoters and their record companies (culminating in an entry in the *Guinness Book of Records* for the highest-selling classical album). 'Three' became a talismanic number in music promotion, singers of all sorts appearing in multiples of the magic number for purely commercial reasons.

The three tenors project undoubtedly raised awareness of the tenor voice, and many younger tenors were able to profit as a result of the increased public demand. Vocally, the three stars added little in terms of style or technique: all were proficient in their individual ways, and all were amplified, seemingly with minimal compromise to their existing techniques. Musically too, the ensemble added nothing to the very conservative musical palette at the core of such a large-scale commercial classical phenomenon. If anything, the Three Tenors reinforced the tendency for the public to be offered a very limited musical diet, anthologized in the form of a 'greatest hits' collection, with none of the vagaries of operatic plots or the contortions of recitative to contend with. They also ventured into popular songs. Italian (and some Spanish) tenors have always done this, and in principle the three tenors repertoire was not very different from the excursions of Caruso or Gigli into Neapolitan song. Its greatest appeal was probably to those who like to listen to opera on classical radio stations, while driving, or as background music on social occasions.

The criticisms of the commercial and musical aspects of the three tenors do not detract from their achievements as individuals; their careers on the operatic stage flourished long before they were overtaken by events. Luciano Pavarotti, the oldest of the three, was born in 1935, the son of a baker and amateur tenor from Modena. It was in 1955 while on a highly successful visit to a Welsh Eisteddfod with the Modena chorus that the nineteen-year-old trainee teacher began to think seriously about a career in music. He had a prodigious natural talent (he was never completely at home with staff notation) and went for lessons to Arigo Pola in Modena and then on to Ettore Campogalliani in Mantova, making his début in 1961 as Rodolfo in *La Bohème* in Reggio Emilia. The role became a Pavarotti signature, with repeats for his débuts at Covent Garden (1963), La Scala (1965) and the Met (1968). His first Covent Garden appearances were as a stand-in for Giuseppe di Stefano, and Pavarotti would often in the future find himself taking on the mantle of the increasingly erratic star of the '50s (whom he greatly admired and who became a life-long friend). His Met performances as Tonio in Donizetti's *La Fille du régiment* created a sensation, with nine successive top Cs establishing him as the tenor to watch (his recording of Tonio opposite Joan Sutherland was described by John Steane as 'one of the best performances by any tenor on record'[18]).

Like his immediate Italian predecessors he was essentially a lyric singer with a big voice, which he wielded with inspiration and a remarkable singerly intelligence. He had considerable stage presence (he was a large man who became much larger as he got older) which to some extent made up for his rather basic acting ability. He was often praised for combining a sense of line with great clarity of diction, though this did not prevent him from adapting the language to his vocal needs, especially towards the end of his career (adding an extra syllable in 'vin-ne-cero, for example, to launch himself into the final phrase of 'Nessun dorma'). His top notes, once he got there, were effortless and he was marketed as the king of the high Cs but he was reluctant to stretch himself, confining his stage roles in the main to Donizetti, Bellini, Puccini and the less onerous Verdi parts. Pavarotti was greatly loved by the public, and gave them what they wanted even when his terminal pancreatic cancer made it impossible to deliver in real time. His last public performance, at the opening of the Turin Winter Olympics in 2006, used 'video trickery, careful lipsynching and a compliant orchestra that pre-recorded its backing track days earlier'. Such was the great tenor's craft and presence, and such was the public's determination to hear and see what they wanted, that nobody noticed that he was miming.[19]

Plácido Domingo's experience has been very different, his total number of roles upwards of 120. He was born in Madrid in 1941 to a performing family who moved to Mexico when Plácido was eight. He attended the National Conservatory in Mexico City, studying piano, conducting and singing (one of relatively few operatic tenors to have had a broader musical education beyond the vocal). His first adult singing was as a baritone in Mexican zarzuelas, and he has always considered his tenor voice to be the product of nurture rather than nature.[20] He auditioned for the Mexican National Opera as a baritone but was hired as a tenor, and in 1962 joined the Israeli National Opera in Tel Aviv. After almost three years during which he gave some 280 performances of eleven different roles he moved to New York, and his international career took off. Domingo is not only one of the most musically intelligent tenors to grace the operatic stage but he is also one of its finest actors, aware that in an age of television, audiences expect more realism and less formality in the emotional delivery of any role. He mastered all of the dramatic-lyric roles and his career trajectory eventually took him to the heights of Tristan (on disc) as well as stage works by contemporary composers. As he gets older, there is the possibility of a new career as a Verdi baritone, in addition to his work as a conductor and opera administrator. History may well judge him to be the greatest tenor of his era.

José Carreras was the most lyrical of the Three. He has sung (so far) only about half the number of roles that Domingo has accumulated, but many more than Pavarotti managed. Born in Barcelona in 1946, he became obsessed with singing from the age of six, when he saw Mario Lanza in *The Great Caruso*.[21] He had a fine treble voice and actually made his stage début as a boy soprano at the Gran Teatre del Liceu at the age of eleven, returning there in 1970 for his début as a tenor in Donizetti's *Lucrezia Borgia* with Montserrat Caballé, who was very supportive of the young tenor at the start of his career. Winning the Giuseppe Verdi Competition in Parma in 1971 soon brought him to the attention of the major European and American opera houses and eventually he won a recording contract. In 1988 Carreras discovered that he had leukaemia, which could have proved fatal but from which he made a full recovery. This defining moment of his life and career occurred at an age when his voice was in any case beginning to darken. This has not prevented him from taking on lighter roles by Bernstein, Lloyd Webber and others (his voice reacts well to the microphone) in addition to weightier operas such as *Samson et Dalila* and *Stiffelio*. Like Domingo, his musical horizons are expanding as he gets older. There are few tenors who would say 'At this stage in my career it's only worthwhile singing something new. Singing Alfredo in *La traviata* for the umpteenth time would be boring for myself and the audience.' Perhaps even more remarkably, he is recorded as saying that singing Siegmund (rather than listening to someone else singing the role) would be worth the risk of losing his voice. These are the remarks of a man whose close encounter with death has left him relishing the creative and artistic possibilities of his life.[22]

Life after Three

The Three Tenors phenomenon skewed the tenor market, with both positive and negative effects. On the plus side was the fact that many more people became aware of good singing for the first time. On the other hand, many fine tenors were at least partially eclipsed, especially those whose roles and repertoire took them beyond the small number of commercially viable 'hits' that were so successful for the Three.

Andrea Bocelli is perhaps the most successful single tenor associated with the Three Tenor era. A pupil of Franco Corelli, he subsequently became a Pavarotti protégé (he sang at Pavarotti's funeral in 2007). Bocelli places himself in an Italian tradition that includes both Gigli and Del Monaco, and he has something of the lyricism of one and the power of the other. Prevented by blindness from having the stage career that his voice would certainly have commanded, he became a multi-million selling recording artist, with a conservative repertoire that such a volume of sales inevitably implies.

The post-trinital world is currently shared between new young opera singers (many from Latin America) and a number of other singers who inhabit a musically dubious but commercially successful studio-to-stadium world somewhere between Mario Lanza and middle of the road pop music. The most successful are subject to clinical marketing strategies by record companies desperate to maintain the viability of their products at a time of rapid technological change. Previous technological advances have worked to record companies' advantage by encouraging consumers to replace recordings that they already own with equivalents in the new format; the downloading phenomenon is having unpredictably democratic consequences in what is fast becoming a consumer-led industry. Having grown up in the age of twenty-four hour television, the new singers are above all media-friendly: it is no coincidence that the star tenors of the early twenty-first century are charismatic personalities, and for the target audience they are as watchable as they are listenable.[23]

The collaboration between the Argentinean Marcelo Álvarez and the Italian Salvatore Licitra is an example of a successful marriage of tenorial talent and efficient promotional machinery. Marketed as DUETTO and hailed by a willing press as 'the heirs to Pavarotti and Domingo', their first joint appearance was at the Coliseum in Rome, and was filmed for television broadcast in Europe and the USA, where they subsequently performed in New York's Central Park. Both are singers who came relatively late to the professional life, having followed non-musical careers and found themselves singers if not entirely by accident then with the benefit of serendipity. Álvarez, born in 1962, managed the family furniture factory in Cordoba until at the age of thirty, when he first had singing lessons. On the advice of Giuseppe di Stefano he tried his luck in Italy, where after winning a competition in Pavia in 1995 he was soon offered roles all over the country. He was fortunate on two occasions to stand in for Alfredo Kraus in 1997 and a year later was taken up by Sony Classical. Licitra was a graphic artist before turning to the serious study of singing, finishing his training under Carlo Bergonzi. He made a promising start in Italy, but his big break came in 2002 when he stood in for Luciano Pavarotti at what was supposed to be the latter's farewell performance of *Tosca*. Licitra was then also signed up to Sony Classical and has gone on to success in opera houses throughout the world. Both, it should be said, are serious singers, and among the finest lyric singers of their generation, but their careers appear to be dictated in large part by publicity departments and consumer response rather than by their own tenorial considerations of repertoire or vocal development.

New South Americans

Licitra and Álvarez are by no means the only Italian and South American tenors to achieve international fame, and only time will reveal who will survive the effects of intensive marketing.[24] Success in Hispanic America has always been a mark of true international worth among opera singers of all voices. Argentina and Mexico in particular have welcomed European and North American tenors since the early nineteenth century, but until the latter part of the twentieth century there were few home-grown singers to match the imported stars. The favoured repertoire of Spanish America was firmly Italian and French, and international success for Mexican or Argentinean singers almost always meant the lyric or dramatic roles in European or North American opera houses. One of the earliest was José Mojica, whose visit to New York in 1916 coincided with the Edison Company's wish to expand into Latin America. His test pressing was not a success but he did eventually record for both Edison and Victor, and went on to star in several films (in three of which he played himself). He died in 1974 at the age of seventy-nine, having become a priest some years earlier. He can be heard on CD with two of his near-contemporaries Alessandro Bonci and Giuseppe Anselmi; all three have a fast vibrato, and all are unmistakably 'Italian' in style, technique and repertoire.[25] More prominent internationally was the extraordinary Chilean Ramón Vinay, whose palindromic career began as a baritone in Mexico before he turned himself into a distinguished Wagner and Verdi tenor; he then reverted to baritone for the latter part of his life.

With media success an essential element in the mass marketing of tenors, the vacuum left by the end of the Three Tenors project began to be filled by energetic, handsome singers who were touched by not only Italianate warmth but also an exotic trans-Atlantic heat. Many of them had few preconceptions about opera singing and were the willing recipients of guidance from marketing executives. They often came to the notice of conductors and agents by winning prestigious singing competitions, which then fast-track them to the world's opera houses. Ramón Vargas' experience is typical: he sang as a boy chorister, subsequently became a tenor, made his début in Mexico City in 1983, and went on to win the Caruso Competition in Milan three years later. He made the first of many visits to the Met in 1992 (in *Lucia di Lammermoor*) and made his La Scala début as Fenton the following year. Fellow Mexican Rolando Villazón also sang as a child, joining the Espacios Performing Arts Academy at the age of eleven. His main musical interest was in romantic pop tunes until he acquired an album of Plácido Domingo singing with John Denver, and it was singing for Domingo while on Pittsburgh Opera's training programme, and subsequently winning a prize in Domingo's Operalia competition that first brought him to public notice. He made his European début in 1999 as Des Grieux in Genoa, and from then on has had the world's opera houses at his feet. Hugh Canning considered his 2004 Covent Garden début as Hoffman the finest interpretation (both musically and as an actor) since Domingo's almost twenty-five years before.[26] A truly modern tenor, Villazón uses his past experience of pop ballads and microphone technique to inform his classical persona; his finely controlled mezza voce was originally developed in the studio and then applied to the theatre.[27] Although his voice is reminiscent of Domingo's he has been careful, like his great Mexican predecessor, to take responsibility for his own technique rather than place himself exclusively in the hands of a voice-teaching guru. He is aware that this strategy is not risk-free ('probably, at the end of my life, I'll think "how stupid", but I don't feel I need one now'[28]). Villazon appeared to suffer a crisis of vocal confidence in the middle of 2007 and stopped performing for the rest of the year, worried that he was approaching burn-out. He is a tremendously energetic and emotionally committed performer, but since his enforced sabbatical has (perhaps) learned to pace himself more carefully. He has been prepared to sing Monteverdi and Handel and hold back on the heavier Verdi, so time will tell.

Mexico and Argentina have probably provided a majority of international Latin American tenors at the start of the century (Argentina's contributions have included Luis Lima, José Cura and Dario Schmunck) but there are no discernible musical traits that could be called a national style. The stylistic differences between Vargas, Alvarez and Villazón are relatively small, and all three sing a similar repertoire. The Peruvian Juan Diego Flórez is something of an exception, emerging as a *tenore di grazia* with the elegance of an Alfredo Kraus (even though his first exposure to serious tenor singing was listening to recordings of Domingo and Pavarotti). Flórez' voice did not break in the traumatic manner that sometimes produces a changed voice overnight, but gradually sank from treble to tenor. This left him with a remarkable top register that has made him one of the few modern singers able to tackle the Rubini repertoire of Bellini, Donizetti and Rossini without resort to chest voice.[29] Flórez, like many of his South American contemporaries, grew up listening to pop and folk music and had little experience of classical music until adolescence. He learned the basis of his technique in Lima with Andrés Santa Maria and subsequently refined his breathing with Ernesto Palacio, who also gave him a sense of style that suited the pre-verismo composers. Flórez' European début, standing in for Bruce Ford in a performance of Rossini's *Matilde di Shabran* in the 1996 Palafestival in Pesaro, was such a success that he has been considered the leading Rossini tenor ever since. This is not a repertoire that is likely to appeal to the stadium audience (although the potential is there for competitive virtuosic display), but his dedication to a repertoire which comes naturally to few modern tenors has led to great critical acclaim and success in all of the world's leading opera houses.[30]

In the last quarter of the twentieth century Germany has produced some distinguished baritones and many fine tenors in contemporary and early music, but relatively few international opera tenors. With the German operatic infrastructure having a uniquely wide and deep base it was only a matter of time before a native talent emerged, and at the beginning of the new century Jonas Kaufmann is being hailed as the best German tenor for generations. He has been compared with Fritz Wunderlich, and is charting a career path dictated by his musical instincts:

> I don't want to be identified as the classical guy who did a crossover album, which I'm sure is what they'll want. I'd be happy one day to record operetta and songs like Granada that Fritz Wunderlich sang beautifully, but not now. Lloyd Webber? Pop ballads? Probably not.[31]

Even before he graduated from the Munich Hochschule für Musik he was singing smaller roles at the Munich Staatsoper and the Gärtnerplatz Theater. In 1994 he moved to Saarbrücken, where he gained valuable experience in lyric roles, which he continued to play in Zurich from 2001, while singing with increasing success all over the world. Recent roles have included Cavaradossi and José (Carmen) at Covent Garden, Alfredo at the Met, La Scala, Zurich and the Bastille, and he continues to sing Mozart and Verdi as well as venturing into the lighter Wagner roles; he has an increasing reputation as a Lieder singer in the Wunderlich mould. Although his international fame has come relatively quickly, it follows from a sound grounding in provincial German opera houses, which gave him the stamina and experience necessary to create a serious career. With his charisma, substantial honeyed tone and ability to sing convincingly in several languages, he may well be able to maintain a career that plays to his vocal strengths, retaining the lyric repertoire while adding heavier roles as his voice matures, hopefully avoiding the musical dilution that so often comes with success in the mass market.

Opera as anthology: tenors as easy listening

More recently a different sort of tenor phenomenon has emerged: the amateur singer 'discovered' as a result of popular acclaim, often by winning a television talent contest. The classical music industry has learned to adopt and adapt the marketing strategies of pop music, and in its most extreme manifestation can create success using the boy band formula. Il Divo, which featured two tenors in its line-up of four young singers, was created by music entrepreneur Simon Cowell, who has established the group in a hugely successful market positioned somewhere between Barbra Streisand and Andrea Bocelli. At the time of writing ex-Il Divo tenor Jonathan Ansell has just become the youngest tenor to top the classical charts, with his album *Tenor at the Movies*. Similar techniques have been deployed to promote tenors such as Russell Watson and Paul Potts; these media-friendly singers are a gift to marketing men, for whom a voice is only one part of their commercial appeal. Russell Watson was a steel worker who sang in clubs and pubs until a lucky break led to an appearance before a match at Old Trafford, the home of Britain's most famous football team, Manchester United. He made something of a speciality of singing at football stadiums à la Pavarotti until he was signed by Decca, and his first album became one of the fastest selling classical albums of all time. Although he is frequently described as an opera singer, his repertoire would not be classed as such by most opera-goers, consisting of arrangements that some-times have a connection to operatic originals and sometimes not. Paul Potts was an amateur singer and mobile phone salesman before winning a televi-sion talent contest in the UK (the video of his audition was one of the most frequently watched YouTube clips).[32] There are, of course, parallels with opera singers winning singing competitions, the essential difference being that Watson and Potts won by public acclamation rather than having their audi-tion legitimised by a panel of specialist musicians. They have also been accused of being poor imitations of greater singers such as Pavarotti or Carreras. Imitation in itself is not a crime against the tenorhood, however: as we have seen above, many of the finest tenors of the twentieth century were able to identify specific roles or arias by other tenors that they had shamelessly made their own.

Singers such as Ansell, Watson and Potts who defy tenorial convention are problematic for critics, who find it difficult to engage with tenors who have had little formal training, do not create stage roles and have only a tenuous connec-tion to the historic tradition.[33] And yet the TV tenor does tell us something about public taste, and may give us clues about the reputations and repertoire choices of 'real' tenors. The word 'opera' still carries with it a certain kudos (Il Divo called themselves an 'international operatic supergroup'[34]) and the default description for male winners of TV talent contests is 'opera singer', and yet these are opera singers in name only. The appeal of opera for modern audiences is very much to do with its tunefulness (opera as drama has to compete with tele-vision and film). The commercial decontextualisation of operatic arias (removing them from both operas and opera houses) has gone hand in hand with the phenomenon of celebrity classical singers who are more famous than the music they sing. It is not opera as we used to know it, and in many respects it is closer to middle of the road pop music. The 'crossover' phenomenon is also related to the fossilisation of the operatic repertoire in seeking to prolong the life of great opera tunes in the absence of new ones within the genre. It is perhaps little surprise that in the search for novelty and tunefulness, singers, promoters and mass audiences take refuge in the pop music repertoire.

There is an absence of an awareness of sense of craft among tenors promoted as pop musicians, and this may have implications for their voices in the longer term. Singing with amplification as a matter of course, stadium tenors rarely experience the live acoustic feedback that enables singers instantly to monitor what they do. Pavarotti famously took great pains to ensure his PA systems had very sophisticated stage monitoring (which often meant he had to stand as still as possible in large arenas) but his starting point was his knowledge of his own voice, which came from years of listening to it live in the world's opera houses. If you start your career in stadiums, the chances of a retreat into an actual opera theatre are rather remote, as Mario Lanza found (ultimately to his cost). Although the success of post-Pavarotti stadium tenors depends very much on record sales, there is little to connect them with the great tenors of recording history, who have generally grown into new roles as they matured. The stadium tenor is likely to grow sideways into 'crossover' rather than risk his reputation on more challenging music. The Three Tenors knew their Verdi; few of their young successors aspire to such dramatic heights.

Tenors as mega stars are not entirely new phenomena, as we have seen. Caruso, Gigli, Tauber and many others ruthlessly exploited their talents and their music with enormous commercial success, and all of them brought whole towns to a standstill when they died. The twenty-first century paradigm is different, however, not just in scale but in nature. Pavarotti was the first tenor to transcend the aesthetic and musical world in which he matured as an artist; as Jürgen Kesting put it:

> This voice has long ceased to be synonymous with the voice of music. It has become entertainment. Pavarotti himself is no longer a singer, but the subject as well as the object of that entertainment, that gigantic industry whose sole purpose is to produce human happiness.[35]

This has popularised a certain sort of tenor singing, but it has had a debilitating effect on opera: Pavarotti was heard increasingly rarely in the opera house, and most of his fans would in any case rather have paid a relatively small sum to hear him on a football pitch than the vastly inflated prices to be paid for seats in an opera theatre.

New times, new singing

If operatic tenors appeared to flourish in the second half of the twentieth century and into the twenty-first, the wider vocal picture was more complicated. The long lens of history may eventually show a different picture of singing during this period from that visible under the microscope of today. Outside the insular and predictable world of opera, the impact of the war was responsible for new thinking among singers. For the young Dietrich Fischer-Dieskau, who had fought in the German army and first experienced singing as an adult in a prisoner-of-war camp, singing was something entirely different from the comfortable world of the Liederabend. The young baritone's starting point was not the voice, but the text. This resulted in a way of singing characterised by fastidious attention to poetic detail, if necessary at the expense of what might be perceived as the musical line. His older contemporaries and predecessors, for whom the production of a beautiful sound was paramount, began to seem decadent by comparison. Fischer-Dieskau could certainly produce an exquisite line when he wanted to, but traditional singerly techniques were only used where the music and text required them, and were not essential to his vocal persona.[36] Vocally, this is much easier for a baritone to do than a tenor, as baritones generally sing in a tessitura that overlaps with speech. Much of the appeal of the tenor voice is its instrumental colour, the fundamental sound quality that distinguishes the voice from that of a baritone, and for acoustic reasons the soaring tenor high notes can only be achieved at the expense of a certain textual clarity.[37] Yet the Fischer-Dieskau approach to text has become the underlying sensibility of much modern singing and has influenced many singers across the classical spectrum.

There was still room for pure vocalism – the new style was more appropriate for nineteenth-century repertoire than Bach and Mozart, and in Fritz Wunderlich, Peter Schreier and Helmut Krebs the newly divided Germany had brilliant interpreters of the eighteenth-century canon (not forgetting the Swiss Ernst Haefliger). The son of a conductor, Wunderlich grew up to be a multi-instrumentalist who discovered he had a voice only after singing and playing in dance bands. He retained an enthusiasm for certain favourite instrumental parts, and Fischer-Dieskau tells the story of the two singers touring with *Das Lied von der Erde* with both giving impromptu renderings of the horn literature in the dressing room.[38] Dieskau himself was touched by Wunderlich's singing and gave him much encouragement. His career began slowly, but was crucially influenced by two female teachers, Käthe Bittel-Valckenberg in Kaiserslauten (to whom he cycled twenty miles each day once a week for a year) and Margarethe von Winterfeldt, with whom he studied for four years at the Freiburg Music Hochschule. As we have seen so often before, the combination of female teacher and lyric tenor produced a very individual voice that had few obvious predecessors. His first public performance was in *Die Zauberflöte*, and Tamino became almost a signature role for him (it was also the last opera he sang before his death). He went on to record prolifically, taking in Bach, Handel and Haydn as well as the Mozart roles that he was perhaps most at home in, and also heavier parts in Strauss and Mahler. Rather than gravitate towards significantly weightier roles he chose to become a Lieder singer, exploring the great Schubert cycles under the collaborative tutelage of Hubert Giesen. His death in 1966 (from a fall at the age of thirty-five) was described by Nigel Douglas as 'the greatest tragedy to strike the operatic profession since the end of the Second World War'.[39]

Peter Schreier was also an eloquent exponent of Mozart and Bach, and one of Germany's finest Lieder singers, recording extensively, before turning to conducting. He was the son of a Kantor and his musical career began early as a boy soprano (later alto) in the Dresdner Kreuzchor, with whom he toured extensively while still a child. As a tenor he joined the Dresden Staatsoper in 1959 and his lyrical warmth earned him success in the major European houses as well as the Met and the Teatro Colón, principally in Mozart. His singing was meticulously phrased and his background as a boy chorister gave him a keen sensitivity to acoustics, something that could surprise those who heard him live only after experiencing him on record.[40] If Schreier has a successor it is perhaps Hans-Peter Blochwitz, who has had considerable success as a Mozart and Bach singer and more recently in Lieder. Helmut Krebs' career encompassed the staple Bach cantatas and Mozart concert arias as well as the great Schubert song-cycles. He was not a great opera singer, but his performances included Schoenberg's *Moses and Aaron* and among his many recordings is the first Monteverdi *Orfeo* on LP. The Danish tenor Aksel Schiøtz also made his mark primarily outside the realm of opera; another sometime student of John Forsell, he went on to become one of the most subtle of Lieder singers, and an intelligent interpreter of Mozart, before a brain tumour disrupted his career, which he eventually resumed as a baritone.

Alternative voices

In both Europe and the USA, once post-war recovery had become a reality there was a considerable broadening of ideas of what constituted music and singing. The baby-boom generation had less time for the extravagance of grand opera, and in any case the supply of singers eventually outstripped demand, so creative musical entrepreneurship was needed if all of the musicians who aspired to a career were actually to have one. This phenomenon made itself felt in two significant areas outside the vocal mainstream, both involving the use of the voice in what at the time were considered to be unconventional ways. In contemporary music the experiments of the avant-garde began to look at non-standard ways of producing the voice. This area of endeavour became known as extended vocal techniques (or 'evt'). These new sounds often required the use of a microphone to amplify the very small and often para-linguistic sounds that composers such as Stockhausen and Berio were exploring. This tended to blur the distinction between voices of the same gender, as many of the sounds were related to speech and often did not demand vocal tract formations that produced recognisable tenor or bass tone colours. In the case of both of these composers the traditional tenor voice was retained in their operas, while 'evt' tenors are required for amplified ensemble music. Berio's *Opera*, for example, has a substantial tenor role (premièred by Gerald English) while the amplified voices of the Swingle Singers (including two tenors) sang from the pit with the instrumental ensemble. Stockhausen's opera cycle *Licht* has substantial tenor roles (many of them premièred by Julian Pike), whereas his *Stimmung* is for six amplified voices singing reinforced harmonics.[41]

In Britain the steady supply of ex-Oxbridge male voices, increasingly augmented by female voices towards the end of the century, encouraged an entrepreneurial spirit that led to the setting up of a large number of vocal ensembles. These were very much at home in the renaissance repertoire and were a significant part of the engine which drove the early music movement. The Tallis Scholars, Hilliard Ensemble, Gothic Voices and The Sixteen all used ex-choral scholar tenors, which contributed to the characteristic English early music sound. These groups featured tenors who had been trained with a modern technique, but in the context of élite professional choirs which required minimal vibrato so that chords could be tuned with considerable refinement. The growth of early music since its commercial beginnings in the 1970s has been spectacular. For tenors it meant a chance to explore repertoires that had not been sung for generations, and the opportunity to re-envision canonic composers such as Bach, Handel and Mozart. Early music has its own specialist tenors; one of the earliest and most significant was Nigel Rogers, who for many years was one of the few possessors of a throat technique that could cope with the very fast music required for virtuosic seventeenth-century music. He has been followed by many tenors in mainland Europe (such as Guy de Mey and Christophe Prégardien) and the USA, with a notable number of Americans (such as Howard Crook) finding more opportunities in Europe.

Much of this music requires tenors to sing in small ensembles with only one voice to a part, and one of the quirks of the early music movement is that this same principle has been applied fairly indiscriminately to renaissance choral music too, providing plenty of work for agile tenors who are quick sight-readers. Ensemble singing, responding to the demand created by record companies and festivals, has been one of the few areas in which creative singers can have the expectation of a career outside the realm of opera. This is something that conservatoires in Britain and the USA have almost universally failed to acknowledge. By focusing almost exclusively on producing opera singers, many of whom will never find the kind of work that their training has equipped them for, music colleges miss an important opportunity to rationalise the supply of new singers. In mainland Europe, especially in the Low Countries, Germany and Switzerland, the Hochschule system has been far more realistic in serving the potential interests of their students by enabling early music singers to function both as soloists and as capable ensemble singers. The Schola Cantorum in Basel, the Royal Conservatoire in the Hague, and German Musik Hochschüle, such as those in Bremen and Trossingen, have produced many successful early music tenors.

The future

Conventional wisdom has it that demand for good tenors almost always outstrips supply. The number of people born with a pre-disposition to a tenorial vocal tract formation is, as far as we know, constant per head of population. The variables in the production of tenors are opportunities to train and then opportunities to work. The training of tenors is now very sophisticated, and young singers not only have the whole of recorded vocal history to call on, but are able to access any contemporary models almost instantly via CD or DVD, radio and television, and the internet. As we have seen with the current crop of aspiring opera tenors, there is little to distinguish one nationality from another: all are aiming to achieve broadly the same thing within a limited repertoire. All have had very similar training, which increasingly relies on real scientific knowledge: if you know how to maximise the acoustic space in your mouth you are likely to be able to sing more efficiently than a tenor who does not understand the principles. With so much objective knowledge available for all, tenors are likely to sound more similar (as is indeed the case with many who are currently successful). They are likely to have learned the trade at a conservatory. These compete in 'excellence' – the visible and aural sign of a certain quality or standard, and high standards almost always mean a high degree of standardisation, especially where 'excellence' is an end in itself. There is often funding available to research ways of creating even better performers, and so efficient are most national conservatories at producing singers across the spectrum of voices, that far more students complete their courses than are likely to find work in the profession. Because tenors are still considered to be very marketable, perhaps more so than baritones or basses, they have an advantage over other male voices. But if we take the UK as an example, and posit that each of seven conservatories produces only one 'excellent' tenor per year, then over the period of a three-year course more than twenty competing tenors will come on to the market. In a ten-year period some seventy tenors would need to be accommodated in the UK alone. We cannot estimate a meaningful figure for the annual international supply of recently graduated tenors, but we can be sure that it is much greater than the opportunities available. The effects of this may take a generation or two to become apparent, but eventually there will be a price to pay for the over-production of operatic excellence. One likely effect is shorter careers (why pay a huge fee to an established tenor when you can get a recent graduate or début-tant to do virtually the same job for a fraction of the price?). For certain areas of the tenor repertoire this is a particularly alarming prospect: there is a risk that the lyric-to-dramatic progression will dry up, as singers are priced out of the profession before they have a chance to mature; Heldentenors can take half a lifetime to grow into the *Fach*.

For the general public, unaware of the niceties of tenor production, there will no doubt be a steady supply of decontextualised stadium tenors to main-tain a semblance of something that may still be called opera singing, but we are likely to see very little further development in the voice of the operatic tenor unless there is some sort of democratic re-envisioning of opera as a genre. A more positive prognosis might suggest greater entrepreneurial spirit. There are signs of this in Europe and America, with small touring companies doing new work. If this kind of enterprise were to be applied in opera on the same scale as the dynamic new thinking that characterised the early music movement towards the end of the twentieth century, then perhaps more tenors will be able to earn a living in the future.

The central focus of this book has been on opera tenors, because it has been in opera that the key developments have taken place. The most significant singers have almost always made their names on the operatic stage, and from there been able to explore other repertoires. In contrast to the narrowing of repertoires that occurred from the end of the nineteenth century onwards there has been a certain broadening of scope from the last decades of the twentieth century onwards. This has taken the form of what is sometimes referred to as 'crossover', where singers from classical music attempt to sing popular music (and vice-versa). The artistic value of these enterprises is hard to measure. On the one hand, a singer of the stature of José Carreras singing popular ballads can be said to increase appreciation for good singing and may encourage new listeners to sample his more serious repertoire. This was prob-ably the case too with the Heldentenor Peter Hofman's parallel career as a rock musician. In the age of the iPod, repertoires of extraordinary diversity seem to sit happily beside each other, a phenomenon which surely encourages experiments in eclectic listening. This process of consumer diversification probably also occurs when pop singers make forays into classical repertoire, attracting new audiences for more serious music. Freddie Mercury's high camp duetting with Montserrat Caballé undoubtedly brought a certain energy to his quasi-operatic performances, using the microphone as an extension of himself. More recently Sting's CD of music by John Dowland excited great interest in the early music world.

Musical theatre

One area in which positive developments can be seen is that of the musical theatre, which in some respects fulfils some of the functions of pre-twentieth century opera, both in terms of the artistic creativity of the performers and the expectations of audiences. Singers cannot depart from the composer's score or conductor's direction in opera and concert works, but there are increasingly creative possibilities in musicals. Off-Broadway tenors are fast re-inventing the voice for their particular medium. Often these singers have grown up with a plurality of vocal styles which might include some opera training for technique, which is then put into the service of creating a sound closer to that of rock musicians. This enables them to sustain roles night after night in much the same way as an opera singer, while the use of amplification gives them the opportunity to experiment with expressive tone colour without the need to project. In theory at least, tenors in musicals have a tonal range that encompasses the barely audible intimate whisper, to full-blooded Puccini-type high notes.[42]

Coda

A history of the tenor can never be very comprehensive or in any way definitive, but if there is an appropriate time to attempt one the beginning of the twenty-first century may be about right. The silent history of the tenor voice before the recording watershed will continue to be refined and re-interpreted, and the more recent tenorial narrative from the twentieth century onwards will be sifted, filtered and argued over as the voice continues to evolve. Recordings of almost all significant tenors of the last century are available in digital format (currently CD but not likely to be for much longer) and radio, television and the world-wide web enable those interested in the voice to be more up to date than ever before. I hope I have explained something of how things came to be as they are; interested readers can now make their own journeys into the tenorial past, enjoy the present and make their own predictions about the future.

NOTES

Chapter 1

1. The larynx and its associated muscles consist of soft tissue so do not survive in the archaeological record, unlike skeletal remains. The anthropological consensus is that the vocal mechanisms of *homo sapiens* are essentially unchanged since the evolution of language.
2. Research currently at the University of York suggests that many singers specialising in early music use a scaled-down version of modern technique.
3. The sources for singing in the medieval period are covered comprehensively in Timothy McGee, *The Sound of Medieval Song* (Oxford, 1998) and there is a concise overview from a different perspective in Joseph Dyer, 'The Voice in the Middle Ages' in John Potter (ed.), *The Cambridge Companion to Singing* (Cambridge, 2000): 165–77. See also John Potter, 'Reconstructing Lost Voices', in Tess Knighton and David Fallows (eds), *Companion to Medieval and Renaissance Music* (Oxford, 1998).
4. Sting's performances of Dowland (*Songs from the Labyrinth* DGG 06025 170 3139) are an example of a more speech-like delivery within the tenor range, where clarity of text and the singer's individual vocal persona are essential to the performance. A performance by a modern classically trained singer will have elements of both of these, but not at the expense of an equally essential tenorial sound quality.
5. See the work of Anna Maria Busse Berger, especially *Medieval Music and the Art of Memory* (Berkeley, 2005).
6. See Craig Wright, *Music and Ceremony at Notre Dame of Paris 500–1550* (Cambridge, 1990).
7. *Medieval Music and the Art of Memory* provides insights into how this very creative process may have worked.
8. See David Fallows 'Alanus, Johannes', *Grove* 1: 276 for a detailed account of this particular piece.
9. Eleanor M. Beck, *Singing in the Garden: Music and Culture in the Tuscan Trecento* (Innsbruck, 1998).
10. Lewis Lockwood, *Music in Renaissance Ferrara 1400–1505* (Cambridge, Mass., 1984), especially Chapter 10, 'Pietrobono and the improvisatory tradition': 95–108.
11. Howard Mayer Brown, *Embellishing Sixteenth-Century Music* (Oxford, 1984). Brown focuses on ten treatises published between 1535 and 1600.
12. 'Dedicated' meaning a specialist as opposed to a courtly amateur. There was no 'profession' of singer as such; see John Rosselli, 'From princely service to the open market: singers of Italian opera and their patrons, 1600–1850', *Cambridge Opera Journal*, 1/1: 1–32.
13. *Embellishing Sixteenth-Century Music*: 48.
14. *Trattato della musica scenica* (1635), translated in Carol MacClintock, *Readings in the History of Music in Performance* (Bloomington, 1982): 202–3.
15. *The Book of the Courtier*, trans. Charles Singleton (New York, 1959): 104. The fact that such etiquette handbooks existed confirms that there was potential upward social mobility for those in a position to capitalise on their talent. The reluctance to

be associated with work also extended to composition. Marco da Gagliano tells us in the preface to his opera *Dafne* that three of the songs were written by 'a great protector of music and a great expert in it' but cannot reveal that it was in fact his patron Ferdinando Gonzaga. See Edmond Strainchamps, 'Gagliano, Marco da', *Grove* 9: 416–21.

16. Echoes tickled the fancy of listeners and musicians alike, and they feature in many compositions of the period (notably the Monteverdi *Vespers* of 1610). A double echo is not unusual, and presupposes echoing tenors of a less exalted kind; Peri's example is one of the earliest known.

17. From the preface to *Dafne* translated in Carol MacClintock, *Readings*: 189. For the Italian original see Warren Kirkendale, *The Court Musicians in Florence during the Principate of the Medici* (Florence, 1993): 206. Gagliano set his version of Rinuccini's libretto in 1608, some eight or nine years after Peri's. Peri was one of several singers whose performance of their own music was said to be particularly captivating; Sigismondo d'India was another charismatic singer (also known to us now primarily as a composer) whose exquisite singing had a similar effect. See Nigel Fortune, 'Italian seventeenth-century singing' *Music & Letters*, 35/3 (July, 1954): 210.

18. Quoted in Tim Carter, 'Jacopo Peri', *Music & Letters*, 61/2 (April, 1980):123.

19. From the preface to *Euridice*, trans. Oliver Strunk, in *Source Readings in Music History* III (London, 1981): 15.

20. From *Discorso della musica dell'età nostra* (1640); this extract quoted in Fausto Razzi, 'Polyphony of the *seconda prattica*: performance practice in Italian vocal music of the mannerist era', *Early Music*, 8/3 (July, 1980):304.

21. *Le nuove musiche* (1602), trans. H. Wiley Hitchcock (Madison, 1970): 43. Howard Mayer Brown, in his 'The geography of Florentine monody: Caccini at home and abroad' (*Early Music*, 9/2, April 1981) considered Palla to be a countertenor, based on the description by Luigi Dentrice of a gathering of musicians supposedly in order of voices. If this order is correct (Palla being the third voice up from the bass), he is more likely to have been a high tenor, since part music of the period more usually required two tenors as inner voices, rather than an alto and a tenor.

22. Brown (*ibid.*) quotes in full a fascinating letter to Caccini from his fellow musician Piero Strozzi, who is trying to convince the singer not to move from Florence to Genoa; Strozzi's letter is a remarkable insight into the life of a renaissance musician and the human foibles of one in particular ('The geography of Florentine monody': 159–62).

23. *Le nuove musiche*: 44–5.

24. As Kirkendale points out, more documentary evidence exists for Rasi's career than for any of his contemporaries, yet this is not reflected in the attention given to him by current musicology (*The Court Musicians in Florence*: 556, n.14).

25. *The Court Musicians in Florence*: 570–71. Kirkendale's section on Rasi (pp. 556–603) gives an overview of his life and works with many illuminating quotations (in Italian).

26. Carol MacClintock, 'The monodies of Francesco Rasi', *Journal of the American Musicological Society*, 14/1 (Spring, 1961): 34.

27. Or it may be that the genuine virtuoso would have improvised from the plain version, with the elaborate version being more in the nature of a model for those unsure of how virtuosic to be.

28. Musicianly murder was not uncommon at the time, Rasi's probable sometime employer Gesualdo being perhaps the most famous example, having murdered his wife and her lover.

29. Susan Parisi, 'Campagnolo', *Grove* 4: 884. See also *The Letters of Claudio Monteverdi* ed./ trans. Denis Stevens (London, 1980): 305.

30. *Discorso sopra la musica* (1628), trans. Carol MacClintock, *Musicological Studies and Documents* 9 (American Institute of Musicology, 1962): 71.

31. Readers who sing tenor or bass will know that attempts to extend their ranges almost always involve a loss of tone colour. Consistency over a wider range is likely to lead to a consistently less rich sound, but one compensation may well be a more flexible throat technique. For more on how to sing music of this period see Richard Wistreich, 'Reconstructing pre-Romantic singing technique', in John Potter (ed.), *The Cambridge Companion to Singing* Cambridge, 2000): 178–91.

32. The practice may have begun by bass singers extending themselves upwards. For more on the tenor-bass phenomenon see Richard Wistreich, *Warrior, courtier, singer: Giulio Cesare Brancaccio and the performance of identity in the late Renaissance* (Aldershot, 2007): 176–85; 193–203.

33. See the multi-authored Section 4 of the *Grove* entry on 'Tenor', *Grove* 25: 285–6.

34. As I pointed out in my *Vocal Authority*, a modern rock singer such as Sting could make an ideal performer of music from this period. Sting's recorded performances of Dowland are compromised by his awareness of other performances by modern tenors, and show unfortunate signs of having been coached by an 'early music' specialist; his speech-like approach to text can be appreciated in much of his other work, such as his version of 'Around Midnight' on the Andy Summers album *Green Chimneys* (Rare RAR 1002).

35. See the note on pitch p. 196 n.5 below. The Purcell counter-tenor 'tenor' did not flourish in England much beyond the early years of the next century; within twenty years of Purcell's death Handel had settled in London and *opera seria*, which was underpinned entirely by Italian singing, soon became entrenched in British theatres. The falsettist counter-tenor survived in English cathedrals as the male alto until Alfred Deller revived the voice for solo repertoire in the twentieth century, paving the way for the modern counter-tenor as a substitute for castrati.

36. See note 4 below for an explanation of terminology relating to registers. Rogers Covey-Crump was among the first modern tenors to revive this technique in early music – so successfully that from the 1980s onwards tenors of similar range were sometimes informally referred to as 'crump-tenors'. He also has the distinction of being one of the most misprinted tenors in history; see the Hilliard Ensemble's *Newsletter* No. 2 (Spring 1991), where he is described as 'a typesetter's nightmare'.

37. Bénigne de Bacilly, *Remarques curieuses sur l'art de bien chanter* (Paris, 1668), trans./ed. Austin B. Caswell as *A Commentary upon the Art of Proper Singing* (New York, 1968).

38. Bacilly, *Remarques*: 42.

39. Nyert embodied the French concept of 'politesse', which required restraint rather than the over-indulgence in dramatic rhetoric, but is otherwise reminiscent of the courtly ideal espoused in Castiglione's *Book of the Courtier*. See Don Fader, 'The *honnête homme* as music critic: taste, rhetoric, and politesse in the 17th-century French reception of Italian music', *The Journal of Musicology*, 20/1 (Winter, 2003): 3–44.

Chapter 2

1. *Voyage en Italie* (1786), quoted in Mary Cyr, 'On performing eighteenth-century *haute-contre* roles', *Musical Times*, 118/1610 (April, 1977): 292. Lalande goes on to make clear that these *haute-contres* were tenors and not contraltos.

2. *Ibid.*

3. 'la puissance de la voix d'homme [et] toute la douceur et le charm de la voix de femme.' Gilbert-Louis Duprez, *L'Art du chant* (Paris, 1846; facs *Méthodes & Traités*, Serie II/II, Paris, 2005): 3.

4. There is no general agreement on a comprehensive definition of registers, and the terminology used to describe their number and nature is confusing. Johan Sundberg

describes a register as 'a phonation frequency range in which all the tones are perceived as being produced in a similar way and which possess a similar voice timbre' (J. Sundberg, *The Science of the Singing Voice* (Dekalb, 1987): 49). Sundberg also makes a distinction in male voices between the 'normal or *modal* register' used for lower frequencies, and *falsetto*, a set of higher phonation frequencies that may 'imitate the female voice character' (p. 50). Singers generally refer to the modal register as their chest voice as this is where the sounds are felt, and the falsetto register is often referred to as 'head voice' because this is where singers experience the resonance (these terms are metaphorical rather than acoustic: there is no significant resonance in either head or chest cavities). Before the end of eighteenth century Italian (or Italian influenced) tenors would sing up to the 'break' between registers in chest voice (around E or F above middle C) and use falsetto for anything higher. There is an overlap of several notes which can be sung with either disposition, and this range is often experienced as a separate register or a mixture of the two (*la voix mixte*). A central part of all singers' technique was to be able to change seamlessly from one register to another.

5. Pitch standards varied, and in general rose to something closer to modern pitch over the course of the nineteenth century (the 440 *A* was not formally adopted internationally until 1975). Singers must have been used to local variations but the gradual rise could produce problems, especially with the increasingly higher use of the chest register: Berlioz complains about tenors who have 'shattered their voices on the high Cs and Bs of the chest register' (see Hector Berlioz, 'The rise in concert pitch', in *The Art of Music and Other Essays,* trans. and ed. Elizabeth Csicsery-Rónay (Bloomington, 1994): 193–9 and n.19, 263), while in England Henry Chorley observes that 'in these days [writing in 1862 of 1848] everyone will sing altissimo – basses where tenors used to disport themselves, tenors in regions as high as those devoted by Handel to his contralti . . .' *Thirty Years' Musical Recollections* (London, 1862; repr. 1972): 232.

6. For *haute-contre* see Chapter 1 above: 19. The evidence from later French treatises confirms that they were tenors rather than counter-tenors. Mengozzi observes that the tenor voice, known in the eighteenth century as 'taille', was only about one note lower than the *haute-contre*; see Bernardo Mengozzi *et al.*, *Méthode de chant du conservatoire de musique* (Paris, 1804, facs *Méthodes & Traités*, serie II/1, Paris, 2005). Garaudé says that the 'first tenor' used to be known as *haute-contre* (Alexis de Garaudé, *Méthode complète de chant* (Paris, 1841; facs *Méthodes & Traités*, serie II/II, Paris, 2005): 16. Mengozzi (1758–1800) and Garaudé (1779–1852) were both successful singers and composers who taught at the Paris Conservatoire.

7. 'second register' or 'head sounds'. Garaudé *Methode*: 9.

8. See B. Brewer, 'Rubini – king of Tenors', *Opera* XXX (1979): 326–9.

9. See G. Buelow, 'Mattheson, Johann', *Grove* II: 832–6.

10. For the story of the re-composition of the role of Bazajet, see S. LaRue, *Handel and his Singers* (Oxford, 1995): 17–79. The role as originally conceived involved a relatively high tessitura and angular leaps, whereas Borosini was more effective (and dramatic) in the middle of his voice.

11. Winton Dean, 'Pinacci, Giovanni Battista', *New Grove* 19: 748–9. Pinacci was a shrewd negotiator; see W. Holmes, 'Giovanni Battista Pinacci and his two contracts in Rome (1726)', *Opera Observed: Views of a Florentine Impresario in the Early Eighteenth Century* (Chicago, 1993): 118–30.

12. Henry Pleasants, *The Great Singers* (London, 1967): 124.

13. Winton Dean, 'Fabri [Fabbri], Annibale Pio ['Balino']', *Grove* 8: 491–2.

14. Winton Dean, 'Gordon, Alexander', *Grove* 10: 156; see also C. Morey, 'Alexander Gordon, scholar and singer', *Music & Letters*, 46/4 (October, 1965): 332–5.

15. Winton Dean, 'Lowe, Thomas', *Grove* 15: 255.

16. See J. Wignall, 'Guglielmo d'Ettore: Mozart's first Mitridate', *Opera Quarterly*, 10/3 (1994): 93–112.

17. 'Mozart's first Mitridate': 93–112.
18. *The Letters of Mozart and his Family* (3rd edn), ed. Emily Anderson, rev. Stanley Sadie and Fiona Smart (London, 1997): 497.
19. *Ibid.*
20. *Ibid.* 551–2.
21. *Ibid.* 698–9. See also D. Heartz, 'Raaff's last aria: a Mozartian idyll in the spirit of Hasse', *Musical Quarterly,* 60/4 (October, 1974): 517–43.
22. *Letters*: 682.
23. The Jesuit churches in the larger cities of Austria and Germany produced and employed many successful singers; Karl Friberth was Kapellmeister to Vienna's two Jesuit churches from 1776 until his death in 1816.
24. Valesi was an accomplished teacher whose pupils included the composer Carl Maria von Weber. See Hans Schmid, 'Valesi, Giovanni', *Grove* 26: 217.
25. R. Mount Edgcumbe, *Musical Reminiscences of the Earl of Mount Edgcumbe: Containing an Account of the Italian Opera in England from 1773* (4th edn, London, 1834; repr. New York, 1973): 16.
26. *Letters*: 426.
27. *Letters*: 807–8.
28. See Thomas Bauman and Paul Corneilson, 'Adamberger, (Josef) Valentin', *Grove* 1: 134–5.
29. Thomas Baumann, 'Mozart's Belmonte', *Early Music*, 19/4 (November, 1991): 560.
30. See Laura E. DeMarco, 'The fact of the castrato and the myth of the countertenor', *Musical Quarterly* 86/1 (2002): 174–85.
31. John Rosselli's chapter 'Castrati' in his *Singers of Italian Opera* (Cambridge, 1995): 32–55 is perhaps the best succinct account of the castrato phenomenon. See also P. Barbier, *The World of the Castrati* (London, 1996) on the schooling of castrati.
32. Rossini and the tenor Duprez are late examples of trebles for whom castration was a possibility; see p. 200, n.24 below.
33. This still happens today, Juan Diego Flórez being a currently successful example of a tenor whose voice seems to have metamorphosed quite gradually from treble to tenor (see Tom Sutcliffe, 'Juan Diego Flórez – a profile', liner notes to Decca 473 440–2). There are many similar twentieth-century examples: Edward Lloyd's voice 'never broke, but gradually deepened from treble to tenor' (J. Jarrett, M. Reddy, and J. Richards, 'Edward Lloyd' *Record Collector,* 12/10 (1959): 221).
34. Michael Kelly, *Solo Recital* (London, 1972): 52.
35. *Solfeggio* exercises (using solfa note-names as a means of developing basic aural and vocal skills) would often be taught by a 'master of lower rank' (Pier Francesco Tosi, *Observations on the Florid Song,* trans. John Galliard, London 1743, facs London, 1967): 11.
36. Kelly: 55.
37. See H.C. Robbins Landon, *Haydn in England* (London, 1994).
38. W.T. Parke, *Musical Memoirs* (London, 1830): 140. Parke was principle oboist in the Covent Garden orchestra from 1790 to 1830, so was able to observe singers at close quarters both in performance and socially. There were several other tenors who managed to make a successful living as performers or teachers but who were not part of the international elite, including Domenico Corri, who had been a pupil of Porpora and whose daughter was good enough to sing duets with David. Parke entertained lavishly, and was host to Attwood, Dussek, and probably Haydn himself during the latter's stay in London.
39. Olive Baldwin and Thelma Wilson, 'Leoni, Michael', *Grove*.14: 564–5. The Jewish cantorial tradition has been a significant factor in the history of singing, especially from the twentieth century onwards. See Stephen Banfield, 'Stage and screen entertainers in the twentieth century' in John Potter (ed.), *The Cambridge Companion to Singing* (Cambridge, 2000): 69–72 and p. 111 below.

40. See Mollie Sands, 'These were singers', *Music & Letters*, 5/2 (April, 1944): 106.
41. Theodore Fenner, *Opera in London: Views of the Press 1785–1830* (Illinois, 1994): 169.
42. Quoted in 'These were singers': 104.
43. Some years earlier Mrs Billington had been the loser in a similar competitive encounter with Miss George in Dublin. In *The Beggar's Opera* Billington had been much applauded in her verse of the strophic 'Why now, madame flirt', whereupon Miss George sung her verse an octave higher, to huge public acclaim. See W.T. Parke, *Musical Memoirs* (London, 1830): 128.
44. *Musical Memoirs*: 325.
45. Quoted in 'These were singers': 105.
46. R. Mount Edgcumbe, *Musical Reminiscences*: 274.
47. John Levien, *The Singing of John Braham* (London, 1944):15. As Example 7 shows, the published score differs from Heywood's description; either Heywood was so overcome that his memory failed him, or Braham changed the score (which he was more than capable of doing).
48. Incledon named his son Venanzio after Rauzzini.
49. As Haydn noted in his London notebook for 1791. See Robbins Landon, *Haydn in England 1791–1795* (London, 1994): 114.
50. Theodore Fenner, *Leigh Hunt and Opera Criticism* (Lawrence, Kansas, 1972): 95 (13 July, 1817). The Scottish tenor John Sinclair, however (who would later create the florid tenor part in Rossini's *Semiramide*) 'glides into the falsetto, without suffering you to distinguish where he quitted his natural tones. . .' Fenner, *Opera in London*: 529. Falsetto is clearly recognized as such when the singer is well clear of the register change, so we can assume a certain difference between top and bottom, but the two registers seem to have been similar in sound for several notes on either side of the break.
51. *Musical Memoirs*: 175.
52. *Ibid.* 332–3.
53. *Ibid.*330.
54. The source of this story is François Joseph Fetis' *Curiosités historiques de la musique* (Paris, 1830); for a translation of the relevant section see Henry Pleasants, *Great Singers*: 67. According to Edmond Michotte, Marietta Alboni studied one page for three years (Michotte, *Rossini's visit*: 113).
55. Pier Francesco Tosi, *Observations on the Florid Song* (trans. John Galliard, London 1743); *Introduction to the Art of Singing by Johann Friedrich Agricola*, ed and trans. J. Baird, (Cambridge, 1995); *Practical Reflections on the Figurative Art of Singing by Giambattista Mancini*, trans. Pietro Buzzi (Boston, 1912); *Treatise on Vocal Performance and Ornamentation by Johann Adam Hiller*, ed. and trans. S. Beicken (Cambridge, 2001).
56. Domenico Corri mentions that he and Rauzzini were students together in Rome but it is unclear whether Rauzzini joined Corri under Porpora's tutelage in Naples or not. See 'Life of Domenico Corri' in his *Singer's Preceptor* (London, 1810, repr. ed. Richard Maunder, London & New York, 1995).
57. Title page to Venanzio Rauzzini, *24 Solfeggi or Exercises for the Voice to be Vocalised, Composed and Dedicated to his Scholars* (Bath, 1808), from which subsequent quotes are taken.
58. The Cambridge University Library copy has crescendo/decrescendo marks on many of these, added in pen by an early user of the book.
59. Girolamo Crescentini, *25 Nouvelles vocalises* (Paris, c. 1818–23).
60. See Chapter 3 below: 50ff.
61. R. Mount Edgcumbe *Musical Reminiscences*: 281–2. The first performance of 'He was despised' was actually given by Mrs Cibber, an actress whom even Handel admitted could not really sing. The varied fortunes of this piece during and immediately after Handel's lifetime are in strong contrast to the bland offerings of the twenty-first century early music movement.

62. Henry Chorley, *Thirty Years' Musical Recollections* (London, 1862; repr. 1972): 23.

63. There have been many attempts to recover the Rubini repertoire, none of which uses a true Rubini technique. Some of the most significant are listed in Stelios Galatopoulos, *Bellini: Life, Times, Music* (London, 2003): 384–5. For interpreters of Meyerbeer, many of whose works pose similar problems of altitude, see D. Clampton, 'L'Histoire d'un jeune et gallant postillon', *Record Collector*, 43/4 (December, 1998): 270–4. The norm in modern performances is to make transpositions and/or substantial cuts.

64. Closed at the time of writing. Always worth checking before planning a visit.

Chapter 3

1. See James Radomski, *Manuel García (1775–1832): Chronicle of the Life of a Bel Canto Tenor at the Dawn of Romanticism* (Oxford, 2000).

2. In a letter from Milan to his sister (26 January, 1770) Mozart says of the tenor Otini that 'He does not sing badly, but rather heavily, like all Italian tenors.' *Letters*: 110.

3. Radomski, *Manuel García*: 111.

4. 7 June 1981, quoted in Theodore Fenner, *Leigh Hunt and Opera Criticism* (Lawrence, 1972): 216.

5. Manuel Garcia, *Exercises pour la voix* (Paris, c. 1835; facs *Méthodes & Traités*, Serie II/III, Paris, 2005).

6. Manuel Garcia II's reputation has somewhat eclipsed that of his father. For an attempt to balance the credit between the two Garcias see Harold Bruder, 'Manuel Garcia the Elder: his school and his legacy', *Opera Quarterly*, 13/4 (1997): 19–46. Bruder sees the elder Garcia as a prototype dramatic tenor who first defined the voice inherited by Nourrit and, later, Jean de Reske.

7. Henry Pleasants, *The Great Singers* (London, 1967): 161.

8. Louis Quicherat, *Adolphe Nourrit: sa vie, son talent, son caractère, sa correspondance* (3 vols, Paris, 1867): 3, n.2.

9. Quicherat, *Nourrit*: 7.

10. Ernest Legouvé, *Soixante ans de souvenirs* (Paris, 1886): 241–2 (translation from Radomski, 200: 266–7); see Quicherat, *Nourrit*: 11.

11. *Ibid.* 13.

12. *Ibid.* 14. This was great encouragement for Nourrit even though Talma died in 1826 and never saw the tenor in any of his major roles.

13. See A. Macaulay, 'Tenor of the three glorious days', *Opera* (August, 1989): 922–9.

14. See David Tunley, *Salons, Singers and Songs: A background to Romantic French Song 1830–1870*, especially 49–51; 89–91.

15. Henry Pleasants, *The Great Tenor Tragedy: The Last Days of Adolphe Nourrit as told (mostly) by himself* (Portland, 1995): 105. Pleasants' book is based largely on the third volume of Quicherat (the Nourrit correspondence) and is a moving testimony to the tenor's last days.

16. Pleasants, *Great Tenor Tragedy*: 123.

17. See John Rosselli, 'Grand Opera' in John Potter (ed.), *Cambridge Companion to Singing* (Cambridge, 2000): 98.

18. 'come ornamento' – see M. Modugno, 'Domenico Donzelli e il suo tempo', *Nuovo rivista musicale italiana* (1984): 208.

19. Henry Chorley, *Thirty Years' Musical Recollections* (London, 1972): 4. See Modugno, 'Domenico Donzelli e il suo tempo', 200–16, for Donzelli's baritenor roles.

20. Giovanni Pacini, *Le mie memorie artistiche* (Florence, 1875): 28–9.

21. Quoted in Galatopoulos, *Bellini*: 215.

22. See Edmond Michotte, *Rossini's Visit to Beau Séjour*: 98.

23. Antoine Elwart, *Duprez: sa vie artistique avec une biographie authentique de son maitre Alexandre Choron* (Paris, 1838): 6.

24. Gilbert-Louis Duprez, *Souvenirs d'un chanteur* (Paris, 1880):31. The castration of trebles was by now very rare (and had never been practised in France) but it is interesting to speculate on how the operation may or may not have altered the course of vocal history. Rossini was another fine treble who managed to escape the knife; his uncle suggested that the operation would be a long-term financial investment but his mother declined the opportunity (see Michotte, *Rossini's Visit:* 109–10). Had these two figures actually been castrated there would perhaps have been a late flowering of the castrato tradition (with Rossini writing castrato parts for himself and he and Duprez becoming serious rivals to Velluti) and the 'ut de poitrine' would not have appeared until later in the century (with the results perhaps captured by the earliest recording machines).

25. Elwart, *Duprez:* 84.

26. Chorley, *Musical Recollections:* 168.

27. The 'darkening' of French voices by exposure to Italian techniques could have serious consequences: the tenor François Wartel, a sometime student of Nourrit left France to study in Italy with Pasini and returned as a high baritone.

28. Elwart, *Duprez:* 212.

29. Literally 'tenorino of yesterday' – i.e. no longer a tenorino, and implying something much more powerful. *Souvenirs:* 75.

30. He attempted part of Rigoletto in 1858, and heard Tamberlik the same year. See T.J. Walsh, *Second Empire Opera: the Theatre Lyrique Paris 1851–1870* (London, 1981).

31. Michotte, *Rossini's Visit:* 99.

32. Chorley *Musical Recollections:* 283–4.

33. *Ibid.* 284–5.

34. Heinrich Panofka, *L'Art de chanter* (Paris, 1854, , facs *Méthodes & treaté,* serie II/VII Paris, 2005).

35. Gilbert-Louis Duprez, *L'Art du chant* (Paris, 1846, facs *Méthodes & treaté,* serie II/II Paris, 2005).

36. 'to darken the sounds'.

37. Edmond Michotte, *Richard Wagner's Visit to Rossini* (Paris 1860), trans. Herbert Weinstock (Chicago, 1968): 39–40.

38. See William Ashbrook, 'The Donizettian tenor-persona', *Opera Quarterly,* 14/3 (Spring 1998), 24–32, for a summary of the influence of Duprez on Donizetti and *vice versa.*

39. Hector Berlioz, *Evenings with the Orchestra,* trans. and ed. Jacques Barzun (Chicago, 1973): 64–75.

40. *Evenings with the Orchestra:* 232.

41. Chorley, *Musical Recollections:* 222.

42. The composition of *Le Prophète* was heavily influenced by the singers Meyerbeer had in mind. For a fascinating account of the relationship between a composer and his singers, and of how he re-cast the Duprez music for Roger, see Alan Armstrong, 'Gilbert-Louis Duprez and Gustave Roger in the composition of Meyerbeer's *Le Prophète*', *Cambridge Opera Journal,* 8/2: 147–65.

43. Pleasants, *Great Singers:* 169–70.

44. At Mario's request Meyerbeer composed an additional cabaletta for him, and which only Mario ever sang. It remained in manuscript until first performed in 1988 at Carnegie Hall in New York by Chris Merritt. See Clarissa Lablache's interview with Merritt at http://www.meyerbeer.com/merritt.htm.

45. Mario's career is dealt with in detail in Elizabeth Forbes, *Mario and Grisi: A Biography* (London, 1985).

46. This purity of tone was achieved despite his passion for cigars, a vice to which many tenors succumbed without apparent ill-effects. Charles Santley tells of a meeting with Mario on a ship in the Irish Sea where the tenor smoked five cigars before breakfast. His normal consumption was said to be twenty-five to thirty-five Havanas a day (or up

to one hundred smaller Cavours if these were not available). See Charles Santley, *Student and Singer: the Reminiscences of Charles Santley* (London, 1893): 44. Jean de Reszke (see Chapter 4, p. 68) was another tenor partial to tobacco but found that cigars were not good for his voice. The cigarettes which bear his name were a blend of tobacco created especially for singers. When a call went out for cigarettes from hospitals for cigarettes for the wounded in World War 1, de Reszke donated fifty thousand. See Clara Leiser, *Jean de Reszke* (New York, 1934): 254 and 289. Lauritz Melchior endorsed Lucky Strike cigarettes but did not smoke them, preferring 'big, black, lethal cigars that smelled like buggy whips' (Shirlee Emmons, *Tristanissimo* (New York, 1990: 164–5)). The late Giuseppe di Stefano was among many more recent tenors to smoke heavily.

47. Chorley, *Musical Recollections*: 177.
48. *Ibid.* 180. Chorley makes more references to Mario than any other tenor.

Chapter 4

1. George Bernard Shaw, *Music in London: Vol. 2, 1890–94* (London, 1956): 145. Shaw is talking (in 1892) of the need for intelligent singers such as the Heldentenor Max Alvary, son of the painter Andreas Achenbach, who was the first Siegfried in the USA (and who was to die six years later as the result of a fall while rehearsing the role at Mannheim). Shaw exaggerated only slightly: Tamagno was the son of a restaurateur; the mother of the great Italian Wagnerian Giuseppe Borgatti died giving birth to him in a field (he grew up illiterate and was first heard singing in a stonemason's yard); of the later generation, Caruso's father was a mechanic, Gigli was the son of a shoemaker and Galliano Masini's father worked in a pasta factory. See John Rosselli, *Singers of Italian Opera* (Cambridge, 1992): 179–80.
2. The significance of this was considerable, and confirmed the idea of tenor as hero. See Rosa Salinas, 'Ernani: the tenor in crisis', *The Cambridge Companion to Verdi* (Cambridge, 2004): 185–96.
3. *Singers of Italian Opera*:176. Chapter 8 'The Age of the Tenor' (pp. 176–95) summarises the story of the ascent of the new tenor.
4. John Rosselli, 'Guasco, Carlo' *Grove* 10: 483.
5. Henry Chorley, *Thirty Years' Musical Recollections* (London, 1972): 190–1.
6. Herman Klein, 'The gramophone and the singer', in *Herman Klein and the Gramophone*, ed. William R. Moran (Portland, 1990): 76–7. Adelina Patti, whose recordings are considerably more controversial than Tamagno's, was similarly enraptured when she first heard her own recorded voice. See Landon Ronald, *Variations on a Personal Theme* (London, 1922): 102–4.
7. See Geoffrey and Ryan Edwards, *The Verdi Baritone* (Bloomington, 1994), especially the chapter on *Otello*: 118–37.
8. London saw only seven Otellos between the first performance there in 1889 and the World War I, the first of whom was Tamagno himself. See A. Notcutt, 'The role of Otello', *Musical Times* (April, 1917): 160–2. The history of subsequent inheritors of the role is detailed in Giorgio Gualerzi, 'Otello: the legacy of Tamagno', *Opera* (February, 1987): 122–7 and 'Postscript' (June, 1987): 628–30.
9. Blanche Roosevelt is quoted at length in Charles Osborne, *The Complete Operas of Verdi* (London, 1969): 412–16; the rather more critical anonymous review is in the *Musical Times* (1 March, 1887): 148–50; Shaw's review is reprinted in *London Music in 1888–9* (London, 1956): 161 and 171. According to the American baritone David Bispam (who was to play Iago opposite Tamagno's Otello in London in 1901), Vannuccini, Tamagno's teacher, thought his excessive volume caused him to bleat like a goat (David Bispham, *A Quaker Singer's Recollections* (New York, 1920): 69.

10. Roland Gelatt, *The Fabulous Phonograph* (London, 1956): 84.

11. Nellie Melba, *Melodies and Memories* (Melbourne, 1980): 93–5. In Tamagno's defence it should be pointed out that many highly successful tenors from poor backgrounds were equally famous for their meanness.

12. For further detail on the life and career of Tichatschek and succeeding Heldentenors see Carla-Maria Verdino-Süllwold's comprehensive study *We need a Hero! Heldentenors from Wagner's Time to the Present*' (New York, 1989), to which the following pages are much indebted.

13. 'My recollections of Ludwig Schnorr of Carolsfeld', in *Richard Wagner's Prose Works*: Vol. 4 *Art and Politics*, trans. W. Ashton Ellis (London, 1895, repr. 1972): 239.

14. *We Need a Hero*: 50. It was Tichatschek's dramatic failings that led Wagner to write his essay on the proper performance of Tannhäuser. See *We Need a Hero*: 52. Wagner's early obsession with the voice of the soprano Wilhelmine Schröder-Devrient was a significant factor in his decision to become a composer; her ability to convey a sense of drama while not losing sight of the traditional bel-canto line may have been the catalyst that enabled him to envision a new type of dramatic singing.

15. Verdino-Süllwold draws attention (*We Need a Hero*, p. 64) to the discussion at the Dresden Opera in 1860 as to whether or not Schnorr was a Heldentenor or a lyric tenor, so varied were his roles.

16. 'My Recollections': 232.

17. 'My Recollections': 239.

18. *The Diary of Richard Wagner 1865–1882: The Brown Book*, ed. Joachim Bergfeld, trans. George Bird (London, 1980).

19. Michael Kennedy has suggested that the Wagner/Schnorr artistic collaboration was unique in the opera world until that between Benjamin Britten and Peter Pears in the twentieth century. See his review of *The Brown Book* (*Music & Letters*, 61/3–4 (July 1980): 378–80).

20. For a list of Tristans during Wagner's lifetime see http://www.francoisnouvion.net/ wagnertenors/wagner2.html

21. Verdino-Süllwold draws attention to the distinction (pp. 20–1) between *echt* and *schwer* Heldentenors. The former is a conventional tenor with a larger voice, while the latter has a darker, baritonal quality (and may have started life as a baritone before being 'pushed up' to a tenor). Tichatschek was an *echt* tenor, whereas Niemann was undoubtedly a *schwer*. Both traditions have continued into the present day; for a diagrammatic view of how the two strands relate to each other over succeeding generations of Heldentenors see *We Need a Hero*, Appendix 1.

22. See *We Need a Hero*: 53–61 and Elizabeth Forbes, 'Niemann, Albert', *New Grove* 13:232.

23. Jens Malte Fischer, 'Towards a history of singing Wagner', *Wagner Handbook*, ed. Ulrich Müller and Peter Wapnewski, trans. John Deathridge (Cambridge, Mass., 1992): 527.

24. Julius Hey, *Deutsche Gesangunterricht* (Mainz, 1885); the condensed version (*Der Kleine Hey*) appeared in 1912.

25. H. De Curzon, 'Cosima Wagner and Bayreuth', *Musical Times* (September 1930): 795. Cosima did eventually mellow a little and came to see that there was music in her husband's work as well as drama. David Bispham recalls Cosima's visit to Covent Garden in the 1890s to hear *Lohengrin* sung by the de Reszke brothers, Schumann-Heink, Nordica and himself, all of whom had 'learned to sing in the best Italian manner', when she commented that it was the first time that she had heard Wagner's music performed 'from a melodious standpoint' (*A Quaker Singer's Recollections*: 130).

26. 'Towards a history': 529.

27. *Music in London*, vol 3: 279–80.

28. *Heldentenöre* Lebendige Vergangenheit Preiser PR89947.

29. *Ibid.*

30. Oswald Bauer, 'Performance history: a brief survey', *Wagner Handbook*: 508. Wagner thought Battistini's 1881 Wolfram in Rome, sung in Italian, the most perfect performance he had ever heard. See Michael Scott, *The Record of Singing, Vol. 1: to 1914* (Boston, 1977): 17.

31. Voytek Matushevski, 'Jean de Reske as pedagogue: his ideas, their development, and their results', *Opera Quarterly*, 12/1 (1995): 49–50.

32. 'Jean de Reske as pedagogue': 52. Matushevski's article contains much information on the singer's life and teaching. See also *We Need a Hero*: 81–92 and Henry Pleasants, *The Great Singers* (London, 1967): 254–62.

33. Scott, *The Record of Singing*, Vol. 1: 62.

34. He is known to have recorded arias by Gounod and Massenet in April 1905, but the records were never released and despite extensive searches over the years have never been found. See Roland Gelatt, *The Fabulous Phonograph* (London, 1956): 91–2.

35. Nellie Melba, *Melodies and Memories* (London, 1980): 30. They subsequently fell out when Melba unwisely attempted Wagner roles that were beyond her.

36. *Melodies and Memories*: 82.

37. *A Quaker Singer's Recollections*: 292.

38. Herman Klein, 'Jean de Reszke and Marie Brema: some reminiscences', *Musical Times*, 66/987 (May, 1925): 406.

39. Herman Klein, *Thirty Years of Musical Life in London* (London, 1903): 243–4.

40. 'Jean de Reske as pedagogue': 53.

41. Amherst Webber, 'Jean de Reszke: his manner of life', *Music & Letters*, 6/3 (July, 1925): 201. The impresario Mapleson's experience with the tenor Angelo Masini in 1879 is a similar sign of the times: he is outraged that Masini should assume that he could dictate his preferred tempi to the conductor, adding for the benefit of his English readers that such heathen practices are still common in Italy (*The Mapleson Memoirs*, ed. Harold Rosenthal (London, 1966): 129–30).

42. George Bernard Shaw, *London Music* (London, 1950): 122.

43. Quoted in Michael Henstock, *Fernando de Lucia: Son of Naples* (London, 1990): 31.

44. The Donizetti was planned for 1840 as *Le Duc d'Albe* but Rosine Stolz refused to sing it, so the composer abandoned it unfinished in 1839. It was finally completed by Matteo Salvi, a sometime Donizetti pupil, with a revised libretto in Italian, and received its first performance at the Teatro Apollo, Rome, in 1882. See William Ashbrook, *Donizetti and his Operas* (Cambridge, 1984): 434–5 and 567–8.

45. Giorgio Gualerzi's two informative articles 'Spain, Land of Tenors', *Opera* (Nov/Dec 1987) encapsulate the history of the tenor in Spain in terms of the core operatic repertoire and do not mention the Spanish repertoire at all; similarly Giancarlo Landini's brief survey of 'canto spagnola' in *Alfredo Kraus* (Parma, 2005).

46. Masini was to outlive him by thirty-six years.

47. Gayarre has been the subject of three films (see Biographical list of tenors, p. 242) and his reputation is kept alive by the Fundación Julián Gayarre, who own his birthplace, now a museum, in Roncal.

48. Shaw, *Music in London* (London, 1937): 337. Shaw did relent on hearing of Gayarre's death, and acknowledged that Wagner thought him a great Lohengrin (see also *ibid.*: 288). Klein, too, drew attention to his unique artistry, but referred to the 'Gayarre bleat' (*Thirty Years of Musical Life in London*: 99–100).

49. Michael Henstock, *Fernando De Lucia* (London, 1990): 54. Henstock's comprehensive and moving biography of De Lucia contains much useful information about Gayarre and also Masini and Stagno.

50. Herman Klein notes that he was one of a number of singers of whom it was said that you could hear him holding a note as you left La Scala to walk round the piazza for a smoke, and return to the theatre to find him still holding the same note. Herman Klein (ed. William Moran), *Herman Klein and the Gramophone* (Portland, 1990): 249.

51. Campanini would eventually christen his son Lohengrin seven years later. Jim McPherson, 'Italo Campanini: one of a kind', *Opera Quarterly*, 19/2 (Spring, 2003): 254.

52. *Ibid.: 259*

53. John Rosselli quotes a letter in which Stagno reports that his audience had never heard 'anyone sing with such sweet tone, such elevated and generous style, and such correct diction.' *Singers of Italian Opera* (Cambridge, 1995): 179.

54. Henstock, *Fernando De Lucia*: 47.

55. Henstock, in *Fernando De Lucia*, makes a strong case for De Lucia's being influenced in specific ways by Stagno, Gayarre and Masini, and quotes many newspaper reports of comparisons between De Lucia and his rivals.

56. Henstock, *Fernando De Lucia*: 159.

57. Henstock, *Fernando De Lucia* contains many press quotes in which similar criticisms surface periodically.

58. As an example of just how free he could be, it is instructive to listen to de Lucia's 'Che gelida la manina' in the context of the 36 performances of this aria recorded between 1906 and 1962 and available on *Che gelida la manina*, Vols 1 & 2, Bongiovanni GB 1156–2 and 1157–2. As Michael Henstock put it, 'If some of his textual and musical changes raise eyebrows in a more conformist age, many of his alterations strike us as totally in character. His singing of the rising orchestral phrase on the opening words . . . is perhaps the most striking solecism of all.' (Liner notes to *Fernando De Lucia: Operatic Recordings 1902–21* Pearl GEMM CDS 9071)

59. Henstock, *Fernando De Lucia*: 273.

Chapter 5

1. Friedrich Kittler, *Discourse Networks 1800/1900*, trans. Michael Metteer (Stanford, 1990): 238.

2. Michael Scott, *The Record of Singing*, Vol. 1: *to 1914* (Boston, 1977): 137.

3. It is a bizarre fact of history that many tenors owe their start in life to enlightened commanding officers, especially those of the armies of Italy and the old Austro-Hungarian Empire.

4. See Michael Scott, *The Great Caruso* (London, 1988): 6–10.

5. Nigel Douglas, *Legendary Voices* (London, 1995): 32.

6. The event is well covered in the Caruso literature, including Roland Gellat, *The Fabulous Phonograph* (London, 1956): 80–81, and Fred Gaisberg, *The Music Goes Round* (New York, 1942): 48, with perceptive commentary from Michael Scott in *The Great Caruso*: 56–7 and from Nigel Douglas in *Legendary Voices*: 34. Douglas points out that Leoncavallo and Cilea accompanied their own pieces. By the time of Caruso's death his records were earning Victor $2500,000 a year (Gelatt, *Fabulous Phonograph*: 160).

7. Scott, *The Record of Singing*, Vol. 1: 139.

8. *Ibid.*: 141.

9. He was also very superstitious man. He kept beside his bed a book given to him by a man whose tongue had been cut out, and he never went on stage without his good luck charms: a twisted coral horn, some holy medallions and old coins on a chain. Before leaving the dressing room he would call upon his dead mother for help and no one was allowed to wish him luck for fear of certain disaster; see Dorothy Caruso, *Enrico Caruso, his Life and Death* (London, 1946): 76 and 78. He was not alone in his singerly superstition: Michael Henstock points out that many Neapolitans carried charms to ward off the Evil Eye, a notion subscribed to by Jean de Reszke, Adelina Patti and Puccini, among others (*Fernando De Lucia*: 40–1).

10. J.B. Steane, *Voices, Singers and Critics* (London, 1993): 65–71.

11. For an explanation of the various additional sub-categories that some have found useful, see the entries in *Grove* for 'tenor' and the following sub-genres.

12. *Voices, Singers and Critics:* 76–7.

13. There is also an argument that the need for detailed and precise categorisation dates from a time when people were more likely to think in terms of 'facts' and certainties, as opposed to the more relaxed ideology of today, which is more at ease with doubt.

14. Frances Alda, *Men, Women and Tenors* (Boston, 1937): 176.

15. Helena Matheopoulos, *The Great Tenors* (New York, 1999): 17.

16. C. Williams, T. Hutchinson, and E. Rees, 'Giacomo Lauri-Volpi', *Record Collector*, 9/11 (1957): 244–72.

17. Verdi called Cotogni 'ignorantino' because of his extreme modesty, and was so moved by his audition that he almost wept. See E. Herbert-Caesari, *Tradition and Gigli* (London, 1963): 80.

18. C. Williams, T. Hutchinson, and E. Rees, 'Giacomo Lauri-Volpi': 250. The rivalry between them only ended when Lauri-Volpi sang at Gigli's funeral in 1957.

19. He recorded excerpts from *Otello* in 1941, available on *Giacomo Lauri-Volpi: Public Performances 1928–1955*, Memories HR 4195/96.

20. See the extract from *Meetings on the Operatic Stage*, the memoirs of Bulgarian mezzo-soprano Ilka Popova, published in Bulgarian in 1972 and in Russian in 2001, English translation from Russian by Olga Besprozvannaya made available on Grandi-Tenori.com by Alexey Bouliguine (http://www.grandi-tenori.com/articles/articles_popova_lauri-volpi_03.php). Although Lauri-Volpi would not countenance imitation, he became a friend and mentor to Franco Corelli. See pp. 173ff. below.

21. There is a video clip of him singing 'Nessun dorma' at the age of 80, recorded at the Teatro del Liceo de Barcelona, January 26, 1972 (http://www.youtube.com/watch?v=1WjURfDzeys).

22. Gerunda's composition lessons stood Schipa in good stead: he went on to compose tangos and an opera.

23. Schipa's youth and career are described in detail in Tito Schipa Jnr's *Schipa* (Dallas, 1996).

24. He attempted to teach his pet monkey to sing, and at one point became the surprised owner of 45,000 automobile heaters; see Robert Baxter (1997) liner notes to *Tito Schipa: The Early Years: The Complete Gramophone and Pathé Recordings (1913–1921)*, Marston MR 52008.

25. Lauritz Melchior, not often compared with Gigli, also shared his birthday: 20 March 1890.

26. The story of the perceptive Colonel Delfino is told by Nigel Douglas in *More Legendary Voices* (New York, 1995): 85.

27. E. Herbert Caesari, in *Tradition and Gigli* (London, 1958), attempts to relate Gigli's technique to that of Caccini and other pre-nineteenth-century singers while at the same time maintaining that he had a completely 'natural' voice.

28. *More Legendary Voices*: 85.

29. When researching my article 'Beggar at the door: the rise and fall of portamento' (*Music & Letters*, 87/4, 2006: 523–50) I was both astounded and moved by hearing Gigli sing first Schubert's 'Ständchen' and then Sullivan's 'Lost Chord' in quick succession. As far as Gigli was concerned they were clearly both Puccini and demanded total commitment.

Chapter 6

1. His replacement at Manhattan was Giovanni Zenatello. See Michael Scott, *The Record of Singing*, Vol. 1 (Boston, 1977): 137.

2. Freddie Stockdale, *Emperors of Song: Three Great Impresarios* (London, 1998): 125.
3. Pietro Buzzi (trans.), *Practical Reflections on the Figurative Art of Singing by Giambattista Mancini* (Boston, 1912).
4. Frieda Hempel, for example, seems to have been almost in awe of him. See *My Golden Age of Singing* (Portland, 1998): 213,
5. Joyce was actually in line for the gold medal but refused to sing at sight, thereby disqualifying himself from anything but an honorable mention; when the second prize winner was also disqualified Joyce was given the bronze. Richard Ellmann, *James Joyce* (New York, 1959): 157.
6. Joyce scholars are divided about the relationship between singer and author. There are references, coded or otherwise, to McCormack in several Joyce works, notably *Ulysses* and *Finnegan's Wake* (in which the character of Shaun is said to be based on aspects of McCormack). Joyce was perhaps painfully aware of McCormack's international success while he himself continued to struggle as an author, and his later promotion of John O'Sullivan may well have its roots in Joyce's envy of McCormack's stardom. See Carole Brown and Leo Knuth, *The Tenor and the Vehicle: a Study of the John McCormack/James Joyce Connection* (Colchester, 1982): 23.
7. Gordon Lebetter, *The Great Irish Tenor John McCormack* (Dublin, 2003): 70.
8. Nigel Douglas, *More Legendary Voices* (London 1995): 144.
9. Gerald Moore, *Am I too Loud?* (London, 1962): 110–16.
10. J.B. Steane, *The Grand Tradition* (London, 1974): 302.
11. Michael F. Bott, *John O'Sullivan, Tenor,* liner notes to Symposium 1152.
12. See p. 155 below.
13. Richard Ellmann *James Joyce* (New York, 1959): 633. One of O'Sullivan's *Tell* top Cs can be heard on Symposium 1152. Authorial support for tenors appears to include a right to alter their names: Joyce insisted O'Sullivan drop the 'O', which he considered unmusical (Ellmann: 632n); Walpole preferred to call Lauritz Melchior David (Rupert Hart-Davis, *Hugh Walpole* (London, 1952): 197).
14. Ellman, *James Joyce:* 638.
15. *John O'Sullivan, Tenor,* liner notes – in contrast to the opinion of fellow record collector John Steane, above.
16. Joe Winstanley, liner notes to *Tom Burke Centennial Edition,* Pearl GEMM 9411.
17. *Ibid.*
18. Nigel Douglas, *Legendary Voices* (London, 1995): 177.
19. Alan Jefferson, *Lotte Lehmann: A Centenary Biography* (London, 1988): 59.
20. Douglas. *Legendary Voices* : 169.
21. *Ibid.*
22. The Earl of Harewood, *The Tongs and the Bones* (London, 1981): 36.
23. See Nigel Douglas' moving account in *Legendary Voices:* 176.
24. See, for example, the tributes by London Green, William Ashbrook, Owen Lee, and Robert Baxter in 'Jussi Björling (1911–1960): A Remembrance' (*Opera Quarterly* 16/2, Spring 2000): 180–9.
25. Nigel Douglas, 'Jussi Björling' *Legendary Voices:* 3.
26. J.B. Steane, *The Grand Tradition* (London, 1974): 373.
27. Helena Matheopoulos, *The Great Tenors from Caruso to the Present* (New York, 1999): 47.
28. Martin Oehmann, 'The Discovery', reprinted from the Memorial Book in the newsletter of the Jussi Björling Appreciation Society (Winter, 2005): 17. Oehmann's international career included many Wagner roles and the first American performance of Janacek's *Jenufa.* He can be heard on *Four Scandinavian Singers of the Past, LV* 89986; for biographical details and photographs see http://www.cantabile-subito.de/Tenors/Oehman__Carl_Martin/oehman__carl_martin.html. See also Harald Henrysson, *A Jussi Björling Phonography* (2nd edn, Stockholm, 1993):16. Henrysson also gives a chronology of the life of Björling, pp. 14–52.

29. *Ibid.* Hislop likened Björling's phrasing to that of Heifetz' violin playing.
30. *The Erik Odde Pseudonym Recordings and Other Popular Works (1931–1935)* Naxos 8.110790.
31. Desmond Shawe-Taylor and Alan Blyth, 'Björling, Jussi', *Grove* 3: 658–9.
32. I am very grateful to Eric Wimbles for letting me see the unpublished English translation by Gail Campain.
33. Gedda discusses Oehmann's teaching in Jerome Hines *Great Singers on Great Singing* (New York, 2003): 118–25.
34. Letter to *High Fidelity* magazine, 7 March 1973, quoted in *Walter Legge: Words and Music*, ed. Alan Sanders (London, 1998): 204–5.
35. Gedda gives examples of his exercises with Novikova in Jerome Hines, *Great Singers.*
36. *Singers of the Century,* 3: 33.
37. Kraus is discussed in Chapter 11, pp. 176ff. below.
38. The two articles by Giorgio Gualerzi entitled 'Spain, Land of Tenors', *Opera* (November, 1987: 1257–63; December, 1987: 1387–91) are concerned solely with Italian, French and German music. Hispanic composers have tended to feel more drawn towards the zarzuela tradition.
39. *The Complete Francisco Viñas,* Marston 53006–2 (3 CDS) contains arias from *Rienzi, Lohengrin, Meistersinger, Tristan, Tannhäuser, Parsifal* and *die Walküre,* all sung in Italian. Michael Aspinall's liner notes are comprehensive and perceptive; further detailed information on Vinas' performing and recording career can be found in Larry Lustig and Clifford Williams, 'Francisco Viñas', *Record Collector,* 34/5–7 (July 1989). The German word 'Fach' literally means 'subject' or specialism. In singing it is applied to categories of voices, especially in the USA.
40. For Paoli see Scott, *The Record of Singing,* Vol. 1: 138; for Calleja, *The Record of Singing,* Vol. 2: 112–13.
41. Giorgio Gualerzi, 'Spain, Land of Tenors', part 2, *Opera* (December, 1987): 1387.
42. *New York Times,* 1 February 1918.
43. For example, *Hipólito Lázaro,* Lebendige Vergangenheit Preiser PR89147.
44. *The Record of Singing,* Vol. 2: 107.
45. *Ibid.* Examples are to be found on *Miguel Fleta,* Lebendige Vergangenheit Preiser PR89002, and the second and third volumes, PR89093 and PR89149.
46. A *comprimario* role is a secondary one.
47. See 'New York' (4), *Grove* 17:821–6.
48. Alan Bilgora lists the principal twentieth-century American and Canadian tenors in his liner note to Nimbus *Charles Kullman* NI 7938.
49. *Musical Times,* 51/808 (1.8.10): 444.
50. Carlo Bassini, *Bassini's Method for Tenor* (New York, 1866). I am grateful to Richard Wistreich for drawing my attention to this treatise.
51. Scott, *Record of Singing,* Vol. 2: 164.
52. See Lawrence Holdridge's liner notes to *Charles Hackett,* Marston 51005–2 (with the personal recollections of Charles Hackett Jnr).
53. Tim Brooks, *Lost Sounds: Blacks and the Birth of the Recording Industry 1890–1919* (Urbana, 2004): 448. Brooks' chapter 'Black recording artists 1916–19' contains the most comprehensive short overview of Hayes' recording career.
54. See the online Georgia Encyclopaedia: http://www.georgiaencyclopedia.org/nge/Article.jsp?id=h-1671
55. Reproduced in Tim Brooks, *Lost Sounds:* 437.
56. See the 1993 interview between Shirley and Dennis Speed, archived at http://sumarts.com/roster/shirley_interview.html
57. The tenor voice is still overwhelmingly white. The USA has a number of successful black tenors, some of whom have achieved a high profile through distinctive promotion (such as Crook, Dixon and Young); in the UK Wills Morgan is a rare success as a recitalist and in the theatre.

58. Both Kullman and Crooks recorded Italian arias in German.
59. His English was often criticised by the London critic Herman Klein, who thought his vowels were over-enunciated. Klein preferred his German or French. See Herman Klein (ed. William R. Moran), *Herman Klein and the Gramophone* (Portland, 1990): 571, 575.
60. Jerome Hines: 'To what do you attribute your enormously long and successful career?' Jan Peerce: 'Being religious.' *Great Singers on Great Singing*: 226. In 1956 Peerce became the first American to sing at the Bolshoi since the war, and he marked the occasion by singing a service in the Great Synagogue in Moscow. Tucker always turned down engagements that clashed with High Holy Days or Passover. See Studs Terkel, *And they All Sang* (London, 2005); 68.
61. *Ibid.*
62. Both Peerce and Tucker can be heard in *Four Famous Met Tenors of the Past* Preiser 89952 and on the curiously named *The Three Singers* CDVS 1952 (the third singer being Robert Merrill, or Moishe Miller, as his parents knew him).
63. Very few successful screen singers would actually describe themselves as tenors. See Stephen Banfield 'Stage and screen entertainers in the twentieth century' in John Potter (ed.) *Cambridge Companion to Singing* (Cambridge, 2000): 63–82.
64. Both Martinelli and Caruso can be heard on *The Art of Singing*, Warner Music Vision DVD 0630–15898–2 with commentary by John Steane. Significantly, many of the recordings on this anthology were originally for television; *Great Tenor Performances* (Warner Music Vision DVD 0630–18626–2) is an anthology mostly taken from live performances.
65. Recordings of Schmidt's cantorial singing survive; see the discography by Hansfried Sieben (*Record Collector, 45/2* July, 2000): 132– 3).
66. Bel Canto Society have reissued *My Song goes around the World* (BCS 529) and the 1934 *A Star Fell from Heaven* (http://www.belcantosociety.org/). See Jan Neckers' 'Joseph Schmidt' (*Record Collector 45/2* July, 2000): 90–107 and the accompanying discography by Hansfried Sieben (*ibid.* 108–45).
67. There is, as yet, no authoritative biography of Tauber in English, most of the earlier efforts relying heavily on material provided by his wife, the actress Diana Napier. The most reliable short survey is still Nigel Douglas' *More Legendary Voices* (New York, 1995): 279–312, which includes a discussion of the recordings.
68. D. Napier Tauber, *My Heart and I* (London, 1959): 45.
69. *More Legendary Voices*: 289.
70. *Ibid.*: 293.
71. D. Napier Tauber, *My Heart and I*: 69.
72. Andrew Lamb, 'Lehár, Franz', *Grove* 14: 490–3.
73. One strand of Tauber's multi-faceted love-life – his relationship with soprano Mary Losseff – is revealed in Nicky Losseff, 'Mary Losseff and Richard Tauber', *Record Collector* 51/4 (December 2006): 305–14. I am grateful to Nicky Losseff for a sight of the unpublished correspondence between Tauber and her grandmother.
74. D. Napier Tauber, *My Heart and I*: 79
75. Released on DVD as Bel Canto Society BCS 413.
76. http://www.joseflocke.co.uk/. In 1997 EMI released an album entitled *Three Great Tenors* – Richard Tauber, Webster Booth and Josef Locke.
77. Raymond Strait and Terry Robinson, *Lanza: His Tragic Life* (Englewood Cliffs, 1980): 20.

Chapter 7

1. A similar case could be made for East European or Scandinavian traditions. Anthologies of tenors (such as Helena Matheopoulos' *The Great Tenors*) often contain no French or British singers.

2. Henry Chorley, *Thirty Years' Musical Recollections* (London, 1862; repr. New York, 1972): 216.
3. Herman Klein, 'Sims Reeves: Prince of Tenors', *Herman Klein and the Gramophone*, ed. William R. Moran (Portland, 1990): 334–6.
4. The reputation that star tenors had for awkwardness was not lost on Bispham. He devotes several pages of his memoirs to his recollections of 'the grand old boy'; David Bispham, *A Quaker Singer's Recollections* (New York, 1920), especially pages 83–8.
5. Bispham notes that promoters would cover themselves against the risk of a non-appearance by Reeves by engaging a tempting line-up of additional artists. On one occasion fourteen other singers were hired plus the band of the Scots guards and an orchestra of 150 players (Bispham: 83–4). Klein suggests that the tenor may have lost more money through unfilled engagements than any tenor in history (Klein, 'Sims Reeves: Prince of Tenors': 461).
6. Sims Reeves, *Sims Reeves on the Art of Singing* (London, 1900): 25–6.
7. There were in fact two Edward Lloyds; to avoid confusion with *the* Edward Lloyd the younger man changed his name to Lloyd Chandos at the suggestion of Joseph Barnby. He became a successful oratorio singer and can be heard on *Lloyd Chandos* Cheyne CHE 44422 (reviewed by Robert Bunyard in *Record Collector*, 52/3 (Summer, 2007): 215–16).
8. *Santley and Lloyd: The Complete Recordings*, Cheyne Records CHE 44372–3.
9. Bispham, *A Quaker Singers' Recllection*: 121; George Bernard Shaw, *Music in London 1890–94*, Vol. 3 (London, 1932): 255.
10. Klein, *Herman Klein and The Gramaphone*: 465.
11. He actually sang in English. H. J. Kimbell, 'British players and singers: No. X Walter Hyde', *Musical Times* (December, 1923): 830.
12. See Charles Hooey, 'Walter Hyde' *Record Collector*, 52/3 (September, 2007): 180–212 (which also includes a comprehensive discography by Alan Kelly *et al.* and an appreciation by Alan Bilgora).
13. *Musical Times* (December, 1911): 775.
14. The Belgian baritone Bouhy was teaching in Paris and New York, after a performing career that included the creation of Escamillo in *Carmen*. Gervase Elwes also took lessons with him at about the same time.
15. Gerald Moore *Am I too Loud?* (London, 1962): 35; Michael Scott, *The Record of Singing*, Vol. 2 (boston, 1979): 172.
16. A selection of his recordings has been reissued on Cheyne CHE 44402–3 (2 CDs), reviewed by Larry Lustig in *Record Collector*, 52/1 (March, 2007): 23–4.
17. Winefride Elwes and Richard Elwes, *Gervase Elwes: The Story of His Life* (London, 1935): 115.
18. John Steane, *The Grand Tradition* London, 1974): 255.
19. Henry Wood, *My Life of Music* (London, 1938): 330.
20. The work was recorded a year later by the original team of soloists and is re-released on Pearl GEMM CD 9342.
21. Klein: 336. For a discography of Titterton see C. Morgan, 'Frank Titterton', *Record Collector*, 27/11 (1983): 244–63).
22. For a review of a substantial number of the recorded Gerontii see Walter Essex's *The Recorded Legacy* at http://www.elgar.org/3gerontr.htm on the website of the Elgar Society.
23. He can be heard on *Tudor Davies: Songs & Arias*, Cheyne CHE 44446–7 (2 CDS).
24. Klein: 416
25. Steane, *The Grand Tradition*, Chapter 17, 248–65. Steane also comments eloquently on Hislop's recorded legacy from the viewpoint of someone who grew up listening to this tenor and deeply appreciated his artistry; see pages 275–6.
26. Though Covent Garden did absorb the British National Opera Company when it ran into difficulties in 1929.

27. See Valerie Parker, *Walter Widdop: His Life and Achievements*, unpublished dissertation, Royal Northern College of Music (April, 2001).
28. Charles Reid, *Thomas Beecham: An Independent Biography* (London, 1962): 189.
29. Klein: 207.
30. *My Life of Music*: 82–3.
31. The young Borgioli can be heard on Lebendige Vergangenheit 89508. He has all the authentic waywardness of a *tenore di grazia*, but never actually relapses into the paralinguistic sobbing of Gigli.
32. 'Discus' in *Musical Times* (January, 1924): 61.
33. Re-released on Membran 220856 (2 CDs).
34. Alan Blyth, 'Pears, Sir Peter (Neville Luard)' *Grove* 19: 261–2.
35. See Christopher Headington, *Peter Pears: A Biography* (London, 1992).
36. Bostridge's staged Lieder performances and Padmore's conductorless approach to the *St John Passion* are examples of the kind of enterprise that goes far beyond the ego-driven careers of many more conventional tenors. These two tenors discuss the role of the Evangelist in Bach's passions in 'Mark Padmore versus Ian Bostridge in St John Passions', *The Times*, 15 February, 2008 (Times Online tp://entertainment.timesonline.co.uk/tol/arts_and_entertainment/stage/opera/article3370176.ece).

Chapter 8

1. Serge Escalaïs and Larry Lustig, 'Léon Escalaïs', *Record Collector*, 9/2 (June, 2004): 82–3.
2. *Léonce Escalaïs*, Lebendige Vergangenheit Preiser PR89527, or *Harold Wayne Collection*, Vol. 15 Symposium 1128.
3. J. B. Steane, 'Dalmorès, Charles', *Grove* 6: 866.
4. The story is told engagingly by Scott in *The Record of Singing*, Vol. 2 (Boston, 1979): 33.
5. Alfred de Cock, 'Léon David', *Record Collector*, 52/1 (March, 2007): 2–21.
6. New York Times, March 20, 1910. Italian and French tenors often found it problematic to sing in each other's language. Caruso famously pronounced 'des anges' (angels) as though it were 'des inges' (sounds like 'des singes' = monkeys) in his first attempt at *Samson et Dalila* at the Met in 1915, much to his own horror and everyone else's amusement (Michael Scott, *The Great Caruso* (London, 1988): 145–6).
7. Both can be heard on *Edmond Clément: Complete Pathé recordings (1916–25); Léon David: Complete recordings (1904–08)* Romophone 82016 (2 CDs).
8. Both Corsica and its neighbour Sardinia have a tradition of male polyphonic folk music, which fulfils a similar cultural function to the male voice choir in Wales. The Sardinian songs are known as *tenores*.
9. His recordings are available on *The Complete César Vezzani*, Vols 1 and 2 Marston 52034–2/52045–2 with comprehensive liner notes by Tom Kaufman, Vincent Giroud and Ward Marston, which are the main source of easily available information about Vezzani.
10. He later discovered that the Caruso records had been played too fast, making the arias a semi-tone higher than Caruso actually sang them. Given Thill's clarion upper register and less honeyed tone than Caruso, this probably made the inimitable tenor a little more imitable; see Robert Bunyard, 'Georges Thill', *Record Collector*, 52/2 (June, 2007): 83.
11. See the extract from a letter from Thill to Michael Henstock in the latter's *Fernando De Lucia* (London, 1990): 389–91.
12. Bunyard, 'Georges Thill': 85.
13. *Ibid.*: 107. *Record Collector* 52/2 is a special Thill issue, and the most authoritative source of information in English, including a discography by David Mason and an appreciation of the recordings by Alan Bilgora.

14. The April 2008 issue of *BBC Music Magazine* featured a list of twenty most important tenors of all time; it included no French tenors.
15. *The Grand Tradition*: 435–6.
16. For an example of how effective this 'pre-Duprez' technique was, see Vanzo's performance of 'Je crois entendre encore' from *Les Pecheurs de perles*, on *Great Tenors Vol. 2* BCS 012.

Chapter 9

1. There is a rare example of a Russian tenor coming the other way: in 1830 Nicola Ivanoff (1810–80), a tenor in the imperial chapel in St Petersburg, was given permission to travel with Glinka to Italy, where he studied with Eliodoro Bianchi, Andrea Nozzari and Heinrich Panofka (later to write a treatise on singing for the Paris Conservatoire). He sang successfully in Paris and London before returning to Italy, where he impressed both Rossini and Verdi, the older composer commissioning the younger to write Ivanoff extra arias for *Ernani* and *Attila*. See Elizabeth Forbes, 'Ivanoff, Nicola', *Grove* 12: 682.
2. Although this is mitigated to some extent by the fact that the Russian tenors almost invariably sing in Russian (with its characteristically liquid consonants) making direct comparison with earlier western singers less easy than with native Russian singers.
3. For an overview see Michael Scott, 'Singers of Imperial Russia' in *The Record of Singing*, Vol; 1: *to 1914* (Boston, 1979): 210–27 and 'Revolution and Russian Singing' in *The Record of Singing*, Vol. 2 *1914–1925* (Boston, 1979): 11–30.
4. Sergei Levik, *The Levik Memoirs: an Opera Singer's Notes,* trans. Edward Morgan (London, 1995), from the 2nd revised edn (Moscow, 1962): 54 *ff.*
5. Levik, *Memoirs*: 256. See also *The Record of Singing*, Vol. 1: 215–16. Yerschov can be heard on *Tenors of Imperial Russia*, Vol. 1, Pearl GEMM 0217 and on the companion CD to the Levik *Memoirs, Singers of Russia 1900–1917: Sergei Levik and his Contemporaries* Symposium 1151.
6. See the website of the Sobinov Memorial House Museum http://www.sobinov.yar.ru/english/index.htm
7. *Greatest Voices of the Bolshoi*, Melodiya 74321 39505 2.
8. *The Record of Singing*, Vol. 1: 18.
9. See the section on Kozlovsky in Bel Canto Society video, *The Tenors of the 78 Era* 4.
10. A post-Soviet artiste, of course, who studied at the Bucharest Conservatory, a typically conservative institution which had been producing similar (if less charismatic) singers for several generations.
11. *The Tenors of the 78 Era* 4.
12. The 1954 film of Kozovsky's Simpleton is available on VAI DVD 4253 (Georgi Nelepp sings the false Dmitri). There are, of course, many interpretative strands in Kozlovky's history, about which he himself refused to talk. Surpringly, he was a member of Orthodox church and may even have considered becoming a priest. I am grateful to Doug Fox for this information.
13. *Ivan Kozlovsky* RCD 16002.
14. 'Kozlovsky . . . sings well but spoils his performances by indulging in excessive *rubato*: no Covent garden conductor would accept his rendering of the 'Chanson Hindu' in *Sadko.*' Geoffrey Bennet, 'The Bolshoi Theatre 1856–1956' in Harold Rosenthal (ed.), *Opera Annual* (London, 1956): 144.
15. See I.M. Yampol'sky, 'Kozlovsky, Ivan Semyonovich', *Grove* 13: 000.
16. There are many examples of Caruso and Tauber on film. Georges Thill described De Lucia's teaching in a letter to Michael Henstock; this included putting a cork in his mouth to ensure that it was open wide enough (see Michael Henstock, *Fernando De Lucia*: 390).

17. *The Tenors of the 78 Era* 4.
18. All three performances can be heard on *Sergei Lemeshev,* Lebendige Vergangenheit Preiser PR 89164.
19. *The Russian Legacy: Georgi Vinogradov,* Guild GHCD 2250/3. I am grateful to Nick Morgan for drawing my attention to this recording.
20. *Nikandr Khanayev* Lebendige Vergangenheit PR 89650.

Chapter 10

1. See Michael Scott, *The Record of Singing,* Vol. 1 (Boston, 1979): 195–205 for a survey of the earliest recorded Heldentenors.
2. Leo Sezak, *Song of Motley: Being the Reminiscences of a Hungry Tenor* (London, 1938): 24.
3. *Leo Slezak,* Nimbus NI 7909.
4. Herold, a former pupil of Sbriglia in Paris, was hailed as a possible successor to Jean de Reszke and was considered one of Denmark's finest Heldentenors until his retirement in 1915. In 1922 he became the director of the Royal Opera. See Leo Riemens, 'Herold, Vilhelm', *NGDO* 2: 706 and Michael Scott, *The Record of Singing,* Vol. 1 (Boston, 1977): 200–1.
5. Shirlee Emmons, *Tristanissimo* (New York, 1990): 16.
6. Walpole paid two-thirds of Beigel's fees, with the rest to be paid by Melchior from his future earnings (Rupert Hart-Davis, *Hugh Walpole* (London, 1952): 218–19). This investment by a teacher in his pupils had been common in the nineteenth century, often enabling poorer students to experience a high standard of teaching. Beigel (1870–193) also taught a number of English tenors, including Gervase Elwes and Hubert Eisdell. For an insight into Beigel's teaching see Winefride Elwes and Richard Elwes, *Gervase Elwes: The Story of his Life* (London 1935): 129–32.
7. Desmond Shawe-Taylor, 'Bahr-Mildenburg', *Grove* 2: 486–7.
8. Emmons, *Tristanissimo*: 52–3. The connection between the Wagner family and Nazism has been well documented elsewhere. Melchior was dismayed by the activities of Hitler.
9. He would eventually sing 233 Tristans, 183 Siegmunds, 144 Tannhäusers, 128 young Siegfrieds, 107 elder Siegfrieds, 106 Lohengrins and 81 Parsifals (*Tristanissimo:* 331).
10. *Tristanissimo:* 249.
11. Shirlee Emmons is particularly revealing about these years, having been a member of the Lauritz Melchior Show cast. See *Tristanissimo,* especially Chapter 16, 'Vacation from Valhalla'.
12. Desmond Shawe-Taylor, 'Melchior, Lauritz', *Grove* 16: 340–1; J.B. Steane, *The Grand Tradition* (London, 1974): 244–7.
13. *Tristanissimo* documents this in 'Melchior and the Heldentenor Crisis', especially 313ff.
14. The Swedish tenorocracy included the Ralf brothers Oscar and Torsten. Oscar Ralf was also a student of Forsell and became the first Swedish tenor to sing at Bayreuth; Torsten sang at the Met 1945–8 and would famously end 'Celeste Aida' with a pianissimo top B-flat pianissimo as Verdi intended, rather than the applause-generating fortissimo most found hard to resist. See Harold Rosenthal and Alan Blyth, 'Ralf, Torsten (Ivar)', *Grove* 20: 776–7.
15. Carla Maria Verdino-Süllwold, *We Need a Hero: Heldentenors from Wagner's Time to the Present* (New Jersey, 1989): 179–80.
16. Verdino-Süllwold considers him to be the greatest Heldentenor actor since Schnorr and de Reszke, with the possible exception of Peter Holfmann. See *We Need a Hero:* 204, also 179–204 for an analysis of Svanholm's singing and career.
17. Pistor, Wolff, Hartmann and Kötter can be heard on *Four German Heldentenors of the Past,* Lebendige Vergangenheit 89975; a selection of Seider, the first German tenor to

be invited back to Covent Garden after the war, is available on Lebendige Vergangenheit 89543.

18. Grenzebach (1871–1936) also taught the lyric tenor Peter Anders among others.
19. See 'The Bayreuth Festival and the Wagner Family', *Wagner Handbook*, ed. Müller and Wapnewski, trans. John Deathridge (Harvard, 1992): 485–501.
20. See *We Need a Hero*: 416 n.3, for a list of the most successful Bayreuth tenors.
21. *Ibid.*: 207–33.
22. *Ibid.*: 264.
23. Jens Malte Fischer, 'Towards a history of singing Wagner', *Wagner Handbook*, ed. Ulrich Müller and Peter Wapnewski, trans. John Deathridge (Cambridge, Mass., 1992): 542
24. *Ibid.*: 319.
25. See Alan Blyth's obituary of Bonisolli in *The Guardian*: 6 November 2003.
26. *We Need a Hero*: 319.
27. *Ibid.*: 329.
28. *Opera* (Autumn, 1976).
29. Hofmann's early career is dealt with in almost hagiographic detail in *We Need a Hero*: 335–89.
30. Bernheimer, M., 'Thomas, Jess (Floyd)', *Grove* 25: 410; *We Need a Hero*: 237–60.
31. Lambert also taught fellow Canadian Ermanno Mauro; Mauro stood in for Vickers at the Met in January 1978 in the role of Canio, before making his official début three weeks later as Radamès.
32. 'Liebestod' in Studs Terkel, *They All Sang* (London, 2005): 29. The debate is intelligently summarised in Michael Linton's review of Jeannie Williams' *Jon Vickers: A Hero's Life* (Boston, 1999) published in *First Things* (December 2000): 49–54.
33. Martin Kettle, 'I thought I was going to die', *The Guardian*, 24 June 2005.
34. *New York Times*, 22 Feb. 1960.
35. 'Liebestod': 25.

Chapter 11

1. The historiography of tenors and Fascism gets more complicated as post-war memories and research seek to re-interpret the era; Tito Schipa Jnr's biography of his father says four times on one page that he was not a Fascist (*Schipa* (Dallas, 1996): 139).
2. Steane, *The Grand Tradition*: 443. Italian critics were generally kinder (the definitive biography, *Mario Del Monaco: Monumentum Aere Perennius* is unavailable in English translation). A DVD of the 1955 *Andrea Chénier*, originally produced for Italian television, is available on Bel Canto Society BCS3.
3. See *Monumentum Aere Perennius*, especially 627–34, for Del Monaco and Wagner.
4. Helena Matheopoulos, *The Great Tenors from Caruso to the Present* (New York, 1999): 65.
5. *Ibid.*: 67.
6. Corelli to Stefan Zucker, quoted in the booklet included with the DVD *Corelli in Concert* (BCS-D0091): 30.
7. *Corelli in Concert*: 22. Corelli would always be aware of the artistry of others, and would have no qualms about letting significant interpretations influence his own. Zucker quotes Corelli as admitting to basing his rendering of individual arias on aspects of specific singers (his *Trovatore* and *Carmen* owed something to Pertile, and he incorporated elements of Fleta's 'E lucevan le stelle' into his own version). Much of the biographical information on Franco Corelli given here has been pieced together from the writings and radio broadcasts of his friend and fellow tenor Stefan Zucker, whose dedication to the tenor voice in general and Corelli's in particular can be experienced at BelCantoSociey.org. I am also grateful for Stefan Zucker's personal communications in connection with Corelli's career.

8. Corelli told this story many times. See his interviews with Stefan Zucker (*Opera News*, reprinted in the Bel Canto Society Newsletter June, 2004) and Jerome Hines (*Great Singers on Great Singing*, New York, 1982/2003: 59–60). For a succinct overview of Corelli's career see Alan Blyth's obituary in *The Guardian* (31 October, 2003): 29.

9. Corelli's worries about high notes were not entirely to do with things vocal. He claimed that as a young singer he had three addictions: singing, sport and sex, the last of the three being incompatible with the other two. He considered that orgasms were debilitating, with a particularly deleterious effect on his ability to reach and sustain high notes (*Corelli in Concert* : 22). Corelli also claimed that Francesco Merli believed that if he could have managed without sex for a month he would have had a voice of steel (interview with Stefan Zucker, 12 May 1990 *Bel Canto Society*). Mario Lanza's experience was rather different: he claimed to have had an orgasm while performing (Raymond Strait and Terry Robinson *Lanza: His Tragic Life* (New Jersey, 1980): 103). Lanza, like Corelli, was well aware of the connection between tenors and sex, informing Terry Robinson that 'It's all sex . . . it comes right out of my balls' (*Lanza: His Tragic Life*: 3). A significant number of the tenors discussed in this book have not felt bound by conventional ideas of sex and marriage though there are notable exceptions, such as Jon Vickers, whose work is driven by a moral imperative. For a more general discussion of sexuality in singing see my *Vocal Authority* (Cambridge, 1998): 175–82.

10. These exchanges were, of course, in Italian. See Matheopoulos, *The Great Tenors*: 72.

11. Radio interview (in Italian) with Stefan Zucker as interviewer/translator (WKCR 12 October, 1985).

12. *Ibid*. René Seghers' new Corelli biography appeared too late for this volume.

13. Bergonzi's mixture of chagrin, embarrassment and relief is captured in René Seghers' article and interview 'Carlo Bergonzi after *Otello*', *Opera Quarterly*, 17/1 (Winter, 2001): 3–9.

14. The tenor lead was taken by Aureliano Pertile.

15. http://www.jcarreras.homestead.com/RRKrausMasterclass.html.

16. In conversation with Robert Baxter reported in Baxter, Burroughs, Farkas, Jellinek and Pines, 'Alfredo Kraus, 1927–1999: In memoriam', *Opera Quarterly*, 18/3 (Summer, 2000): 314.

17. The *Observer* newspaper's third leader on the occasion of Pavarotti's death observed (perhaps not entirely seriously) that the singer, far from 'dumbing down' opera, had 'brought class to the game of football.' 'Pitch Perfect', *The Observer*, 9 September 2007: 24.

18. Steane, *The Grand Tradition*: 458.

19. Tom Kington, *Guardian*, 7 April, 2008.

20. Zarzuela is the Spanish form of operetta that his parents specialised in (as have many Spanish and Latin American tenors).

21. José Carreras, *Singing from the Soul: An Autobiography* (London, 1991): 84–5.

22. Matheopoulos, *The Great Tenors*: 120.

23. The showbizification of singing includes trappings of celebrity that go well beyond the singing itself. A typical example is Joseph Kaiser's photograph in *Opera News Online*, (www.metoperafamily.org/operanews/issue/article.aspx?id=1897) which includes a double credit for 'grooming', and the revelations of his shopping habits to be found in *The Guardian*, 7 December 2007.

24. The younger tenors discussed in this chapter are only a sample of the many lyric and dramatic lyric tenors with prominent careers in the first decade of the twenty-first century.

25. *Three Edison Tenors*, Marston 51002–2, with informative liner notes by Lawrence Holdridge, includes all the sides these three singers recorded for Edison. Mojica's 'Mi par d'udir ancora', recorded in 1925, sounds like a younger version of that by Giuseppe Anselmi, who recorded it in 1913.

26. Hugh Canning, 'Rolando Villazon: why I needed to pause for breath', *Sunday Times*, 8 March, 2008 (Times on line: http://entertainment.timesonline.co.uk/tol/arts_and_entertainment/stage/opera/article3492166.ece).

27. Warwick Thompson, 'Clown Prince', *The Gramophone* (March, 2006): 27.

28. Michael White, 'The sound of one voice mending', *New York Times*, 16 March, 2008 (http://www.nytimes.com/2008/03/16/arts/music/16whit.html?pagewanted=1&_r=1).

29. See the Tom Sutcliffe's profile of Juan Diego Flórez in the liner notes to *Una furtiva lagrima*, Decca CD 473 440–2.

30. He was No. 13 of the '20 Greatest Tenors' in the BBC Music Magazine's April 2008 issue – the only South American singer in the list.

31. Rupert Christiansen, 'This sexy singer is sticking to opera', *Daily Telegraph*, 30 November, 2006 (http://www.telegraph.co.uk/arts/main.jhtml?xml=/arts/2006/11/30/bmjonas30.xml). For a comparison with Wunderlich see Michael Tanner's review of *Romantic Arias*, Decca 475 9966, *BBC Music Magazine* (April, 2008): 98.

32. Radio or television talent contests have provided life-changing opportunities for aspiring tenors since broadcasting began. The 'Wolverhampton Tenor' John McHugh won the BBC Amateur Hour Radio Completion 1936 and was able to give up his job as a pattern-maker to study in Italy. He subsequently made records and a film, and was a resident singer with the London Philharmonic Orchestra.

33. There is also a purely musical problem: there is very little originality in the stadium repertoire, which often includes 'crossover' arrangements that would make Puccini turn in his grave.

34. http://www.ildivo.com/biography/biography.html.

35. Jürgen Kesting, *Luciano Pavarotti: The Myth of the Tenor* (London, 1996): ix.

36. See my 'Beggar at the Door: the rise and fall of portamento in singing', *Music & Letters*, 87/4 (2006): 545–7.

37. See Harm K. Schutte, Donald G. Miller and Mark Duijnstee, 'Resonance strategies revealed in recorded tenor high notes', *Folia Phoniatrica et Logopaedica*, 57/5–6 (September–December, 2005): 292–307, which deals with the high register of some thirty named tenors.

38. See D. Fischer-Dieskau, *Reverberations* (New York, 1989): 302

39. Nigel Douglas, *Legendary Voices* (London, 1995): 265.

40. John Steane considered his voice as manifest on LP to be 'chicken . . . rather than roast beef, eglantine rather than red rose', but was surprised by the purity of Schreier's tone in the flesh (*Singers of the Century*, Vol. 3 (London, 2003): 164).

41. The vast range of extended vocal techniques is demonstrated by Trevor Wishart in his *On Sonic Art* (Amsterdam, 1998) and Michael Edgerton's *The 21st-Century Voice* (Lanham, Maryland, 2004); both books include a comprehensive CD of recorded examples.

42. 'Off' Broadway should also include the various multiple extrapolations that may feature several 'offs'. I should like to thank Stephen Ziegler for first making me aware of the new developments in this genre.

BIOGRAPHICAL LIST
OF TENORS

Abbreviations:

Farkas	Andrew Farkas, *Opera and Concert Singers: An Annotated International Bibliography of Books and Pamphlets* (New York, 1985)
Grove	*The New Grove Dictionary of Music and Musicians*, ed. S. Sadie and J. Tyrrell (London: Macmillan, 2001)
NGDO	*The New Grove Dictionary of Opera*, ed. S. Sadie (London, 1992)
Scott 1	Michael Scott, *The Record of Singing*, vol. 1: *to 1914* (Boston, 1993)
Scott 2	Michael Scott, *The Record of Singing*, vol. 2: *1914–1925* (Boston, 1993)
Steane 1	John Steane, *Singers of the Century*, vol. 1 (London, 1996)
Steane 2	John Steane, *Singers of the Century*, vol. 2 (London, 1998)
Steane 3	John Steane, *Singers of the Century*, vol. 3 (London, 2003)

The biographical list combines the functions of select bibliography, discography and videography, and is intended to be a convenient means of accessing the most important works on the most significant tenors up to 2008 (many of whom have not been included in the main text for reasons of space). Most of the titles are in English but significant works in the singers' own languages have also been included. English readers are referred to the entries in *Farkas* (up to 1985) and *The New Grove Dictionary of Opera* (up to 1992 and online thereafter) for fuller bibliographies. German readers will find similar information in the comprehensive Personteil of *Die Musik in Geschichte und Gegenwart*, ed. Ludwig Finscher *et al.* (Basel, 1999–2003, 17 volumes, with supplementary volume 2008) and the more variable K. Kutsch and L. Riemens, *Grosses Sängerlexicon*, 3rd edn 1991, revised in 7 vols (Munich: Sauer Verlag, 2004; also available on CD-ROM Directmedia Publishing, Digitale Bibliothek Band 33).

This is not intended to be a gazetteer of tenors; the essential criterion for inclusion was the existence of at least one major article or recording. The articles and books listed are intended to be reasonably comprehensive for most entries but I have been selective with those singers whose careers have generated substantial reference material. This is also the case for the discographical and videography elements: I have tried to select a small number of representative recordings (all on CD) but many singers have substantial catalogues, and interested readers are encouraged to explore further by using the published discographies where these are indicated.

The internet is a ready source of information, much of which is unverifiable and should be used with care. It is increasingly used as a publishing tool, however (discographies and other forms of lists are especially likely to be web-based in the future), so I have included links to sites where these may augment or anticipate print sources. The net is also invaluable as a source of pictures and soundfiles, and there are links to a number of dedicated tenor websites which I know to be run by extremely knowledgable and passionate enthusiasts (not all of whom agree with each other). All the links given here were current in January 2008. I have generally not included links to video clips on social networking sites, nor to Wikipedia, but readers are encouraged to seek these out (and to edit the latter where appropriate). I have also included contact details for a number of societies devoted to individual singers.

Lorenzo Abruñedo *1836–1904*
> Gualerzi, G., 'Spain: Land of Tenors', *Opera* (November, 1987): 1257–63 (December, 1987): 1387–91.

Valentin Adamberger *1740–1804*
> Angermüller, R., 'Ein Mozart Tenor aus Niederbayern: Johann Valentin Adamberger zu seinem 260. Geburtstag', *Musik in Bayern Halbjahresschrift der Gesellschaft für Bayerische Musikgeschichte e.V 59* (Munich, 2000): 93–110.
> Barak, H., 'Valentin Adamberger-Mozarts Belmonte und Freund', *Internationaler Musikwissenschaftlicher Kongress zum Mozartjahr 1991* (Baden–Vienna): 463–74.
> Bauman, T., 'Mozart's Belmonte', *Early Music* 19/4 (November 1991): 556–63.
> Bauman, T., 'Adamberger, (Josef) Valentin', *Grove* 1: 134.
> Bauman, T., 'Adamberger, (Josef) Valentin', *NGDO* 1: 16–17.

Charles Adams *1834–1900*
> Wiley Hitchcock, H., 'Adams, Charles', *NGDO* 1: 16–17.
> Wiley Hitchcock, H. and Ottenberg, J., 'Adams, Charles', *Grove* 1:43.

Agustarello Affre *1858–1921*
> Dennis, J., 'About the Records', *Record Collector,* 3/8 (1948): 131–3.
> Steane, J.B., 'Affre, Agustarello', *NGDO* 1: 30–1.
> Vellacott, Mrs, 'M. Gustarello Affre: tenor de l'opéra Paris 1889–1911', *Record Collector,* 3/6 (1948): 82–8.

Discography
> *Agustarello Affre* Truesound TT-2009.

Paul Agnew *1964*
Web
> http://www.bach-cantatas.com/Bio/Agnew-Paul.htm.

Discography
> *Bach: Cantatas* Vol. 10 Challenge CHL 72210.
> See http://www.hyperion-records.co.uk/a.asp?a=A568.

Giuseppe Agostini *1874–1951*
> Forbes, E., 'Agostini, Guiseppe', *NGDO* 1: 36.

Douglas Ahlstedt *1945*
Web
> http://www.yarochester.info/services/artist.php?id=75.

Videography
> *Rossini: L'Italiana in Algeri* DGG 044007342619.

John Mark Ainsley *1963*
> Jolly, J., 'Ainsley, John Mark', *Grove* 1: 252.

Web
> http://www.bach-cantatas.com/Bio/Ainsley-John-Mark.htm [Galina Kolomietz].
> http://www.musicweb-international.com/sandh/2002/Mar02/Ainsley.htm [Melanie Eskenazi interview].

Discography
> *Remember your Lovers (Tippett, Britten)* Signum SGK 066.
> *Peter Warlock songs* Hyperion 66736.
> *Rameau: Dardanus* DGG 4634762.
> *Hyperion French Song Edition – L'Invitation au voyage* Hyperion 67523.

Videography
> Mozart *Zaide* DGG DVD 044007342527.
> *Great Tenor Performances* Warner 0630-18626-2.
> *Monteverdi: Orfeo* BBC Opus Arte BOA 0929.

Roberto Alagna *1963*

Alagna, R., *Je ne suis pas le fruit de hazard: autobiographie* (Paris, 2007).
Blyth, A., 'Roberto Alagna', *Opera* (December, 1997): 1403–09.
Blyth, A., 'Alagna, Roberto', *Grove* 1: 267.
Steane 3: 248–52.

Web

http://www.grandi-tenori.com/tenors/alagna.php [Anthonisen].
http://www.jcarreras.homestead.com/Alagna1.html [Jean Peccei].

Discography

Bel Canto: Bellini, Donizetti EMI 5573022.
Berlioz EMI 5574332.
C'est Magnifique: Songs of Luis Mariano DGG 4775569.
Robert Alagna Artists Edition EMI 4767002.

Francesco Albanese *1912*

Bilgora, A., review of *Francesco Albanese arias* (Tima Club CD-30).
Record Collector, 43/1 (March, 1998): 60–3.
Forbes, E., 'Albanese, Francesco', *NGDO* 1: 49
Hughes, J., review of *The Cetra Tenors* (Pearl GEMS 0120) *Record Collector*, 46/2 (June, 2001): 153–6.

Discography

Verdi: La traviata Naxos 8.110300–01.
The Cetra Tenors Pearl GEM 0120.

Carlo Albani *1872–1938*

Web

http://www.francoisnouvion.net/italian/albani1.html.

Discography

Edison Grand Opera Series, Vol.ume 6 (1910–1911) Truesound TT2470.
Souvenirs of Donizetti Operas: Rare Recordings IRC CD 817.

Tomaz Alcaide *1901–1967*

Moreau, M., *Tomás Alcaide* (Lisbon, 2001).

Web

http://www.grandi-tenori.com/tenors/alcaide.php [Anthonisen].

Discography

Tomaz Alcaide Bongiovanni GB 1095–2.

John Aler *1949*

Clampton, D., 'L'Histoire d'un jeune et galant postillon', *Record Collector*, 43/4 (December, 1998): 270–4.
Walsh, M., 'Aler, John', *NGDO* 1: 77.

Web

http://members.aol.com/opsingers/jaler.html (with discography).

Discography

Berlioz: L'Enfance du Christ Hyperion CDA66991/2.

John Alexander *1923–1990*

Bernheimer, M., 'Alexander, John', *NGDO* 1: 82.
Hines, J., *Great Singers on Great Singing* (New York, 2003): 25–9.

Videography

Donizetti: Roberto Devereux VAI 4204.

Luigi Alva *1927*

Rosenthal, H., 'Alva, Luigi', *Grove* 1: 430.
Rosenthal, H., 'Alva, Luigi', *NGDO* 1: 99.

Discography

Ay ay ay: Spanish and Latin-American Songs Decca 028947564102.

Videography
 Il barbiere di Siviglia DGG 044007340394.
Albert Alvarez *1861–1933*
 Forbes, E., 'Alvarez, Albert', *NGDO* 1: 99.
Discography
 Albert Alvarez 22 Pathé recordings (1905) / 4 Maplesons (1902–3) Truesound
 TT2450.
Marcelo Álvarez *1963*
Web
 http://www.marceloalvarez.com/.
Discography
 A Tenor's Passion Sony Classical 1SK92937.
 Bel Canto Sony Classical 1SK60721.
 French Arias Sony Classical 1SK89650.
Max Alvary *1856–1898*
 Rosenthal, H., 'Alvary [Achenbach], Max(imilian)', *Grove* 1: 432.
 Rosenthal, H., 'Alvary [Achenbach], Max(imilian)', *NGDO* 1: 99.
Web
 http://www-scf.usc.edu/~gishii/ahis001/wagner/artists/tenor/alvary.html.
Angelo Amorevoli *1716–1798*
 Hansell, S., 'Amorevoli, Angelo (Maria)', *NGDO* 1: 112
 Hansell, S. and Lipton, K., 'Amorevol.i, Angelo (Maria)', *Grove* 1: 514.
Aloys Ander *1821–1864*
 Ashbrook, W., 'The First Singers of *Tristan und Isolde*', *Opera Quarterly*, 3 (1985):
 11–23.
 Forbes, E., 'Aloys, Ander', *NGDO* 1: 121.
 Strell-Anderle, H., *Alois Ander: aus dem Leben eines grossen Tenors: das Lebensbild
 eines europäischen Tenors* (Horn, 1996).
Peter Anders *1908–1954*
 Clampton, D., 'L'Histoire d'un jeune et galant postillon', *Record Collector*, 43/4
 (December, 1998): 270–4.
 Farkas: 9.
 Kosters, F., *Peter Anders: Biographie eines Tenors* (Stuttgart, 1995).
 Pauli, F.W., *Peter Anders* (Berlin, 1963).
 Steane, J.B., 'Anders, Peter', *Grove* 1: 610.
 Steane, J.B., 'Anders, Peter', *NGDO* 1: 122.
Web
 http://www.cellconcept.de/Carlem/ysinger1.html (with discography).
Discography
 Dramatische Tenor – Arien Gebhardt GEB 0014.
 Peter Anders Vols 1–3 Berlin Classics BER 2166–8.
 Wagner: Lohengrin Myto MYT 93485.
Konstyantyn Andreyev *1971*
 Jeal, E., 'Great Expectations', *Gramophone* (August 2005): 27.
Web
 http://classicalplus.gmn.com/story.asp?sc=1&id=73624.
Angelo Angioletti *1862–1909*
 Gualerzi, G., 'Spain: Land of Tenors', *Opera* (November, 1987): 1257–63.
Giovanni Ansani *1744–1826*
 Libby, D., 'Ansani, Giovanni', *NGDO* 1: 144.
 Rice, J., 'Benedetto Frizzi on singers, composers, and opera in late eighteenth-century
 Italy', *Studi musicali*, 23 (1994): 367–93.

Giuseppe Anselmi *1876–1929*

> Lustig, L. and Williams, C., 'Giuseppe Anselmi', *Record Collector*, 32/3–5 (1987): 51–109 (with discography).
> Lustig, L., 'A Giuseppe Anselmi postscript', *Record Collector*, 36/2 (1991): 137–8.
> *Scott* 1:129–30.
> Shawe-Taylor, D., 'Anselmi, Giuseppe', *Grove* 1: 710.
> Shawe-Taylor, D., 'Anselmi, Giuseppe', *NGDO* 1: 144–5.
> Steane, J., 'A century of singing: John Steane on Verdi's interpreters', *Opera* (January, 2001): 25–31.

Web

> http://www.cantabile-subito.de/Tenors/Anselmi__Giuseppe/hauptteil_anselmi_giuseppe. htm.

Discography

> *Three Edison Tenors* Marston 51002–2.
> *Giuseppe Anselmi* The Harold Wayne Collection 20 Symposium 1076174.
> *Giuseppe Anselmi* GEMM 9227.

Fernand Ansseau *1890–1972*

> De Cock, A. (trans D. Newson), 'Fernand Ansseau', *Record Collector*, 9/1 (1954): 4–20 (with discography).
> *Scott* 2: 32–4.
> Tubeuf, A. and Forbes, E., 'Ansseau, Fernand', *NGDO* 1: 145.

Web

> http://artfuljesus.0catch.com/artists/ansseau.html.
> http://www.cantabile-subito.de/Tenors/Ansseau.

Discography

> *The Art of Fernand Ansseau* 9240 GEMM.
> *Fernand Ansseau* Lebendige Vergangenheit Preiser PR89022.

Giovanni Apostolu *1860–1905*

> Dzázopulos, J., 'Giovanni Apostolu', *Record Collector*, 50/1 (March, 2005): 50–8.

Web

> http://www.grandi-tenori.com/tenors/apostolou.php [Dzazópulos].

Jaime (Giacomo) Aragall *1939*

> Blyth, A., 'Aragall (y Garriga), Giacomo', *Grove* 1: 833.
> Blyth, A., 'Aragall (y Garriga), Giacomo', *NGDO* 1: 160.
> Gualerzi, G., 'Spain: Land of Tenors', *Opera* (November, 1987): 1257–63 (December, 1987): 1387–91.
> Sugden, D., *Giacomo Aragall: A Life on Stage* (Bushmoor, 2003).

Web

> http://www.grandi-tenori.com/tenors/aragall.php [Joern Anthonisen].

Francisco Araiza *1950*

> Zucker, S., 'Francisco Araiza', *Bel Canto Society Newsletter*, 2/15 (2005).

Web

> http://www.francisco-araiza.ch/ (with discography).

Videography

> *[see http://movies2.nytimes.com/gst/movies/filmography.html?p_id=2049 http://www.imdb.com/name/nm0032845/].*

Antonio Arámburo *1839–1912*

> Dales, J., 'The Viuda de Arámburo cylinders', *Record Collector*, 44/2 (June 1999): 167–8.
> Gualerzi, G., 'Spain: Land of Tenors', *Opera* (November, 1987): 1257–63 (December, 1987): 1387–91.
> Kaufman, T., 'Antonio Arámburo', *Record Collector*, 44/1 (March, 1999): 83–4.
> Kaufman, T., 'Antonio Arámburo chronology', *Record Collector*, 44/4 (December, 1999): 298–305.

Lopez, V., *Pasajes de la vida del tenor Aramburo* (Madrid, 1998).

Suárez, H., 'Antonio Arámburo: the enigmatic "missing link" between Manuel García Sr and Julián Gayarré' *Record Collector*, 43/4 (December, 1998): 285–306 (with discography).

Discography

Rare and Unique Early Cylinders 1900–1903 Symposium 1306.

Paul Asciak *1923*

Freestone, J., review of *Paul Asciak: Arias and Songs* KTA (Malta) 111 and 112 *Record Collector*, 43/1 (March, 1998): 59–60.

Web

http://www.paulasciak.com/.

http://www.grandi-tenori.com/tenors/asciak.php [Albert Storace].

Discography

Paul Asciak: Arias and Songs KTA (Malta) 111 and 112.

Eduardo Asquez *1919–1998*

Web

http://www.grandi-tenori.com/tenors/asquez.php [Joern Anthonisen].

Vladimir Atlantov *1949*

Web

http://www.vor.ru/English/Music_Portraits/Music_Portraite_23.html.

Discography

Mussorgsky: *Khovanshchina* Naxos 100310.

Filmography

The Queen of Spades (1987).

Gregorio Babbi *1708–1768*

Eive, G., 'Babbi, Gregorio (Lorenzo)', *NGDO* 1: 267.

Eive, G., 'Gregorio (Lorenzo) Babbi', *Grove* 1: 281–2

Matteo Babbini *1754–1816*

Brighenti, P., *Elogio di Matteo Babini ditto al Liceo filarmonico di Bologna nella solenne distribuzione dei premi musicali il 9 luglio 1819* (Bologna, 1821).

Farkas: 15.

Fenner, T., *Opera in London: Views of the Press 1785–1830* (Illinois, 1994): 164–5.

Forbes, E., 'Babbini, Matteo', *NGDO* 1: 267.

Rice, J., 'Benedetto Frizzi on singers, composers, and opera in late eighteenth-century Italy', *Studi musicali*, 23 (1994): 367–93.

Barry Banks

Web

http://www.imgartists.com/?page=artist&id=29&c=4.

http://www.musicalcriticism.com/interviews/banks-christy-0208.shtml.

Discography

Barry Banks Sings Bel Canto Arias Chando CHAN 3112.

Videography

Rimsky-Korsakov: Le Coq d'or TDK DVD DV-OPLCO.

Edmund Barham *1952–2008*

Web

http://www.independent.co.uk/new/obituaries/edmund-barham-stylish-dramatic-tenor-82547.html.

http://www.guardian.co.uk/music/2008/jul/01/obituaries.culture.

Discography

Verdi: *Requiem* EMI 759362.

Rule Britannia Nimbus NIM 7067.

Kurt Baum *1908–1981*

Hines, J., *Great Singers on Great Singing* (New York, 2003): 35–9.

Oestreich, J., obituary, *New York Times*, 29.12.1989.

Web

http://www.grandi-tenori.com/articles/articles_kurtzman_operanight_01.php [Neil A Kurtzmann].

http://www.answers.com/topic/kurt-baum?cat=entertainment [Erik Eriksson].

Bénigne de Bacilly *c. 1625–1690*

Caswell, A., 'Bacilly [Basilly, Bassilly], Bénigne de', *Grove* 2: 443–4

Antonio Baglioni *fl. 1780s-90s*

Hansell, S. and Mackenzie, B. D., 'Baglioni, Antonio', *Grove* 2: 469.

Mackenzie, B. D., 'Baglioni, Antonio', *NGDO* 1: 278.

Rice, J., *W.A. Mozart: La Clemenza di Tito* (Cambridge, 1991): 54–9.

Davidde Banderali *1789–1849*

Forbes, E., 'Banderali, Davidde', *Grove* 2: 651–2.

Daniele Barioni *1930*

Web

http://www.grandi-tenori.com/tenors/barioni.php [Anthonisen and Dzazópulos].

Giovanni Basadonna *1806–1850*

Gualerzi, G., 'Tipologia del tenore serio Donizettiano', *International Conference on the Operas of Gaetano Donizetti* (Bergamo, 1992): 353–8.

Amadeo Bassi *1874–1949*

Steane, J. B., 'Bassi, Amadeo', *Grove* 2: 871.

Steane, J. B.,'Bassi, Amadeo', *NGDO* 1: 345–6.

Scott 1: 136.

Francesco Battaglia *1893–1968*

Padoán, P. (trans. Peter Dempsey), 'Francesco Battaglia', *Record Collector*, 42/3 (September, 1997): 195–209 (with discography by Alan Bilgora and Michael F. Bott).

John Beard *1717–1791*

Dean, W., 'Beard, John', *Grove* 3: 19.

Dan Beddoe *1863–1937*

Lewis, G., 'Dan Beddoe, 1863–1937', *Record Collector*, 33/1 (1988): 2–16 (with discography by Clifford Williams).

Scott 1: 50–1.

Discography

Dan Beddoe 23 recordings (1911–1928) (incl. an unpublished Edison disc). Truesound TT2484.

Dan Beddoe Cheyne CHE 44414.

Pierre Ignac Begrez [Begri] *1787–1863*

Fenner, T., *Opera in London: Views of the Press 1785–1830* (Illinois, 1994): 322–3.

Forbes, E., 'Begrez [Begri] Pierre Ignac', *Grove* 3:142.

Antonio Benelli *1771–1830*

Fenner, T., *Opera in London: Views of the Press 1785–1830* (Illinois, 1994): 319.

Forbes, E., 'Benelli, Antonio (Pellegrino)', *Grove* 3: 248.

Carlo Bergonzi *1924*

Gualerzi, G., 'Bergonzi – 75 and not out', *Opera* (July, 1999): 782–6.

Marchesi, G ., *Carlo Bergonzi, i suoi personaggi* (Parma, 2003).

Matheopoulos, H., *The Great Tenors* (New York, 1999): 74–9.

Rosenthal, H. and Blyth, A.,'Bergonzi, Carlo (ii)', *Grove* 3: 345.

Seghers, R., 'Ora e per sempre, Addio: the tragic end of Carlo Bergonzi's career', *Record Collector*, 45/3 (September, 2000): 246–7.

Seghers, R., 'Carlo Bergonzi after *Otello*', *Opera Quarterly*, 17/1 (2001): 3–9.

Steane, J., 'A century of singing: John Steane on Verdi's interpreters', *Opera* (January, 2001): 25–31.

Steane 1: 91–5.

Web

  http://www.carlobergonzi.it.

Discography

  Carlo Bergonzi in concerto Bongiovanni GB 2502–2.

  Le grandi voci: Carlo Bergonzi Frequenz 046–003.

Videography

  Carlo Bergonzi live in concert Fabula Classica FAB 29912.

Willi Birrenkoven *1865–1955*

Web

  http://www.rahlstedter-kulturverein.de/Jahrbuch2002/Birrenkoven.pdf
  [Dietmar Möller].

Discography

  Willi Birrankoven Truesound TT-2020.

Jussi Björling *1911–1960*

  Björling, A-L. and Farkas, A., *Jussi* (Portland, Oregon, 1996).

  Björling, G., *Jussi, boken om storebror* (Stockholm, 1945).

  Björling, J., *Med bagaget i strupen* (Stockholm, 1945).

  Douglas, N., *Legendary Voices* (New York, 1995): 1–24.

  Farkas, A., 'Björling and *Ballo*: "The most unkindest cut of all"', *Opera Quarterly*, 16/2 (2000): 190–203.

  Farkas: 23–4.

  Green, L., Ashbrook, W., Owen Lee, M. and Baxter, R., 'Jussi Björling (1911–1960): a remembrance', *Opera Quarterly*, 16/2 (2000): 180–9.

  Hagman, Bertil (ed.), *Jussi Björling, en minnesbok* (Stockholm, 1960).

  Henrysson, H., *A Jussi Björling Phonography* 2nd edn (Stockholm, 1993).

  Shawe-Taylor, D., 'Björling, Jussi [Johan]', *NGDO* 1: 490–1.

  Shawe-Taylor, D. and Blyth, A., 'Björling, Jussi [Johan]', *Grove* 3: 658–9.

  Steane 2: 68–72.

Web

  http://www.geocities.com/Vienna/Strasse/3468/bjorling.htm.

Jussi Björling Museum, Borlänge

  http://www.borlange.se/templates/BlgUnitStartPage_6972.aspx.

Jussi Björling Societies

  www.jussibjorlingsociety.com.

  http://www.jussibjorlingsallskapet.com.

Discography

  Lieder and Songs (1939–1952), Naxos 8.110789.

  Opera and Operetta Recordings (1930–1938), Naxos 8.110722.

  Opera Arias (1936–1948), Naxos 8.110701.

  Opera Arias and Duets (1936–1944), Naxos 8.110754.

  Opera Arias and Duets (1945–1951), Naxos 8.110788.

  Songs in Swedish (1929–1937) Naxos 8.110740.

  The Erik Odde Pseudonym Recordings and Other Popular Works (1931–1935), Naxos 8.110790.

  Björling 1 Pearl GEMM 9041.

  Björling 2 Pearl GEMM 9041.

  Björling 3 Pearl GEMM 9041.

  Jussi Björling Preiser PR89553.

Filmography

  Fram för framgång (Head for Success) 1937.

  Resan till dej (The Journey to You) 1953.

Beno Blachut *1913–1985*

  Coxen, C., 'Beno Blachut', *Record Collector*, 51/4 (December, 2006): 248–81 (with discography by Jan Králík).

Beno Blachut Society
> Spole_nost Beno Blachuta, T_nská uli_ka 8, 110 02 PRAHA 1 (Staré m_sto).

Web
> http://www.belcanto.cz/Blachut/Blachut_his_recordings.htm#Czech%20Radio.
> http://www.answers.com/topic/beno-blachut?cat=entertainment.

Discography
> *Operatic Recital* Suprafon SU34323.

Rockwell Blake *1951*
> Clampton, D., 'L'Histoire d'un jeune et galant postillon', *Record Collector*, 43/4 (December, 1998): 270–74.
> Crutchfield, W., 'Lending an ear to the strains of bel canto', *New York Times*, 12.06.1988.
> Ellison, C., 'Blake, Rockwell' *NGDO* 1: 495–96.

Web
> http://www.bruceduffie.com/blake.html [Bruce Duffie].

Discography
> *Rockwell Blake: Rossini for Tenor* Renata Records CD 1911.
> *The Rossini Tenor* Arabesque Z6582.

Hans-Peter Blochwitz *1949*
Web
> http://www.bach-cantatas.com/Bio/Blochwitz-Hans-Peter.htm.

Discography
> *Alexander Zemlinsky* DGG 427 3482 (2 CDs).
> *Così fan tutte* DGG 423 8972 (3 CDs).
> *Bach Sacred Choral Works* DGG 69 7692 (9 CDs).

Andrea Boccelli *1958*
> Felix, A., *Andrea Boccelli: A Celebration* (New York, 200).
> Steane, J., 'A century of singing: John Steane on Verdi's interpreters', *Opera* (January, 2001): 25–31.

Web
> http://www.andreabocelli.org/.

Discography
> *The Best of Andrea Bocelli* Universal 1746680.
> *Sacred Arias* Philips 4626002.

Alfie Boe *1973*
Web
> http://www.alfie-boe.com/aboutalfie.php.
> http://www.alfie-boe.com/index.php.

Discography
> *La Passione* EMI Classics 504 4112.

Alexander Bogdanovich *1874–1950.*
> *Tenors of Imperial Russia* vol. 2 *Pearl* GEMM 0218.

Alessandro Bonci *1870–1940*
> Bennati, N., *Alessandro Bonci: impressioni* (Ferrara, 1901).
> Brenesal, B., review of *Alessandro Bonci* Cheyne CHE 44387–88, *Record Collector*, 49/2 (2004): 124–6.
> *Farkas*: 25.
> Hutchinson, T., 'Alessandro Bonci', *Record Collector*, 11/7 (1957): 148–62 (with discography).
> Inzaghi, L., *Il tenore Alessandro Bonci (1870–1940)* (Rimini, 2001).
> *Scott* 1: 128–9.
> Shawe-Taylor, D., 'Bonci, Alessandro', *Grove* 3: 850.
> Shawe-Taylor, D., 'Bonci, Alessandro', *NGDO* 1: 536.
> Springer, C., 'Alessandro Bonci and his machinations', *Record Collector*, 50/1 (March, 2005): 59–60.

Steane, J., 'A century of singing: John Steane on Verdi's interpreters', *Opera* (January, 2001): 25–31.

Discography

    Three Edison Tenors Marston 51002–2.

    Alessandro Bonci GEMM CD 9168.

    Alessandro Bonci Preiser PR89525.

Lorenzo Bonfigli *c. 1805–1876*

    Gualerzi, G., 'Tipologia del tenore serio Donizettiano', *International Conference on the Operas of Gaetano Donizetti* (Bergamo, 1992): 353–8.

    La Spina, R., 'Bonfiglio, Lorenzo', *Grove 3*: 857.

Franco Bonisolli *1935–2003*

    Blyth, A., obituary, *The Guardian*, 6.11.2003.

Web

    http://www.grandi-tenori.com/tenors/bonisolli.php [Joern Anthonisen].

Discography

    Recital – Franco Bonisolli Myto MYT 066339.

Webster Booth *1905–1984*

    Ziegler, A. and Booth, W., *Duet* (London, 1951).

Web

    http://math.boisestate.edu/GaS/whowaswho/B/BoothWebster.htm.

    http://ziegler-booth.blogspot.com/2007/01/webster-booths-birthday.html.

Discography

    Stars of English Opera Dutton CDLX 7018.

    Along the Road of Dreams ASV 5365.

    Webster Booth sings Songs of Romance Pavilion 9709.

Filmography

    The Invader (1935).

    George Bizet, Composer of Carmen (1938).

    Waltz Time (1945).

    The Laughing Lady (1946).

    The Story of Gilbert and Sullivan (1953).

    Kimberley Jim (1965).

Giulio Bordogni *1789–1856*

    Fenner, T., *Opera in London: Views of the Press 1785–1830* (Illinois, 1994): 327.

    Forbes, E., 'Bordogni, Giulio (Marco)', *Grove 3*: 893–4.

    Forbes, E., 'Bordogni, Guilio (Marco)', *NGDO* 1: 546.

Giuseppe Borgatti *1871–1950*

    Borgatti, G., *La mia vita d'artista, ricordi e anedotti* (Bologna, 1927).

    Celletti, R., 'Borgatti, Giuseppe' *NGDO* 1: 550.

    Celletti, R. and Gualerzi, A. P., 'Borgatti, Guiseppe', *Grove 3*: 897.

    Farkas: 26.

    Scott 1: 133–4.

Web

    http://www.operaitaliana.com/autori/interprete.asp?ID=759.

Discography

    Fonotipia: A Centenary Celebration (1904–2004) Symposium 1261.

Dino Borgioli *1891–1960*

    Shawe-Taylor, D., 'Borgioli, Dino', *Grove 3*: 900–1.

    Shawe-Taylor, D., 'Borgioli, Dino,' *NGDO* 1: 551.

Web

    http://chalosse.free.fr/masterpieces/step-one/borgioli.htm.

Discography

    Dino Borgioli Preiser LV 89508.

Antonio Borosini *c. 1655–c. 1721*
>Vitali, C., 'Antonio Borosini [Boresini, Borosino]', *Grove* 3: 918.
>Vitali, C., 'Antonio Borosini [Boresini, Borosino]', *NGDO* 1: 562.

Francesco Borosini *1690–1747*
>Brandenburg, I., 'Borosini, Francesco', *MGG* 3: 441–3.
>Dean, W., 'Francesco Borosini', *Grove* 3: 918–19.
>Dean, W., 'Francesco Borosini', *NGDO* 1: 562–3.
>Johengen, C., 'Francesco Borosini: First among tenors', *Journal of Singing*, 63/3 (Jan–Feb 2005): 253–60.
>LaRue, S., *Handel and his Singers* (Oxford, 1995).

Ian Bostridge *1964*
>Blyth, A., 'Bostridge, Ian (Charles)', *Grove* 4: 77–8.
>Cook, C., 'Ian Bostridge, the Must-have English tenor', *Steane 3:* 158–62.

Web
>http://www.geocities.com/Vienna/1185/bostridge.html.
>http://www.virelai.net/disco/bostridge/.
>http://www.gramophone.co.uk/interviews_detail.asp?id=911.

Discography
>*Schubert: Die schöne Müllerin* Hyperion CDJ33025.
>*Winterreise* EMI Classics 0724355779021.
>*Ian Bostridge: Great Handel* EMI Classics 0094638224327.
>*The English Songbook* EMI Classics 0724355683021.

Luca Botta *1882–1917*
>Alda, F., *Men, Women and Tenors* (Boston, 1937): 177–8.

Kenneth Bowen *1932*
>Bowen, K. and Pratley, G., The Handel Opera Repertory, Book 2: Tenor (London, 1989).

Web
>http://www.londonwelshchorale.org.uk/e_kenneth_bowen.htm.

Discography
>*Great Welsh Tenor Solos* Sain SCD2019.
>*Mathias: Ave Rex, Elegy, This Worlde's Joie* Lyrita LYTA324.

John Braham *1774–1856*
>Crichton, R., 'Braham, John' *NGDO* 1: 580.
>*Farkas*: 27.
>Fenner, T., *Opera in London: Views of the Press 1785–1830* (Illinois, 1994): 168–70; 518–25.
>Hogarth, G., *Memoirs of the Opera*, vol. 2 (London, 1851): 280–4; 365–6.
>Levien, J. M., *The Singing of John Braham* (London, 1944).
>Rice, J., 'Benedetto Frizzi on singers, composers, and opera in late eighteenth-century Italy', *Studi musicali*, 23: (1994): 367–93.
>Sands, M., 'These were singers', *Music & Letters*, 25/2 (April, 1944): 103–6.

Achille Braschi *1909–1983*
Web
>www.grandi-tenori.com/tenors/braschi.php.

Discography
>*Mascagni: Cavalleria rusticana* 8573 87271–2.

John Brecknock *1937.*
>Brecknock, J. L. and Melling, J. K., *Scaling the High Cs* (London, 1996).
>Goodwin, N., 'Brecknock, John', *NGDO* 1: 591.

Discography
>*Evening Scene: Elgar Songs* Meridian CDE 84173.

Filmography
>*Barber of Seville* (1984).

Otto Briesemeister *1866–1910*
Discography
  Otto Briesemeister Preiser LV PR89947.
Helge Brilioth *1931*
  Rosenthal, H., 'Brilioth, Helge', *NGDO* 1: 603.
Discography
  Götterdämmerung DGG 415 155–2 (4 CDs).
Antonio Brizzi *1774–1851*
  Rice, J., 'Benedetto Frizzi on singers, composers, and opera in late eighteenth-century
    Italy', *Studi musicali*, 23 (1994): 367–93.
Friedrich Brodersen *1873–1926*
  Scott 2: 222–3.
Wilfred Brown *1921–1971*
  Stevens, John, obituary, *The Musical Times*, 112/1539 (May, 1971): 478.
Web
  http://www.bach-cantatas.com/Bio/Brown-Wilfred.htm.
Discography
  Songs for Voice and Guitar CBS 61126.
  Folksongs Belart 461 4892.
  Finzi: Dies Natalis EMI 65588.
Philip Brozel *c. 1868–1928*
  Hymos, H., 'The ones who got away: Philip Brozel, the forgotten tenor', *Record
    Collector*, 51/1 (March, 2006): 46–9.
Hans Buff-Giessen *1862–1907*
Discography
  Gustav Walter/Hans Buff-Gießen/Felix Senius Complete recordings (1904–1911):
    Truesound TT-1905.
Karel Burian *1870–1924*
  Dennis, J., 'Karel Burian', *Record Collector*, 18/7 (1969): 148–64 (with discography).
  Shawe-Taylor, D., 'Burian, Karel [Burrian, Carl]', *Grove* 4: 624.
Web
  http://www.karelburian.cz/english/index.php.
Tom Burke *1890–1969*
  Bott, M., 'Tom Burke in Opera', *Record Collector*, 29/9–12 (1984): 262–6.
  Bott, M., 'Tom Burke in Kansas City', *Record Collector*, 50/3 (2005): 186–7.
  Winstanley, F., 'Tom Burke', *Record Collector*, 35/11–12 (1990): 287–97 (with discog-
    raphy).
  Farkas: 28.
  Rosenthal, H., 'Burke, Thomas [Tom] (Aspinall)', *NGDO* 1: 647.
  Rosenthal, H. and Blyth, A., 'Burke, Thomas [Tom] (Aspinall)', *Grove* 4: 624.
  Vose, J. D., *The Lancashire Caruso: The Life of Tom Burke* (Blackpool, 1982).
Discography
  Tom Burke Centennial Edition Pearl GEMM CD9411.
Stuart Burrows *1933*
  Blyth, A., 'Burrows (James), Stuart', *Grove* 4: 645–6.
  Blyth, A., 'Burrows (James), Stuart', *NGDO* 1: 652.
Web
  http://www.stuartburrows.f9.co.uk/.
Discography
  Mozart: Famous Arias Decca 4213112.
  Stuart Burrows: Favourite Ballads Decca 4300902.
Giulio Caccini *1586–1618*
  Carter, T. and Wiley Hitchcock, H., 'Giulio Romolo Caccini', *Grove* 4: 769–75.
  Hanning, B. R., 'Caccini, Giulio', *NGDO* 1: 668–9.

Kirkendale, W., *The Court Musicians in Florence during the Principate of the Medici* (Florence, 1993): 119–80.

Pompeo Caccini *b. 1578/9*

Kirkendale, W., *The Court Musicians in Florence during the Principate of the Medici* (Florence, 1993): 162–3.

Icilio Calleja *1882–1941*

Scott 2: 112–13.

Web

http://www.grandi-tenori.com/tenors/calleja/calleja.php [Emy Scicluna].

Discography

Rare Records of Famous Tenors vol. 3 Symposium CD 1370.

Joseph Calleja *1978*

Jeal, E., 'Great Expectations', *Gramophone* (August 2005): 25–9.

Web

http://www.josephcalleja.net/.

Discography

Tenor Arias: Joseph Calleja Decca 475 250–2 (2 CDs).

The Golden Voice Decca 475 6931 (2 CDs).

Vincenzo Calvesi *1771–1811*

Fenner, T., *Opera in London: Views of the Press 1785–1830* (Illinois, 1994): 316–17.

Link, D. and Rice, J. A., 'Calvesi, Vincenzo', *Grove* 4: 843–4.

Raeburn, L. and Link, D., 'Calvesi, Vincenzo', *NGDO* 1: 693.

Leon Campagnola *1875–1955*

De Cock, A., 'Leon Campagnola', *Record Collector*, 48/4 December 2003: 250–87 (with discography).

Holdridge, L., 'Leon Campagnola', *Record Collector*, 45/4 (December, 2000): 325–6.

Discography

Léon Campagnola Malibran CDRG138.

Francesco Campagnolo *1584–1630*

Parisi, S., 'Campagnolo, Francesco', *Grove* 4: 884.

Parisi, S., 'Campagnolo, Francesco', *NGDO* 1: 703.

Stevens, D. (ed./trans.) *The Letters of Claudio Monteverdi* (London 1980): 305.

Italo Campanini *1845–1896*

Forbes, E., 'Campanini, Italo', *NGDO* 1: 704.

Forbes, E., 'Campanini, Italo', *Grove* 4: 886.

McPherson, J., 'Italo Campanini: one of a kind', *Opera Quarterly*, 19/2 (2003): 251–71.

Carlo Carpi *1842–1930*

Monson, D. E., 'Carpi, Carlo', *NGDO* 1: 732.

Fernando Carpi *1876–1959*

Scott 2: 101–2.

Discography

The Harold Wayne Collection vol. 29 Symposium 1399.

José Carreras *1946*

Bernheimer, M., 'Carreras, José', *NGDO* 1: 744.

Carreras, J., *Singing from the Soul: An Autobiography* (London, 1991).

Web

http://www.josepcarreras.com/index_en.php.

http://www.jcarreras.homestead.com/Carreras1.html [Jean Peccei].

http://www.carrerascaptures.com/.

Discography

José Carreras: the Golden Years Philips 462892.

The Very Best of José Carreras EMI 7243 5 75903 2 7.

Video

José Carreras por José Carreras. Perfil de un Hombre, 1990 (recorded 1984), Classic Media/ Selecta Vision.

José Carreras: A Life Story, 1993 Decca Records/Iambic Productions.

Filmography

Romanza Final 1986 (as Julián Gayarre).

Manuel Carrión *1817–1876*

Gualerzi, G., 'Spain: Land of Tenors', *Opéra* (November, 1987): 1257–63 (December, 1987): 1387–91.

Enrico Caruso *1873–1921*

Barthelemy, R. (trans. James Camner), *Memories of Caruso* (Plainsboro, 1979).

Bello, J., *Enrico Caruso; A Centennial Tribute* (Providence, 1973).

Bolig, J.R., *The Recordings of Enrico Caruso; A Discography* (Dover, 1973).

Caruso, D., *Enrico Caruso: His Life and Death* (London, 1955).

Caruso, E. (Jr) and Farkas, A., *Enrico Caruso, My Father and My Family* (Portland, Oregon, 1990).

Caruso, E. and Tetrazzini, L., *Caruso and Tetrazzini on the Art of Singing* (New York, 1975).

Celletti, R., 'Caruso, Enrico', *NGDO* 1: 746–7.

Celletti, R. and Blyth, A., 'Caruso, Enrico', *Grove* 5: 213–14.

Daspuro, N., *Enrico Caruso* (Milan, 1977).

Douglas, N., *Legendary Voices* (New York, 1995): pp. 25–54.

Farkas, A., 'Enrico Caruso: tenor, baritone and bass', *Opera Quarterly,* 4/4 (Winter 1896/7): 53–60.

Farkas 40–51.

Favia-Artsay, A., *Caruso on Records. Pitch, Speed and Comments for All the Published Recordings of Enrico Caruso* (New York, 1965).

Fink, H.T., *The Secret of Caruso's Glorious Voice* (Philadelphia, 1929).

Gerald Fitzgerald (ed.) '*Caruso 1981*' *The Opera Engagement Calendar* (New York, 1980).

Flint, M. H., *Impressions of Caruso and His Art as Portrayed at the Metropolitan Opera House* (New York, 1917).

Freestone, J. and Drummond, H. J., *Enrico Caruso; His Recorded Legacy* (London, 1960).

Fucito, S. and Beyer, B. J., *Caruso and the Art of Singing, Including Caruso's Vocal Exercises and His Practical Advice to Students and Teachers of Singing* (New York, 1922).

Gara, E., *Caruso, storia di un emigrante* (Milan, 1947).

Greenfeld, Howard., *Caruso* (New York, 1983).

Marafioti, P.M., *Caruso's Method of Voice Production* (New York, 1981).

Scott 1: 138–41.

Steane 3: 248–52.

Ybarra, T. R., *Caruso: The Man of Naples and the Voice of Gold* (New York, 1953).

Vaccaro, R., 'Caruso' (Naples, 1995).

Discography

Naxos Complete Recordings (1902–1920) in 12 volumes.

Richard Cassilly *1927–1998*

Blyth, A., 'Cassilly, Richard', *Grove* 5: 243–4.

Blyth, A., 'Cassilly, Richard', *NGDO* 1: 754.

Louis Cazette *1887–1922*

Ashbrook, W., 'Three tenors of the Opéra-comique', *Record Collector,* 45/2 (June, 2000): 149–51.

Hall, L., 'Louis Cazette', *Record Collector,* 27/1 (December, 1981): 5–23.

Holdridge, L., 'Charles Dalmorès and Louis Cazette', *Record Collector*, 45/3 (September, 2000): 227–8.

Scott 2: 38–9.

Steane, J. B., 'Cazette, Louis', *NGDO* 1: 792.

Web

http://www.cantabile-subito.de/Tenors/Cazette_Louis/cazette_louis.html.

Discography

Three Tenors of the Opéra-Comique: Louis Cazette, Charles Friant and Jean Marny. Marston MR 51006.

Mario Chamlee *1892–1966*

Dennis, J., 'Thumbnail Sketches', *Record Collector*, 8/11–12 (1953): 273.

Riemans, L., 'The Brunswick Hall of Fame', *Record Collector*, 5/4 (1950): 88–9.

Steane, J. B., 'Chamlee, Mario', *NGDO* 1: 816.

Scott 2: 164.

Mario Chamlee Preiser PR89591.

Lloyd Chandos *1861–c. 1939*

Lloyd Chandos Cheyne Records CHE 44422.

Jean Baptiste Chollet *1798–1892*

Farkas: 61.

Robinson, P., 'Chollet, Jean Baptiste (Marie)', *Grove* 5: 704–5.

Robinson, P., 'Chollet, Jean Baptiste (Marie)', *NGDO* 1: 849.

Ercole Ciprandi *c. 1725–1790*

Rosselli, J., 'Ciprandi, Ercole', *NGDO* 1: 872.

Pablo Civil *1899–1987*

Hughes, J., review of *The Cetra Tenors* (Pearl GEMS 0120), *Record Collector*, 46/2 (June, 2001): 153–6.

Discography

The Cetra Tenors Pearl GEMS 0120.

Edmond Clément *1867–1928*

McKee, E., 'Edmond Clément: the complete Pathé recordings (1916–25)', *Record Collector*, 45/4 (December, 2000): 327–9.

Scott, M., 1: 68.

Steane, J.B., 'Clément, Edmond', *Grove* 6: 34.

Steane 2: 128–32.

Discography

Edmond Clément: French Opera and Mélodies Pearl GEMM CD 9161.

John Coates *1865–1941*

Anon, 'John Coates', *Musical Times* (December, 1911): 773–6.

Foreman, D., 'John Coates', *Record Collector*, 38/2 (1993): 82–119 (with discography).

Moore, G., *Am I Too Loud?* (London, 1962): 33–43.

Moore, G. and Forbes, E., 'Coates, John', *NGDO* 1: 889.

Scott 2: 170–2.

Discography

John Coates Cheyne CHE 44402–3 (2 CDs).

Florencio Constantino *1869–1919*

Arnosi, E., 'Florencio Constantino' *Record Collector*, 37/4 (1992): 242–67 (with discography).

Goyen-Aguado, J., *Florencio Constantino, 1868–1919: El hombre y el tenor – milagro de una voz* (Bilbao, 1993).

Gualerzi, G., 'Spain: Land of Tenors', *Opera* (November, 1987): 1257–63 (December, 1987): 1387–91.

Moran, W., review of *El hombre y el tenor: miagro de una voz*, *Record Collector*, 42/3 (September, 1997): 218–21.

Steane, J. B., 'Constantino, Florencio', *NGDO* 1: 921.

Discography
> *Florencio Constantino: Opera and Zarzuela* Truesound TT-2022.

Franco Corelli *1921–2003*

> Blyth, A., 'Franco Corelli', *Guardian*, 31.10.03.
>
> Boagno, M. with Starone, G. (trans. Teresa Brentegani and Samuel Chase), *Corelli: A Man, A Voice* (chronology and discography by Gilberto Starone, tapeography by Federico Rota, videography and filmography by Gilberto Starone, Mark Schiavone and Stephen R. Leopold; 2nd edn, Fort Worth, 2006) with CD.
>
> Celletti, R., 'Corelli, Franco', *NGDO* 1: 949.
>
> Celletti, R. and Blyth, A., 'Corelli, Franco', *Grove* 6: 463.
>
> Downs, J., 'Franco Corelli' in Breslin, Herbert H. (ed.), *The Tenors* (New York, 1974): 83–125.
>
> Gualerzi, G., 'Di Stefano and Corelli at 75', *Opera* (October, 1996): 1137–44.
>
> Hines, J., *Great Singers on Great Singing* (New York, 2003): 57–68.
>
> Rubin, S., 'Franco Corelli', in Breslin, Herbert H. (ed.) *The Tenors* (New York 1974): 83–125.
>
> Seghers, R., *Franco Corelli Prince of Tenors* (Amadeus Press, 2007).
>
> *Steane 2*: 1–6.

Web
> Seghers, R., http://www.francocorelli.nl/.
>
> http://chalosse.free.fr/masterpieces/step-one/corelli-2.htm.

Discography
> *Legendary Performances of Franco Corelli – 7 Operas* Opera d'Oro ODO 5602 (7 CDs).
>
> See *http://www.belcantosociety.org* for extensive audio, video and interview material.

Pierre Cornubert *1863–1922*

> Barnes, H., 'Pierre Cornubert', *Record Collector*, 40/2 (1995): 127–131 (with discography).

Discography
> *Early French Tenors: Émile Scaramberg, Pierre Cornubert, and Adolphe Maréchal* Marston 52059–2.

Antonio Cortis *1891–1952*

> Bilgora, A., review of *Antonio Cortis: Arias* (Pearl GEMM 0047), *Record Collector*, 44/2 (June, 1999): 161–3.
>
> Favia-Artsay, A., Léon, J. and Dennis, J., 'Antonio Cortis', *Record Collector*, 20/3 (1971): 52–69 (with discography).
>
> Gualerzi, G., 'Spain: Land of Tenors', *Opera* (November, 1987): 1257–63 (December, 1987): 1387–91.
>
> Rosenthal, H., 'Cortis [Corts], Antonio', *NGDO* 1: 963–4.
>
> Rosenthal, H. and Blyth, A., 'Cortis [Corts], Antonio', *Grove* 6: 509–10.
>
> *Steane 1*: 146–150.

Discography
> *Antonio Cortis* Preiser PR89043.
>
> *Cortis* Nimbus NI 7850.

Jean Cox *1922*

> Heldt, G. (ed.), *Ein Leben fur die Oper* (Laaber, 1982).
>
> Rosenthal, H., 'Cox, Jean', *NGDO* 1: 1002.

Discography
> *Siegfried* Myto 055318.

Charles Craig *1920–1997*

> Forbes, E., obituary, *The Independent*, 25.01.1997.

Discography
> *Charles Craig: Puccini Arias and Favourite Ballads* Testament.
>
> *Charles Craig: Operatic Arias and Italian Songs* Testament.

Giulio Crimi *1885–1939*
> Steane, J. B., 'Crimi, Giulio', *NGDO* 1: 1007.
> *Scott* 2: 107–8.

Gaetano Crivelli *1768–1836*
> Fenner, T., *Opera in London: Views of the Press 1785–1830* (Illinois, 1994): 176–7.
> Forbes, E., 'Crivelli, Gaetano', *Grove* 6: 699.
> Forbes, E., 'Crivelli, Gaetano', *NGDO* 1: 1014.

Richard Croft
Web
> http://www.richardcroft.net/.

Videography
> Mozart: *Mitridate* Decca 00440 074 3168.

Howard Crook *1947*
Web
> *http://www.operalafayette.org/howard_crook.html.*

Discography
> *Lully: Armide* Harmonia Mundi 901456.57.
> *Lully: Phaëton* Erato 4509917372.

Filmography
> *Atys* (1987).
> *Tarare* (1988).
> *Le malade imaginaire* (1990).
> *Castor et Pollux* (1991).
> *Revenez plaisirs exiles* (1992).

Richard Crooks *1900–1972*
> De Scheuensee, M., 'Crooks, Richard (Alexander)', *Grove* 6: 719–20.
> Mackiggan, K., 'Richard Crooks in opera and concert', *Record Collector*, 31/11–12 (1986): 243–56.
> Morgan, C., 'Reminiscing with Richard Crooks', *Record Collector*, 20/11 (1972): 258–70.
> Morgan, C., 'Richard Crooks discography', *Record Collector*, 47/3 (2002): 257–79.
> Pearce, J, 'Richard Crooks, tenor opera arias and songs, 1918–19', *Opera Quarterly*, 14 (1998): 130–4.

Web
> http://www.maurice-abravanel.com/crooks.html.

Discography
> *Richard Crooks* Delos DE 5501 (2 CDs).
> *Richard Crooks* GEMM CD 9093.
> *Richard Crooks: Only a Rose* GEMM CD 9244.
> *Richard Crooks in Songs and Ballads* Nimbus NI 7888.

Rogers Covey-Crump *1944*
> Pratt, G., 'Covey-Crump, Rogers', *Grove* 6: 618.

Web
> http://www.bach-cantatas.com/Bio/Covey-Crump-Rogers.htm.

Discography
> *Bach St John Passion* EMI 5620192 (2 CDs).
> *Ancient Airs and Dances* Hyperion CDA66228.
> *Music for St Paul's* Hyperion CDA67009.

Hughes Cuénod *1902*
> Blyth, A., 'Cuénod, Hughes', *NGDO* 1:1023.
> Blyth, A., 'Cuénod, Hughes', *Grove* 6: 772.
> Hudry, F., *Hugues Cuénod with a Nimble Voice: Conversations with François Hundry* (Pendragon Press, 1999).

Steane 2: 211–15.

Westphal, M., 'The World's Oldest Living Tenor Celebrates His 105th Birthday (And He's a Newlywed, No Less!)', *Playbill Arts* 26 June 2007 [http://www.playbillarts.com/news/article/6704.html]

Discography

Satie *Socrate* Nimbus NI 5027.

Hugues Cuénod: Le Maître de la Mélodie Nimbus NI 5337.

A Tribute to Hughes Cuénod Cascavelle CAS 3080.

Alberto Cupido *1976*

Web

http://www.albertocupido.it/.

Discography

Alberto Cupido canta arie di Donizetti Denon CD-79785.

José Cura *1962*

Allison, J., 'José Cura', *Opera* (October, 1999): 1137–43.

Blyth, A., 'Cura, José', *Grove* 6: 781.

Web

http://www.josecura.com/.

http://kira.romeoandjuliet.net/kireannasweb/Biography/biography.htm.

http://www.jcura-connexion.com/.

Discography

José Cura Artist's Portrait Warner Classics.

José Cura: Verdi Arias Erato.

Alberico Curioni *1785–1875*

Fenner, T., *Opera in London: Views of the Press 1785–1830* (Illinois, 1994): 192–5.

Forbes, E., 'Curioni, Alberico', *Grove* 6: 783.

Forbes, E., 'Curioni, Alberico', *NGDO* 1: 1030.

Charles Dalmorès *1871–1939*

Holdridge, L., 'Charles Dalmorès and Louis Cazette', *Record Collector*, 45/3 (September, 2000): 227–8.

Scott 1: 63–4.

Steane, J. B., Dalmorès, Charles', *Grove* 6: 866.

Steane, J. B., Dalmorès, Charles', *NGDO* 1: 1054.

Discography

Charles Dalmorès Preiser PR89506.

Vasili Damaev *1878–1931*

Discography

Tenors of Imperial Russia vol. 1 Pearl GEMM 0217

Charles Daniels *1960*

Web

http://www.bach-cantatas.com/Bio/Daniels-Charles.htm.

Discography

Lute Songs ATMA 22548.

Orfeo Fantasia ATMA 22337.

Senfl: Im Maien Harmonia Mundi HAR 907334.

See http://www.hyperion-records.co.uk/a.asp?a=A118&name=daniels.

André D'Arkor *1901–1971*

Web

http://www.cantabile-subito.de/Tenors/D_Arkor_Andre/d_arkor_andre.html.

Discography

Lebendiger Vergangenheit Preisr LV 89541.

Léon David *1867–1962*

David, L., *La vie d'un tenor* (Fontenay-le-Conte, 1950).

Forbes, E., 'David, Léon', *Grove* 7: 54.

Forbes, E., 'David, Léon', *NGDO* 1: 1088.

McKee, E., 'Léon David: the complete recordings (1904–08),' *Record Collector*, 45/4 (December, 2000): 327–9.

Discography

Léon David: The Complete Recordings (1904–08) Romophone 82016–2.

Giacomo David(de) *1750–1830*

Forbes, E., 'Davide [David], Giacomo', *NGDO* 1: 1088.

Rice, J., 'Benedetto Frizzi on singers, composers, and opera in late eighteenth-century Italy', *Studi musicali*, 23: (1994): 367–93.

Giovanni Davide *1790–1864*

Celletti, R., *Voce di tenore* (Cremona, 1989): 79–81.

Forbes, E., 'Davide [David], Giovanni', *Grove* 7: 55.

Forbes, E., 'Davide, Giovanni', *NGDO* 1: 1088.

Zucker, S., *The Origins of Modern Tenor Singing* (New York, nd).

Aleksandr Davidoff *1872–1944*

Scott 1: 219.

Steane, J. B., 'Davidoff [Levinson], Aleksandr', *Grove* 7: 55.

Steane, J. B., 'Davidoff [Levinson], Aleksandr', *NGDO* 1: 1089.

Discography

Tenors of Imperial Russia, vol. 2 Pearl GEMM 0218.

Ben Davies *1858–1943*

Anon *Musical Times* (August, 1899): 513–18.

Dales, J., 'The Ben Davies Cylinders', *Record Collector*, 42/1 (March, 1997): 54–5.

Foreman, D., 'Ben Davies', *Record Collector*, 41/3 (September, 1996): 163–88.

Discography

Ben Davies Cheyne CHE 44370–1 (2 CDs).

Ryland Davies *1943*

Blyth, A., 'Davies, Ryland', *Grove* 7: 72.

Blyth, A., 'Davies, Ryland', *NGDO* 1: 1091.

Web

http://www.rylanddavies.info/.

Discography

Handel: Judas Maccabaeus Deutsche Grammophon DTGM 4476922.

Mozart: Così fan tutte Decca B000064312.

Videography

Janáček: Kat'A Kabanova KUL 36.

Die Entführung aus dem Serail Arthaus AHM 101091.

Tudor Davies *1892–1958*

Badrock, A., 'Tudor Davies: a discography', *Record Collector*, 45/3 (September, 2000): 249–54.

Steane, J. B., 'Davies, Tudor', *Grove* 7: 72–3.

Steane, J. B., 'Davies, Tudor', *NGDO* 1: 1091.

Discography

Tudor Davies: Operatic and Song Recital (London, 1922–1927) Truesound 2456.

Tudor Davies: Songs and Arias Cheyne CHE 44446–7 (2 CDS).

Paul Elliott *1950*

Web

http://www.bach-cantatas.com/Bio/Elliott-Paul.htm.

Discography

Bach: Cantatas 195 and 215 Rondeau RDAU 2006.

Gay: The Beggar's Opera Harmonia Mundi HAR 1951071.

Handel: Messiah Decca DEC 4304882.

Isidoro de Fagoaga *1893–1976*
> Gualerzi, G., 'Spain: Land of Tenors', *Opera* (November, 1987): 1257–63 (December, 1987): 1387–91.

Scipione Delle Palle *d. 1569*
> Carter, T., 'Delle Palle [Dalle Palle, Del Palla, Vecchi detto Delle Palle]', *Grove* 7: 176.

Mario Del Monaco *1915–1982*
> Chedorge, A., Mancini, R. and Caussou, J. L., *Mario del Monaco* (Paris, 1965).
> Del Monaco, M., *La mia vita e i miei successi* (Milan, 1982).
> Romagnolo, E., *Mario del Monaco: Monumentum aere perennius* (Parma, 2002), with discography and filmography.
> *Farkas*: 68–9.
> Rosenthal, H., 'Del Monaco, Mario', *NGDO* 1: 1115–16.
> Rosenthal, H. and Blyth, A., 'Del Monaco, Mario', *Grove* 7: 182.
> *Steane 3*: 83–7.

Web
> http://www.mariodelmonaco.net/index3.html [Roberto Scandurra-official site].

Fernando De Lucia *1860–1925*
> Henstock, M., *Fernando De Lucia: Son of Naples, 1860–1925* (London, 1990).
> Shawe-Taylor, D., 'De Lucia, Fernando', *Grove* 7: 186–7.
> Shawe-Taylor, D., 'De Lucia, Fernando', *NGDO* 1: 1117.
> Steane, J., 'A century of singing: John Steane on Verdi's interpreters', *Opera* (January, 2001): 25–31.
> *Steane 1*: 41–5.
> Steinson, P., review of *Fernando De Lucia*, *Record Collector*, 46/3 (September, 2001): 185–6.

Discography
> *Fernando De Lucia* Pearl GEMM CDS 9071.
> *Fernando De Lucia* OPAL 9845 (2 CDs).
> *Fernando De Lucia*, vols 1–4: Truesound TT2218–21.
> *Fernando De Lucia – Italian Song Recital* (Naples, 1920–21) Truesound TT2302.
> *Fernando De Lucia*, vol. 6: Phonotype recordings (Naples, May–June 1917) Truesound TT2491.
> *Fernando De Lucia*, vols 7–12 Truesound TT2492–97.

Emilio De Marchi *1861–1918*
> Luther, E., 'De Marchi, Emilio', *MGG*. 5: 796–7.
> Steane, J. B., 'De Marchi, Emilio', *Grove* 7: 192.
> Steane, J. B., 'De Marchi, Emilio', *NGDO* 1: 1118.

Guy de Mey *1955*
Web
> http://www.bach-cantatas.com/Bio/Mey-Guy-de.htm [Aryeh Oron].
> http://www.goldbergweb.com/en/interpreters/vocals/10594.php.

Discography
> *Bach: Johannes Passion* Erato ERA 94675.
> *Handel: Judas Maccabaeus* Harmonia Mundi HAR 2907374.

Bernardo de Muro *1881–1955*
> Arnosi, E., 'Bernardo de Muro', *Record Collector*, 18/3 (1968): 52–69 (with discography and recording commentary by J. A. Léon).
> De Muro, N., 'Bernardo de Muro: a personal recollection by his daughter Nina', *Record Collector*, 40/3 (1995): 224–30.
> *Farkas*: 69–70.
> Steane, J. B., 'de Muro, Bernardo', *NGDO* 1: 1122.

Discography
> *Bernardo de Muro* Preiser PR89572.

Enzo de Muro Lomanto *1902–1952*

> Feliciotti, G. with Rideout, B., 'Enzo de Muro Lomanto' (with discography by Tom Peel), *Record Collector*, 45/3 (September, 2000): 2257–89.

Jean de Reszke *1850–1925*

> *Farkas*: 215–16.
>
> Forbes, E., 'de Rezke, Jean', *NGDO* 1: 1127.
>
> Forbes, E., 'de Rezke, Jean', *Grove* 7: 225
>
> Klein, H., 'Jean de Reszke and Marie Brema: some reminiscences', *Musical Times*, 1 May 1925: 405–8.
>
> Leiser, C., *Jean de Reszke and the Great Days of Opera* (London, 1933).
>
> Matushevski, V., 'Jean de Reske as pedagogue: his ideas, their development, and their results', *Opera Quarterly*, 12/1 (1995): 47–70.
>
> Pleasants, H., *The Great Singers* (London, 1967): 254–62.
>
> *Scott* 1: 84–6.
>
> Verdino-Süllwold, C., *We Need a Hero: Heldentenors from Wagner's Time to the Present, A Critical History* (New York, 1989): 81–92.
>
> Webber, A., 'Jean de Reszke: his Manner of Life', *Music & Letters*, 6/3 (July, 1925): 195–202.

Anton Dermota *1910–1989*

> Dermota, A., *Tausendundein Abend: mein Sängerleben* (Vienna, 1978).
>
> *Farkas*: 70.
>
> Rosenthal, H., 'Dermota, Anton', *NGDO* 1: 1128.
>
> Rosenthal, H. and Blyth, A., 'Dermota, Anton', *Grove* 7: 227.

Web

> http://www.bach-cantatas.com/Bio/Dermota-Anton.htm.

Discography

> *Anton Dermota* Preiser PR89623.

David Devriès *1882–1934*

> Bilgora, A., 'David Devriès: the voice', *Record Collector*, 49/4 (2004): 266–8.
>
> De Cock, A., 'David Devriès (1882–1934)' *Record Collector*, 49/4 (2004): 242–66 (with discography by Paul Steinson).
>
> Forbes, E., 'Devriès, David', *NGDO* 1: 1151.
>
> *Scott* 2: 35–6.

Discography

> *David Devriès* Symposium SYM 1220.

Rafaelo Diaz *1885–1943*

> Bott, M., 'Rafaelo Diaz', *Record Collector*, 46/4 (December, 2001): 301–7 (with discography with Tom Peel).

Andreas Dippel *1866–1935*

> Baily, D., 'Dippel, Andreas', *NGDO* 1: 1181.
>
> *Scott* 1: 198.

Giuseppe Di Stefano *1921–2008*

> Blyth, A., obituary, *The Guardian* (5.3.08): 38.
>
> *Farkas*: 72.
>
> Gualerzi, G., 'Di Stefano and Corelli at 75', *Opera* (October, 1996): 1137–44.
>
> Rosenthal, H., 'Di Stefano, Giuseppe', *NGDO* 1: 1182.
>
> Rosenthal, H. and Blyth, A., 'Di Stefano, Giuseppe', *Grove* 7: 380–1.
>
> Semrau, T., 'Giuseppe di Stefano', *Record Collector*, 39/3 (1994): 165–229 (with discography by Tom Peel and John Holohan).
>
> *Steane* 1: 66–70.

Web

> http://www.giuseppedistefano.it/.
>
> http://www.grandi-tenori.com/tenors/distefano/distefano_p3.php [Joern Anthonisen].

Discography
>Giuseppe Di Stefano: The Early Recordings 1944–1950 Historia VA 3003.
>Giuseppe Di Stefano: Historical Recordings 1952–1963 Gala GL 303.
>Maria Callas/Giuseppe Di Stefano: Italian Opera Duets EMI 7 69543 2.
>Met Legends: Giuseppe Di Stefano RCA MET 224.

Plácido Domingo *1941*
>Allison, J., (ed.) *Forty Years of Domingo in Opera*, supplement to *Opera* (September, 2001).
>Domingo, P., *My First Forty Years* (New York, 1983).
>*Farkas*: 73.
>Hines, J., *Great Singers on Great Singing* (New York, 2003): 99–108.
>Jeal, E., 'Great Expectations', *Gramophone* (August 2005): 25–9.
>Rosenthal, H., 'Domingo, Placido', *NGDO* 1: 1194.
>Rubin, S., 'Placido Domingo', in Herbert H. Breslin (ed.), *The Tenors* (New York 1974): 126–60.
>Steane, J. B., 'A century of singing: John Steane on Verdi's interpreters', *Opera* (January, 2001): 25–31.
>*Steane 2*: 138–42.

Web
>http://www.placidodomingo.com/.

Discography
>*Domingo the Verdi Tenor* DGG 471 4782.
>*The Best of Plácido Domingo* DGG 415 3662.
>*Pasión Español* DGG 477 6590.
>*Wagner: Tristan und Isolde* EMI 7243 5 58006 2 6.

Domenico Donzelli *1790–1873*
>Fenner, T., *Opera in London: Views of the Press 1785–1830* (Illinois, 1994): 195–8.
>Forbes, E., 'Donzelli, Domenico', *Grove 7*: 500–1.
>Forbes, E., 'Donzelli, Domenico', *NGDO* 1: 1228.
>Gualerzi, G., 'Tipologia del tenore serio Donizettiano', *International Conference on the Operas of Gaetano Donizetti* (Bergamo, 1992): 353–8.
>Modugno, M., 'Domenico Donzelli e il suo tempo', *Nuova rivista musicale italiana* XVIII/2 (April–June 1984): 200–16.
>Pleasants, H., 'A new kind of tenor', in *The Great Singers* (London, 1967): 158–76.

Nigel Douglas *1929*
>Douglas, N., *Legendary Voices* (New York, 1992).
>Douglas, N., *More Legendary Voices* (New York, 1994).

Web
>http://www.josef-weinberger.com/mw/starring.html.

Ronald Dowd *1914–1990*
>Blyth, A., 'Dowd, Ronald', *NGDO* 1:1236.

Discography
>Berlioz: *Requiem, Grande Messe des Morts* Philips 416 283–2 (2 CDs).

Gilbert-Louis Duprez *1806–1894*
>Armstrong, A., 'Gilbert-Louis Duprez and Gustave Roger in the Composition of Meyerbeer's *Le Prophète*', *Cambridge Opera Journal*, 8/2 (1996): 147–65.
>Corti, S., 'Duprez, Gilbert (-Louis)', *Grove 7*: 731.
>Duprez, G., *L'Art du chant* (Paris, 1846).
>Duprez, G., *A Treatise on the Art of Singing* . . . trans. and ed. J.W. Mould (London 1847).
>Duprez, G., *Souvenirs d'un chanteur* (Paris, 1880).
>Elwart, A., *Duprez: sa vie artistique avec une biographie authentique de son maître Alexandre Choron* (Paris, 1838).

Farkas: 75.

Pleasants, H., 'A new kind of tenor', in *The Great Singers* (London, 1967):158–76.

Warrack, J. and Corti, S., 'Duprez, Gilbert-Louis', *NGDO* 1: 1281.

Zucker, S., *The Origins of Modern Tenor Singing* (New York, nd).

Peter Dvorsky *1951*

Stilichová, D., *Peter Dvorsky* (Bratislava, 1991).

Web

http://www.grandi-tenori.com/tenors/dvorsky.htm [Joseph Fragala].

http://www.naxosdirect.com/Peter-Dvorsky-Operatic-Recital/title/8550343/.

Discography

Peter Dvorsky: Italian and French Opera Arias Naxos 8550343.

Vivere: Famous Italian Canzonettas SU3577–2 231.

Filmography

Rigoletto 1981.

Lucia di Lammermoor 1983.

Evgeny Onegin 1984.

Madama Butterfly 1986.

Adriana Lecouvreur 1989.

Ignacy Dygas *1881–1955*

Scott 2: 243.

Discography

Cavalleria rusticana – Siciliana Historic Masters 118.

Hubert Eisdell *1882–1948*

Web

http://www.collectionscanada.ca/4/4/m2–1074–e.html.

Discography

Hubert Eisdell Cheyne CHE 44421.

Richard Elford *1677–1714*

Baldwin, O. and Wilson, T., 'Elford, Richard', *Grove* 8: 114–15.

Gervase Elwes *1866–1921*

Elwes, W. and Elwes, R., *Gervase Elwes: The Story of His Life* (London, 1935).

Farkas: 78.

Fuller Maitland, J. A. and Colles, H. C., 'Elwes, Gervase (Cary)', *Grove* 8: 174.

Hyde, J., 'Gervase Elwes', *Record Collector*, 17/8 (1967): 182–191 (with discography).

Scott 2: 172–3.

Discography

Gervase Elwes (complete recordings) Cheyne CHE 44418–9.

Gervase Elwes OPAL 9844.

Gerald English *1925*

http://www.move.com.au/artist.cfm/130.

http://www.answers.com/topic/gerald-english-classical-musician?cat=entertainment.

http://www.bach-cantatas.com/Bio/English-Gerald.htm.

Discography

Schumann Lieder Tall Poppies TPO 23.

Sweeter than Roses Tall Poppies TP122.

Kurt Equiluz *1929*

Web

http://www.bach-cantatas.com/Bio/Equiluz-Kurt.htm.

Discography

Mozart: The Complete Masonic Music Vox Box VOX 5055 (2 CDs).

Bach: Schleicht, spielende Wellen BVW 206 Musicaphon MRLC 51354.

Videography

Bach: Johannes Passion DGG DVD-VIDEO NTSC 073 4291.

Karl Erb *1877–1958*
> Branscombe, P., 'Erb, Karl', *Grove* 8: 283.
> Branscombe, P., 'Erb, Karl', *NGDO* 2: 59–60.
> Dennis, J., 'Karle Erb', *Record Collector*, 24/3 (1978): 53–86 (with discography).
> *Farkas*: 78.
> Müller-Gögler, M., *Karl Erb: das Leben eines Sängers* (Offenburg, 1948).
> *Discography*
>> *Karl Erb* Preiser PR89095.
>> *Karl Erb Liederalbum*, vol. 2 Preiser PR89239.

Léon Escalaís *1859–1942*
> Bilgora, A., 'Léon Escalaís: ténor extraordinaire', *Record Collector*, 49/2 (2004): 89–94.
> Escalaís, S. and Lustig, L., 'Léon Escalaís', *Record Collector*, 49/2 (2004): 74–89 (with discography).
> Steane, J. B., 'Escalaís, Léon', *NGDO* 2: 76.
> *Web*
>> http://www.escalais.com/leon/biographie.html.
> *Discography*
>> *Léonce Escalaís* Preiser PR89527.
>> *Harold Wayne Collection* vol. 15 Symposium 1128.

Guglielmo d'Ettore *c. 1740–1771*
> Wignall, H., 'Ettori [d'Ettore] Giuglelmo', *Grove* 8: 413–14.
> Wignall, H., 'Ettori [d'Ettore] Guiglelmo', *NGDO* 2: 84.
> Wignall, H., 'Giuglelmo d' Ettore: Mozart's first Mitridate', *Opera Quarterly*, 10/3 (1994): 93–112.
> Wignall, H., *Mozart, Guglielmo d' Ettore and the Composition of Mitridate* (Ann Arbor, 1995).

Wynford Evans
> *Web*
>> http://www.bach-cantatas.com/Bio/Evans-Wynford.htm [Teddy Kaufman].
> *Discography*
>> *Can y Tenoriaid/Great Welsh Tenors of Wales* SAIN SCD2019.
>> *Hugh the Drover* Hyperion CDD2 2049.

Annibale Pio Fabri *1697–1760*
> Dean, W., 'Fabri [Fabbri], Annibale Pio ['Balino']', *Grove* 8: 491–2.
> Dean, W., 'Fabri [Fabbri], Annibale Pio ['Balino']', *NGDO* 2: 100.

Giuseppe Fancelli *1833–1887*
> Forbes, E., 'Fancelli, Giuseppe', *Grove* 8: 541.
> Forbes, E., 'Fancelli, Giuseppe', *NGDO* 2: 117.

Edourado Ferrari-Fontana *1878–1936*
> Bott, M., 'Edoardo Ferrari-Fontana', *Record Collector*, 36/1 (1991): 3–10 (with discography by Michael Bott and William Moran).
> Steane, J. B., 'Ferrari-Fontana, Edourado' *NGDO* 2: 165.

Augusto Ferrauto *1903–1986*
> Feliciotti, G. (trans. Peter Dempsey) 'Augusto Ferrauto: a short biography', *Record Collector*, 40/2 (1995): 91–112 (with discography).
> Hughes, J., review of *The Cetra Tenors* (Pearl GEMS 0120), *Record Collector*, 46/2 (June, 2001): 153–6.

Nikolay Figner *1857–1918*
> Barnes, H., 'Figner, Nikolay Nikolayevich', *Grove* 8: 789–90.
> Barnes, H., 'Figner, Nikolay Nikolayevich', *NGDO* 2: 191–2.
> *Farkas*: 87.
> *Scott* 1: 215.
> Yankovsky, M., 'Nikolai N. Figner', *Record Collector*, 35/1 (1990): 2–19 (with discography by J. Dennis and commentary by Boris Semeonoff).

Discography
    Tenors of Imperial Russia, vol. 1 Pearl GEMM 0217.
Benvenuto Finelli *1910–1987 born Bennet Flynn*
    Central Opera Service Bulletin 28/1–2 (Fall/Winter 1987–8): 92.
Discography
    Bellini and Donizetti Bel Canto Club BCC 451.
Anton Fischer *1778–1808*
    Branscombe, P., 'Fischer, Anton', *Grove* 8: 890.
    Branscombe, P., 'Fischer, Anton', *NGDO* 2: 218.
Salvatore Fisichella *1943*
    http://www.grandi-tenori.com/tenors/fisichella/.
    http://www.salvatorefisichella.it.
Miguel Fleta *1893–1938*
    Bilgora, A., 'Miguel Fleta: his voice and art on record', *Record Collector*, 38/1 (1993): 27–40.
    Celletti, R., 'Fleta, Miguel', *Grove* 8: 939.
    Celletti, R., 'Fleta, Miguel', *NGDO* 2: 228.
    Dzazopoulos, J., 'Miguel Fleta', *Record Collector*, 37/3 (1992): 161–217 (with discography).
    Farkas: 90.
    Gualerzi, G., 'Spain: Land of Tenors', *Opera* (November, 1987): 1257–63 (December, 1987): 1387–91.
    Saiz-Valdivielso, A., *Miguel Fleta: Memoria de una voz* (Bilbao, 1997).
    Scott 2: 106–7.
Discography
    Miguel Fleta Preiser PR89002.
    Miguel Fleta, vol. 2 Preiser PR89093.
    Miguel Fleta, vol. 3 Preiser PR89149.
Juan Diego Flórez *1973*
    Jeal, E., 'Great Expectations', *Gramophone* (August 2005): 25–9.
    Sutcliffe, T., 'Juan Diego Flórez: a profile', liner notes to *Una furtiva lagrima* Decca CD 473 440–2.
Web
    http://www.jcarreras.homestead.com/Florez1.html [Jean Peccei].
    http://www.deccaclassics.com/artists/florez/index.html [official Decca site].
    http://www.juandiegoflorez.com/index.htm.
    http://homepage.mac.com/juandiegoflorez/Menu3.html [personsal homepage].
    http://www.ernestopalacio.com/Florez_ing.htm.
Discography
    Arias for Rubini Decca CD 475 907–9.
    Rossini Arias Decca CD 470 0242.
    Una furtiva lagrima Decca CD 473 440–2.
Bruce Ford *1956*
    Forbes, E., 'Ford, Bruce', *NGDO* 2: 256.
    Loppart, M., 'Ford, Bruce', *Grove* 9: 86
    Milnes, R., 'Bruce Ford', *Opera* (August, 1998): 900–7.
Web
    http://www.bruce-ford.com/.
Discography
    Bruce Ford – Romantic Heroes Opera Rara ORR202.
    Bruce Ford – Serious Rossini ORR218.
Fernand Francell *1880–1966*
    Scott: 2:36–7.

Paul Franz *1876–1950*

Rosenthal, H., 'Franz, Paul', *NGDO* 2: 288.

Rosenthal, H. and Blyth, A., 'Franz, Paul', *Grove* 9: 209–10.

Scott 2: 31–2.

Pines, R., review of *Great French Heroic Tenors, Opera Quarterly*, 19/3 (Summer, 2003): 608–12.

Web

http://www.cantabile-subito.de/Tenors/Franz_Paul/franz_paul.html.

Discography

Great French Heroic Tenors Record Collector TRC 9.

Gaetano Fraschini *1816–1887*

Forbes, E., 'Fraschini, Gaetano', *Grove* 9: 213–14.

Forbes, E., 'Fraschini, Gaetano', *NGDO* 2: 289.

Gualerzi, G., 'Tipologia del tenore serio Donizettiano', *International Conference on the Operas of Gaetano Donizetti* (Bergamo, 1992): 353–8.

Landini, G., 'Fraschini: Tenor without heirs?' *Opera*, 51/6 (June 2000); 649–54.

Paul Frey *1941*

Web

http://www.thecanadianencyclopedia.com/index.cfm?PgNm=TCE&Params=U1AR TU0001283.

http://www.encyclopedia.com/doc/1G1-100106940.html.

Discography

Ariadne auf Naxos Philips 422–084–1.

Filmography

Die Meistersinger von Nürnberg (1989).

Lohengrin (1991).

Charles Friant *1890–1947*

Ashbrook, W., 'Three tenors of the Opéra-comique', *Record Collector*, 45/2 (June, 2000): 149–51.

Scott, 2: 37–8.

Steane, J. B., 'Friant, Charles', *Grove* 9: 258.

Steane, J. B., 'Friant, Charles', *NGDO* 2: 302.

Discography

Three Tenors of the Opéra-Comique: Louis Cazette, Charles Friant and Jean Marny Marston MR 51006.

Carl Friberth *1736–1816*

Hunter, M., 'Friberth [Friebert, Friberth, Friedberg], Carl', *Grove* 9: 259–60.

Hunter, M., 'Friberth [Friebert, Friberth, Friedberg], Carl', *NGDO* 2: 302.

Maurizio Frusoni *1941–2000*

Chilcote, K., *Maurizio e Katerina* (Bloomington, 2006).

Edouardo Garbin *1865–1943*

Steane, J. B., 'Garbin, Edouardo', *Grove* 9: 520.

Steane, J. B., 'Garbin, Edouardo', *NGDO* 2: 345.

Discography

Eduardo Garbin: Recordings 1902–13 Bongiovanni GB1018–2.

Manuel del PopuloVicente Garcia *1775–1832*

Bruder, H., 'Manuel García the Elder: his school and his legacy', *Opera Quarterly*, 13/4 (1997): 19–46.

Farkas: 98.

Fenner, T., *Opera in London: Views of the Press 1785–1830* (Illinois, 1994): 181–5.

Garcia, M. del P. V., *Exercises and method for singing, with an accompaniment for the piano forte, composed and dedicated to Miss Francis Mary Thompson, by Manuel Garcia* (London, 1824).

Garcia, M. del P. V., *340 exercices, thèmes variés et vocalises, composés pour ses élèves par Manuel Garcia (père)* (Paris, 1868).

Radomski, J., *Manuel García (1775–1832)* (Oxford, 2000).

Radomski, J., 'Manuel (del Pópulo Vicente Rodríguez) García (i)', *Grove* 9: 520–2.

Radomski, J., 'Manuel (del Pópulo Vicente Rodríguez) García (i)', *NGDO* 2: 345–7.

Julian Gayarre *1844–1890*

Farkas: 99–101.

Forbes, E., 'Gayarre, Julian', *NGDO* 2: 365.

Gualerzi, G., 'Spain: Land of Tenors', *Opera* (November, 1987): 1257–63/(December, 1987): 1387–91.

Muñoz- Salvoch, O., *Juliàn Gayarre: Come el de casa ninguno* (Roncal, 1999).

Web

http://en.wikipedia.org/wiki/Juli%C3%A1n_Gayarre [Jean Peccei].

http://www.francoisnouvion.net/19century/gayarre.html [Francois Nouvion].

Filmography

Il canto del ruiseñor 1932 (with José Romeu).

Guayarre 1959 (with Alfredo Kraus).

Romanza Final 1986 (with Jose Carreras).

Nicolai Gedda *1925*

Farkas: 101.

Gedda, N. (with Aino Sellermark Gedda), *My Life and Art* (New York, 1999).

Hines, J., *Great Singers on Great Singing* (New York, 2003): 118–25.

Osborne, C., ' "Flawless technique" – Nicolai Gedda at 70', *Opera* (March 1996): 264–8.

Rosenthal, H., 'Gedda [Ustinoff], Nicolai (Harry Gustaf)', *NGDO* 2: 369.

Rosenthal, H. and Blyth, A., 'Gedda [Ustinoff], Nicolai (Harry Gustaf)', *Grove* 9: 622.

Steane, J. B., *The Grand Tradition* (London, 1974): 471–3.

Steane 3: 33–7.

Web

http://www.nicolai-gedda.de/.

Discography

Nicolai Gedda – The Early Records 1952–1956 Archipel ACP 0354.

Great Moments of . . . Nicolai Gedda EMI CMS5 67445 2 (3 CDs).

The Very Best of Nicolai Gedda EMI 850902.

Arias, Duets and Trios Bella Voce BVC 7212.

Costanzo Gero

Hughes, J., review of *The Cetra Tenors* (Pearl GEMS 0120), *Record Collector*, 46/2 (June, 2001): 153–6.

Discography

The Cetra Tenors Pearl GEMS 0120.

Giuseppe Giacomini *1940*

Bott, M., review of *Giuseppe Giacomini: arias* (Bongiovanni GB 2525–2), *Record Collector*, 44/1 (March, 1999): 74–5.

Forbes, E., 'Giacomini, Giuseppe', *NGDO* 2: 403.

Web

http://www.grandi-tenori.com/tenors/giacomini.php [Joern Anthonisen].

Discography

Giuseppe Giacomini: arias Bongiovanni GB 2525–2.

Beniamino Gigli *1890–1957*

Collins, W., 'Beniamino Gigli: non-commercial recordings', *Record Collector*, 35/8 (1990): 190–240 (with filmography).

Gigli, B., *Memoirs*, trans. Darina Silone (London, 1957).

Gigli, B., *Memorie* (Milan, 1957).

Chuilon, J., 'Beniamino Gigli: an appreciation', *Opera Quarterly*, 15/4 (1999): 697–717.

Cronstrom, A. and G., 'Beniamino Gigli – the king of tenors', *Record Collector*, 9/9–11 (1955): 198–240; 246–69 (with discography).

Douglas, N., *More Legendary Voices* (New York, 1995): 81–106.

Farkas: 103–6.

Herbert-Caesari, H., *Tradition and Gigli* (London 1963).

Peel, T. and Holohan, J., 'Beniamino discography', *Record Collector*, 35/5 (1990): 110–58.

Scott 2: 102–4.

Shawe-Taylor, D., 'Gigli, Beniamino', *NGDO* 2: 411–12.

Shawe-Taylor, D. and Blyth, A., 'Gigli, Beniamino', *Grove* 9: 847–8.

Steane 3: 113–17.

Discography

Naxos Gigli Edition in 15 volumes (1918–1955) 8.110262–72, 8.111101–04.

Gigli: American and European Recordings 1925–35 Pearl GEMM 9033.

Gigli: Arias, Duets amd Songs 1926–1937 Pearl GEMM 9176 (2 CDs).

Gigli: The Complete Operatic Acoustical Recordings Pearl GEMM 9423 (2 CDs).

James Gilchrist *1966*

Web

http://www.jamesgilchrist.co.uk/home.html.

Discography

Owen Wingrave Chandos CHA 10473.

Finzi: Intimations of Mortality Naxos USA NXS 8557863.

Francis Pott: The Cloud of Unknowing Signum SGK 105.

see http://www.bach-cantatas.com/Bio/Gilchrist-James.htm

Raúl Giménez *1950*

Crutchfield, W., 'Lending an ear to the strains of bel canto', New York Times, 12.06.1988

Discography

Rossini Operatic Arias Nimbus NI15106

Mozart Arias Nimbus NI 5300

Aristodemo Giorgini *1879–1937*

Lustig, L., 'Aristodamo Giorgini', *Record Collector*, 395/4 (1994): 242–72 (with discography and critical analysis by Larry Lustig and Paul Steinson).

Scott 1: 130.

Steane, J. B., 'Giorgini, Aristodemo', *NGDO* 2: 427.

Steane, J. B., 'A century of singing: John Steane on Verdi's interpreters', *Opera* (January, 2001): 25–31.

Fiorello Giraud *1868–1928*

Scott 1: 134–6.

Steane, J.B., 'Giraud, Fiorello', *NGDO* 2: 431.

Discography

The Harold Wayne Collection, vol. 3 Symposium SYM 1073.

Antonio Giuglini *1827–1865*

Forbes, E., 'Guiglini, Antonio', *NGDO* 2: 434.

Gualerzi, G., 'Tipologia del tenore serio Donizettiano', *International Conference on the Operas of Gaetano Donizetti* (Bergamo, 1992): 353–8.

Rosenthal, H., 'The tenor, Giuglini and Madame Puzzi', *The Mapleson Memoirs* (London, 1966): 41–5.

Alexander Gordon *c. 1692–1754/5*

Dean, W., 'Gordon, Alexander', *Grove* 10: 156.

Dean, W., 'Gordon, Alexander', *NGDO* 2: 489–90.

Morey, C., 'Alexander Gordon, scholar and singer', *Music & Letters*, 46/4 (October, 1965): 332–5.

Gunnar Graarud *1886–1960*

Bilgora, A., review of *Four Scandinavian Tenors of the Past* (Preiser LV 89986), *Record Collector*, 42/3 (September, 1997): 213–15.

Steane, J. B., 'Graarud, Gunnar', *NGDO* 2: 504–05.

John Graham-Hall

Web

http://www.glyndebourne.com/operas/albert_herring/creative_team_cast_members/john_graham_hall.

http://www.operabase.com/listart.cgi?id=none&lang=en&name=John%20[Graham-Hall].

Discography

Carmina Burana Membran Multichannel SACD 222862–203.

Georges Granal *fl. c. 1910–1930*

Pines, R., review of *Great French Heroic Tenors*, in *Opera Quarterly*, 19/3 (Summer, 2003): 608–12.

Discography

Georges Granal Malibran MR572.

Great French Heroic Tenors Record Collector TRC 9.

Louis Graveure *1888–1965*

Steane, J. B.,'Graveure, Louis [Douthitt, Wilfried]', *NGDO* 2: 521.

Lustig, R., 'Louis Graveure', *Record Collector* 52/2, (June, 2007): 152.

Discography

Men of Empire AE001 (CD ROM).

Filmography

Es gibt nur eine Liebe (1933).

Ich sehne mich nach dir (1934).

Ein Walzer für dich (1934).

Ein Lied klagt an (1936).

Vittorio Grigolo *1977*

Web

http://www.vittoriogrigolo.com/.

Gegam Grigorian *1951*

Web

http://www.mariinsky.ru/en/opera/soloist/zguest/grigorian_gegam.

http://profile.myspace.com/index.cfm?fuseaction=user.viewprofile&friendid=248540646.

Filmography

Sadko (1994).

Forza del Destino (1997).

Pique Dame (2002).

Herbert Ernst Groh *1905–1982*

Bilgora, A., liner notes to *Herbert Ernst Groh in Opera* (Nimbus NI 7934).

Discography

Herbert Ernst Groh Preiser PR89140.

Herbert Ernst Groh in Opera Nimbus NI 7934.

Filmography

Das Lied vom Glück (1933).

Schön ist es, verliebt zu sein (1934).

Monika (1937).

Casanova heiratet (1939).

Hochzeitsreise zu drit (1939).

Die keusche Geliebte (1940).

Sechs Tage Heimaturlaub (1941).

So ein Früchtchen (1942).

Paul Groves *1964*
Web
 http://www.bruceduffie.com/grovesja.html.
Discography
 Duparc Chansons Naxos 8.557219.
Domenico Guardasoni *1731–1806*
 Angermuller, R., 'Domenico Guardasoni, Mozarts Impresario', *Mitteilungen der Internationalen Stiftung Mozarteum*, 50 (June 2002): 1–15.
 Volek, T., 'Guardasoni, Domenico', *Grove* 10: 476.
 Volek, T., 'Guardasoni, Domenico', *NGDO* 2: 560.
Carlo Guasco *1813–1876*
 Forbes, E., 'Guasco, Carlo', *NGDO* 2: 560.
 Gualerzi, G., *Carlo Guasco: Tenore Romantico fra mito e realtà* (Alessandria, 1976).
 Rosselli, J., 'Guasco, Carlo', *Grove* 10: 483.
Heinrich Gudehus *1845–1909*
 Forbes, E., 'Gudehus, Heinrich', *Grove* 10: 492–3.
 Forbes, E., 'Gudehus, Heinrich', *NGDO* 2: 562–3.
Charles Hackett *1887–1942*
 Dyer, R. and Forbes, E., 'Hackett, Charles', *Grove* 10: 645.
 Dyer, R. and Forbes, E., 'Hackett, Charles', *NGDO* 2: 591.
 Holdridge, L., 'Charles Hackett', *Record Collector*, 22/8 (1975): 174–214 (with discography).
 Pearce, J., review of *Charles Hackett* (Marston 51005–2), *Record Collector*, 44/2 (June 1999): 159–60.
 Scott 2: 161–4.
Discography
 Charles Hackett Marston 51005–2.
Ernst Haefliger *1909–2007*
 Blyth, A., 'Haefliger, Ernst', *Grove* 10: 652–3.
 Blyth, A., 'Haefliger, Ernst', *NGDO* 2: 593.
 Haefliger, E., *Die Singstimme* (Berne,1983).
 Haefliger, E., *Die Kunst des Gesangs* (Mainz, 2000).
Web
 http://www.bach-cantatas.com/Bio/Haefliger-Ernst.htm.
Discography
 Bach: Grosse geistliche Werke Archiv POCA-9025.
 Schubert Song Cycles Claves CD 50–8900/4 (4 CDs).
 Mozart: Opera and Concert Arias Claves CD 50–8305.
Anton Haizinger *1796–1869*
 [Uncredited] *NGDO* 2: 597.
 Hilmar, E., 'Karl Goldmark über den Schubert-Sanger Anton Haizinger', *Schubert durch die Brille: Internationales Franz Schubert Institut Mitteilungen*, 15 (June 1995): 100–2.
 Warrack, J. and Forbes, E., 'Haizinger [Haitzinger], Anton', *Grove* 10: 680.
George Hamlin *1868–1923*
 Bott, M., 'George Hamlin, a Musical Tenor' (with discography by William Moran) *Record Collector*, 45/3 (September, 2000): 297–319.
 Hamlin, A., *Father was a Tenor* (New York, 1978).
 Miller, P. L., 'Hamlin, George', *NGDO* 2: 612.
 Trott, J., *George Hamlin: American Singer* (Denver, 1925).
Discography
 Haydn: In Native Worth VRS Acoustics 74250.
Samuel Harrison *1760–1812*
 Sands, M. and Cowgill, R., 'Harrison, Samuel', *Grove* 11: 68.

William Harrison _1813–1868_

> Husk, W., Rosenthal, H. and Biddelcombe, G., 'Harrison, William', _Grove_ 11: 68–9.
> [Uncredited] 'Harrison, William', _NGDO_ 2: 651.

Orville Harrold _1878–1933_

> _Scott 2:_ 161
> Alda, F., _Men, Women and Tenors_ (Boston, 1937, repr. New York, 1971).

Discography

> _Lohengrin – Mein lieber Schwann_ VRS Acoustics 74813.

Roland Hayes _1887–1977_

> Brooks, T., 'Black recording artists 1916–19', _Lost Sounds: Blacks and the Birth of the Recording Industry 1890–1919_ (Urbana, 2004): 436–51.
> De Schauensee, M., 'Hayes, Roland', _Grove_ 11: 284.
> _Farkas:_ 115.
> Hayden, R., _Singing for All People: Roland Hayes, A Biography_ (Boston, 1989).
> Helm, M., _Angel Mo' and her son Roland Hayes_ (Boston, 1942).
> Knight, A., 'Roland Hayes', _Record Collector_, 10/2 (1955): 27–45 (with discography).

Web

> http://www.georgiaencyclopedia.org/nge/Article.jsp?id=h-1671.
> http://www.afrovoices.com/rhayes.html.

Discography

> _The Art of Roland Hayes_ Smithsonian RD 041.

Uwe Heilmann _1960_

Web

> http://www.bach-cantatas.com/Bio/Heilmann-Uwe.htm.

Discography

> _Don Giovanni_ Erato PID 670209

Ruby Helder _1880–1938_

> http://www.thestage.co.uk/features/feature.php/9701.

Discography

> _Ruby Helder: The Girl Tenor_ GEMM CD 9035.

Heinrich Hensel _1874–1935_

> Rosenthal, H., 'Hensel, Heinrich', _NGDO_ 2: 694–5.
> Rosenthal, H. and Blyth, A., 'Hensel, Heinrich', _Grove_ 11: 383.

Discography

> _The Edison Legacy_, vol. 1 Marston MR 52042 (2 CDs).

Ben Heppner _1956_

> Forbes, E., 'Heppner, Ben', _Grove_ 11: 398.
> Forbes, E., 'Heppner, Ben', _NGDO_ 2: 697.
> Dyson, P., 'Ben Heppner', _Opera_ (October, 1995): 1146–53.
> Steane, J., 'A century of singing: John Steane on Verdi's interpreters', _Opera_ (January, 2001): 25–31.
> _Steane 3:_ 73–7.

Web

> http://www.benheppner.com/.
> http://www.mvdaily.com/articles/2004/05/benhep1.htm.
> http://www.musicweb-international.com/classrev/2001/Aug01/Heppner.htm.

Discography

> _Ben Heppner sings Lohengrin_ RCA 09026 68239 2.
> _Great Tenor Arias_ RCA 09026 62504 2.
> _Airs français_ Deutsche Grammophon 4713722.

Vilhelm Herold _1865–1937_

> Bergmann, P., 'Vilhelm Herold', _Record Collector_, 38/4 (1993): 271–97 (with discography).

Farkas: 118.

Riemens, L., 'Herold, Vilhelm', *NGDO* 2: 706.

Riemens, L. and Blyth, A., 'Herold, Vilhelm Kristoffer', *Grove* 11: 435.

Discography

Velhelm Herold Nimbus NI 7880.

Martyn Hill *1944*

Web

http://www.bach-cantatas.com/Bio/Hill-Martyn.htm.

http://www.owenwhitemanagement.com/tenors/Martyn-Hill/.

Discography

Finzi Song Cycles Hyperion CDA661612.

Schubert Lieder Hyperion CDJ33010.

Grainger Songs Chandos CHAN 9610.

A French Collection Meridian CDE84417.

Joseph Hislop *1884–1977*

Bott, M., 'Joseph Hislop', *Record Collector*, 23/9 (1977): 196–237 (with discography).

Bott, M., 'Joseph Hislop – an Addendum', *Record Collector*, 25/1 (1979): 36–42.

Hislop, J., 'Some reminiscenses of my life', *78 rpm*, 4 (1969): 2.

Pearce, J., review of *Joseph Hislop* (Cheyne CHE 44473/4), *Record Collector*, 52/2 (June, 2007): 154–5.

Scott 2: 167–8.

Steane 1: 76–80.

Turnbull, M.T.R.B., 'Hislop, Joseph', *Grove* 11: 546.

Turnbull, M.T.R.B., 'Hislop, Joseph', *NGDO* 2: 726.

Turnbull, M.T.R.B., *Joseph Hislop: Gran Tenore* (Aldershot, 1992).

Discography

Joseph Hislop Pearl GEMM 9956.

Joseph Hislop Cheyne CHE 44473/4 (2 CDS).

Filmography

The Loves of Robert Burns (1930).

Peter Hofmann *1944*

Goodwin, N., 'Hofmann, Peter', *NGDO* 2: 735.

Türschmann, M., *Peter Hofmann: Singen aus Leidenschaft* (Uster, 2002).

Verdino-Süllwold, C., *We Need a Hero: Heldentenors from Wagner's Time to the Present, A Critical History* (New York, 1989): 333–90.

Discography

Parsifal Deutsche Grammophon DGG 4133472 (4 CDS).

Tristan und Isolde Philips CD 410 447–2.

Die Walküre CBS MK 39745.

Der fliegende Holländer EMI 2 CD 7 47054 8.

The Best of Rock Classics Columbia (Sony) LP/CD 496132.

Das Phantom der Oper Polydor LP/CD 847514–2.

Love me Tender: Peter Hofmann singt Elvis Columbia (Sony) CD 471327 2.

Web

http://www.peterhofmann.com/index.html (with discographies & videography).

Filmography

Wagner (1983).

Die Walküre (1980).

Der Ring des Nibelungen (1980).

Stars in der Manege (1984).

Wetten, dass..? aus Ravensburg (1984).

Verstehen Sie Spaß (1990–3).

Videography

Lohengrin Euroarts DVD 207202 TT (1986).

Lohengrin Deutsche Grammophon DVD B0006727 TT (1982).
Der Ring des Nibelungen / Patrice Chéreau Philips (7 discs).

Ian Honeyman
Web
> http://ecc.isuisse.com/solistes/ihoneyman.htm.

Discography
> *Monteverdi Rognoni, Bonelli* Alba ABA 198.
> *Hasse: Requiem* Naïve NAI 30464.
> *Charpentier: Leçons de ténèbres* Virgin Veritas PID 757646.

Charles Horn *1786–1849*
> Fenner, T., *Opera in London: Views of the Press 1785–1830* (Illinois, 1994): 525–7.
> Montague, R., *Charles Horn: His Life and Works* (unpublished PhD dissertation, Florida State University, 1959).
> Preston, K., *Opera on the Road: Travelling Opera Troupes in the United States* (Illinois, 2001).
> Temperley, N., 'Horn, Charles Edward', *NGDO* 2: 752–4.

Walter Hyde *1875–1951*
> Hooey, C., 'Walter Hyde', *Record Collector*, 52/3 (Summer, 2007): 180–212 (includes discography).
> Kimbell, H.J., 'British Players and Singers: No X Walter Hyde', *Musical Times* (December, 1923): 829–32.
> Rosenthal, H., 'Hyde, Walter', *Grove* 12: 10.
> Rosenthal, H., 'Hyde, Walter', *NGDO* 2: 777–7.
> *Scott* 2: 173–5.

Discography
> *Walter Hyde* Cheyne CHE 44420.

Georges Imbart de la Tour *1865–1911*
> Pines, R., review of *Great French Heroic Tenors*, in *Opera Quarterly*, 19/3 (Summer, 2003): 608–12.
> Scott 1: 71

Discography
> *Great French Heroic Tenors* Record Collector TRC 9.

Charles Incledon *1763–1826*
> Baldwin, O. and Wilson, T., 'Incledon, Charles [Benjamin]', *Grove* 12: 146
> Baldwin, O. and Wilson, T., 'Incledon, Charles [Benjamin]', *NGDO* 2: 791.
> Fenner, T., *Opera in London: Views of the Press 1785–1830* (Illinois, 1994): 515–17.
> Hogarth, G., *Memoirs of the Opera*, vol. 2 (London, 1851): 364–5.

Luigi Infantino *1922*
Discography
> *Luigi Infantino* Lebendige Vergangenheit Preiser PR89674.

Nicola Ivanoff *1810–1888*
> Forbes, E., 'Ivanoff [Ivanov], Nicola [Nikolay] (Kuz'mich)', *Grove* 12: 682.
> Forbes, E., 'Ivanoff [Ivanov], Nicola [Nikolay] (Kuz'mich)', *NGDO* 2: 860.
> Gualerzi, G., 'Tipologia del tenore serio Donizettiano', *International Conference on the Operas of Gaetano Donizetti* (Bergamo, 1992): 353–8.

Hermann Jadlowker *1877–1953*
> Frankenstein, A., 'Hermann Jadlowker', *Record Collector*, 19/1 (1970): 5–32 (with discography by Tom Kaufman and Dennis Brew and commentary by Dennis Brew).
> Nicholson, R., review of *Hermann Jadlowker* Symposium 1286, *Record Collector*, 46/2 (June, 2001): 151–3.
> *Scott* 2: 240–2.
> Riemens, L. and Blyth, A., 'Jadlowker, Hermann', *Grove* 12: 750.
> Riemens, L. and Blyth, A., 'Jadlowker, Hermann', *NGDO* 2: 870.

Discography
> Hermann Jadlowker, vols 1–5 Truesound TT2428–32.
> *Hermann Jadlowker* Preiser PR89113.
> *Hermann Jadlowker* Symposium 1286.

Herbert Janssen *1892–1965*
> Shawe-Taylor, D., 'Janssen, Herbert', *NGDO* 2: 880.
> Shawe-Taylor, D. and Blyth, A., 'Jansen, Werner', *Grove* 12: 814.
> *Steane 3*: 43–7.

Discography
> *Herbert Janssen* Preiser PR89640.

Neil Jenkins *1945*
> Forbes, E., 'Jenkins, Neil', *NGDO* 2: 888.

Web
> http://www.neiljenkins.com/.

Discography
> *Jubilee!* Claudio CS0072.

Siegfried Jerusalem *1940*
> Blyth, A., 'Siegfried Jerusalem', *Opera* (August, 1992): 904–9.
> Forbes, E., 'Jerusalem, Siegfried', *Grove* 13: 17–18.
> Forbes, E., 'Jerusalem, Siegfried', *NGDO* 2: 894–5.
> Verdino-Süllwold, C., *We Need a Hero: Heldentenors from Wagner's Time to the Present, a Critical History* (New York, 1989):3 19–32.

Web
> http://www.neue-stimmen.de/en/siegfried_jerusalem/.

Discography
> *Siegfried Jeruslalem: Great Tenor Arias* Sony 60526.
> *Wagner: Der Ring des Nibelungen* Warner Classics 2564–62317–2 (7 DVDs).

Filmography
> *Der Ziegeunerbaron* (1975).
> *Der Ring des Nibelungen* (1980).
> *Das Rheingold* (1980 and 1990).
> *Parsifal* (1982 and 1993).
> *Die Meistersinger von Nürnberg* (1984).
> *Götterdämmerung* (1990/1992).
> *Tristan und Isolde* (1995).

Raoul Jobin *1906–1974*
> Tubeuf, A., 'Jobin, Raoul', *NGDO* 2: 900.
> Tubeuf, A. and Blyth, A., 'Jobin, Raoul', *Grove* 13: 131–2.

Web
> http://www.thecanadianencyclopedia.com/index.cfm?PgNm=TCE&Params=U1AR
> TU0001762.

Discography
> *Romantic Arias from French Operas: Raoul Jobin* Parnassus PAR-1013.
> *Raoul Jobin Live / en concert* Analekta AV2 7803.

Edward Johnson *1878–1959*
> *Farkas*: 124.
> Mercer, R., *The Tenor of His Time: Edward Johnson of the Met* (Clarke, 1976).
> Mercer, R., 'Johnson, Edward', *NGDO* 2: 902–3.
> *Scott 2*: 164–6.

Web
> http://www.bach-cantatas.com/Bio/Johnson-Edward.htm.

James Johnston *1903–1991*
> Blyth, A., 'Johnston, James', *Grove* 13: 172
> Gilmore, L., *At Last a Great Tenor: James Johnston* (Belfast, 1994).

Gilmore, L., 'James Johnston, Belfast's Tenor', *Ireland Land of Welcomes*, July/Aug 2004.
Rosenthal, H., 'Johnston, James', *NGDO* 2: 904.

Web

http://www.ulsterhistory.co.uk/johnston.htm.

Discography

Stars of English Opera Dutton CDLX 7018.
Messiah (1946) Membran 220856 (2 CDs).

John Johnstone *1759?-1828*

Baldwin, O. and Wilson, T., 'Johnstone, John', *NGDO* 2: 904.
Fenner, T., *Opera in London: Views of the Press 1785–1830* (Illinois, 1994): 649–50.
Fiske, R., *English Theatre Music in the Eighteenth Century* (Oxford, 1986): 629–70.

Parry Jones *1891–1963*

Rosenthal, H., 'Jones, Parry', *NGDO* 2: 914–15.
Woolf, J., review of *Elijah* (The Divine Art 27802), *Record Collector, 51/3 (2006)*: 235–6.

Web

http://yba.llgc.org.uk/en/s2–JONE-PAR-1891.html.

Discography

Mendelssohn: Elijah (first complete recording) Divine Art 27802.
Parry Jones Cheyne CHE 44478–9 (2 CDs).

Joseph Kaiser *1978*

Web

http://www.metoperafamily.org/operanews/issue/article.aspx?id=1897.

Filmography

The Magic Flute (2006).
Eugene Onegin (2007).

Kaludi Kaludov *1953*

Web

http://www.ucis.pitt.edu/opera/IFGO/stars/kal01.htm.

Discography

Kaludi Kaludov Verdi Recital Gega New 271.

Jonas Kaufmann *1969*

Christiansen, R., 'This Sexy Singer is Sticking to Opera', *Daily Telegraph*, 30.11.2006
(http://www.telegraph.co.uk/arts/main.jhtml?xml=/arts/2006/11/30/bmjonas30
.xml).

Web

http://www.jonas-kaufmann.com/.
http://www.jkaufmann.info/.

Discography

Romantic Arias Decca B001083702.
Strauss Lieder Harmonia Mundi HAR 901879.

Michael Kelly *1762–1826*

Farkas: 126–7.
Fenner, T., *Opera in London: Views of the Press 1785–1830* (Illinois, 1994): 166–7;
517–18.
Hyatt King, A., 'Kelly, Michael (William)', *Grove* 13: 465–6.
Hyatt King, A., 'Kelly, Michael (William)', *NGDO* 2: 973–5.
Kelly, M., *Solo Recital* (London, 1972).

William Kendall

Web

http://www.bach-cantatas.com/Bio/Kendall-William.htm.

Discography

Elgar: The Dream of Gerontius Naxos USA NXS 8553885.
See http://www.hyperion-records.co.uk/a.asp?a=A643&name=kendall.

Nikander Sergeevich Khanaev *1890–1974*
  Farkas: 128.
Discography
  Nikandr Khanayev Lebendige Vergangenheit 89650.
Solomon Khromchenko *1907–2002*
  Sikorsky, N., 'Solomon Kyromchenko: lyric tenor', *Record Collector*, 49/4 (2004): 272–304 (with discography).
  Sikorsky, N., 'Solomon Markovich Kromchenko: Bolshoi Tenor and Pedagogue', *Opera Quarterly*, 21/1 (Winter, 2005): 133–81, 21/2 (Spring, 2005), 303–60.
Web
  http://www.russia-in-us.com/Music/GRV/ (with MP3 samples).
Jan Kiepura *1902–1966*
  Farkas: 128.
  Kiepura, M., 'My father Jan Kiepura', *Record Collector*, 38/2 (1993): 151–60.
  Ramage, J., *Jan Kiepura* (Paris, 1969).
Web
  http://www.grandi-tenori.com/tenors/kiepura.php [Pawel A. Pachniewski].
Discography
  Jan Kiepura I Pearl GEMM 1976.
  Jan Kiepura Preiser PR89138.
Filmography
  O czem sie nie mysli (1926).
  Die singende Stadt (1930).
  Das Lied einer Nacht (1932).
  Ein Lied für Dich (1933).
  Mein Herz ruft nach Dir (1934).
  Ich liebe alle Frauen (1935).
  Opernring/Im Sonnenschein (1936).
  Zauber der Bohème (1937).
  Das Abenteuer geht weiter (1939).
  My Song for You (1940).
  Addio Mimi (1947).
  Walzer der Liebe (1949).
  Ihre wunderbare Lüge (1950).
  Das Land des Lächelns (1952).
Andrew King
Web
  http://www.bach-cantatas.com/Bio/King-Andrew.htm.
James King *1925–2005*
  Bernheimer, M., 'King, James', *NGDO* 2: 991.
  Bernheimer, M. and Blyth, A., 'King, James (Ambros)', *Grove* 13: 606.
  Blyth, A., 'James King', *The Guardian*, 23 November 2005.
  King, J., *Nun sollt Ihr mich befragen* (Berlin, 2000).
  Verdino-Süllwold, C., *We Need a Hero: Heldentenors from Wagner's Time to the Present, A Critical History* (New York, 1989).
Web
  http://www.geocities.com/rmlibonati/jking.html.
Discography
  Galakonzert Leonie Ryansek and James King Golden Melodram GM 4.0065.
  Das Lied von der Erde Eloquence 468 182–2.
  Die Walküre Philips 464 751–2.
  Parsifal Arts Music 43027–2.
Filmography
  Fidelio (1970).

Die Tote Stadt (1983).
Il ritorno d'Ulisse in patria (1985).
Ariadne auf Naxos (1988).
Elektra (1989 & 1994).

Walter Kirchhoff *1879–1951*

Forbes, E., 'Kirchoff, Walter', *NGDO* 2: 999.
Scott 2: 246–8.

Discography

    Walter Kirchhoff Preiser PR89686.
    Der Ring des Nibelungen – Excerpts Gebhardt JGCD0016 (3 CDs).

Heinrich Knote *1870–1953*

Farkas: 129.
Scott 1: 199.
Shawe-Taylor, D., 'Knote, Heinrich', *Grove* 13: 699.
Wagernann, J. H., *Der sechzigjährige deutsche Meistersänger Hienirch Knote in seiner stimmbilderischen Bedeutung und im Vergleich mit anderen Sängern* (Munich, 1931).

Discography

    Heinrich Knote – Wagner Recital (1906–1910) Truesound TT2227.
    Heinrich Knote – Arias and Songs (1905–1912) Truesound TT2228.

René Kollo *1937*

Farkas: 129.
Forbes, E., 'Kollo, René', *Grove* 13: 757–8.
Kayser, B., 'René Kollo', *Opera* (December, 1989): 1415–21.
Verdino-Süllwold, C., *We Need a Hero: Heldentenors from Wagner's Time to the Present, A Critical History* (New York, 1989): 299–319.

Web

    http://www.kollo.com/kollographie-rene.htm.

Discography

    René Kollo Artone 222608 (4 CDs).

Filmography

    Tannhäuser 1995/2000.

Videography

    Ariadne auf Naxos Universal Classics DVD.
    Tristan und Isolde TDK UK DVD.

Sándor Kónya *1923–2002*

Blyth, A., 'Konya, Sandor', *NGDO* 2: 1026.
Kozinn, A., obituary, *New York Times*, 6.06.2002.
Verdino-Süllwold, C., *We Need a Hero: Heldentenors from Wagner's Time to the Present, A Critical History* (New York, 1989): 263–72.

Web

    http://www.sandor-konya.com/home/index.html.

Discography

    Lohengrin Gala GL 100.656 4.
    Verdi Requiem BBC Legends BBCL 4144–2.

Ivan Kozlovsky *1900–1993*

Ardoin, J., 'Ivan Kozlovsky, a voice from behind the iron curtain', *Opera Quarterly*, 11/4 (1995): 95–102.
Farkas: 130.
Friedman, L., 'Ivan Kozlovsky', *Record Collector*, 44/3 (September, 1999): 170–81.
Peel, T., 'Ivan Kozlovsky Discography', *Record Collector*, 44/3 (September, 1999): 181–212.
Steane 3: 128–32.

Yampol'sky, I. M., 'Kozlovsky, Ivan', *Grove* 13: 854
Yampol'sky, I. M., 'Kozlovsky, Ivan', *NGDO* 2: 1036–7.

Web

http://russia-in-us.com/Music/GRV/Kozlovsky/index.htm.

Discography

Gounod: Roméo et Juliette Guild GHCD 2264/65.
La traviata Guild GHCD 2205/06.
Ivan Kozlovsky RCD16001.
Ivan Kozlovsky RCD16002.

Filmography

Boris Godunov 1954 VAI (VAI DVD 4253).

Videography

The Tenors of the 78 Era 4 Bel Canto Society.

Alfredo Kraus *1927–1999*

Baxter, R., Burroughs, B., Farkas, A., Jellinek, G. and Pines, R., 'Alfredo Kraus, 1927–1999, in memoriam', *Opera Quarterly*, 18/3 (2002): 313–27.
Celletti, R., 'Kraus, Alfredo', *NGDO* 2: 1039.
Celletti, R. and Blyth, A., 'Kraus, Alfredo', *Grove* 13: 874–5.
Daguzan, S., 'Aristocrat of tenors', *Opera Quarterly*, 18/3 (2002): 329–76.
Gualerzi, G., 'Spain: Land of Tenors', *Opera* (November, 1987): 1257–63/(December, 1987): 1387–91.
Landini, G., *Alfredo Kraus: I suoi personaggi* (Parma, 2005).
Steane 3: 17–21.

Web

http://www.answers.com/topic/alfredo-kraus?cat=entertainment.
http://www.grandi-tenori.com/feat/kraus.htm [Joseph Fragala].

Discography

The Art of Alfredo Kraus: The Recital Discs Bongiovanni GB 536–2 (5 CDs).
The Very Best of Alfredo Kraus EMI 863412 (2 CDs).
Arie antiche Nimbus NI 5102.

Filmography

Guayarre (1959).
Vagabundo y la estrella (1960).
Lucrezia Borgia (1980).
Lucia di Lammermoor (1980).
Faust (1989).
Rigoletto (1989).

Helmut Krebs *1913–2007*

Anderson, N., 'Krebs, Helmut', *Grove* 13: 886.
Goodwin, N., 'Krebs, Helmut', *NGDO* 2: 1042.

Web

http://www.angelfire.com/tx2/theorbo/HELMUT_KREBS.html.
http://www.bach-cantatas.com/Bio/Krebs-Helmut.htm.

Discography

Monteverdi: L'Orfeo Berlin Classics Eterna 0033142BC.
St Matthew Passion Music and Arts CD1091.
Bach Cantatas Apex 0927498042.

Werner Krenn *1943*

Blyth, A., 'Krenn, Werner', *NGDO* 2: 1047.

Web

http://www.bach-cantatas.com/Bio/Krenn-Werner.htm.

Charles Kullmann *1903–1983*

Blyth, A., 'Kullmann, Charles', *Grove* 14: 20.

Morgan, I., 'Charles Kullman', *Record Collector*, 20/11(1972): 245–58 (with discography).

[Uncredited], 'Kullmann, Charles', *NGDO* 2: 1057.

Discography

Charles Kullmann – Complete European Recordings 1931–38 Nimbus NI 7938.

Charles Kullmann Preiser PR89057.

Filmography

Bomben auf Monte Carlo (1931).

Schön ist jeder Tag den Du mir schenkst, Marie Luise (1934).

La Paloma (1934).

The Goldwyn Follies (1938).

Song of Scheherazade (1947).

Andrei Labinsky *1871–1941*

Web

http://www.grandi-tenori.com/tenors/labinsky.php [Keith Shilcock].

Discography

Tenors of Imperial Russia, vol. 2 Pearl GEMM 0218.

Eyvind Laholm *1894–1958*

Bott, M., 'Eyvind Laholm: American Heldentenor', *Record Collector*, 42/1 (March, 1997): 44–8 (with discography).

Discography

Tannhäuser (1939) Symposium CD 1178/9.

Forrest Lamont *1881–1937*

Bott, M., 'Forrest Lamont: Bravo for a House Tenor', *Record Collector*, 48/3 September 2003: 222–35 (with discography).

Web

https://www.collectionscanada.gc.ca/gramophone/m2–1077–e.html.

Philip Langridge *1939*

Jeal, E., 'His dark materials', *Guardian* 18.06.04.

Web

http://www.musicomh.com/classical_features/philip-langridge_0307.htm.

http://www.bach-cantatas.com/Bio/Langridge-Philip.htm.

http://www.musicomh.com/classical/features/philip-langridge_0307.htm.

Discography

Britten: St Nicolas Naxos 8.557203.

Britten: Serenade Naxos 8.557199.

Britten: Death in Venice Chandos CHAN 10280 (2 CDs).

Songs for tenor and guitar Chandos CHAN 10305.

Videography

Turn of the Screw (1982).

Idomeneo (1983).

Midsummer Marriage (1984).

Wozzeck (1987).

Billy Budd (1988).

Jenufa (1989).

La clemenza di Tito (1991).

From the House of the Dead (1992).

Oedipus Rex (1993).

Peter Grimes (1995).

Das Rheingold (2005).

Mario Lanza *1921–1959*

Cesari, A., *Mario Lanza: An American Tragedy* (Fort Worth, 2003), discography and CD (preface by Placido Domingo).

Farkas: 133–4.

Mannering, D., *Mario Lanza, Singing to the Gods* (Jackson, 2005), discography and filmography.

Strait, R. and Robinson, T., *Lanza: His Tragic Life* (New Jersey, 1980).

Web

> http://www.mariolanza.it/index2.html [Roberto Scandurra].
> http://www.lanzalegend.com/welcome.htm [Bob Dolfi and Damon Lanza].
> http://www.rense.com/excursions/lanza/index.htm [Jeff Rense].
> http://www.mario-lanza-institute.org/ [Mario Lanz Institute].
> http://www.grandi-tenori.com/tenors/lanza/lanza.php [Derek McGovern].

Discography

> *Mario Lanza Legendary Tenor* RCA RD86218.
> *Mario Lanza: the Great Caruso* RCA GD60049.

Filmography

> *That Midnight Kiss* (1949).
> *The Toast of New Orleans* (1950).
> *The Great Caruso* (1951).
> *Because You're Mine* (1952).
> *The Student Prince* (1953).
> *Serenade* (1956).
> *The Seven Hills of Rome* (1957).
> *For the First Time* (1959).

Ulysse Lappas *1881–1971*

Bigora, A., review of TIMAClub CLAMA CD-48, *Record Collector*, 50/2 (June, 2005): 122–6.

Dzazopoulos, J., 'Ulysses Lappas', *Record Collector*, 50/3 (September, 2005): 170–85 (with discography).

Scott 2: 108–9.

Steane, J. B., 'Lappas, Ulysse', *NGDO* 2: 1101.

Web

> http://www.grandi-tenori.com/tenors/lappas.php [Juan Dzazópulos].

Giacomo Lauri-Volpi *1892–1979*

Collins, W., 'Giacomo Lauri-Volpi: Live and private recordings', *Record Collector*, 34/11 (1989): 234–52

Farkas: 135–6.

Lauri-Volpi, G., *L'equivoco (così è, e non vi pare)* (Milan, 1938; R1953).

Lauri-Volpi, G., *Voci parallele* (Milan, 1955).

Lauri-Volpi, G., *A viso aperto* (Milan, 1953; R Bologna 1983), with discography.

Rosenthal, H., 'Lauri-Volpi, Giacomo', *NGDO* 2: 1109–10.

Rosenthal, H. and Blyth, A., 'Lauri-Volpi [Vol.pi], Giacomo', *Grove* 14: 383.

Steane 1: 86–90

Williams, C., Hutchinson, T. and Rees, E., 'Giacomo Lauri-Vol.i', *Record Collector*, 9/11 (1957): 244–72.

Web

> http://www.giuseppedeluca.it/index3.html (with discography).
> http://www.grandi-tenori.com/articles/articles_popova_lauri-volpi_03.php.

Discography

> *Giacomo Lauri-Volpi: Public Performances 1928–1955* Memories HR 4195/96.
> *Giacomo Lauri-Volpi* Pearl GEMM 9010.
> *Giacomo Lauri-Volpi* Preiser PR89012.
> *Lauri-Volpi* Nimbus NI 7845.

Hipólito Lázaro *1887–1974*

Farkas: 137–8.

Gualerzi, G., 'Spain. Land of Tenors', *Opera* (November, 1987): 1257–63 (December, 1987): 1387–91.

Richards, J., 'Hipolito Lazaro', *Record Collector*, 15 (1964): 52–84 (with discography). *Scott* 2: 104–6.

Steane, J. B., 'Lázaro, Hipólito', *Grove* 14: 414.

Steane, J. B., 'Lázaro, Hipólito', *NGDO* 2: 1113–14.

Discography

Hipólito Lázaro Preiser PR89147.

Richard Leech *1958*

Milnes, R., 'Richard Leech', *Opera* (June, 1997): 641–8.

Web

http://richardleech.com/.

http://www.ffaire.com/leech/index.html.

Discography

From the Heart Telarc International CD-80432.

Robin Leggate *1946*

Forbes, E., 'Leggate, Robin', *NGDO* 2:1126.

Web

http://www.robinleggate.com/.

http://www.bruceduffie.com/leggate.html.

Discography

Stravinsky: Pulcinella, Le baiser de la fée Naxos (USA) 8557503.

Sergey Lemeshev *1902–1977*

Farkas: 145.

Yampol'sky, I. M., 'Lemeshyov, Sergey (Yakovlevich)', *Grove* 14: 540.

Yampol'sky, I. M., 'Lemeshev, Sergey (Yakovlevich)', *NGDO* 2: 1142.

Discography

Sergei Lemeshev Preiser PR89164.

Russian Vocal School – Sergey Lemeshev: 25 Russian Folk Songs RCD16047 (2 CDs).

Michael Leoni *c. 1755–97*

Baldwin, O. and Wilson, T., 'Leoni, Michael', *NGDO* 2: 1150.

Fiske, R., *English Theatre Music in the Eighteenth Century* (Oxford, 1986): 629–70.

Leon Leonov *1813–1872*

Forbes, E., 'Leonov, Leon Ivanovich (Charpentier)', *NGDO* 2: 1150.

Richard Lewis *1914–1990*

Blyth, A., 'Lewis, Richard [Thomas, Thomas]', *Grove* 14: 620–1.

Blyth, A., 'Lewis, Richard [Thomas, Thomas]', *NGDO* 2: 1162.

Ross-Russell, N., *There Will I Sing – The Making of a Tenor: A Biography of Richard Lewis CBE* (London, 1996).

Steane 3: 148–52.

Web

http://www.richardlewis-tenor.co.uk/.

http://www.bach-cantatas.com/Bio/Lewis-Richard.htm.

Discography

Handel Arias Dutton CDCLP 4003.

Tippett: Midsummer Marriage Gala 524.

Paul Lhèrie *1844–1937*

Forbes, E., 'Lhèrie, [Lèvy] Paul', *NGDO* 2: 1162.

Web

http://opera.stanford.edu/Bizet/Carmen/history.html.

Salvatore Licitra *1968*

Web

http://www.salvatorelicitra.com/.

http://www.grandi-tenori.com/tenors/new/licitra.php [Joern Anthonisen].

Discography
　　La traviata Sony Classical SK 89553.
Max Lichtegg *1910–1992*
　　Operetta and Lieder Dutton CDBP 9769.
Aroldo Lindi *1888–1944*
　　Bilgora, A., 'Aroldo Lindi: the records', *Record Collector*, 46/4 (December, 2001):
　　　　250–8.
　　Lustig, L. and Lindau, R., 'Aroldo Lindi', *Record Collector*, 46/4 (December, 2001):
　　　　234–50 (with discography by Tom Peel).
Web
　　http://community-1.webtv.net/rjlindau/AROLDOLINDI/.
Discography
　　Aroldo Lindi TIMA Club-CLAMA CD-27.
Alan Lindquest *1891–1984*
　　http://www.voiceteacher.com/lindquist.html.
David Lloyd *1913–1969*
　　Lloyd, W., 'David Lloyd', *Record Collector*, 31/6–7 (1986):127–38.
Web
　　http://www.archivesnetworkwales.info/cgi-
　　　　bin/anw/fulldesc_nofr?inst_id=1&coll_id= 20038&expand=.
Discography
　　Stars of English Opera Dutton CDLX 7018.
　　Caneuon Cynnar/Early Songs SAIN SCD2076.
　　Y Canwr Mewn Lifrai/The Singer in Uniform SAIN SCD2098.
　　Y Llais Arian SAIN SCD2128.
Edward Lloyd *1845–1927*
　　Jarrett, J., Reddy, M. and Richards, J., 'Edward Lloyd', *Record Collector*, 12/10 (1959):
　　　　220–37 (with discography).
　　Klein, H., Thirty *Years of Musical Life in London* (New York, 1903): 460–5.
　　Grove
　　Scott 1: 49–50.
Web
　　http://encyclopedia.jrank.org/LEO_LOB/LLOYD_EDWARD_1845_.html.
Discography
　　Edward Lloyd: 25 Gramophone Co. recordings (1904–1908) Truesound TT2434.
　　Santley and Lloyd: The Complete Recordings Cheyne Records CHE 44372–3.
Josef Locke *1917–1999*
Web
　　http://www.joseflocke.co.uk/.
　　The Very Best of Josef Locke EMI 7243 8 53438 2 7.
Enzo de Muro Lomanto *1902–1952*
Web
　　http://chalosse.free.fr/masterpieces/step-one/enzo-de-muro.htm.
Discography
　　Famous Tenors of the Past Preiser PR89229.
Max Lorenz *1901–1975*
　　Branscombe, P., 'Lorenz, Max', *Grove* 15: 184.
　　Branscombe, P., 'Lorenz, Max', *NGDO* 3: 46.
　　Farkas: 159.
　　Verdino-Süllwold, C., *We Need a Hero: Heldentenors from Wagner's Time to the
　　　　Present, A Critical History* (New York, 1989).
Web
　　http://www.grandi-tenori.com/tenors/lorenz/ [Daniele Godor].

Discography
> *Max Lorenz* Preiser PR89053.
> *Max Lorenz: The Complete Electrola Recordings 1927–1942* PR89232 (2 CDs).

Thomas Lowe *c. 1719–1783*
> Dean, W., 'Lowe, Thomas', *Grove* 15: 255.
> Dean, W., 'Lowe, Thomas', *NGDO* 3: 64.
> Fiske, R., *English Theatre Music in the Eighteenth Century* (Oxford, 1986): 629–70.

José Luccioni *1903–1978*
> *Farkas*: 160.
> Mancini, R., *José Luccioni* (Paris, 1978).
> Pines, R., review of *Great French Heroic Tenors* in *Opera Quarterly*, 19/3 (Summer, 2003): 608–12.

Discography
> *José Luccioni* Malibran CDRG147.
> *Great French Heroic Tenors* Record Collector TRC 9.

Web
> http://www.cantabile-subito.de/Tenors/Five_French_Tenors/five_french_tenors.html.

Walter Ludwig *1902–1981*
Web
> http://www.bach-cantatas.com/Bio/Ludwig-Walther.htm.

Discography
> *Grosse Sänger der Vergangenheit: Walter Ludwig* Berlin Classics BC 3310.

Giuseppe Lugo *1898–1980*
> Bilgora, A., review of *Giuseppe Lugo* (TIMACLUB CLAMA CD-31/1–3), *Record Collector*, 43/2 (June, 1998): 131–2.
> Steane, J. B., 'Lugo, Giuseppe', *NGDO* 3: 79.

Web
> http://www.opera-gems.com/recalls/giuseppe_lugo.htm.

Discography
> *Giuseppe Lugo* Preiser PR89034.
> *Giuseppe Lugo* Malibran CDRG139.
> *Giuseppe Lugo* TIMACLUB CLAMA CD-31/1–3 (3 CDs).

Giovanni Malipiero *1906–1970*
> Hughes, J., review of *The Cetra Tenors* (Pearl GEMS 0120), *Record Collector*, 46/2 (June, 2001): 153–6.
> Steane, J.B., 'Malipiero, Giovanni', *NGDO* 3: 171.

Discography
> *Lucia di Lammermoor* Naxos Historical 8.110150–51 (2 CDs).
> *The Cetra Tenors* Pearl GEMS 0120.

Giovanni Manurita *1895–1984*
> Bilgora, A., review of *Giovanni Manurita* (Bongiovanni GB 1147/50–2), *Record Collector*, 43/4 (December, 1998): 281–2.
> Defraia, A., *Giovanni Manurita: tenore di grazia* (Bologna, 1997) with CD.

Discography
> *Il mito dell'opera: Giovanni Manurita* Bongiovanni BGV 1147.

Ottokar Mařák *1872–1939*
> Cummings, D., 'Mařák, Otakar', *Grove* 15: 798.
> Cummings, D., 'Mařák, Otakar', *NGDO* 3: 199.
> *Scott* 2: 243.

Aurelio Marcato
> Hughes, J., review of *The Cetra Tenors* (Pearl GEMS 0120), *Record Collector*, 46/2 (June, 2001): 153–6.

Discography
> *The Cetra Tenors* Pearl GEMS 0120.

Émile Marcelin *1885–1947*
Lustig, L., 'Émile Marcelin', *Record Collector*, 46/1 (March. 2001): 34–5.
Discography
Émile Marcelin Malibran CDRG165.
Francesco Marconi *1853/5–1916*
Liff, V., review of *Harold Wayne Collection*, vol. 2 Symposium 1069, *Collector*, 35/7 (1990): 164–5.
Discography
Harold Wayne Collection, vol. 2 SYM 1069; vol. 3 SYM 1073.
The Golden Age of Singing, vol. 1: 1900–1910 Nimbus NIM 7050.
Richard Margison *1953*
Allison, J.,*Opera* (October, 2001): 1182–8.
Web
http://www.richardmargison.com/.
Discography
On the Threshold of Hope RCA 87769.
Giovanni Mario *1810–1883*
Chorley, H., *Thirty Years' Musical Recollections* (London, 1862, repr. New York, 1972): 177–81.
Farkas: 173–4.
Forbes, E., *Mario and Grisi* (London, 1985).
Forbes, E., 'Mario, Giovanni Matteo', *Grove* 15: 866–7.
Forbes, E., 'Mario, Giovanni Matteo', *NGDO* 3: 218–19.
Pearse, C., *The Romance of a Great Singer: A Memoir of Mario* (London, 1910, repr. New York, 1977).
Jean Marny *1885–after 1949*
Ashbrook, W., 'Three tenors of the Opéra-comique', *Record Collector*, 45/2 (2000): 149–51.
Discography
Three Tenors of the Opéra-Comique: Louis Cazette, Charles Friant and Jean Marny Marston MR 51006.
Jean Marny Malibran CDRG166.
Riccardo Martin *1874–1952*
Le Suer, R. and Forbes, E., 'Martin, Ricardo', *NGDO* 3: 233.
Giovanni Martinelli *1885–1969*
Collin, W., 'Giovanni Martinelli: forward to the biography', *Record Collector*, 25/7–12 (1979–80): 149–255.
Padoan, P. and Tiberi, M., *Giovanni Martinelli: un leone al Metropolitan* (Rome, 2007) with discography and 2 CDs.
Scott 2: 113–17.
Shawe-Taylor, D. and Blyth, A., 'Martinelli, Giovanni', *Grove* 15: 915–16.
Steane, J.B., 'Giovanni Martinelli', in *Voices: Singers and Critics* (London, 1992):173–8.
Steane 3: 1–5.
Web
http://www.giovannimartinelli.net/.
Discography
Giovanni Martinelli: His Last Otello Grammofono 2000 GMFN 78935.
Giovanni Martinelli: The Acoustic Recordings 1913–1923 Preiser 89213.
Giovanni Martinelli: Edison recordings (1912 and 1929) Truesound TT2472.
Giovanni Martinelli: The Great Victor Recordings 1925–29 Pearl GEMS 0030.
Nino Martini *1902–1976*
Bilgora, A., 'Nino Martini: the recordings', *Record Collector*, 46/1 (March 2001): 24–7.
MacPherson, J., 'The films of Nino Martini', *Record Collector*, 46/1 (March 2001): 9–11 (with chronology).

MacPherson, J., 'Nino Martini on the radio', *Record Collector*, 46/1 (March 2001): 20–4 (with chronology).

Martini, P., 'Nino Martini', *Record Collector*, 46/1 (March 2001): 2–9.

Filmography

Here's to Romance (1935).

The Gay Desperado (1936).

One Night with You 1948 [Bel Canto Society 668].

Nicola Martinucci *1941*

Web

http://www.nicolamartinucci.it/.

http://www.grandi-tenori.com/tenors/martinucci.htm.

Angelo Masini *1844–1926*

Forbes, E., 'Masini, Angelo', *Grove* 16: 30.

Forbes, E., 'Masini, Angelo', *NGDO* 3: 248.

Henstock, M., 'Angelo Masini', *Record Collector*, 50/2 (June, 2005): 158–63.

Inzaghi, L., *Il Tenore Angelo Masini* (Rimini, 2002).

Galliano Masini *1896–1986*

Bilgora, A., review of *Galliano Masini: Arias, Duets and Songs* (Tima Club CLAMA CD 29/1–3) *Record Collector*, 43/2 (June, 1998): 133–4.

Calvetti, M., *Galliano Masini: la vita e la carriera artistica del celebre tenore* (Livorno, 1979).

Farkas: 175.

Forbes, E., 'Masini, Galliano', *NGDO* 3: 248.

Hughes, J., review of *The Cetra Tenors* (Pearl GEMS 0120), *Record Collector*, 46/2 (June, 2001): 153–6.

Discography

Galliano Masini: Arias, Duets and Songs (Tima Club CLAMA CD 29/1–3 (3 CDs).

The Art of Galliano Masini Preiser 89154.

Johann Mattheson *1681–1764*

Buelow, G., 'Mattheson, Johann', *Grove* 16: 139–44.

Ermanno Mauro *1939*

Web

http://thecanadianencyclopedia.com/index.cfm?PgNm=TCE&Params=U1ARTU0002258.

Discography

Great Tenor Arias CBC SM-5046.

William McAlpine *1922–2004*

Blyth, A., obituary, *Guardian*, 13.02.04.

Forbes, E., 'McAlpine, William', *NGDO* 3: 110.

James McCracken *1926–1988*

Bernheimer, M., 'McCracken, James', *Grove* 15: 454.

Bernheimer, M., 'McCracken, James', *NGDO* 3: 116–17.

Crutchfield, W., obituary, *New York Times*, 1.05.1988.

Hines, J., *Great Singers on Great Singing* (New York, 2003): 156–63.

Williamson, A., 'James McCracken', *Opera*, xviii (1967).

Web

http://www.grandi-tenori.com/tenors/mccracken.php [Joern Anthonisen].

Discography

McCracken on Stage Decca SXL6201.

Meyerbeer: Le Prophète Omega Opera Archive 1160.

Verdi: Otello EMI CMS 5 65296–2 (2 CDs).

John McCormack *1884–1945*

Banks, J., 'The John McCormack Electrical edition', *Record Collector*, 50/2 (June, 2005): 122–6.

Brown, C. and Knuth, L., *The Tenor and the Vehicle: A Study of the John McCormack/ James Joyce Connection* (Colchester, 1982).

Douglas, N., *More Legendary Voices* (New York, 1995): 131–52.

Farkas: 160–4.

Ledbetter, G.T., *John McCormack* (Dublin, 2003).

Scott 2: 175–9.

Shawe-Taylor, D., 'McCormack, John', *Grove* 15: 453–4.

Shawe-Taylor, D., 'McCormack, John', *NGDO* 3: 116.

Ward, J., 'John McCormack comes to London', Part 1, *Record Collector*, 49/2 (2004): 139–51; Part 2, *Record Collector*, 49/3 (2004): 234–40.

Worth, P. and Cartwright, J., *John McCormack: A Comprehensive Discography* (Westport, CT, 1986).

Steane 1: 121–5.

Web

http://www.mccormacksociety.co.uk/ (with discography).

Discography

Count John McCormack: The Final Recordings Pearl GEMM 9188 (2 CDs).

Count John McCormack Pearl GEMM 9243.

The Kreisler/McCormack Duets Pearl GEMM 9315.

McCormack I: Italian Opera Pearl GEMM 9335.

McCormack II: Irish Song Pearl GEMM 9338.

McCormack III: Lieder and Art Song Pearl GEMM 9343.

John McCormack in English Song Pearl GEMM 9970.

John McCormack in American Song Pearl GEMM 9971.

Count John McCormack, vol. VII OPAL 9847 (2 CDs).

John McCormack Edition, vols 1–4 Naxos 8.110328–31.

Barton McGuckin *1852–1913*

Musical Times, obituary, 01.06.1913: 388.

Rosenthal, H., 'M' Guckin, Barton', *Grove* 15: 475.

John McHugh *1912–2004*

Carey, R., 'John McHugh', *Record Collector*, *51/3 (2006)*: 245.

Web

http://www.grandtheatre.info/content/dynamic/NewsCompetition_Details.asp?ID=7.

Discography

Stars of English Oratorio, vol. 2 Dutton CDLX 7029.

Filmography

I'll Walk Beside You (1943).

Kenneth McKellar *1927*

Horricks, R., liner notes to *The Decca Years 1955–1975* Decca 466 415–2.

Web

http://www.rampantscotland.com/famous/blfammckellar.htm.

Discography

Kenneth McKellar: The Rosette Collection Decca 9859272.

Kenneth McKellar: The Decca Years 1955–1975 Lismor LCOM466415–3 (2CDs).

Kenneth McKellar: A Scottish Journey Lismor LCOM6037.

Kenneth McKellar:A Scottish Journey Part 2 Lismor LCOM6044.

To Robert Burns: A Tribute Lismor LCOM 6019.

Antonio Melandri *1891–1970*

Discography

Antonio Melandri Preiser 89134.

Cavalliera Rusticana Bongiovanni GB 1050–2.

Lauritz Melchior *1890–1973*

Albright, W., 'Great Dane in the morning: musings on the centenary of Lauritz Melchior', *Opera Quarterly*, 7/4 (1990/91): 110–32.

Douglas, N., *More Legendary Voices* (New York, 1995): 153–82.

Emmons, S., *Tristanissimo, The Authorized Biography of Heroic Tenor Lauritz Melchior*, with discography by Hans Hansen (New York, 1990).

Heckner, A., *Lauritz Melchior, Die kommentierte Diskographie des Wagner-Heldentenors* (Bayreuth, 1995).

Melchior, I., *Lauritz Melchior: The Golden Years of Bayreuth* (Fort Worth, 2003).

Scott 2: 248–50.

Shawe-Taylor, D., 'Melchior, Lauritz (Lebrecht Hommel)', *Grove* 16: 340–1.

Shawe-Taylor, D., 'Melchior, Lauritz (Lebrecht Hommel)', *NGDO* 3: 320–1.

Verdino-Süllwold, C., *We Need a Hero: Heldentenors from Wagner's Time to the Present, A Critical History* (New York, 1989).

Web

http://wap03.informatik.fh-wiesbaden.de/weber1/melchior/melframe.html.

http://www.heroictenor.com/.

http://www.maurice-abravanel.com/lauritz_melchior.html#engels.

Discography

Lauritz Melchior, vol. 1–3 Danacord DACO115–120.

Lauritz Melchior Pearl GEMM 9500.

Lauritz Melchior: American Recordings (1946–47) Naxos 8.111239.

Wagner: Opera Scenes EMI References CDH7 69789–2.

Wagner: Operatic Scenes Claremont CDGSE78–50–33.

Wagner: Der Ring des Nibelungen (abridged) Pearl GEMMCDS9137 (7 CDs).

Wagner: Tristan und Isolde EMI References CHS7 64037–2 (3 CDs.)

Filmography

Thrill of a Romance (1945).

Two Sisters from Boston (1946).

This Time for Keeps (1947).

Luxury Liner (1948).

The Stars are Shining (1953).

Bernardo Mengozzi *1758–1800*

Fenner, T., *Opera in London: Views of the Press 1785–1830* (Illinois, 1994): 317.

Noiray, M., 'Mengozzi [Mengocci, Mingozzi], Bernardo', *Grove* 16: 430

Modest Menzinsky *1875–1935*

Sawycky, R., 'Tracking Menzinsky records', *Record Collector*, 24/9 (1978): 216–33.

Web

http://www.ukrweekly.com/Archive/2001/130123.shtml.

Discography

Modest Menzinsky Preiser PR89199.

Francesco Merli *1887–1976*

Lustig, L., 'Francesco Merli', *Record Collector*, 43/2 (June, 1998): 82–130 (with post-script by Giogio Gualerzi, discography by Tom Peel and recordings commentary by Alan Bilgora).

Rosenthal, H., 'Merli, Francesco', *NGDO* 3: 343.

Rosenthal, H., 'Merli, Francesco', *Grove* 16: 463.

Web

http://www.grandi-tenori.com/tenors/merli.php [Joern Anthonisen]

Discography

Francesco Merli, vol. 1 Preiser PR89026.

Francesco Merli, vol. 2 Preiser PR89091.

Chris Merritt *1952*

Crutchfield, W., 'Lending an ear to the strains of bel canto', *New York Times*, 12.06.1988

Forbes, E., 'Merrit, Chris (Allan)', *Grove* 16: 467–8.

Forbes, E., 'Merrit, Chris (Allan)', *NGDO* 3: 345.

Web

http://www.brainyday.com/chrismerritt/.

Discography

The Heroic bel canto Tenor Philips CD 434–102–2.

Chris Merritt in Concert Bongiovanni GB 2508–2.

see http://www.geocities.com/vienna/8917/Chris.html

Benzion Miller *1946*

Web

http://www.thecantors.com/miller.htm.

Discography

Cantor Benzion Miller: Cantorial Concert Masterpieces Naxos 8.559416.

Costa Milona *1897–1949*

Dzazopoulos, J., 'Costa Milona (Kostas Mylonas)', *Record Collector*, 50/3 (September 2005): 205–17 (with discography).

Bilgora, A., 'Costa Milona: the records', *Record Collector*, 50/3 (September 2005): 217–22.

Web

http://www.grandi-tenori.com/tenors/milona.php.

Discography

Costa Milona vol. 1 Truesound Transfers TT-3006.

Angelo Minghetti *1887–1957*

Rideout, B., 'Angelo Minghetti', *Record Collector*, 44/4 (December 1999): 283–97 (with discography and note by Alan Bigora).

Web

http://chalosse.free.fr/masterpieces/step-one/MINGHETTI.htm.

Raffaele Mirate *1815–1895*

Forbes, E., 'Mirate, Raffaele', *NGDO* 3: 408.

Rosselli, J., 'Mirate, Raffaele', *Grove* 16: 748.

John Mitchinson *1932*

Forbes, E., 'Mitchinson, John', *NGDO* 3: 413.

Discography

Das Lied von der Erde BBC Legends BBCL 4042–2.

Jose Mojica *1896–1974*

Mojica, J., *I – a Sinner* (Chicago, 1963).

Discography

Three Edison Tenors Marston 51002–2.

Filmography

See http://us.imdb.com/name/nm0596267/#a1950.

Domenico Mombelli *1751–1835*

Forbes, E. and Timms, C., 'Mombelli, Domenico', *Grove* 16: 910.

Forbes, E. and Timms, C., 'Mombelli, Domenico', *NGDO* 3: 426.

Wills Morgan

Web

http://www.philipglass.com/music/recordings/three_songs-songs_from_liquid_days_vessels.php.

Discography

Coleridge Taylor: *My Heart is like a Singing Bird* Musaeus MZCD101.

Alan Bush: *To all a Future World May Hold* Musaeus MZCD102.

Philip Glass: *Songs from Liquid Days* Silva SILKCD 6023

Videography

Jerry Springer: the Opera – Story of a Musical (2005).

Napoleone Moriani *1806/8–1878*

Budden, J., 'Moriani, Napoleone', *Grove* 17: 119

Budden, J., 'Moriani, Napoleone', *NGDO* 3: 467.

Gualerzi, G., 'Tipologia del tenore serio Donizettiano', *International Conference on the Operas of Gaetano Donizetti* (Bergamo, 1992): 353–8.

Louis Morrisson (Ludovicus Moyson) *1888–1970*

Haesen, F., 'Luis Morrisson', *Record Collector*, 19/3 (1970): 52–76 (with discography).

Frank Mullings *1881–1953*

Farkas: 189.

Fryer, J. and Richards, J., 'Frank Mullings', *Record Collector*, 7/1 (1952): 5–19 (with discography).

Scott 2: 169–70.

Steane, J.B., 'Mullings, Frank', *Grove* 17: 382.

Steane, J.B., 'Mullings, Frank', *NGDO* 3: 516.

Discography

Pagliacci Cheyne CHE 44378.

Petre Munteanu *1916–1988*

Hughes, J., review of *The Cetra Tenors* (Pearl GEMS 0120) *Record Collector* 46/2 (June, 2001): 153–6.

Lustig, L., review of *Petre Munteau* Symposium 1332 *Record Collector* 49/2 (2004): 126–7.

Discography

Petre Munteanu: Song cycles by Schubert and Schumann Preiser PR89306.

Petre Munteanu Preiser PR89662.

Petre Munteanu, vol. 2 Preiser PR89682.

Petre Munteau Symposium 1332.

The Cetra Tenors Pearl GEMS 0120.

Lucien Muratore *1876–1954*

Blyth, A., 'Muratore, Lucien', *Grove* 17: 405.

Scott 1: 64–5

Discography

Lucien Muratore 1: 27 Recordings (Paris, 1904–1907) Truesound TT 2444.

Lucien Muratore 2: 27 Pathé recordings (Paris and New York, 1907–1918) Truesound TT 2444.

Filmography

The Shadow of her Past (1916).

Le chanteur inconnu (1931).

Le chant du destin (1933).

Franz Nachbaur *1835–1902*

Forbes, E., 'Nachbaur, Franz (Ignaz)', *Grove* 17: 586–7.

Forbes, E., 'Nachbaur, Franz (Ignaz)', *NGDO* 3: 546.

Heddle Nash *1894–1961*

Blyth, A., 'Nash, Heddle', *Grove* 17: 647.

Capell, R. and Shawe-Taylor, D., *NGDO* 3: 560.

Lustig, L., 'Heddle Nash', *Record Collector*, 41/1 (March, 1996): 1–32 (with discography by David Mason and recollections by Eric Rees).

Steane 3: 148–52.

Web

http://www.cantabile-subito.de/Tenors/Nash__Heddle/nash__heddle.html.

Discography

Heddle Nash: Serenade Pearl GEMM 9175.

Heddle Nash: II Pearl GEMM 9473.

Cavalleria rusticana Cheyne CHE 44374.

Douglas Nasrawi *1959*

Web

http://www.douglasnasrawi.com/.

http://www.bach-cantatas.com/Bio/Nasrawi-Douglas.htm.
Discography
> *Werner Egk: Der Revisor* Arte Nova 74321 85294 2.
> *Chausson: Le Roi Arthus* Koch Schwann 3–6542–2

Kenneth Neate *1914–1997*
Web
> http://www.operafolks.com/Cooke/valeken.html.

Georgei Nelepp *1904–1957*
> Blyth, A., 'Nelepp, Georgy', *Grove* 17: 748.

Discography
> *Georgy Nelepp* Lebendige Vergangenheit Preiser PR89081.
Filmography
> *Boris Godunov* 1954 VAI (VAI DVD 4253).

Albert Niemann *1831–1917*
> *Farkas:* 191–2.
> Forbes, E., 'Niemann, Albert,' *Grove* 17: 899–900.
> Verdino-Süllwold, C., *We Need a Hero: Heldentenors from Wagner's Time to the Present, A Critical History* (New York, 1989).

Antonio Notariello *1892–1975*
> Bilgora, A., 'Antonio Notariello (tenor)', *Record Collector*, 43/2 (June, 1998): 141–8.

Adolphe Nourrit *1802–1839*
> *Farkas:* 195.
> Macaulay, A., 'Tenor of the Three Glorious Days', *Opera* (August, 1989): 922–9.
> Pleasants, H., *The Great Tenor Tragedy* (Portland, Oregon, 1995).
> Pleasants, H., 'A New Kind of Tenor', in *The Great Singers* (London 1967): 158–76.
> Quicherat, L. M., *Adolphe Nourrit; sa vie, son talent, son charactère, sa correspondance*, 3 vols (Paris, 1867).
> Walker, E., 'Nourrit, Adolphe', *NGDO* 3: 625–6.
> Walker, E. and Hibberd, S., 'Nourrit, Adolphe', *Grove* 18: 206–7.

Louis Nourrit *1780–1831*
> Robinson, P., 'Nourrit, Louis', *NGDO* 3: 626.
> Robinson, P. and Hibberd, S., 'Nourrit, Louis', *Grove* 18: 207

Andrea Nozzari *1775–1832*
> Forbes, E., 'Nozzari, Andrea', *Grove* 18: 227.
> Forbes, E., 'Nozzari, Andrea', *NGDO* 3: 631.

Carl-Martin Oehman *1887–1967*
> Bilgora, A., review of *Four Scandinavian Tenors of the Past* (Preiser LV 89986), *Record Collector* 42/3 (September, 1997): 213–15.
> Steane, J. B., 'Oehman, Carl-Martin', *Grove* 18: 343.
> Steane, J. B., 'Oehman, Carl-Martin', *NGDO* 3: 652.

Web
> http://www.cantabile-subito.de/Tenors/Oehman_Carl_Martin/oehman_carl_martin.html.
Discography
> *Four Scandinavian Tenors of the Past* Preiser LV 89986.
> *Carl Martin Oehmann* Preiser PR89197.

Joseph O'Mara *1864–1927*
> Potterton, R. and O'Mara Carton, E., 'Joseph O'Mara', *Record Collector*, 19/1 (1970): 33–42.

Dennis O'Neill *1948*
> Forbes, E., 'Dennis O'Neill', *Opera* (March, 1994): 285–92.
> Goodwin, N., 'O'Neill, Dennis', *NGDO* 3: 670.

Web
> http://www.dennisoneilltenor.com/.

Louis Orliac

Pines, R., review of *Great French Heroic Tenors* in *Opera Quarterly*, 19/3 (Summer, 2003): 608–12.

Discography

Great French Heroic Tenors Record Collector TRC 9.

John O'Sullivan *1878–1955*

Bott, M., 'John O'Sullivan', *Record Collector*, 39/4 (1994): 278–92 (with discography by Michael Bott and Thomas Kaufman).

Dempsey, P., review of Symposium CD1152, *Record Collector*, 40/1 (1995): 42–3.

Forbes, E., 'O'Sullivan, John', *NGDO* 3: 749.

Scott 2: 168–9.

Discography

John O'Sullivan Symposium SYM 1152.

Mark Padmore *1961*

Padmore, M., 'Dream Weaver' (on singing Britten's *Nocturne*), *Guardian* 21.10.2008: 18.

Web

http://www.markpadmore.com/.

http://www.bach-cantatas.com/Bio/Padmore-Mark.htm.

Discography

Britten/Finzi/Tippett Hyperion CDA67459.

Handel: As Steals the Morn Harmonia Mundi HMU907735.

Britten and Dowland Lute Songs Hyperion CDA67648.

José Palet *1877–1946*

Gualerzi, G., 'Spain: Land of Tenors', *Opera* (November, 1987): 1257–63 (December, 1987): 1387–91.

Discography

Great Singers at the Gran Teatro del Liceo Nimbus NI 7869.

Domenico Panzacchi *c. 1730–1805*

Libby, D. and Corneilson, P., 'Panzacchi [Pansacchi], Domenico, *Grove 19*: 48–9.

Antonio Paoli *1870–1946*

Gualerzi, G., 'Spain: Land of Tenors', *Opera* (November, 1987): 1257–63 (December, 1987): 1387–91.

López, J. and Arnosi, E., 'Antonio Paoli', *Record Collector*, 22/1 (1974): 5–38 (with discography by J. Dennis and commentary by Luis Alvarado).

López, J., *El León de Ponce* (Waterbury, Conn., 1997).

Main, W., review of *Antonio Paoli: Arias, Duets and Ensembles* Pearl GEMM 0028, *Record Collector*, 43/4 (December, 1998): 282–3.

Scott 1: 138.

Thompson, D., 'Paoli, Antonio', *NGDO* 3: 848.

Discography

Antonio Paoli: Arias, Duets and Ensembles Pearl GEMM 0028.

Ian Partridge *1938*

Loppert, M., 'Partridge, Ian', *Grove* 19: 176.

Partridge, I., *Songs Every Tenor Sings* (Stowmarket, nd).

Web

http://www.ianpartridge.pwp.blueyonder.co.uk/.

http://music.barnesandnoble.com/features/interview.asp?NID=130946&userid=2I O9IIJOXV&srefer=.

Discography

Romantic Songs for Tenor and Guitar Pearl 608.

Spirit of Love Meridian CDE 84395.

Songs by Finzi and his Friends Helios CDH55084.

Kálmán Pataky *1896–1964*
Várnai, P., 'Pataky, Kálmán', *NGDO* 3: 915.
Farkas: 201.
Web
http://www.grandi-tenori.com/tenors/pataky.php.
Discography
Koloman von Pataky Preiser PR89111.

Tino Pattiera *1890–1966*
Scott 2: 244–6.
Steane, J. B., 'Pattiera, Tino', *Grove* 19: 239.
Steane, J. B., 'Pattiera, Tino', *NGDO* 3: 918.
Vincenti, A., 'Tino Pattiera', *Record Collector*, 17/12 (1968): 268–5 (with discography).
Discography
The Voice of Tino Pattiera Preiser PSR 89222.

Julius Patzak *1898–1974*
Branscombe, P., 'Patzak, Julius', *Grove* 19: 239–40.
Dennis, J., 'Julius Patzak', *Record Collector*, 19/9 (1971): 197–222 (with discography by Dennis Brew).
Sharpe, R., 'Treasures from Tegernsee', *Record Collector*, 48/4 December 2003: 288–90.
Steane, J. B., 'Patzak, Julius', *NGDO* 3: 918–19.
Discography
Julius Patzak Pearl GEM 0156.
Julius Patzak Preiser PR89075.
Julius Patzak, vol. 2 Preiser PR89174.

Luciano Pavarotti *1935–2007*
Blyth, A. and Sadie, S., 'Pavarotti, Luciano', *Grove* 19: 253.
Blyth, A. and Sadie, S., 'Pavarotti, Luciano', *NGDO* 3: 922.
Farkas: 205–6.
Hines, J., *Great Singers on Great Singing* (New York, 2003): 212–23.
Kesting, J. (trans. Susan H. Ray), *Luciano Pavarotti* (London, 1996).
Pavarotti, L., *My Own Story* (Garden City, 1981).
Rubin, S., 'Luciano Pavarotti', in Herbert H. Breslin (ed.), *The Tenors* (New York 1974): 161–96.
Steane, J., 'A century of singing: John Steane on Verdi's interpreters', *Opera* (January, 2001): 25–31.
Steane 2: 143–8.
Web
http://www.lucianopavarotti.com/.
http://www.pavarotti-forever.com/.
Discography
Luciano Pavarotti: The EMI Recordings EMI 139372B (7 CDs).
Luciano Pavarotti: The Studio Albums Decca B001001702 (12 CDs).
Videography
Pavarotti: the DVD Collection Decca 074 3188.

William Pearman *b. 1792*
Fenner, T., *Opera in London: Views of the Press 1785–1830* (Illinois, 1994): 658–60.

Peter Pears *1910–1986*
Blyth, A., 'Pears, Sir Peter (Neville Luard)', *Grove* 19: 261–2.
Blyth, A., 'Pears, Sir Peter (Neville Luard)', *NGDO* 3: 924–5.
Headington, C., *Peter Pears: A Biography* (London, 1993).
Pears, P., *The Travel Diaries of Peter Pears 1936–1978*, ed. Philip Reed (Rochester NY, 1999)
Steane 2: 33–7.

York, S., 'Sir Peter Pears: An Annotated Bibliography', *Notes* 63/1 (September, 2006): 43–66.

Web

http://www.its.caltech.edu/~tan/Britten/britpears.html.
http://www.brittenpears.org/.

Discography

The Land of Lost Content Belart 461 5502 10.
Britten: Peter Grimes Universal Classics 467 682–2 (2 CDs).
Schubert: Winterreise Universal Classics 466 382–2.

Videography

Benjamin Britten: In Rehearsal and Performance with Peter Pears VAI DVD 4277.

Jan Peerce *1904–1984*

Bernheimer, M., 'Peerce, Jan', *Grove* 19: 282–3.
Bernheimer, M., 'Peerce, Jan', *NGDO* 3: 931.
Farkas: 206.
Hines, J., *Great Singers on Great Singing* (New York, 2003): 224–30.
Peerce, J. and Levy, A., *The Bluebird of Happiness: The Memoirs of Jan Peerce* (New York, 1976).

Discography

Jan Peerce Lebendige Vergangenheit Preiser PR89562.
Jan Peerce, vol. 2 Lebendige Vergangenheit Preiser PR89571.
Bluebird of Happiness Pearl GEMM 9297.
Richard Tucker, Robert Merrill and Jan Peerce Dutton CDVS 1952.

Filmography

Carnegie Hall (1947).
Goodbye Columbus (1969).
If I were a Rich Man: the Life of Jan Peerce (1991).

Jacopo Peri *1561–1633*

Kirkendale, W., *The Court Musicians in Florence during the Principate of the Medici* Florence, 1993): 189–243.
Mayer Brown, H., 'Peri, Jacopo' *NGDO* 3: 956–8.
Porter, W. and Carter, T., 'Peri, Jacopo ['Zazzerino']', *Grove* 19: 397–401.

Aureliano Pertile *1885–1952*

Celletti, R., 'Pertile, Aureliano', *NGDO* 3: 974.
Celletti, R. and Gualerzi, A., 'Pertile, Aureliano', *Grove* 19: 466–7.
Silvestrini, D., *I tenori celebri: Aureliano Pertile e il suo metodo di canto* (Bologna, 1932).
Farkas: 207.
Morby, P., 'Aureliano Pertile', *Record Collector*, 7 (1952): 244–60, 267–83.
Steane, J., 'A century of singing: John Steane on Verdi's interpreters', *Opera* (January, 2001): 25–31.
Steane 1:
Tosi, B., *Pertile: una voce, un mito* (Venice, 1985).

Web

http://chalosse.free.fr/masterpieces/step-one/pertile-2.htm.

Discography

Aureliano Pertile Preiser PR89007.
Aureliano Pertile, vol. 2 Preiser PR89072.
Aureliano Pertile, vol. 3 Preiser PR89116.

Thomas Phillips *1774–1841*

Fenner, T., *Opera in London: Views of the Press 1785–1830* (Illinois, 1994): 654–5.

Nino Piccaluga *1890–1973*

Bilgora, A., Nino Piccaluga: Verismo and a Tenor voice', *Record Collector*, 47/3 (2002): 200–10.

Bott, M., 'Nino Piccaluga', *Record Collector*, 47/3 (2002): 163–73.
Kaufman, T., 'Nino Piccaluga: Chronology', *Record Collector*, 47/3 (2002): 173–90.
Nouvion, F., 'Nino Piccaluga Discography', *Record Collector*, 47/3 (2002): 191–99.
Steane, J. B., 'Piccaluga, Nino (Filippo)', *NGDO* 3: 1000.

Discography
Nino Piccaluga Preiser PR89179.

Alfred Piccaver *1884–1958*
Dennis, J., 'Alfred Piccaver', *Record Collector*, 22/5 (1974): 100–55 (with discography).
Douglas, N., *Legendary Voices* (New York, 1995): 155–78.
Rosenthal, H., 'Piccaver [Peckover], Alfred', *NGDO* 3: 1000.
Rosenthal, H. and Blyth, A., 'Piccaver [Peckover], Alfred', *Grove* 19: 706.
Scott 2: 166–8.

Discography
Alfred Piccaver Pearl GEMM 9412.
Alfred Piccaver Preiser PR89060.
Alfred Piccaver, vol. 2 Preiser PR89601.

Julian Pike *1958*
Web
http://de.wikipedia.org/wiki/Julian_Pike

Discography
Examen RCA Red Seal 74321 73671 2 (7 CDs).
Mondeva Stockhausen Complete Edition 32 (3 CDs).
Geburts-Arien Stockhausen Complete Edition 38 (CDs).
Dienstag aus Licht Stockhausen Complete Edition 40 (2 CDs).

Giovanni Battista Pinacci *c. 1695–1750*
Dean, W., 'Pinacci, Giovanni Battista', *Grove* 19: 748–9.
Holmes, W., 'Giovanni Battista Pinacci and his two contracts in Rome (1726)', *Opera Observed: Views of a Florentine Impresario in the Early Eighteenth Century* (Chicago, 1993): 118–30.

Gotthelf Pistor *1887–1947*
Steane, J., 'Pistor, Gotthelf', *NGDO* 3: 1022–3.

Discography
Gotthelf Pistor Preiser PR89195.
Four German Heldentenors of the Past Preiser 89975.

Antonio Poggi *1806–1875*
Forbes, E., 'Poggi, Antonio', *NGDO* 3: 1040.
Gualerzi, G., 'Tipologia del tenore serio Donizettiano', *International Conference on the Operas of Gaetano Donizetti* (Bergamo, 1992): 353–8.

Gianni Poggi *1921–1989*
Forbes, E., 'Poggi, Gianni', *NGDO* 3: 1040.

Discography
Gianni Poggi Preiser PR89644.

Paul Potts *1971*
Web
http://www.paulpottsuk.com/intro/.
http://www.paulpottsopera.org/.

Discography
One Chance Sony 715517.

Courtice Pounds *1862–1927*
Ganzl, K., 'Pounds, (Charles) Courtice', *NGDO* 3: 1080.

Web
http://math.boisestate.edu/gas/whowaswho/P-Q/PoundsCourtice.htm.

Discography
   The Savoy Connection Circa ATM 101.
Giacinto Prandelli *1914*
   Forbes, E., 'Prandelli, Giacinto', *NGDO* 3: 1087.
   Hughes, J., review of *The Cetra Tenors* (Pearl GEMS 0120), *Record Collector*, 46/2
      (June, 2001): 153–6.
Discography
   Giacinto Prandelli Preiser PR89661.
   Giacinto Prandelli, vol. 2 Preiser PR89680.
   The Cetra Tenors Pearl GEMS 0120.
Christophe Prégardien *1956*
Web
   http://www.pregardien.com/.
   http://www.bach-cantatas.com/Bio/Pregardien-Christoph.htm.
Discography
   Die Schöne Müllerin Challenge CC72292.
   Britten: Nocturne and Serenade BIS CD 504.
Giovanni Puliaschi *d. 1622*
   Fortune, N. (with Hill, J.W.), 'Puliaschi, Giovanni', *Grove* 20: 596.
Anton Raaff *1714–1797*
   Everist, M., 'Anton Raaff', in Rushton, J., *W.A. Mozart: Idomeneo* (Cambridge, 1993):
      50–4.
   Farkas: 212.
   Friedberger, H., *Anton Raaff, 1714–1797. Sein Leben und Wirken als Beitrag zur
      Musikgeschichte des 18. Jahrhunderts* (Cologne, 1929).
   Heartz, D., 'Raaff's last aria: a Mozartian idyll in the spirit of Hasse', *Musical
      Quarterly*, lx (1974): 517–43.
   Heartz, D. (with Corneilson, P.), 'Raaff [Raff], Anton', *Grove* 20: 694–5.
   Heartz, D., (with Corneilson, P.), 'Raaff [Raff], Anton', *NGDO* 3: 1207.
   Petrobelli, P., 'The Italian years of Anton Raaff', *Mozart-Jahrbuch* (Salzburg,1973–74):
      233–73.
Gianni Raimondi *1923*
   Celletti, R., 'Raimondi, Gianni', *NGDO* 3: 1217.
   Celletti, R. and Gualerzi, V.P., 'Raimondi, Gianni', *Grove* 20: 765.
   Farkas: 212.
   Rubboli, D., *Gianni Raimondi: Felicemente tenore* (Berlin, 2003).
Web
   http://www.grandi-tenori.com/tenors/raimondi.php [Joern Anthonisen].
Discography
   Gianni Raimondi Bongiovanni GB 1187–2.
Filmography
   La bohème (1965).
Oscar Ralf *1881–1964*
   Farkas: 213.
   Rosenthal, H., 'Ralf, Oscar (Georg)', *NGDO* 3: 1225.
Discography
   *Wagner in Stockholm: Great Wagnerians of the Royal Swedish Opera Recordings,
      1899–1970* Bluebell ABCD 091 (4 CDs).
Torsten Ralf *1901–1954*
   Bilgora, A., review of *Four Scandinavian Tenors of the Past* (Preiser LV 89986), *Record
      Collector*, 42/3 (September, 1997): 213–15.
   Rosenthal, H., 'Ralf, Torsten (Ivar)', *NGDO* 3: 1225.
   Rosenthal, H. and Blyth, A., 'Ralf, Torsten (Ivar)', *Grove* 20: 776–7.

Web

> http://www.answers.com/topic/torsten-ralf?cat=entertainment.

Discography

> *Torsten Ralf* Preiser PR89152.
>
> *Four Scandinavian Tenors of the Past* Preiser LV 89986.
>
> *Wagner in Stockholm: Great Wagnerians of the Royal Swedish Opera Recordings, 1899–1970* Bluebell ABCD 091 (4 CDs).

Francesco Rasi *1574–1621*

> Kirkendale, W., *The Court Musicians in Florence during the Principate of the Medici* Florence, 1993): 556–603.
>
> Porter, W., 'Rasi, Francesco', *Grove* 20: 838–9.

John Sims Reeves *1818–1900*

> *Farkas*: 214.
>
> Klein, H., 'Sims Reeves: Prince of English Tenors', *Herman Klein and the Gramophone* ed. William R. Moran (Portland, Oregon, 1990): 334–6.
>
> Pearce, C.E., *Sims Reeves; Fifty Years of Music in England* (New York, 1980).
>
> Rosenthal, H. and Biddlecombe, G., 'Reeves, Sims (John)', *Grove* 21: 77.

Alberto Remedios *1935*

Web

> http://www.answers.com/topic/alberto-remedios-classical-musician?cat=entertainment.

Discography

> *Wagner: Twilight of the Gods* Chandos (5 CDs).
>
> *Wagner: the Valkyrie* Chandos (4 CDs).

David Rendall *1948*

> Davies, M., 'David Rendall', *Opera* (September, 1998): 1044–51.
>
> Forbes, E. and Goodwin, N., 'Rendall, David', *NGDO* 3: 1289.

Web

> http://www.intermusica.co.uk/artists/tenor/david-rendall/biography.

Discography

> *Elgar: Dream of Gerontius* LSO Live 583.

Filippo Rochetti *fl. 1724 – 1753*

> Dean, W., 'Rochetti, (Gaetano) Filippo', *Grove* 21: 484
>
> Dean, W., 'Rochetti, (Gaetano) Filippo', *NGDO* 3: 1364.

Gustave Roger *1815–1879*

> Armstrong, A., 'Gilbert-Louis Duprez and Gustave Roger in the Composition of Meyerbeer's *Le Prophète*', *Cambridge Opera Journal*, 8/2 (July, 1996): 147–65.
>
> *Farkas*: 223.
>
> Macdonald, H., 'Roger, Gustave-Hippolyte', *Grove* 21: 514
>
> Macdonald, H., 'Roger, Gustave-Hippolyte', *NGDO* 4: 2.
>
> Roger, G. H., *Le carnet d'un tenor* (Paris, 1880).

Nigel Rogers *1935*

> Anderson, N., 'Rogers, Nigel', *NGDO* 4: 3.
>
> Sadie, S., 'Rogers, Nigel (David)', *Grove* 21: 519–20.

Web

> http://www.bach-cantatas.com/Bio/Rogers-Nigel.htm.
>
> http://www.musicweb-international.com/SandH/2005/Jan-Jun05/rogers0305.htm.

Discography

> *Monteverdi: Orfeo* EMI CDCB-47141 (2 CDs).
>
> *Earyl Music Festival* Decca 2894529672 (2 CDs).

Anthony Rolfe Johnson *1940*

Web

> http://www.bach-cantatas.com/Bio/Rolfe-Johnson-Anthony.htm.

Goodwin, N., 'Rolfe Johnson, Anthony', *NGDO* 4:12.
Goodwin, N., 'Rolfe Johnson, Anthony', *Grove* 21: 529.
Discography
    A Shropshire Lad Hyperion CDA66471/2.
    Bach: Sacred Choral Works DGG 69 7692 (9 CDs).
    Britten: Michelangelo Sonnets and Winter Words Hyperion CDH55067.

Endre Rösler *1904–1963*
Várnai, P., 'Rösler, Endre', *NGDO* 4: 49.
Farkas: 223.
Discography
    Beethoven: Fidelio Urania URN 22.246.

Pablo Mariano Rosquellas *1790–1859*
Bourligeux, G., 'Rosquellas, Pablo (Mariano)', *NGDO* 4: 50–1.
Gualerzi, G., 'Spain: Land of Tenors', *Opera* (November, 1987): 1257–63 (December, 1987): 1387–91.

Giulio Rossi (1862–1934)
MacPherson, J., 'Ring-a-ring-O'-Rossis: a Pocket full of Questions', *Record Collector*, 46/1 (2001): 39–58 (with discography).

Tino Rossi *1907–1983*
Web
    http://www.view.com/rossi.html.
Discography
    Chanteur de charme AKCH 75114.
    O Corse, ile d'amour BEST 85755 (2 CDs).

Helge Rosvaenge *1897–1972*
Dennis, J., 'Helge Rosvaenge', *Record Collector*, 23/5 (1976): 100–40 (with discography).
Farkas: 225–6.
Rosenthal, H., 'Rosvaenge [Roswaenge, Rosenvinge Hansen], Helge', *NGDO* 4: 68.
Tassié, F., *Helge Rosvaenge* (Augsburg, 1975).
Discography
    Helge Rosvaenge Preiser PR89018.
    Helge Rosvaenge in Szenen aus André Chenier und Rigoletto Preiser 90272.
    Helge Roswaenge Pearl GEMM 9394.

Charles Rousselière *1875–1950*
    Scott 1: 65–6.
Web
    http://www.malibran.com/acatalog/AD574.htm.
Discography
    Charles Rousseliere – Ténor Malibran MR574.

Giovanni-Battista Rubini *1794–1854*
Brewer, B., 'Rubini – King of Tenors', *Opera*, xxx (1979), 326–9
Budden, J., 'Rubini, Giovanni Battista', *Grove* 21: 842–3.
Budden, J., 'Rubini, Giovanni Battista', *NGDO* 4: 79–80.
Cassinelli, B., Maltempi, A. and Pozzoni, M., *Rubini: l'uomo e l'artista* (2 vols, Romano di Lombardia, 1993)
Farkas: 226.
Rubini, G-B., *Le 12 lezioni di canto per tenore e soprano* in Cassinelli *et al.* (1993).
Zucker, S., *The Origins of Modern Tenor Singing* (New York, nd).

Luigi Rumbo
Hughes, J., review of *The Cetra Tenors* (Pearl GEMS 0120), *Record Collector*, 46/2 (June, 2001): 153–6.
Discography
    The Cetra Tenors (Pearl GEMS 0120).

Giuseppe Russitano *b. 1865*

Wolfson, J., 'The Russitano Record(s)', *Record Collector*, 51/2 (June 2006): 152–4 (with discography).

Giuseppe Sabbatini *1957*

Web

http://www.jcarreras.homestead.com/Sabbatini1.html [Jean Peccei].

Videography

Donizetti: Roberto Devereux Image Entertainment.

Konstantin Sadko

Farkas: 230.

Sadko, K., *Das Leben ist köstlich; ein fahrender Sänger erzählt* (Tübingen, 1951).

Thomas Salignac *1867–1945*

Forbes, E., 'Salignac, Thomas', *NGDO* 4: 144.

Discography

Maurice Grau at the Metropolitan Opera: Live Performances 1901–1903 Symposium CD 1284.

Sapio *1792–1851*

Fenner, T., *Opera in London: Views of the Press 1785–1830* (Illinois, 1994): 533–5.

Americo Sbigoli *d. 1822*

Pacini, G., *Le mie memorie artistiche* (Florence, 1875): 28–9.

Pleasants, H., *The Great Singers* (London, 1967): 160.

Emile Scaremberg *1863–1938*

Scott 1: 63.

Discography

Les Introuvables du chant français EMI 585828–2.

Benedikt Schack *1758–1826*

Branscombe, P., 'Schack [Cziak, Schak, Zák, Ziak], Benedikt (Emanuel)', *Grove* 22: 424–5.

Tyler, L., 'Schack [Cziak, Schak, Zák, Ziak], Benedikt (Emanuel)', *NGDO* 4: 210–11.

Tyler, L., 'Benedickt Schack' in Stanley Sadie (ed.) *Mozart and his Operas* (London, 2000): 184–5.

Piero Schiavazzi *1875–1949*

Defraia, A., *Tra mito e verità: il cantante–attore della Giovane Scuola* (Bologna, 1995) (with CD).

Piero Schiavazzi Sings Opera Arias Bongiovanni GB 1003–2.

Aksel Schiøtz *1906–1976*

Blyth, A., 'Schiøtz, Aksel (Hauch)', *Grove* 22: 513.

Blyth, A., 'Schiøtz, Aksel (Hauch)', *NGDO* 4: 227.

Farkas: 234.

Schiøtz, A., *The Singer and His Art* (New York, 1969).

Steane 2: 221–5.

Discography

Axel Schiøtz GEMM CD 9140.

Tito Schipa *1888–1965*

Douglas, N., *Legendary Voices* (New York, 1995): 213–28.

Farkas: 235.

Schipa, T. (jnr), *Schipa: A Biography* (Dallas, 1996), with CD.

Scott 2: 98–101.

Shawe-Taylor, D., 'Schipa, Tito', *NGDO* 4: 227.

Shawe-Taylor, D. and Blyth, A., 'Schipa, Tito', *Grove* 22: 513–14.

Steane, J. B., 'Tito Schipa', in *Voices: Singers and Critics* (London, 1992): 167–72.

Steane 2: 216–20.

Web

http://www.titoschipa.it/pag1srengl.htm.

Discography

    Tito Schipa Pearl GEMM 9183.

    Tito Schipa II Pearl GEMM 9364.

    Tito Schipa III Pearl GEMM 9988 (2 CDs).

    Tito Schipa IV: Operatic Recordings 1913–42 Pearl GEMM 9017.

    Tito Schipa: The Early Years: The Complete Gramophone and Pathé Recordings (1913–1921) Marston MR 52008 (2 CDS).

    Tito Schipa: The Complete Victor Recordings, vol. 1 (1922–1925) Naxos 8.110332.

    Tito Schipa: The Complete Victor Recordings, vol. 2 (1924–1925) Naxos 8.110333.

Filmography

    Vivere (1937).

    Terra di fuoco (1938).

    Chi è più felice di me (1938).

    In cerca di felicità (1943).

    Il Cavaliere del sogno (1946).

    L'inferno degli amanti [Life of Donizetti] (1946).

    Follie per l'opera (1948).

    Trois hommes en habit [I Sing for You Alone] (1932).

    Il faro sulla laguna [I misteri di Venezia] (1950).

Max Schlosser *1835–1916*

    Forbes, E., 'Schlosser, Max [Karl]', *Grove* 22: 524.

    Forbes, E., 'Schlosser, Max [Karl]', *NGDO* 4: 229.

Erik Schmedes *1868–1931*

    Bruun, C. L. and Blyth, A., 'Schmedes, Erik', *Grove* 22: 525.

    Bruun, C. L., 'Schmedes, Erik', *NGDO* 4: 229–30.

    Scott 1: 196–7.

    Welsh, C., 'Erik Schmedes', *Record Collector*, 27/1 (September, 1981): 23–46 (with discography).

Discography

    Heldentenöre Preiser PR89947.

    Mahler's Decade in Vienna: Singers of the Court Opera 1897–1907 Marston 53004–2 (3 CDs).

Joseph Schmidt *1904–1942*

    Farkas: 235.

    Fassbind, A., *Joseph Schmidt: Spuren einer Legende* (Zürich, 1992).

    Neckers, J., 'Joseph Schmidt', *Record Collector*, 45/2 (June, 2000): 90–107.

    Sieben, H., 'Joseph Schmidt Discography', *Record Collector*, 45/2 (June, 2000): 108–45).

    Steane, J. B., 'Schmidt, Joseph', *Grove* 22: 539.

Web

    http://www.dutchdivas.net/tenors/josephschmidt.html (with discography).

Discography

    Joseph Schmidt: The Complete EMI Recordings Vol..1 EMI CHS 7 64673 2 (2 CDs).

    Joseph Schmidt: The Complete EMI Recordings Vol..2 EMI CHS 7 64676 2 (2 CDs).

    Joseph Schmidt Live 1930–1937 Koch 3–1257–2.

    Joseph Schmidt: Rare Early Opera and Song Recordings Pearl GEMS0052 (2 CDs).

    Joseph Schmidt: religiöse Gesänge und Arien Preiser 90145.

Filmography

    Der Liebesexpress/Acht Tage Glück (1931).

    Goethe lebt. . .! (1932).

    Gehetzte Menschen/Steckbrief Z (1932).

    Ein Lied geht um die Welt (1933).

    Wenn du jung bist, gehört dir die Welt (1934).

    Ein Stern fällt vom Himmel (1934).

Ludwig Schnorr von Carolsfeld *1836–1865*

Ellis, W. (trans.), 'My Recollections of Ludwig Schnorr of Carolsfeld', *Richard Wagner's Prose Works*, vol. 4: *Art and Politics* (London, 1895, repr. 1972): 225–43 (originally published as 'Meine Erinnerungen an Ludwig Schnorr von Carolsfeld', *Neue Zeitschrift fuer Musik*, 5/12 June 1868).

Farkas: 235.

Warrack, J., 'Schnorr von Carolsfeld, Ludwig', *Grove* 22: 570–1.

Warrack, J., 'Schnorr von Carolsfeld, Ludwig', *NGDO* 4: 234.

Verdino-Süllwold, C., *We Need a Hero: Heldentenors from Wagner's Time to the Present, A Critical History* (New York, 1989).

Peter Schreier *1935*

[Uncredited] 'Schreier, Peter', *NGDO* 4: 240.

Blyth, A., 'Schreier, Peter', *Grove* 22: 639.

Schmiedel, G., *Peter Schreier: ein Bildbiographie* (Munich, 1982).

Steane 3: 163–7.

Web

http://home.planet.nl/~peter.schreier/biographyengels.htm.

Discography

Schubert and the Strophic Song Hyperion CDJ33018.

Hugo Wolf: Italiensches Liederbuch Hyperion CDA66760.

Harry Secombe *1921–2001*

Secombe, H., *Arias and Raspberries* (London, 1997).

Secombe, H., *Strawberries and Cheam* (London, 2008).

Peter Seiffert *1954*

Blyth, A., 'Seiffert, Peter', *Grove* 3: 51.

Videography

Strauss: Die Frau ohn Schatten TDK DVD DVWW-OPFROS.

Johannes Sembach *1881–1944*

Scott 2: 239–40.

Steane, J. B., 'Sembach [Semfke], Johannes', *Grove* 23: 63.

Steane, J. B., 'Sembach [Semfke], Johannes', *NGDO* 4: 304.

Michel Sénéchal *1927*

Forbes, E.,and Blyth, A., 'Sénéchal, Michel', *Grove* 23: 73.

Tubeuf, A. and Forbes, E., 'Sénéchal, Michel', *NGDO* 4: 313–14.

Web

http://www.answers.com/topic/michel-s-n-chal?cat=entertainment.

Felix Senius *1868–1913*

Scott 1: 205

Discography

Gustav Walter / Hans Buff-Gießen / Felix Senius – Complete recordings (1904–1911) Truesound TT-1905.

Neil Shicoff *1949*

LeSuer, R. and Forbes, E., 'Schicoff, Niel', *NGDO* 4: 353.

Web

http://members.lycos.co.uk/shicoff/.

http://www.shicoff.com/.

Discography

Neil Shicoff Recital HRE 394–1.

George Shirley *1934*

Web

http://www.bruceduffie.com/shirley.html.

http://sumarts.com/roster/shirley_interview03.htm.

http://www.bach-cantatas.com/Bio/Shirley-George.htm [Aryeh Oron].

Discography
> Warren M. Swenson: *Battle Pieces* Albany ALB 606.
> Mozart: *Così fan tutte* RCA 82876877612.

Daniil Shtoda *1977*
> Jeal, E., 'Great Expectations', *Gramophone* (August 2005): 27.

Web
> http://www.mariinsky.ru/en/opera/soloist/shtoda.

Discography
> *Daniil Shtoda* Delos DEL 3348.

Léopold Simoneau *1916–2006*
> Potvin, G., 'Simoneau, Léopold', *Grove* 23: 405.
> Potvin, G., 'Simoneau, Léopold', *NGDO* 4: 384.

Web
> http://www.bach-cantatas.com/Bio/Simoneau-Leopold.htm [Aryeh Oron].
> http://www.thecanadianencyclopedia.com/index.cfm?PgNm=TCE&Params=U1AR
> TU0003217.

Discography
> Mozart: *Opera Arias* Urania URA 923.
> *The Perfect Vocal Marriage* CBC 2022.

John, Sinclair *1791–1857*
> Fenner, T., *Opera in London: Views of the Press 1785–1830* (Illinois, 1994): 527–30.
> Gualerzi, G., 'Tipologia del tenore serio Donizettiano', *International Conference on the Operas of Gaetano Donizetti* (Bergamo, 1992): 353–8.
> Husk, W.H. and Warrack, J., 'Sinclair, John', *Grove* 23: 417.
> [uncredited]'Sinclair, John', *NGDO* 4: 385.

Gino Sinimberghi *1913–1966*
Discography
> Verdi: *Nabucco* Archipel ACP 0001.

Filmography
> *Avanti a lui tremava tutta Roma* (1946).
> *L'elisir d'amore* (1946).
> *Lucia di Lammermoor* (1946).
> *Pagliacci* (1948).
> *La forza del destino* (1949).
> *Il trovatore* (1949).
> *Puccini* (1953).
> *La favorita* (1952).
> *La sonnambula* (1952).
> *Torna piccina mia!* (1955).
> *Agguato sul mare* (1956).
> *La donna più bella del mondo* (1956).
> *L'Angelo delle Alpi* (1957).

Leo Slezak *1873–1946*
> Bilgora, A., review of *Leo Slezak 1873–1946* (GEMM CDS 9299), *Record Collector*, 46/3 (2001): 183–5.
> Dennis, J., 'Leo Slezak', *Record Collector*, 15/9 (nd): 196–235 (with discography by Thomas Kaufman).
> *Farkas*: 244–8.
> *Scott* 1: 202–4.
> Shawe-Taylor, D., 'Slezak, Leo', *Grove* 23: 502–3.
> Shawe-Taylor, D., 'Slezak, Leo', *NGDO* 4: 413–14.
> Slezak, L., *Song of Motley; Being the Reminiscences of a Hungry Tenor* (London, 1938).
> Verdino-Süllwold, C., *We Need a Hero: Heldentenors from Wagner's Time to the Present, A Critical History* (New York, 1989).

Discography
  Leo Slezak Pearl GEMM 9299 (2 CDs).
  Leo Slezak Edition 15 vols Truesound TT2405–19.
Filmography
  Ein toller Einfall (1932).
  Moderne Mitgift (1932).
  Skandal in der Parkstrasse (1932).
  Der Frauendiplomat (1932).
  Kaiser (1933).
  Die Herren vom Maxim (1933).
  Grossfürstin Alexandra (1933).
  La Paloma (1934).
  Die Pompadour (1935).
  Unser Musik im Blut (1934).
  Freut Euch des Lebens (1934).
  Ihr grösster Erfolg (1934).
  Der Herr ohne Wohnung (1934).
  G'schichten aus dem Viennaerwald (1934).
  Die ganze Welt dreht sich um Liebe (1935).
  Die blonde Carmen (1935).
  Tanzmusik (1935).
  Knox und die lustigen Vagabunden (1935).
  Ein Walzer um den Stephansturm (1935).
  Unsterbliche Melodien (1935).
  Eine Nacht an der Donau (1935).
  Herbstmanöver (1935).
  Fasching in Vienna (1935).
  Die Fahrt in die Jugend (1935).
  Konfetti (1936).
  Die lustigen Weiber (1936).
  Rendezvous in Vienna (1936).
  Der Postillon von Lonjumeau (1936).
  Das Frauenparadies (1936).
  Die glücklichste Ehe der Welt (1937).
  Gasparone (1937).
  Liebe im Dreiviertel-Takt (1937).
  Husaren heraus (1937).
  Heimat (1938).
  Die vier Gesellen (1938).
  Frau am Steuer (1939).
  Es war eine rauschende Ballnacht (1939).
  Operette (1940).
  Der Herr im Haus (1940).
  Golowin geht durch die Stadt (1940).
  Rosen in Tirol (1940).
  Alles für Gloria (1941).
  Geliebter Schatz (1943).
  Münchhausen (1943).

Dimitri Smirnov *1881–1944*

  Barnes, H. and Blyth, A., 'Smirnov, Dimitry (Alekseyevich)', *Grove* 23: 562.
  Barnes, H. and Blyth, A., 'Smirnov, Dimitry (Alekseyevich)', *NGDO* 4: 424.
  Juynboll, F., 'Dmitri Smirnov discography', *Record Collector*, 42/3 (September, 1997):
    177–87.

Mason, D., review of *Dmitri Smirnov: Arias and Songs* (Pearl GEMM CD 9241), *Record Collector*, 43/3 (September, 1998): 198–9.

Scott 2: 16–19.

Steane 1:

Stratton, J., 'Dmitri Smirnoff, tenor (1882–1944)', *Record Collector*, 14/11 (nd): 244–77 (with discography).

Discography

Tenors of Imperial Russia, vol. 1 Pearl GEMM 0217.

Dmitri Smirnov Pearl GEMM 9241.

Leonid Sobinov *1872–1934*

Barnes, H. and Blyth, A., 'Sobinov, Leonid Vital'yevich', *Grove* 23: 598.

Barnes, H. and Blyth, A., 'Sobinov, Leonid Vital'yevich', *NGDO* 4: 430.

Farkas: 248–9.

Robertson, J. (trans.), 'Leonid V. Sobinov', *Record Collector*, 24/7 (1978): 149–90 (with discography by J Dennis).

Steane 1:

Scott 1: 217–18.

Web

http://www.cantabile-subito.de/Tenors/Sobinov_Leonid/sobinov_leonid.html.

http://www.sobinov.yar.ru.

Discography

Tenors of Imperial Russia, vol. 1 Pearl GEMM 0217.

Leonid Sobinov: Vocal Recital RCD16033.

Leonid Vitalyevich Sobinov. Early recordings 1900 to 1904 The Harold Wayne Collection 36 Symposium 1238.

José Soler *1904–1999*

Zucker, S., 'José Soler: Among the Last Heroic Tenors', *Bel Canto Society News Letter* 2/6 (October, 2005).

Web

http://www.belcantosociety.org/pages/soler.html.

Roberto Stagno *1840–1897*

Forbes, E., 'Stagno, Roberto', *NGDO* 4: 519.

Farkas: 252.

Web

http://www.francoisnouvion.net/19century/stagno.html.

Ian Storey *1958*

Farmer, B., 'Pit tenor wows the world', *Daily Telegraph*, 8.12.2007:

Kettle, M., 'The Billy Elliot of Opera', *Guardian*, 4.12.07: 28–9.

Web

http://www.ianstorey.com/.

Discography

Smareglia: Nozze Istriane Bongiovanni BGV 2265.

Heinrich Stümer *1789–1856*

Forbes, E., 'Stümer, Heinrich', *NGDO* 4: 589.

Ludwig Suthaus *1906–1971*

Rosenthal, H., 'Suthaus, (Heinrich) Ludwig', *NGDO* 4: 611.

Verdino-Süllwold, C., *We Need a Hero: Heldentenors from Wagner's Time to the Present, A Critical History* (New York, 1989).

Discography

Ludwig Suthaus Preiser PR89539.

Ludwig Suthaus, vol. 2 Preiser PR89677.

Set Svanholm *1904–1964*

Bruun, C. L. and Blyth, A., 'Svanholm, Set (Karl Viktor)', *Grove* 24: 743–4.

Bruun, C. L. 'Svanholm, Set (Karl Viktor)', *NGDO* 4: 612–13.

Verdino-Süllwold, C., *We Need a Hero: Heldentenors from Wagner's Time to the Present, A Critical History* (New York, 1989).
Discography
> Set *Svanholm Live* Preiser PSR 90332.
> Set *Svanholm* PSR 89535.
> Set *Svanholm*, vol. 2 Preiser PR89579.
> Set *Svanholm Sings Wagner* Myto MYT 001039.

Giuseppe Taccani *1885–1959*
Discography
> *Giuseppe Taccani* Preiser PR89173.

Feruccio Tagliavini *1913–1995*
> Baxter, R., 'The last *tenore lyrico*: Ferruccio Tagliavini', *Opera Quarterly* 13/1 (1996): 29–36.
> *Farkas*: 258.
> Hughes, J., review of *The Cetra Tenors* (Pearl GEMS 0120), *Record Collector*, 46/2 (June, 2001): 153–6.
> Sanguinetti, H. and Williams, C., 'Ferruccio Tagliavini', *Record Collector*, 29/9 (1984): 197–255 (with discography).
> Shawe-Taylor, D., 'Tagliavini, Feruccio', *Grove* 24: 925.
> Shawe-Taylor, D., 'Tagliavini, Feruccio', *NGDO* 4: 632.
> Tedeschi, C., *Ferruccio Tagliavini, il signore del canto, nuovo idolo delle folle* (Roma, 1942).

Discography
> *Ferruccio Tagliavini* Preiser PR89163.
> *Ferruccio Tagliavini*, vol. 2 Preiser PR89515.

Jean-Alexandre Talazac *1851–1896*
> Forbes, E., 'Talazac, Jean-Alexandre', *NGDO* 4: 635.

Björn Talén *1890–1947*
> Bilgora, A., review of *Four Scandinavian Tenors of the Past* (Preiser LV 89986), *Record Collector*, 42/3 (September, 1997): 213–15.
Discography
> *Björn Talén* Preiser PSR 89654.
> *Four Scandinavian Tenors of the Past* Preiser LV 89986.

Francesco Tamagno *1850–1905*
> Corsi, M., *Tamagno* (New York, 1977).
> *Farkas*: 258–9.
> Forbes, E., 'Tamagno, Francesco', *Grove* 25: 49–50.
> Forbes, E., 'Tamagno, Franceso', *NGDO* 4: 639–40.
> Gualerzi, G., '"Otello": the Legacy of Tamagno', *Opera* (February, 1987): 122–7 with 'Postscript' (June, 1987): 628–30.
> Lewis, P., 'Tamagno's records', *Record Collector*, 40/2 (1995): 113–22 (with discography).
> *Scott* 1: 131–2.
> *Steane* 2: 149–54.
> Steinson, P., review of *Francesco Tamagno – the complete 12″ recordings* Historic Masters
> FT-1–7, *Record Collector*, 52/4 (December, 2007): 301–3.
> Stratton, J., 'Francesco Tamagno the extraordinary', *Opera Quarterly*, 12/4 (1996): 61–73.
> Wolfson, J., 'The Russitano Record(s)', *Record Collector*, 51/2 (June 2006): 152–4.
Discography
> *Francesco Tamagno* OPAL 9846.
> *Francesco Tamagno: Complete issued recordings (1903–1904)* Truesound TT2425.

Francesco Tamagno: Unissued recordings (1903) Truesound TT2426.
Francesco Tamagno: The complete 12″ recordings Historic Masters FT-1–7 (vinyl 78s).

Enrico Tamberlik *1820–1899.*

Forbes, E., 'Tamberlik [Tamberlick], Enrico', *Grove* 25: 52.
Forbes, E., 'Tamberlik [Tamberlick], Enrico', *NGDO* 4: 640.
Pleasants, H., 'A new kind of tenor', in *The Great Singers* (London 1967): 158–76.

Eric Tappy *1931*

Web
    http://www.bach-cantatas.com/Bio/Tappy-Eric.htm.

Discography
    Regamey: Alpha, Cinq Poèmes de Jean Tardieu Grammont Records SKA 2005.
    Debussy: Pelléas et Mélisande Claves CLV 2415.

Videography
    Mozart: La clemenza de Tito DGG B000617409.

Richard Tauber *1891–1948*

Castle, C. and Diana Napier Tauber, *This was Richard Tauber* (London, 1971).
Dennis, J., 'Richard Tauber discography', *Record Collector*, 18/8 (1969): 171–239.
Dennis, J., 'Richard Tauber', *Record Collector*, 18/11 (1969): 244–65.
Douglas, N., *More Legendary Voices* (New York, 1995): 279–312.
Farkas: 260–1.
Jürgs, M., *Gern hab'ich die Frau'n geküßt* (Munich, 2000).
Losseff, N., 'Mary Losseff and Richard Tauber', *Record Collector*, 51/4 (December 2006): 305–14.
Matheopoulos, H., *The Great Tenors* (New York, 1999): 40–5.
Napier Tauber, D., *My Heart and I* (London, 1959).
Scott 2: 235–8.
Steane, J. B., 'Richard Tauber', *Voices: Singers and Critics* (London, 1992): 179–85.
Steane 1:
Shawe-Taylor, D., 'Tauber, Richard', *Grove* 25: 123.
Shawe-Taylor, D., 'Tauber, Richard', *NGDO* 4: 658.

Web
    http://richardtauber.com/Introduction.htm.
    http://www.richard-tauber.de/index.htm.
    http://film.virtual-history.com/person.php?personid=656.

Discography
    The Vocal Prime of Richard Tauber Pearl GEMM 9327.
    Richard Tauber – Lieder Pearl GEMM 9370.
    Tauber sings Schubert Pearl GEMM 9381.
    Richard Tauber: Light Music of the 20s and '30s Pearl GEMM 9416.
    Richard Tauber: Opera and Operetta Pearl GEMM 9418.
    Richard Tauber: The Singing Dream Pearl GEMM 9444.
    Tauber: The Acoustic Lieder Pearl GEMM 9901.
    Richard Tauber: Lieder (1919–1926) Naxos 8.110739.
    Richard Tauber: Opera Arias (1919–1926) Naxos 8.110729.
    Richard Tauber: Opera Arias (1926–1946) Naxos 8.111001.
    Richard Tauber: Operetta Arias (1921–1932) Naxos 8.110779.

Filmography
    Ich küsse Ihre Hand (1929).
    Ich glaub' nie mehr an eine Frau (1930).
    Die grosse Attraktion (1930).
    Das lockende Ziel (1930).
    Das Land des Lächelns (1930).
    Melodie der Liebe (1932).

Blossom Time/April Romance (1934).
Heart's Desire (1935).
A Clown Must Laugh/Pagliacci (1936).
Land Without Music/Forbidden Music (1936).
The Big Broadcast of 1936 (1936).
Waltz Time (1945).
Lisbon Story (1946).

Robert Tear *1938*

Tear, R., *Tear Here* (London, 1990).
Tear, R., *Singer Beware: A Cautionary Story of the Singing Class* (London, 1995).
Blyth, A., 'Tear, Robert', *Grove* 25: 188.
Blyth, A., 'Tear, Robert', *NGDO* 4: 674.

Web

http://www.bach-cantatas.com/Bio/Tear-Robert.htm [Aryeh Oron].
http://www.concertartist.info/biog/TEA001.html.
http://www.kings.cam.ac.uk/chapel/services/RobertTear.html.

Discography

Schubert: die Winterreise ASV 3053.
British Composers EMI 647312.

Filmography

Lulu 1979.
Les Contes d'Hoffmann 1981.
The Turn of the Screw 1982.
Der Rosenkavalier 1985.
Il ritorno d'Ulisse in patria 1985.
Death in Venice 1990.
Lady Macbeth von Mzensk 1992.
Le nozze di Figaro 1994.
The Makropulos Case 1995.
Amahl and the Night Visitors 2002.
Turandot 2002.

Georges Thill *1897–1984*

Bilgora, A. and Geores Thill, 'The Recording and a Journey of Re-discovery', *Record Collector*, 52/2 (June, 2007): 135–43.
Bunyard, R., 'Georges Thill', *Record Collector*, 52/2 (June, 2007): 82–134 (with discography and filmography by David Mason).
Farkas: 265.
Mancini, R., *Georges Thill* (Paris, 1966)
Morgan, K., 'Georges Thill', *Opera Quarterly*, 15/1 (1999): 73–86.
Steane 2: 133–7.
Tubuef, A., 'Thill, Georges', *Grove* 25: 399.
Tubuef, A., 'Thill, Georges', *NGDO* 4: 725.

Discography

Georges Thill: Airs d'opéra français EMI CDM 7 69548 2.
Georges Thill Pearl GEMM 9947.
Georges Thill Lebendige Vergangenheit Preiser PR89168.

Filmography

Chansons de Paris (1934).
Au Portes de Paris (1934).
Opéra de Paris (1936).
Louise (1939).

Ivor Thomas *1892–1946*

Bott, M., 'Ivor Thomas (Ifor O Fôn), *Record Collector*, 44/3 (September, 1999): 216–21 (with discography); updated in *Record Collector*, 46/2 (June, 2001): 133.

Jess Thomas *1927–1993*

    Bernheimer, M., 'Thomas, Jess (Floyd)', *Grove* 25: 410.

    LeSuer, R. and Forbes, E., 'Thomas, Jess', *NGDO* 4: 728.

    Thomas, J. and Judmann, K., *Kein Schwert Verhiess mir der Vater* (Vienna, 1986).

    Verdino-Süllwold, C., *We Need a Hero: Heldentenors from Wagner's Time to the Present, A Critical History* (New York, 1989): 237–60.

Web

    http://www.richard-wagner.bayern-online.de/01_Wissen/11_Saengerportraits/.

    http://www.geocities.com/rmlibonati/jthomasbio.html.

Discography

    Wagner: Parsifal Philips PHI B000786302.

    Wagner: Tannhäuser MEL 10033.

Adrian Thompson *1955*

Web

    http://www.bach-cantatas.com/Bio/Thompson-Adrian.htm

    http://www.hyperion-records.co.uk/a.asp?a=A101

Discography

    Britten: Serenade & Nocturne Naxos 8.553834

Guiseppe Tibaldi *1729–1790*

    Brofsky, H., 'Tibaldi, Guiseppe (Luigi)', *Grove* 25: 440.

    Brofsky, H., 'Tibaldi, Guiseppe (Luigi)', *NGDO* 4: 732.

Joseph Tichatschek *1807–1866*

    Pleasants, H., 'A new kind of tenor', in *The Great Singers* (London 1967): 158–76.

    Warrack, J., 'Tichatschek, Joseph (Aloys)', *Grove* 25: 463.

    Warrack, J., 'Tichatschek, Joseph (Aloys)', *NGDO* 4: 733.

    Verdino-Süllwold, C., *We Need a Hero: Heldentenors from Wagner's Time to the Present, A Critical History* (New York, 1989).

Frank Titterton *1892–1956*

    Klein, H., 'Sims Reeves: Prince of English Tenors', *Herman Klein and The Gramophone*, ed. William R. Moran (Portland, Oregon, 1990): 336

    Morgan, C., 'Frank Titterton', *Record Collector*, 27/11 (1983): 244–63 (with discography).

Filmography

    Waltz Time (1933).

    Song at Eventide (1934).

    Barnacle Bill (1935).

    British Pathe: http://www.britishpathe.com/thumbnails.php?id=17332&searchword= Frank%20titterton&searchword=Frank%20titterton.

Discography

    Vaughan Williams: Serenade and other works Pearl PRL 9342.

Armand Tokatyan *1894–1960*

Web

    http://www.parev.net/armenian-profile-armand-tokatyan.shtml.

Discography

    Armand Tokatyan Preiser 89170.

Diomiro Tramezzani *c. 1776*

    Fenner, T., *Opera in London: Views of the Press 1785–1830* (Illinois, 1994): 170–2.

Josef Traxel *1916–1975*

Web

    http://www.josef-traxel-society.org/.

    http://www.emiclassics.de/xml/6/551012/discografie.html.

    http://traxel.i-networx.de/de/start.html.

    http://www.bach-cantatas.com/Bio/Traxel-Josef.htm [Aryeh Oron].

Antonin Trantoul *1887–1966*
> Lustig, L., 'The ones who got away: Antonin Trantoul', *Record Collector*, 50/4 December 2005: 267–9.

Günther Treptow *1907–1981*
> Rosenthal, H. and Blyth, A., 'Treptow, Günther', *Grove* 25: 720

Discography
> *Günther Treptow* Preiser PR89550.

Richard Tucker *1913–1975*
> Bernheimer, M., 'Tucker, Richard', *Grove* 25: 871.
> Bernheimer, M., 'Tucker, Richard', *NGDO* 4: 835–6.
> Drake, J., *Richard Tucker* (New York, 1984).
> Jackson, P., *Sign Off for the Old Met* (New York, 1997).
> Tucker, R. *et al.*, *Remembering Richard Tucker* (New York, 2006).
> *Farkas*: 269.
> Rubin, S., 'Richard Tucker', in Herbert H. Breslin (ed.), *The Tenors* (New York 1974): 1–42.
> *Steane 2*: 166–70

Web
> http://www.grandi-tenori.com/articles/articles_kurtzman_tucker_03.htm.

Discography
> *Four Famous Met-Tenors of the Past* Preiser PR89952.
> *Richard Tucker* Preiser PR89552.
> *Richard Tucker*, vol. 2 Preiser PR89637.
> *Richard Tucker, Robert Merrill and Jan Peerce* Dutton CDVS 1952.

Videography
> *Richard Tucker in Opera and Song* Bel Canto Society F2435 (VHS only).

Georg Unger *1837–1887*
> Fuller Maitland, J. A. and Fifeld, C., 'Unger, George', *Grove* 26: 73.
> [uncredited] 'Unger, Georg', *NGDO* 4: 866.

Jacques Urlus *1897–1935*
> Dennis, J., 'Jacques Urlus', *Record Collector*, 26/1 (1981): 245–81 (with discography).
> Bruun, C.L., 'Urlus, Jacques [Jacobus]', *NGDO* 4: 875–6.
> Bruun, C.L. and Blyth, A., 'Urlus, Jacques [Jacobus]', *Grove* 26: 157.
> *Farkas*: 270.
> *Scott* 1: 201–2.

Web
> http://chalosse.free.fr/masterpieces/step-one/urlus.htm.
> http://www.cantabile-subito.de/Tenors/Urlus_Jacques/urlus_jacques.html.

Discography
> *Jacques Urlus* Preiser PR89502.
> *Jacques Urlus, Heroic Tenor: The Complete Edison Recordings* Marston MR 52031 (2 CDs).

Fernando Valero *1854–1914*
Web
> http://www.grandi-tenori.com/tenors/valero.php [Joern Anthonisen].

Discography
> *The Harold Wayne Collection*, vol. 3 Symposium SYM 1073.

Alessandro Valente *1890–1958*
> Bilgora, A., 'The Valente story. . .', *Record Collector*, 34/1 (1989): 2–19 (with discography by
> Alan Kelly).

Discography
> *Alessandro Valente* Preiser PR89126.

Cesare Valletti *1922–2000*

    Hughes, J., review of *The Cetra Tenors* (Pearl GEMS 0120), *Record Collector*, 46/2 (June, 2001): 153–6.

    Rosenthal, H., 'Valletti, Cesare', *NGDO* 4: 888.

    Rosenthal, H. and Blyth, A., 'Valletti, Cesare', *Grove* 26: 221.

Web

    http://www.cantabile-subito.de/Tenors/Valletti_Cesare/valletti_cesare.html.

Discography

    The Cetra Tenors Pearl GEMS 0120.

Ernest van Dyck *1861–1923*

    Dennis, J., 'Ernest Marie Hubert Van Dyck', *Record Collector*, 5/2 (1950): 29–32.

    Forbes, E., 'Van Dyck [van Dijck], Ernest (Marie Hubert)', *Grove* 26: 252.

    Malou, H., *Ernest Van Dyck, un ténor à Bayreuth* (Lyon, 2005).

    Scott 1: 197–8.

Web

    http://www.dutchdivas.net/tenors/ernest_van_dyck.html.

Discography

    Helden an geweihtem Ort – Wagnertenöre in Bayreuth Preiser PSR 89944.

    A Symposium of Major Rareties Symposium SYM 1292.

John van Kesteren *1921*

    Kestern, J. Van, *Notities van een 'notekraker'* (Nieuwkoop, 1978).

Web

    http://www.dutchdivas.net/tenors/john_van_kesteren.html.

Discography

    The Art of John van Kesteren in Opera Gala GL 100.572.

Alain Vanzo *1928–2002*

    Loppert, M., 'Vanzo, Alain (Fernand Albert)', *Grove*. 26: 270.

    Loppert, M., 'Vanzo, Alain (Fernand Albert)', *NGDO* 4: 899.

    Forbes, E., 'Alain Vanzo', *The Independent* ,11/04/2002.

Discography

    Bizet: The Pearl Fishers EMI 677022.

    Meyerbeer: Robert le diable GLA 622.

    Delibes: Lakmé Decca 4254852.

Ramón Vargas *1960*

Web

    Ramonvargas.com.

Discography

    L'amour l'amour RCA 74321 61464 2.

    Arie antiche:17th and 18th-Century Songs RCA 09026–63913–2.

    Verdi arias RCA 7432179603–2.

    Ramon Vargas: Mexico Lindo RCA 7432175478–2.

René Verdière *1899–1981*

    Pines, R., review of *Great French Heroic Tenors* in *Opera Quarterly*, 19/3 (Summer, 2003): 608–12.

Discography

    Great French Heroic Tenors Record Collector TRC 9.

Joseph Vernon *1737–1782*

    Baldwin, O. and Wilson, T., 'Vernon, Joseph', *Grove* 26: 485.

    Fiske, R., *English Theatre Music in the Eighteenth Century* (London, 1973): 629–70.

    Wilson, T., 'Vernon, Joseph', *NGDO* 4: 957.

César Vezzani *1886–1951*

    Bilgora, A., 'César Vezzani chante Manon', *Record Collector*, 46/1 (March, 2001): 33–4.

    Pines, R., review of *Great French Heroic Tenors* in *Opera Quarterly*, 19/3 (Summer, 2003): 608–12.

Steane, J. B., 'Vezzani, César', *NGDO* 4: 980.
Discography
> The Complete César Vezzani vol.1 *(Odeon Recordings 1912–1914, French HMV Recordings 1923–1924)* Marston 52034–2 (2 CDs).
> The Complete César Vezzani vol. 2 *(Complete HMV Acoustics 1924–1925, Selected Electric Recordings 1930–1933)* Marston 52045–2 (2 CDs).

Jon Vickers *1926*
> *Farkas*: 275.
> Rosenthal, H., 'Vickers, Jon(athan Stewart)', *NGDO* 4: 986.
> Rosenthal, H. and Blyth, A., 'Vickers, Jon(athan Stewart)' *Grove* 26: 533.
> Rubin, S., 'Jon Vickers', in Herbert H. Breslin (ed.), *The Tenors* (New York 1974): 43–82.
> *Steane 1*: 211–15.
> Verdino-Süllwold, C., *We Need a Hero: Heldentenors from Wagner's Time to the Present, A Critical History* (New York, 1989).
> Williams, J., 'A sense of awe: the career of Jon Vickers as seen in reviews', *Opera Quarterly*, 7/3 (1990): 36–73.
> Williams, J., *Jon Vickers: A Hero's Life* (Boston, 1999).
Web
> http://www.bruceduffie.com/vickers.html.
> http://thecanadianencyclopedia.com/index.cfm?PgNm=TCE&Params=U1ARTU000 3594.
> http://mlhart.com/WordsMusic/bio_Vickers.htm.
Discography
> *Jon Vickers: a Tribute on his 75th Birthday* VAI 1201.
> *The Very Best of John Vickers* EMI 863382.
Videography
> *Four Operatic Portraits* VAI 4219.
> *John Vickers: Early Telecasts* VAI 4240.
> *Tristan und Isolde* KUL 2230.
> *Peter Grimes* KUL 2255.

Melchior Vidal *1837–1911*
> Gualerzi, G., 'Spain: Land of Tenors', *Opera* (November, 1987): 1257–63 (December, 1987): 1387–91.

Giuseppe Viganoni *1754–1823*
> Fenner, T., *Opera in London: Views of the Press 1785–1830* (Illinois, 1994): 167–8.

Miguel Villabella *1921–1936*
Web
> http://www.cantabile-subito.de/Tenors/Five_French_Tenors/hauptteil_five_french_tenors. html.
Discography
> *Prince of French Lyric Tenors* VAIA 1132.

Rolando Villazón *1972*
> Canning, H., 'Rolando Villazon: why I needed to pause for breath', *Sunday Times*, 8.3.2008 (Times on line: http://entertainment.timesonline.co.uk/tol/arts_and_entertainment/stage/opera/article3492166.ece).
> Jeal, E., 'Great Expectations', *Gramophone* (August 2005): 25–9.
> Thompson, W., 'Clown Prince', *Gramophone* (March, 2006): 20–7.
> White, M., 'The sound of one voice mending', *New York Times* 16.03.2008 (http://www.nytimes.com/2008/03/16/arts/music/16whit.html?pagewanted=1&_r=1).
Web
> http://www.rolandovillazon.com/.
Discography
> *Gitano Zarauela Arias* Virgin Classics 365474.

Opera Recital Virgin Classics 3447332.
Gounod and Massenet Arias Virgin Classics 5457192.
Cielo e mar DG 4777224.

Francisco Viñas *1863–1933*

Gualerzi, G., 'Spain: Land of Tenors' *Opera* (November, 1987): 1257–63 (December, 1987): 1387–91.

Lustig, L. and Williams, C., 'Francisco Viñas', *Record Collector*, 34/5–7 (July 1989) (with discography).

Scott 1: 126–7.

Steane, J. B., 'Viñas, Franciso [Viñas, Frances; Vinas, Francesco]', *NGDO* 4: 1012.

Discography

The Complete Francisco Viñas Marston 53006–2 (3 CDs).

Ramón Vinay *1912–1996*

Carlos Bastías, C. and Dzazópulos, J., *Ramón Vinay: De Chillán a la gloria* (1997).

Rosenthal, H., 'Vinay, Ramón', *Grove* 26: 648.

Rosenthal, H., 'Vinay, Ramón', *NGDO* 4: 1012–13.

Web

http://www.cantabile-subito.de/Tenors/Vinay_Ramon/hauptteil_vinay_ramon.html.

Discography

Ramón Vinay Preiser PR89619.

Four Famous Met-Tenors of the Past Preiser PR89952.

Georgei Vinogradov *1908–1976*

Hussein, K., review of *Georgi Vinogradov* Guild GCD 2250/3–4, *Record Collector*, 49/2 (2004): 127–9.

Web

http://russia-in-us.com/Music/GRV/Vinogradov/ (with sound files and discography by Larry Friedman).

Discography

Georgi Vinogradov: Arias, Songs and Duets Guild GHCD 2250/51/52/53 (4 CDs).

Georgi Vinogradov Preiser PR89118.

Heinrich Vogl *1845–1900*

Farkas: 277.

Forbes, E., 'Vogl, Heinrich', *Grove* 26: 862.

Forbes, E., 'Vogl, Heinrich', *NGDO* 4: 1035.

Franz Völker *1899–1965*

Branscombe, P., 'Völker, Franz', *NGDO* 4: 1038.

Branscombe, P., 'Völker, Franz', *Grove* 26: 882.

Dahmen, U. (ed./trans. Michael Foster), 'Franz Völker', *Record Collector*, 48/3 (September, 2003): 162–215 (includes discography by Ulrich Dahmen and Jakob Vieten, and commentary by Alan Bilgora).

Discography

Franz Völker Preiser PR89005.

Franz Völker, vol. 2 Preiser PR89070.

Alfred von Bary *1873–1926*

Heldentenöre Preiser PR89947.

Koloman von Pataky *1896–1964*

Web

http://www.grandi-tenori.com/tenors/pataky.php' [Joern Anthonisen].

Dmitri Voropaev *1980*

Jeal, E., 'Great Expectations', *Gramophone* (August 2005): 27.

Web

http://www.naxos.com/artistinfo/Dmitry_Voropaev/43800.htm.

Theodor Wachtel *1823–93*

Obituary: *Musical Times*, 1 December 1893.

Gustav Walter *1843–1910*
 Farkas: 279.
 Scott 1: 204–5.
 Steane, J. B., 'Walter, Gustav', *NGDO* 4: 1097–8.
Discography
 Gustav Walter/Hans Buff-Gießen / Felix Senius – Complete recordings (1904–1911)
  Truesound TT-1905.
Russell Watson *1974*
Web
 Moir, J., 'Ha Ha, of course I can Sing!' *Daily Telegraph*.
 http://www.telegraph.co.uk/arts/main.jhtml?xml=/arts/2001/12/21/bmruss21.xml.
 http://www.russell-watson.com/.
Discography
 The Voice Decca 289468695–2.
Walter Widdop *1892–1849*
 Dempsey, P., review of Pearl GEMM CD 9112, *Record Collector*, 39/3 (1994):237–8.
 Parker, V., *Walter Widdop: His Life and Achievements* (unpublished dissertation, Royal
  Northern College of Music, Manchester, April 2001).
 Steane, J. B., 'Widdop, Walter', *Grove* 27: 355–6.
 Steane, J. B., 'Widdop, Walter', *NGDO* 4: 1151.
 Steane 2: 38–42
Web
 http://www.cantabile-subito.de/Tenors/Widdop_Walter/widdop_walter.html.
Discography
 Anthology of Song II Symposium1357.
 Walter Widdop Pearl GEMM 9112.
Ben Williams *1893–1946*
 Bott, M., 'Ben Williams', *Record Collector*, 51/2 (June 2006): 135–47 (includes discog-
  raphy).
Evan Williams *1867–1918*
 Farkas: 281.
 Lewis, G., 'Evan Williams 1867–1918', *Record Collector*, 24/11 (1978): 242–77 (with
  discography by William Moran).
 Williams, G., *Evan Williams* (Akron, OH, 1974).
 Woolf, J., review of Cheyne CHE 44368/9, *Record Collector*, 50/3 (2005): 231–2.
Discography
 Mendelssohn. Arias and Songs, vol. 1 Cheyne CHE 44368.
 Handel, Arias and Songs, vol. 2 Cheyne CHE 44369.
Steuart Wilson *1889–1966*
 Farkas: 281.
 Kennedy, M., 'Wilson, Steuart', *Grove* 27: 426.
 Steward, M., *English Singer: The Life of Steuart Wilson* (London, 1970).
Gösta Winbergh *1943–2001*
 Forbes, E., 'Winbergh, Gösta', *Grove* 27: 428–9.
 Forbes, E., 'Winbergh, Gösta', *NGDO* 4: 1163.
Web
 http://www.bach-cantatas.com/Bio/Winbergh-Gosta.htm [Atyeh Oron].
Discography
 Donizetti: L'elisir d'amore DGG B00045800–2.
 Liszt: A Faust Symphony EMI 09017–2.
Fritz Windgassen *1883–1963*
 Verdino-Süllwold, C., *We Need a Hero: Heldentenors from Wagner's Time to the
  Present, A Critical History* (New York, 1989): 209–10.

Discography
>   *Fritz Windgassen: The Complete Recordings (1925–1952)* Truesound TT2201.

Wolfgang Windgassen *1914–1974*
>   *Farkas*: 281.
>   Natan, A., 'Windgassen, Wolfgang', *Primo Uomo* (Basel, 1963) with discography.
>   Rosenthal, H., 'Windgassen, Wolfgang', *NGDO* 4: 163–4.
>   Rosenthal, H. and Blyth, A., 'Windgassen, Wolfgang', *Grove* 27: 433.
>   Verdino-Süllwold, C., *We Need a Hero: Heldentenors from Wagner's Time to the Present, A Critical History* (New York, 1989): 207–33.
>   Wessling, B., *Wolfgang Windgassen* (Bremen, 1976).

Discography
>   *Wolfgang Windgassen singt Wagner* DGG B000818802.
>   *Wagner: Parsifal* Archipel ACP 0112.
>   *Wagner: Tristan und Isolde* MEL 10020.

Hermann Winkelmann *1849–1912*
>   [Uncredited], 'Winkelmann [Winckelmann], Hermann', *Grove* 27: 436.
>   [Uncredited], 'Winklemann [Winckelmann], Hermann', *NGDO* 4: 1164.
>   *Scott* 1: 195–6.

Discography
>   *Heldentenöre* Preiser PSR 89947.

Marcel Wittrisch *1901–1955*
>   Seddon, J., 'Marcel Wittrisch discography', *Record Collector*, 40/4 (1995): 263–322.
>   Semrau, T., 'Marcel Wittrisch', *Record Collector*, 40/4 (1995): 256–63.
>   Steane, J. B, 'Wittrisch, Marcel', *Grove* 27: 456.
>   Steane, J. B., 'Wittrisch, Marcel', *NGDO* 4: 1168.

Discography
>   *Marcel Wittrisch* Preiser PR89024.
>   *Marcel Wittrisch*, vol. 2 Preiser PR89591.

Otto Wolf *1871–1946*
Discography
>   *Otto Wolf Singt Wagner 1922–25* Gebhardt JGCD 0004.
>   *So Viel der Helden: Wagnerian heroic Tenors* Preiser PSR 89940.

Fritz Wunderlich *1930–1966*
>   Canning, H., 'Fritz Wunderlich: Unforgettable and Unforgotten', *Opera* (September, 1990: 1048–55.
>   Douglas, N., *Legendary Voices* (New York, 1995): 263–85.
>   Giesen, H., *Am Flügel: Hubert Giesen* (Frankfurt-am-Main 1972): 251–60.
>   Pfister, W., *Fritz Wunderlich: Biographie* (Zurich, 1990).
>   Porter, A. and Wigmore, R., 'Wunderlich, Fritz', *Grove* 27: 587–8.

Web
>   http://www.andreas-praefcke.de/wunderlich/ [Andreas Praefcke].

Discography
>   *Original Masters: The Art of Fritz Wunderlich* Deutsch Grammophon / 2005–09–13 (7 CDs).
>   *Fritz Wunderlich, the Great German Tenor* EMI CZS 7 62993 2 (3 CDs).

Ivan Yershov *1867–1943*
>   Steane, J., 'Yerschov, Ivan', *NGDO* 4: 1190.
>   Levik, S., *The Levik Memoirs: An Opera Singer's Notes*, trans. Edward Morgan (London, 1995) from the 2nd revised edn (Moscow, 1962): 251–67, 298–301.
>   Lustig, L., 'Ivan Ershov', *Record Collector*, 42/4 (December, 1997): 234–47 (with discography).

Web
>   http://www.cantabile-subito.de/Tenors/Ershov_Ivan/ershov_ivan.html.

Discography
  Tenors of Imperial Russia, vol. 1 Pearl GEMM 0217.
Alexander Young *1920–2000*
  Forbes, E., obituary, *The Independent,* 23.03.2000
  Rosenthal, H., 'Yong [Youngs], (Basil) Alexander', *NGDO* 4: 1196.
  Rosenthal, H. and Blyth, A., 'Young [Youngs], (Basil) Alexander', *Grove* 27: 671–2.
Web
  http://www.bach-cantatas.com/Bio/Young-Alexander.htm [Aryeh Oron].
Discography
  Handel: Tamerlano Parnassus PRN 96038.
  Haydn: The Seasons EMI 861182B.
  Elgar: The Kingdom EMI 642092.
Renato Zanelli *1892–1935*
  Rosenthal, H. and Blyth, A., 'Zanelli, Renato', *Grove* 27: 741–2.
  Rosenthal, H., 'Zanelli, Renato', *NGDO* 4: 1207.
Discography
  The Unpublished Treasury Pearl PRL 0215
Web
  http://www.grandi-tenori.com/tenors/zanelli.php [Joern Anthonisen].
  http://www.cantabile-subito.de/Baritones/Zanelli__Renato/zanelli__renato.html.
Heinrich Zeller *1856–1934*
  Forbes, E., 'Zeller, Heinrich', *NGDO* 4: 1223.
Giovanni Zenatello *1876–1949*
  Hutchinson, T. and Williams, C., 'Giovanni Zenatello', *Record Collector,* 14/5 (nd): 100–43 (with discography).
  Celletti, R., 'Zenatello, Giovanni', *NGDO* 4: 1226.
  Celletti, R. and Gualerzi, V. P., 'Zenatello, Giovanni', *Grove* 27: 788.
  Farkas: 283–4.
  Scott 1: 136–7.
  Steane 1: 186–90.
Discography
  Giovanni Zenatello Preiser PR89038.
  Giovanni Zenatello, vol. 2 Preiser PR89575.
Alessandro Ziliani *1906–1977*
Discography
  Alessandro Ziliani Preiser PSR 89165.
Giovanni Battista Zingoni *1718/20–1811*
  Bongiovanni, C., 'Zingoni [Singoni, Zingone] Giovanni Battista', *Grove* 27: 847.

AUDIO, VIDEO AND WEBSITE SOURCES

Video anthologies

The Great Tenors Bel Canto Society FD 2443.
Tenors of the Shellac Era (Taurusfilm).
Bel Canto: Tenors of the 78 Era Bel Canto Society (4 VHS + booklet).
Great Tenor Performances Warner 0630–18626–2.

CD-ROM

German tenors: http://www.mrichter.com/ae/fangetan.htm

CD anthologies

Great Tenors in Rare Recordings Symposium 1268.
The Great Tenors I 9337 GEMM CD 9337.
The Great Tenors II 9337 GEMM CD 9344.
Wagner in Stockholm: Great Wagnerians of the Royal Swedish Opera Recordings, 1899–1970
  Bluebell ABCD 091 (4 CDs).

General tenor websites

Voce di tenore:
http://www.jcarreras.homestead.com/index.html
  (Carreras, Sabbatini, Florez, Alagna).

Historical tenors:
http://www.francoisnouvion.net/#index
http://www.cantabile-subito.de/Tenors/tenors.htm
http://www.grandi-tenori.com [Jay Anthonisen]

Operatic tenors on the Web:
http://www.operastuff.com/peopletenor.html

British tenors (pictures + short biographies):
http://www.ram.ac.uk/NR/rdonlyres/9506E285–38FE-658–AF15–0CEE90CFF179/0/british
  tenor.pdf

Cantorial tradition:
http://www.operanostalgia.be/html/Greatest_Cantorial_Voices.htm

Canadian Wagnerians:
http://www.encyclopedia.com/doc/1G1–152872787.html

Wagnerian tenors:
http://www.wagneroperas.com/indexwagnerianstenors.html

Historic recordings

http://www.historicmasters.org/ (vinyl repressings of 78s)
www.cheynerecords.co.uk
http://www.tinfoil.com/default.htm (early cylinders)
http://www.symposiumrecords.co.uk/artists.html
http://www.cantabile-subito.de/Tenors/tenors.htm (photos and sound clips)
Marston: http://www.marstonrecords.com/html/about.htm
http://www.preiserrecords.at/start2.php http://www.truesoundtransfers.de/allissues.htm
http://www.malibran.com/acatalog/TENOR.html
http:// www.cheynerecords.co.uk
http://www.symposiumrecords.co.uk/sym_home.html http://www.bongiovanni70.com/
http://www.bassocantante.com/opera/tenor.html (sound clips)
http://www.naxos.com/labels/naxos_historical-singer.htmPearl
Nimbus Records: http://www.wyastone.co.uk/nrl/pvoce.html
http://www.belcantosociety.org/
http://www.norpete.com/
http://www.holdridgerecords.com/

Pictures on the web

http://www.historicopera.com/index_main.htm

BIBLIOGRAPHY AND
FURTHER READING

General studies of tenors

Ashbrook, W., 'The evolution of the Donizettian tenor-persona', *Opera Quarterly*, 14/3 (1998): 24–32.
Breslin, H., (ed.), *The Tenors* (New York 1974).
Celletti, R., *Voce di tenore* (Milan, 1989).
Celletti, R., *A History of Bel Canto* (Oxford, 1991).
Frisell, A., *The Tenor Voice* (Cambridge, Mass., 1964).
Matheopoulos, H., *The Great Tenors* (New York, 1999) with CD.
Otter, J., *Tenors* (London, 2002).
Rosselli, J., *Singers of Italian Opera* (Cambridge, 1992): Chapter 8 'The Age of the Tenor', pp. 176–95.
Zucker, S., *The Origins of Modern Tenor Singing* (New York 1986).
Clampton, D., 'L'Histoire d'un jeune et galant postillon', *Record Collector*, 43/4 (December, 1998): 270–4.
Rice, J., 'Benedetto Frizzi on singers, composers, and opera in late eighteenth-century Italy', *Studi musicali*, 23: (1994): 367–93.
Fallowes, Jander, Forbes, Steane, Harris and Waldmann, 'Tenor', *Grove* 25: 284–91.
Jander, Forbes and Steane, 'Tenor', *NGDO* 4: 690–6.

Relevant singing history

Nigel Douglas, *Legendary Voices* (New York, 1992).
Nigel Douglas, *More Legendary Voices* (New York, 1994)
Pleasants, H., *The Great Singers* (London, 1967).
Steane, J. B., *The Grand Tradition: Seventy Years of Singing on Record 1900–1970* (London, 1974).
Steane, J. B., *Voices: Singers and Critics* (London, 1993).
Stevens, D. (ed.), *A History of Song* (London, 1971).
Tunley, D., *Salons, Singers and Songs* (Aldershot, 2002).

Nineteenth-century memoirs and general histories

Chorley, H., *Thirty Years' Musical Recollections* (London, 1862; repr. 1982).
Hogarth, G., *Memoirs of the Opera in Italy, France Germany and England*, 2 vols (London, 1851, repr. New York, 1971).
Mount Edgcombe, R., *Musical Reminiscences of the Earl of Mount Edgcombe* (London, 1834, repr. New York, 1973).

Range and acoustics

Clampton, D., 'L'histoire d'un jeune et galant postillon', *Record Collector*, 43/4 (December, 1998): 270–4.

Schutte, H. and Miller, D., 'Acoustic details of vibrato cycle in tenor high notes', *Journal of Voice*, 5 (1990): 217–23.

Schutte, H., Miller, D. and Duijnstee, M., 'Resonance strategies recorded in tenor high notes', *Folia Phoniatrica et Logopaedica*, 57/5–6 (2005): 292–307.

Pedagogy

Carlo Bassini, *Bassini's method for tenor: an analytical physiological and practical system for the cultivation of the tenor voice* . . . (Boston, c. 1861).

Miller, R., *Training Tenor Voices* (USA, 1993).

INDEX

Readers are also referred to the alphabetical Biographical List of Tenors on pages 216–89

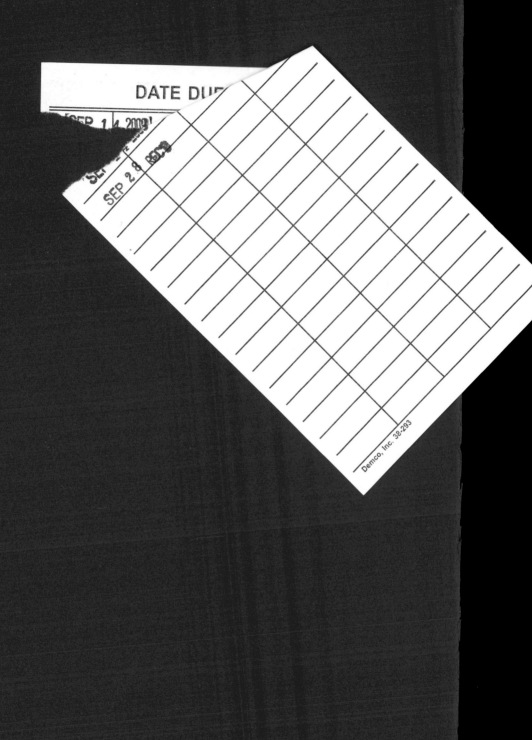